D1573187

Diagrams of the
UNCONSCIOUS

Diagrams of the
UNCONSCIOUS

HANDWRITING AND PERSONALITY IN MEASUREMENT, EXPERIMENT AND ANALYSIS

By WERNER WOLFF, Ph.D.

Professor of Psychology, Bard College, Annandale-on-Hudson

GRUNE & STRATTON
New York   ::   1948

COPYRIGHT 1948
WERNER WOLFF
Bard College
Annandale-on-Hudson, N. Y.

Second printing, November 1965

Printed in U.S.A. (U-M)

To

KATE WOLFF

CONTENTS

PART II. EXPRESSION AND MOVEMENT

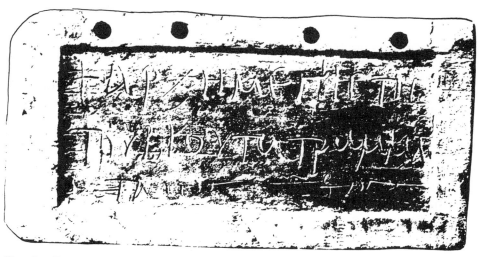

FIG. 1.—From a clay slate of ancient Egypt: "Letters are the true beginning of life."

INTRODUCTION

An ancient clay slate, probably written by a schoolteacher, bears the Greek words: Arche megiste tou biou ta grammata—"letters are the true beginning of life" (Fig. 1). It was through letters that the mental life of man became communicable beyond the boundaries of his immediate environment, conquering the limits of space; it was through letters that man's mental life became immortalized, thrust beyond the boundaries of his immediate existence, conquering the limits of time. Thus, in ancient cultures, letters had a magic value, they were symbols of conjuration said to be brought by a god from the underworld, from the innermost depths of existence. But the written sign is not only a symbol of an object or happening which the writer communicates intentionally: it may also be a symbol of a hidden message, a message without words, frequently not even known to the writer. Written signs, whether letters or ornaments or artists' drawings, are charged with the performer's personal note, with his style of expression. This personal note is like a photograph in which the receiver immediately recognizes the writer or artist. Everybody admits that it is very difficult to imitate it, and since earliest times the signature has been accepted as the seal of an individual. Thus a signature, reflecting the unique movement pattern of a person and accepted socially as his symbol, represents physiologically as well as psychologically the expression of an individual.

The movement pattern has its origin in physiological factors involving hereditary characteristics, and in mental factors conditioned by learning. The fundamental question which arises is whether such a pattern is fixed —that is, physiologically and mentally established at an early time—or whether it changes along with physiological and mental changes. Everybody experiences a change of his total expressiveness in his moods, movements, and activities. But in the case of handwriting most scientists and laymen refuse to accept this assumption, even though it seems to be dictated by our knowledge of the unity of the organism on the one hand and the dynamic changes of the organism on the other. The reasons for this resistance to accepting relationship between graphic movement and the changing personality seems to be of an emotional nature. Resistance against self-revelation, enforced by moral, social, and religious canons, has created a barrier against the assumption that handwriting is a reflection of the changing personality, and has stimulated investigators to disprove this assumption by experiments. It was again the emotional factor which made these investigators blind to the fact that, although their experiments proved the absence of some arbitrary relationships between single graphic signs and single personality traits, they did not disprove a possible relationship between the *total* graphic expression and the *total* personality.

Our movement pattern is based upon physiological and mental processes. The influence of mental processes upon movements was exemplified by M. E. Chevreul's* famous experiment with a pendulum. Anyone can easily repeat this experiment. If we suspend a ring from a hair and hold the other end of the hair motionless between two fingers, and then we think of the ring's possible movements, the thought alone will be sufficient to produce a rotary movement toward the right or toward the left, according to his thought. Chevreul reported that the amplitude of these oscillations increased if he followed them with his eyes. Perception increased the vividness of the idea and hence its motive power. Thus we see that our imagination as well as our perception seems to have an influence upon our movement pattern. Were we to record our bodily movements graphically the patterns would change according to our changing impressions and expressions. The biologist knows that emotional thought may influence glandular functions, and the psychiatrist is familiar with the relationship between thought and disease—the so-called psychosomatic disorders. Movement being a basic expression of the organism, we should expect any one type of movement, such as graphic movement, to be influenced by psychological processes. Thus we state our hypothesis: In his handwriting or artistic expression man not only communicates his conscious thought but also, underlying his thought, a biopsychological pattern of which he is unconscious. We shall try to support our hypothesis by an investigation of a possible relationship between thought and sign. If such relationship were established, graphic signs may be taken as symbolic in character. It is through a systematization of such symbolic signs that we hope to obtain "diagrams of the unconscious."

This concept stimulated the present study, the beginning of which dates back about seventeen years. An earlier treatment was published ten years ago. [463]** In 1929 I read the thirteenth printing of Ludwig Klages' famous book, *Handschrift und Charakter (Handwriting and Char-*

---

*De la baguette divinatoire, du pendule explorateur et des tables tournantes, etc. Paris, 1854.
**Numbers refer to those in the general bibliography.

acter). For a student of psychology this was a puzzling experience. German psychology at that time emphasized, to the exclusion of almost everything else, the phenomena of sensation, perception, and memory; the problems of expression were largely neglected. Nevertheless, university laboratories and scientific circles chose the books by Klages in preference to those, for example, by Sigmund Freud. Several societies and journals were devoted to graphology, and in Germany, Austria, France, Holland, and England many reputable psychologists considered the study of handwriting one of the most promising fields in psychology. In France Alfred Binet, founder of the intelligence tests, did extensive work with handwriting [36-39] which was carried on by Piéron at the Sorbonne [324] and by Rougemont at the Collège Libre des Sciences Sociales [356]. In Germany studies on handwriting were a frequent subject for Ph.D. theses and psychological research [13, 48-50, 265, 414, 415, 436, 444]; American psychologists dealt with this subject reluctantly, although some leading American psychologists such as E. L. Thorndike [418]; J. E. Downey [99-102]; G. W. Allport [7]; H. Cantril [65] and others devoted a great deal of research to the study of handwriting. From 1939-1941 the Department of Hygiene at Harvard University conducted a large experimental investigation about the expressiveness of handwriting [318, 319, 443]. Most investigations in this field have been either studies on specific graphic characteristics, which were not directly relevant to a general theory of graphic expression, or they have presented merely a broad theory, as did Ludwig Klages [205-211, 247], though without any experimental verification. The condemnation of what some psychologists have called the "psychological underworld" [470] hampered a scientific approach to the principles of graphic movement.

Ever since I had become fascinated by the problem of personality, it was my desire to achieve a combination of both experiment and theory. It was necessary to attack the expression of personality by experimental methods. However, experimental methods may become so standardized that we lose sight of individual differences; they may become so rigid that they test only the surface and blind the experimenter to the depth of personality. It was for this reason that I set myself the task of founding an *experimental depth psychology,* planning experiments with a view toward studying the depth of personality.

While the various movement patterns which I investigated [466] reflect a transient expression, graphic movements preserve the projections of bodily movements upon paper, giving us a record, a diagram of expression, which can easily be compared with other graphic expressions of the same person and with graphic expressions of other persons. In graphic movements the origin of expressiveness could be traced back all the way to the first scribblings of the preschool child. I have integrated these studies into a special volume. [467]

The history of the present studies reflects the tumultuous circumstances of our times. My first investigations were interrupted by political catastrophes, starting in 1933, when I left Hitler's Germany and continued my work at the University of Barcelona. Here the studies were brought to a halt by the outbreak of the Spanish Civil War in 1936, when I left for Paris to work at the Sorbonne. After having used German, Spanish, and French resources, I came to this country in 1939. Thus, I was forced to work with graphic specimens of different nationalities and to consult publications in various languages. In preparing three versions of this subject for a German,* a Swiss,** and a Spanish*** publisher, political interventions forced me to start anew each time. My graphic material was taken from photostats made from the collections of autographs in the libraries of the capitals of Europe. I had a list in which each specimen was dated, but unfortunately no copy was made, and the original list was burned in the publishing house Biblioteca Nueva, when the bombs fell on Madrid in 1937. Fortunately, most of the graphic material and copies of the manuscripts were saved. Now, when no outer forces hinder the publication of the present material, I feel some inner inhibitions to presenting it. I am conscious of the fact that this most promising field of investigation is in its beginnings so that it is fully as difficult to cope with the exaggerated skepticism of scientists who expect from handwriting less than from any rat running blindly through a maze, as with the exaggerated expectations of laymen who expect everything from a handwriting analysis. Although many studies have been made on the subject of graphic expression (our bibliography lists about 500 titles), my experimental approach dealt with a virtually uncharted field. Since studies in expressive behavior indicate that an experimentation on single manifestations detached from their larger context do not yield satisfactory results, I felt that the time and energy at my disposal should not be invested in large statistical investigations of a few isolated problems. The first step was to approach the field from many different sides on the basis of a limited number of samples which a single investigator was able to handle. Some observations did not lend themselves to laboratory conditions but had to be made with samples that had originated in spontaneous life situations. However, the quantitative limitation seems to be compensated by qualitative evidence in that we do not deal with isolated but with interrelated data. The simultaneous occurrence of several form-principles in graphic patterns which determine each other seems to exclude the factor of chance. A constancy of expressive principles, allowing us to make certain predictions, yields indications even with a limited number of observations. All observations together give us a united picture which seems to have surprising implications for a new theory on personality. With this new picture of expressive behavior in mind single problems can now be attacked on the basis of very large samples. If, as the present study hopes to establish, the study of graphic movements leads to new concepts on man's expression of personality and to new diagnostic

*Teubner, Leipzig. **Huber, Bern. ***Biblioteca Nueva, Madrid.

tools, hope seems to be justified that further studies from many psychological laboratories will enable us to obtain definite quantitative statements in the direction of laws which seem to govern the expression of personality as reflected in man's graphic patterns.

Combining our quantitative and qualitative investigation, highly positive correlations were indicated between graphic expression and personality. Studies in which the same subjects were analyzed by Dr. Bruno Klopfer through use of the Rorschach and by myself through graphic analysis revealed a significant degree of correlation, although it was found that the Rorschach analysis discovered the structural and enduring qualities, while the graphic analysis detected the short-term problems and disturbances of the individual. Since graphic movements mainly reflect dynamic processes of personality and not static traits, their expressive degree varies with different persons and with the same person at different times. This is the reason why some graphic specimens are not "expressive" and why a diagnosis derived from them may easily be wrong. Graphic movements are especially indicative of inner conflicts and disturbances and in extreme cases the graphic analysis allows us to detect almost unbelievable facts. From the many cases in my own experience I should like to mention three. For Professor Emilio Mira, former director of the Psychological Institute of the University of Barcelona, I detected from handwriting specimens a man who had committed a murder in the Café Oro del Rhin in Barcelona. On the basis of graphic samples I told Dr. Thiebaut of Teachers College, Columbia University, of unsuspected suicidal tendencies in a patient who attempted suicide a month later, and of another patient's beginning cancer, which was discovered several months later. In March 1948 a reporter from Colliers' National Weekly asked me to make a personality diagnosis from doodlings without any indication who the doodlers were. He demonstrated* how my analysis agreed almost in every point with facts known from these personalities who were leading figures at the United Nations Assembly. Although such successes are an exception, they occur too frequently to be explained by chance, and the expressive principles underlying the diagnosis can be demonstrated under controlled experimental conditions.

The studies of graphic movements differ from those of graphology in various respects. The term "graphic movement" is used in order to emphasize that graphic patterns are recorded movements which reflect dynamic processes of personality; they cannot be isolated but must be considered as an integrated whole and not as a sum of single elements. Emphasis is placed on the diagnostic value of configurations rather than of fixed relationships between graphic patterns and personality traits. If our expressiveness is patterned by our personality, graphic expressiveness must show this, whether done by the child, by the average man or by the artist. Therefore, the study of graphic movements does not

---

*O. H. Brandon, "Doodles International." Colliers National Weekly, May 22, 1948, page. 22.

single out handwriting for purposes of interpretation, as does graphology. While graphology is solely interested in the diagnosis of personality, our first aim is to discover the structural quality of expressive behavior in the underlying processes, by methods of experimental depth psychology. The present investigation aims at establishing a scientific foundation for the study of expressive movements in general and for the study of their graphic reflection in particular. Graphic specimens are patterned by two factors: the *form* that is the crystallized movement, comparable to the characteristic style of an artist, and *expression,* comparable to the moods that works of art convey. Both factors led me to different investigations, the form by means of measurements and the expression by means of reaction experiments. The result of these studies are two volumes, united in the present book. Volume I, "Form and Movement," demonstrates that shape, length and position of graphic elements are determined by an unconscious principle of configuration, the discovery of which has deep implications for a new theory of personality. Volume II, "Expression and Movement," demonstrates that graphic expression is patterned by the writer's associations, a finding which leads to new diagnostic applications.

This investigation demands the discussion of statistical, experimental and methodological problems, not essential for a lay reader who may wish to proceed to the material demonstrating the principles that determine everybody's form and expression in his graphic "Diagram of the Unconscious."

I wish to express my thanks to all those who helped me develop the present study; to those who volunteered as subjects for my experiments, to the students who assisted me with measurements and calculations, to institutions which provided me with material, to libraries, especially the Roosevelt Library, whose collections I was kindly permitted to use. I am indebted to the many publishers who very obligingly permitted use of previously published illustrations and text; these sources of material are referred to at the appropriate points in the pages which follow.

My gratitude goes to Dr. Franco Modigliani for his help with the statistical investigation, to Mrs. Paula Mendel, Mrs. Gertrude Schmeidler, Mr. Joseph Precker and Mr. James Holsaert for their help in editing the manuscript.

As usual, my wife shared the thought and labor incorporated in this book; the typing of its many versions as well as the preparation of the complete index is her work alone. My special thanks are offered to my publisher, Mr. Henry M. Stratton, for his continued cooperation and the freedom given me in the presentation of this material.

W. W.

Annandale-on-Hudson, N. Y.
August, 1948.

PART I

FORM AND MOVEMENT

CHAPTER I

GRAPHIC EXPRESSION AND PERSONALITY

CONSCIOUS, PRECONSCIOUS, AND UNCONSCIOUS MOVEMENTS

Writing or drawing occurs when we move our hand as it holds a writing instrument over the paper. These little movement patterns are consciously directed and fulfill a certain purpose, just as our big movement patterns are directed, whether we reach for an object or walk toward a goal. But just as we are not aware of the single steps made by our moving feet, just as we do not deliberately plan the movements of our typing or piano-playing hand, so we are unaware of single writing movements. They are automatized and function almost without direction of the details. Our impulse is: get this object, walk to that goal, play this music, write this document, draw this picture. How the general command which we give to ourselves is fulfilled is usually beyond our attention.

Although we are not aware of the single movements themselves, although they are not in the focus of our consciousness, they can be brought into consciousness. The graphic artist can concentrate upon the performance of each stroke, the pianist can be aware or conscious of the movement of his playing fingers. These movements which are not conscious, but which can be brought to consciousness, we call preconscious movements. We are conscious of the total movement pattern, and we are preconscious of each step with which we achieve the total pattern. The total pattern corresponds to our conscious attention; each single step corresponds to preconscious, reflex-like reactions.

Both conscious and preconscious movements are learned. Even if many children have the same teacher and learn to make letters in the same way, each child's writing will nevertheless show an individual pattern. This variation cannot be explained by the immediate conditions of writing, such as paper, pen, or position of the body, because the variation remains stable, allowing us to identify each child's writing in many repetitions even if we alter the conditions intentionally, as by giving different kinds of paper and pens, and changing the positions of the body.

This observation holds for all kinds of movements: whether different pupils of one piano teacher play the same piece of music, whether various artists draw or paint the same object, we always recognize a definite style of expression. This style of expression cannot be explained entirely by environmental conditions or by factors of learning; it is an expression of the individual personality. The form and the quality of our movement are neither conscious nor preconscious. We cannot bring to consciousness why we incline a certain letter, why we put the dot over the "i" in a certain place, why we emphasize a curve. We are usually able to define neither the forms nor the quality of our movement patterns as they may appear to other people. While the direction of the total movement is conscious and the single steps of movement are preconscious, its form and quality are unconscious.

It is the unconscious pattern of movements which interests us in the present study. [463] Modern psychology has shown that our life is only to a small degree a conscious one, if to be conscious means to be aware of an act, to be able to explain it, and to be able to analyze it. Undirected impulses, strange compulsions, sudden insights, and all the complicated activities which we perform without being aware of them play the greater part in our lives.

Direction, purposefulness, and interrelationship are not solely properties of the conscious mind. Reflex actions and the inner functions of our organs, have direction and purpose. They are part as well as origin of complicated relationships. Equally, unconscious mental patterns, as they appear in dreams, have all the characteristics mentioned. Chance seems to become more and more inadequate as an explanatory term for human activities; for these always seem to follow organized patterns. Just as modern psychiatry tries to interpret the unconscious pattern of dreams, so we attempt to analyze the unconscious pattern of movements. However, such an analysis demands validation. We have three main criteria of validity: the explanation of one manifestation may receive its support from another manifestation by the same person; various observations thus validating each other (we call this co-validation); furthermore, an explanation can be validated by successful prediction (this is pre-validation); and finally, an explanation becomes validated if it explains other phenomena previously observed but not understood (that is, re-validation). These three procedures guide our efforts in explaining unconscious patterns.

THE GRAPHOGRAM

If we move a writing instrument in our hand over paper, the resulting pattern, whether apparently meaningless lines, or letters, or a drawing, is a "graphogram." For an exploration of the unconscious we are not interested in the manifest meaning of this pattern, such as the meaning of a written word or the content of a drawing. This belongs to the field of conscious and preconscious movements. We seek, rather, an explanation of unconscious forms and qualities, hoping to demonstrate the graphogram as a diagram of the unconscious. As mentioned above, a graphic pattern, which is a projection of a movement pattern upon paper, has two main characteristics: its form and its expressive quality. Form is determined by length, height, shape, and position of elements. These elements can be measured. Neither a writer nor an artist can usually explain his individual form elements. He is inclined to say, "This came just by chance," or, "I always make this form, but I don't know why," or, "These patterns fit each other." Nobody constructs such individual form elements intentionally; they are made unconsciously. Measuring the length and position of form elements and analyzing their relationships, we shall try to investigate whether these unconscious patterns originate by chance or by an unconscious organizing principle. Such an unconscious organization would become apparent if the principles of form remained consistent with different form patterns of the same person (co-validation); if they allowed the successful prediction of certain form principles for future movement patterns (pre-validation); and if certain observations, say on the length of movements, also explained others, for instance if one present movement pattern allowed us to validate other movement patterns of the same person, as it becomes necessary in disputed handwritings (re-validation).

The first search for an individual formula of movement determining graphic forms is followed by the search for a possible relationship between graphic forms and personality patterns. Expressive qualities cannot be subjected to measurements in the same way as form patterns. Aesthetics has not yet succeeded in analyzing the expression of beauty and of many emotions and feelings; nevertheless, certain elemental expressions are understood by everybody. The infant and the animal immediately recognize friendly and unfriendly expressions. Children are able to judge expressions of behavior correctly, also in graphic forms [415]. By eliciting the associations that accompany graphic movements we hope to discover the roots of graphic expressiveness.

HISTORICAL SURVEY

The first attempt to recognize a relationship between handwriting and personality was made in 1622 by the Italian physician Camillo Baldo in his *Treatise on a Method to Recognize the Nature and Quality of a Writer from His Letters.* [20] But this study remained rather isolated. A new interest in handwriting arose in the second half of the eighteenth century with Lavater's *Physiognomical Fragments* [233] (1775-78); this includes a chapter on handwriting, which, however, makes only dogmatic statements. Predecessors of the modern scientific approach to this subject are the French Abbé J. H. Michon, with his *System of Graphology* (1875) [284], and his student Crépieux-Jamin [76-82], who enlarged these studies. The German W. Preyer's work, *Psychology of Handwriting* (1895) [333], deals for the first time with the relationship of graphic movements to mental processes. It was Ludwig Klages [205-211] who founded a Graphological Society (1896) and brought, in Germany, this field of study to a scientific and even governmental acceptance. Handwriting experts were used for vocational and diagnostic purposes, they played a considerable role in the fields of education and industry, and they were advisers for the screening of soldiers in the German Army.

But while, especially in Germany, the analysis of handwriting played a greater role than other diagnostic devices such as the Rorschach inkblot

test or other personality tests, graphology found much less consideration in the United States. A study of publications on this subject during
the last ten years indicates a steady decrease of contributions. Listed
in Table 1 is the number of studies made between 1936 and 1945, as
referred to by the *Psychological Abstracts,* which cover the most important psychological journals. The grouping of contributions according to
the different countries indicates the varying interest in the subject.

TABLE 1

Frequency of Publications on Handwriting During the Ten-Year Period from 1936
to 1945 in Various Countries

Year	Germany	America	Japan	France	Hungary	Italy	Poland	Latin America and Spain	China	Holland	Britain
1936	12	7	1	—	—	2	1	2	—	—	—
1937	17	6	1	2	—	2	1	—	2	—	—
1938	16	7	3	1	—	—	—	—	—	1	1
1939	18	7	—	3	4	—	1	—	—	—	—
1940	14	11	2	—	—	—	—	—	—	—	—
Total: 145	77	38	7	6	4	4	3	2	2	1	1
1941	—	8	—	—	—	—	—	—	—	—	—
1942	—	6	—	—	—	—	—	—	—	—	—
1943	1	9	—	—	—	—	—	—	—	—	—
1944	—	8	—	—	—	—	—	—	—	—	—
1945	—	4	—	1	—	—	—	—	—	—	1
Total: 38	1	35	—	1	—	—	—	—	—	—	1

Only the distribution of papers during the five years from 1936 to
1940 is significant, since the war later interfered with the production
of papers and with their communication; from 1936 to 1940 the number of papers produced each year in any one country remained relatively stable. It appears that interest in studies on handwriting is highest
in Germany (77), its number of papers being double that of America.
All the other contributing countries together have fewer studies (30)
than the United States (38). Under the leadership of Robert Saudek
[265, 371], founder of a journal devoted to these studies, British psychologists made significant contributions to the study of handwriting,
but this interest ceased immediately with Saudek's death (1934), putting
Britain at the bottom of the scale of contributors to this subject.

Handwriting is a very complex material for investigation, offering the most varied implications. Grouping the 183 studies referred to by the *Psychological Abstracts* during the ten-year period from 1936 to 1946, we can scale the topics dealt with as shown in Table 2.

TABLE 2

Topics	Frequency of Contributions	
Theories of handwriting analysis		
a. General	16	
b. Textbooks	13	29
Characteristics of handwriting		
a. Forms of connection	4	
b. General characteristics	4	
c. Structure of strokes	2	10
Scales		
a. Ability	2	
b. Dynamic aspects	1	
c. Qualifications	1	4
Physiological factors		
a. Pressure and speed	12	
b. Motor processes	5	
c. Disturbances	4	21
Physiological and developmental factors		
a. Children	2	
b. Kinetic aspects	2	4
Hereditary factors		
a. Handwriting in twins	9	
b. Family similarities	7	
c. Racial characteristics	2	18
Educational factors		
a. Writing ability	17	
b. Errors in writing	4	21
Conscious and unconscious factors		
a. Mental anticipation of writing movements	3	
b. Hypnotic and automatic writing	2	
c. General	1	6
Personality		
a. Traits	4	
b. Errors in writing	3	
c. Sex characteristics	2	
d. Self-identification	2	
e. Intelligence	1	12

Pathological cases

    a. Psychosis 8
    b. Epilepsy 2
    c. Feeble-mindedness 1
    d. Neurological cases 1   12

Criminal cases

    a. General 5
    b. Rhythm 1
    c. Disguise 1
    d. Single case 1   8

Single case studies 7   7

Types

    a. Physical type and handwriting 4
    b. Extraversion-introversion 2   6

Diagnosis

    a. Medical 6
    b. Vocational 5
    c. Psychological 4   15

Validation

    a. Matchings of handwritings to personal data 7
    b. Theoretical studies 3   10

With special reference to these fifteen topics the following observations and theoretical considerations are an attempt to summarize the majority of studies on handwriting.

Theories. Several authors discuss methods in graphology [111, 336] and whether this subject is or may become a science [74, 255, 324, 377, 427, 470]; some stress its physiological basis [64, 116], others its "depth-psychological" foundation [63, 73, 115, 131-133, 190, 201, 270, 279, 336, 410]; some objective techniques and experimentation [114, 123, 128, 187, 255, 276, 316, 324, 329, 330, 367, 414, 415, 436, 444, 460-67], others discuss the applications of a handwriting analysis [29, 38, 39, 41, 45, 111a, 269, 395, 409]. Some authors discuss a "political graphology" based upon the handwriting of politicians [109, 382]; other authors indicate the impact of graphology upon medicine when handwriting may hint at latent physiological disturbances [8, 44, 110, 118, 159, 248, 471]. Some authors discuss the importance of graphology for an understanding of poets [69, 425, 438], painters [162, 270a], musicians [428], and creative intellectuals [429]. The guides or textbooks emphasize different topics, such as the relationship between handwriting and character, handwriting and education, handwriting and crime, handwriting and successful living, and handwriting and unconscious processes [15, 22, 23, 30, 32, 33, 45, 55, 76, 78, 79, 82, 92, 93, 94, 97, 117, 130, .134, 142, 163, 174, 176, 177, 183, 192, 193, 202, 205-11, 213, 216, 231, 242, 256, 271, 273, 278, 279, 282,

283, 284, 296, 309, 312, 333, 336, 337, 339, 345, 348, 351, 356, 365, 366, 374, 397, 400, 406, 408, 413, 419].

Characteristics of handwriting. Special investigations have been made on the character of the graphic stroke, the size, width, length, variations of letters, the angle of inclination [7, 172, 180, 185, 319]. Statistical studies indicate that wideness and marked inclination tend to go together; large script tends to be better connected than small script and to have a greater variation in size [95, 319]. The forms of connection in handwriting movements, such as angular or curved connections, curves in the upper or in the lower part of the letter, are attributed to various personality structures [34, 422, 441, 474, 474a].

Scales. Scales have been designed for judging the quality of handwriting in terms of school standards and in terms of qualifications for employees [21, 249, 325].

Physiological factors. Physiological factors of the writing movement have been observed by cinematographic studies of handwriting, by influencing the kinesthetic sense—e.g., through rotatory experiments—by recordings of the fine tremors in writing, by the measurement of pressure [7, 25, 42, 50, 67, 228, 318, 354, 359, 431, 453, 473], speed [7, 46, 180, 228, 289, 354, 451, 453] and of the muscle tonus [35, 151, 196, 359].

Physiological and developmental factors. Studies in the variability of handwriting were made with reference to the development of writing speed and point pressure in school children [144, 145, 146, 179, 338, 354]; developmental sequences in name writing were analyzed [179], and the kinetic aspects of growth and the principles of motor skill [154, 196, 315, 343] and of muscle tonus [35, 151, 196] were examined.

Hereditary factors. Similarities of handwriting in races and families serve for a discussion of hereditary factors [49, 87, 173, 238, 302, 344, 372]. Some authors demonstrate similarities in twins [48, 50, 67, 144, 155, 166, 178, 218, 237, 306, 307, 354a, 384, 385, 403], others in siblings [241, 407, 416]. Some claim that pressure and speed are determined by heredity, other characteristics by social factors. According to some authors only certain graphic characteristics, such as the angle of writing, seem to have a hereditary basis. Some American students of the subject have not found racial differences in handwriting samples [140], while some German students emphasize that the innervation of writing movements is inherited as a partial function of the motor apparatus in general, being a constant expression of racial factors [221]. According to one author, the handwriting of children conceived when the parents were under the influence of alcohol is likely to show signs characteristic of drunkenness in adults [238]. Some authors discuss psycho-somatic types from the angle of graphic expression [85, 113, 220, 243, 326, 364, 390].

Educational factors. These studies deal with the teaching of handwriting, legibility, deficiencies in writing, calligraphy, practice, writing tools, improvements of handwriting, and other problems of penmanship [165, 181, 197, 236, 430, 448, 450, 456].

Conscious and unconscious factors. Unconscious factors in handwriting were studied by the use of hypnosis [229, 458, 466], hypnagogic states, and automatic writing [96, 115, 115a, 225, 298]. The origins of mistakes in handwriting were studied in their relation to the intentional aims [203, 294, 295, 357, 363, 448]. It was found, also, that letter distortions are related to perceptual processes and to motor inco-ordination. The role of consciousness in the writing process was analyzed by the use of introspective reports, questionnaires, and films.

Personality. Although most topics in the study of handwriting have an indirect bearing upon problems of personality, relatively few papers deal with the direct relationship of personality traits and handwriting. Results of judging isolated traits such as dominance [109, 286], neuroticism [287, 303, 357], sex differences [37, 56, 80, 100, 109, 143, 153, 204, 285, 305, 424, 439, 454], intelligence [37, 143, 152, 232, 288, 313] and personal interests [65, 66] varied in their conclusiveness. An analysis of total personality patterns is more likely to be successful [7, 205, 319, 329, 336, 352].

Pathological cases. Many authors report a significant relationship between handwriting and mental disturbance. Certain characteristics of the handwriting and drawing of feeble-minded children have significance for a mental diagnosis [10, 227, 322]. The outstanding factor in the handwriting of the psychotic is abnormal rhythmic disturbance, rigidity, or extreme irregularity [71, 161, 217, 240, 248, 250a, 256, 265, 334, 379, 402]. In schizophrenic writing a disturbance in the breadth of writing prevails; in paranoid writing it is the depth of handwriting that is predominantly affected; and manic-depressive writing shows an emphasis on disturbances in the height of letters [248, 265, 334]. The graphic pattern shows changes after electrically induced convulsions as they are used in electro-shock treatment [402]. Investigations with the handwriting of deteriorated and nondeteriorated epileptic patients have shown some statistically significant differences: the average height of the small letters as well as the ratio of the height of the small letters to that of the tall letters is greater in the handwriting of deteriorated patients than in the handwriting of nondeteriorated patients. The handwriting of institutionalized epileptic patients shows a greater mean value for the height of the tall letters than does the handwriting of extramural patients [256, 320]. The reflection of psychological disorders upon graphic expression also appears in the handwriting of children, who have not yet reached maturity in their writing [28, 239, 264]. The handwriting of children may give indications of a prepsychotic personality; according to the samples of another author, however, the adolescent writing of persons who later developed psychoses did not show any peculiarities which are not also found in normal adolescents [240]. Several investigations have been made about motor disorders and handwriting. Cases of agraphia have been studied [267, 268], the handwriting of stutterers [86, 353, 398], cases of mirror handwriting [106, 297, 317, 396] and of letter reversals [452]. The indication of diseases in handwritings has been claimed by several authors [105, 117, 248, 278, 419, 435] and characteristic changes in the writing of persons near death [191] have been observed. Some studies are devoted to disturbances of the writing center in the brain [308, 355].

Criminal cases. Graphological investigations of the handwriting of criminals suggest that handwriting analysis can be used to detect actual criminals, to discover individuals with criminal potentialities, and to infer motives behind particular crimes [1, 68, 79, 171, 231, 254, 256, 282, 335, 388, 393, 421, 449]. Disguise in handwriting and forgery may be detected by the fact that certain characteristics of handwriting usually are difficult to change [31, 126, 229, 234, 266, 314, 341, 375].

Single case studies. Studies of single cases describe the most different writing phenomena, such as an unusual case of imitation of handwriting and anonymous writing [341], a case of dual personality in handwriting [275], a case of writing exercises of a senile homosexual as a source of pleasure and infantile regression [201].

Types. Relationships between handwriting and constitutional types are claimed to be based upon size and pressure of letters. Small letters are found more frequently in the writing of asthenics than in that of pyknics and athletics; pressure variations are said to correspond to Kretschmer's phenotypes [220], according to which a definite relationship exists between bodily build and character traits [85, 113, 326, 364]. Also, characteristic differences in handwriting between extraverted and introverted types have been analyzed [243]. According to one investigation the ability to judge handwriting depends on the type of the interpreter; cyclothymics and extraverts being more suited to grasp successfully the personality from handwriting than are schizothymics and introverts.

Diagnosis. Since handwriting is supposed to indicate somatic and psychological disturbances its importance to the physician in general [8, 44, 110, 159, 471] and to the psychiatrist in particular [118, 125, 135, 292, 378] has been stressed. Handwriting became a tool for diagnosis [8, 57, 111a, 125, 471] and played a considerable role in German and Spanish military psychology and psychiatry [291, 292, 347]. Handwriting has been used for a diagnosis of sexual [190, 201, 279, 335, 336] and social problems [370, 383, 410] of the individual.

While the medical use of graphology is controversial, its use for vocational guidance is supported by many testimonials of business and industrial men [17, 18, 91, 167, 223, 226, 423], and its implications for education have been stressed [165, 167, 455].

Validation. Several studies deal with the validation of graphological judgments and theoretical claims of graphologists [83, 377, 387, 409]. Correlations of handwriting characteristics with personality characteristics, carried out in the Harvard Psychological Clinic, led to the conclusion that certain variables of handwriting are related to certain variables of personality [319]. The results of many studies indicate that the varying degrees of success in graphological experiments depend on whether the experimenter is dealing with isolated traits or with patterns; or whether a single characteristic is enforced by other characteristics. The success of matching experiments varies with different characteristics of handwriting and with the expressiveness of specimens used [5, 7, 13, 331, 416, 432, 433, 434, 460, 461].

Relations Between Graphic Movement and Personality

The present ten year survey is significant for the general topics with which students in handwriting deal. Thirty-seven studies were based upon experimental approaches, but of these very few experiments were made to show any relationship between graphic expression and personality. Such experiments were discouraged by studies like those of C. L. Hull and P. Montgomery [187], who in 1919 published their *Experimental Investigation of Certain Alleged Relations Between Character and Handwriting*. They measured microscopically some of the elemental graphic signs from copies of a message obtained from seventeen fraternity members. Each of the subjects was judged according to the significance which certain graphologists attach to these signs; these judgments were compared with personality ratings by the fraternity members. The average correlation between ten such measurements and ratings was set at —.16. The failure of a positive result was grist to the mills of the skeptics. But the results of this experiment are not conclusive at all. Allport and Vernon [7] objected that no modern graphologist would claim that a single graphic sign has a fixed meaning, but that it is considered only as an indicator for certain tendencies which vary with regard to the relationship with other elements. The unreliability of ratings in testing for the diagnosis of certain selected traits is well known; such single criteria are not sufficient for the evaluation of a whole method.

K. T. Omwake [313] demonstrated that his untrained judges were not able to determine intelligence from handwriting. And some other experiments in this line, made by other authors, gave zero correlations. But if we judge only a single feature from a form of expression we destroy the concept of personality itself, because single features do not exist in personality. We cannot speak of the isolated trait "intelligence" without considering in what relationships intelligence manifests itself. Feebleminded persons may be able to show a high intelligence in solving chess problems, and an intelligent philosopher may not be able to solve technical problems which are supposed to test intelligence.

On the other hand, several German and French experimenters were able to distinguish single characteristics of personality. A. Binet [38] shuffled the writings of male and female—of old and young, honest and dishonest persons—and asked judges to sort the writings according to these groups. Success was obtained in 61 per cent to 92 per cent of the cases. The significance of such results depends on their chance factor.

If we distinguish between two factors—e.g., male-female, or honest-dishonest—we might expect to be correct in 50 per cent of the cases if we made blind guesses. Correctness due to chance appears in one out of two; if we made a blind guess of one out of three, a correctness due to chance might appear in 33.3 per cent of the cases, and so forth. Thus, Binet's results were significant.

While "intelligence" is a characteristic which has meaning only in connection with other traits, sex is a biologically defined characteristic; but here we have a new problem, namely, the difference between physiological and psychological sex characteristics. A person with an extremely masculine appearance, as for example, a boxer, may have a feminine personality; while women may have masculine traits. Thus we cannot expect conclusive results in judging sex from the graphic expression of persons in whom biological and psychological sex characteristics are opposite. Hence some authors have achieved very successful results while others have not succeeded, depending on their material.

From this point of view the expressive value of handwriting cannot be decided by diagnosing single features, and R. Arnheim, as well as the present author, studied experimentally whether an interrelated group of traits appears in graphic expression. Arnheim [13] asked different judges to match the handwriting of Michelangelo, Leonardo da Vinci, and Raphael, which they had never seen before, to the corresponding personalities. He obtained on the average 83.6 per cent success instead of the 33.3 per cent expected by chance. The present writer [461] in experiments matching voice records with handwriting, and matching styles of retelling stories with handwriting, obtained successful results about one and a half times as frequently as might be expected by chance.

Regarding an interrelationship of traits, graphology was applied in Germany to personnel investigation. G. von Kügelgen [226] analyzing the writing of forty-eight pupils with regard to nine traits, obtained an agreement with their teachers' ratings in 66 per cent of the cases, as against a chance expectancy of about 20 per cent. K. Seeseman [387], with his diagnosis of twenty miners, established on yes and no answers, got an agreement of 93 per cent with the results obtained by their foremen. C. Bobertag [41], with 450 matchings of 30 personality sketches to handwriting specimens, obtained 80.7 per cent correct answers as against 20 per cent to be expected by chance. Many similar experiments have been published with corresponding results: features of the total personality could be diagnosed from handwriting with a correctness far above chance expectation. In this country, handwriting experts were used successfully in the army, and they have also worked in industrial and personnel investigation.

Allport and Vernon [7] in 1933 made a survey on the status of experimental graphology, which we have supplemented with the present report.

While graphology is recognized as a legitimate psychological approach in Europe, it has aroused skepticism in America, owing to the fact that graphological experts neglect methodology. Students of hand-writing have been satisfied to observe a relationship between certain characteristics of writing and certain attitudes of the writer. Following the founder of graphology, Abbé Michon, they collect a dictionary of signs with their supposed meanings, applying them indiscriminately to a diagnosis of personality. But living phenomena and their reflection in movements and signs are never a sum of static and fixed entities. The same building materials in nature form the most different structures. All materials are like letters with which we can form innumerable words. In the sphere of expression every artist knows that the same color looks different and has different expressive qualities in different backgrounds and different combinations. A picture is more than the sum of its color patches and a musical piece more than the sum of its sounds. What makes the work of art is the unique configuration of its elements. The German school of Gestalt psychology, dealing especially with the problem of con-figuration, showed in many detailed investigations that our perception, the way we deal with impressions, and our expressions are determined by the principle of relationships and of configuration. Thus, the observa-tion and classification of data in isolation is not enough, since any single item has significance only in relation to other items. A classification of elements is not always helpful in seeking an interpretation of an expres-sion as a whole.

Following the modern trend of focusing attention upon relationships and upon the whole expression, several serious students of graphic ex-pression have emphasized that the problem is not so much the understand-ing of elements as of their interplay, the "resultants." [81] The difficulty has been, however, that the numberless resultants could no longer be described exactly. An appeal had to be made to the observer's intuition with which he grasped the total configuration and its degrees of harmony. Klages [211] called this over-all pattern of graphic expression its "level of form," giving some indications for training in ways to grasp it. How-ever, the concept of an over-all pattern is vague if we have no frame of reference from which to judge.

From the two basic methods used up to now, the static classificational one has led to several empirical observations, which, however, have not given us an understanding of the underlying processes. The dynamic method, attempting an understanding, has neglected objective observation. The aim of the first method was to discover the building stones; that of the second method was to unveil the finished structure; but neither of them helps us to recognize the principles according to which the stones were assembled and the structure was finished. What we need is to detect the building plan, the diagram of expression, with which the expression was built.

Certainly, the student of graphic expression should not neglect the results of the two approaches mentioned. The empirical material col-lected by the classifying method shows us, even if the classification itself is disputable, what kinds of material we have to deal with. The keenest attempts in this direction were made by Robert Saudek. He used all kinds of apparatus to attack the single element—microscope, pressure board, motion picture camera. He analyzed the effect of writing instruments and writing surface [367], the influence of training, and the modification of subjective expression by national stereotypes [369] and age factors [371].

But other factors, not intrinsic to the expressive act itself, are the environmental conditions influencing its perception. The psychology of the observer plays a decisive role in all manifestations of expression. An expression highly estimated a hundred years ago may be ridiculed today. A psychology of the observer of graphic expression was the subject of studies made by E. Powers [329] and by Schorn [377]. They emphasize the influence of the written content upon the judgment of the observer. The present author made several studies to investigate the amount of agreement and disagreement among several judges of the same specimen. The evaluation of such studies is difficult. Different judges may point toward the same phenomenon but use different terms of interpretation. Agreement may be high as to descriptive characteristics of secondary importance, such as quickness-slowness, imaginative-conventional forms, but low as to deeper personality characteristics, such as honesty-dishonesty, sexual indications, compulsive trends. Or there may be agreement in the detection of characteristics but disagreement in their evaluation, and *vice versa*. Furthermore, the judgments may be general and not specific, general judgments having validity for a large group of people, and therefore meaning nothing for the description of an individual. The present author took the personality analyses of individual handwriting, as published in graphological books such as those of Klages. He used the same description for a supposed analysis of several subjects selected at random, asking them whether they agreed with this description of their personality. Most of the subjects agreed completely and considered the analysis to the point. This indicates that such general phrases as "an active personality, intelligent, sincere," are accepted by a majority of people as being judgments which are actually true or which, as favorable traits, are desired by the subject concerned.

Finally, the present author analyzed published analyses according to their contradictory statements. In long analyses such as those of Klages, essential statements are submerged by meaningless generalities, so that the reader loses track of the essential statement. When, after a page of generalities, an opposite essential statement, again embedded in generalities, is made, the reader does not recognize the contradiction. However, the human subject of the analysis duly picks out that statement with which he agrees, neglecting its opposite. When such an analysis is broken down into its essentials, the contradictory statements frequently cancel each other out and there remain only empty generalities.

The discoveries of psychoanalysis have influenced investigators of graphic movement such as Max Pulver [336], Anja Mendelsohn [279], Hans Jacobi [190], Nöck Sylvus [410]. In the search for reflections of the inner psychological dynamics elucidated by Freud, Adler, and Jung, new spheres of expression have been discovered. The interrelationship of processes manifest in the body and its movements, as well as in the mind, including its conscious and unconscious phenomena, suggests that every phenomenon observed in man's organism has a replica in his movements. Some of these dynamic processes have even been demonstrated under hypnosis. The conscious intentions which cover unconscious drives and the resistance against their manifestation are here removed; the hypnotized individual acts out his inner stimulations and, expressing them in graphic movements, gives us some insight into the sources of expressiveness. Later we shall discuss some of the observations made with hypnotized subjects, but a study of graphic expression cannot depend entirely on such unnatural conditions.

Methods based on a static experimental approach determine the tools for our investigation; methods founded on a dynamic interpretative approach determine our point of view. Both methods combined form part of the approach which the present author has introduced as *experimental depth psychology* [466].

CHAPTER II

THE CONSISTENCY OF PERSONALITY

THE PROBLEM OF CONSISTENCY

The concept of personality immediately poses an intricate problem. Is personality implanted in us like the works in a clock, so that our reactions remain uniform or consistent? Any social relationship we enter upon is based upon the concept of a consistency of personality. If we do business we suppose that our partner will meet his obligations in the manner we both have agreed upon; in our friendships we trust that the bond of common interests will not change from one day to the other; in marriage we believe that our partner participates consistently in our problems of living. Our habits, duties, and activities follow a consistent pattern so that the people around us can predict our reactions. Certainly, we are frequently disappointed because people do not always behave as we expect them to do. We may even be shocked if a person suddenly reveals traits which seem to be completely inconsistent with the picture we had of him. According to one theory, man's actions and reactions are structurally consistent, but we frequently do not recognize his true behavior. If heredity played a decisive part in our behavior we might assume that man's personality is determined and fixed from birth on.

But there is an opposite viewpoint. We might believe that man's actions and reactions are not determined by his inner personality, that he only reacts to his enviroment. If the environment changes, his reactions change. According to this assumption man has no inner consistency at all; if his behavior appears consistent, this is due to the environment, which forces upon him a routine and a standardization of behavior. Thus, man is conditioned to be consistent, but he is really inconsistent. This thesis of man's inner inconsistency has some support. Everybody experiences self-contradictions. We may smile in the deepest depression; we may even love and hate at the same time.

The problem of consistency is related to that of a constancy of specific traits which form the personality. Studies on infants [58] have shown that babies as young as four months old show certain personality traits by which they can definitely be distinguished from each other. A constancy was found even in the amount of such elemental reactions as smiling, laughing [442] and crying [26]. M. M. Shirley [392], testing twenty behavior items of infants at frequent intervals, observed that babies constantly exhibit certain characteristics, the dominance of which,

17

however, varies from age level to age level. Shirley concludes: [392, p. 56]

> Both constancy and change characterize the personality of the baby.
> Traits are constant enough to make it plausible that a nucleus of personality
> exists at birth and that this nucleus persists and determines to a certain
> degree the relative importance of the various traits; some change is doubt-
> less brought by environmental factors, but this change is limited by the
> limitations of the original personality nucleus.*

A constancy of certain behavior patterns has been observed not only
in the beginnings of personality formation but also at later age levels.
If the constancy appears not only in certain age periods but extends over
a person's development we have an indication of a developmental stability [145].

Consistencies have been investigated by measuring personal manifestations. Some investigators measured the consistency of individual
speed in speaking [7, 51, 440] by counting or reading set passages;
others measured the speed of walking [9, 51], some that of tapping [51,
102, 251, 343, 349, 391]. Many of these investigators concluded from the
consistencies observed that everybody has his consistent "personal tempo."
However, in comparing a person's speed in his different forms of expression it appeared that the tempo may vary with different forms. The consistency of mental reactions has been measured by examining a person's
intelligence quotient during various periods of his development [10, 72,
84, 139, 227, 290, 340, 360]. But here also contradictory observations
have been made [7, p. 98]. There is a high constancy in extreme cases
such as mental defectives and supernormal or genius personalities, but
the fluctuations of the normal are considerable. The fact that a consistency
which appeared within a single form of expression disappeared in a
comparison of various forms of expression of the same person made
it difficult to understand these contradictions of personality.

Trying to explain these contradictory results, we may ask first: Is
our concept of consistency and constancy in personality wrong? Don't
we think in terms of the constancy of a machine, which always performs
the same act? We measure the consistency with the amount of laughing,
and of crying with the speed of talking and walking; the consistency of
the I.Q. with answers to a questionnaire, just as we would test a standardized machine. We believe in consistency if the human machine runs
at the same speed and gives the same response if we push the same buttons. Everybody has experienced the influence of such a concept of a
human machine upon psychological thinking. The use of tests presupposes
that each test question is a key which, if pressed, should produce a certain
reaction in everybody, and if we describe a personality we enumerate its
traits like fixed elements.

But the organism seems to be of a different structure. Nature gives
many examples of how one thing may change into something different.
The larva, the caterpillar, and the butterfly appear as inconsistent mani-

---

*M. Shirley: "The First Two Years." Vol. II. Minneapolis, University of Minne-
sota Press, 1931. Used by permission of the publisher.

festations of the same individual organism, and the lawful transformations are predictable. The development of the embryo goes through many varying stages. In personality equally apparent inconsistencies may be variations of the same theme. But how can we discover the structure of the "theme of personality"? Psychologists who are familiar with the manifestations of a neurotic personality know that the theme of the same neurosis is expressed by the most varied means of expression. If we block one way of expression, if we suppress one symptom, the patient substitutes another. A deeper analysis would show that the same formula of personality can be expressed by different signs.

From this point of view we cannot describe or measure one trait of personality after the other, but we must see them simultaneously, in their interrelationships. The personality traits no longer appear as a mosaic but as many rays shooting from one center. How can we approach these centers? A human being usually shows us only the surface of his personality. Psychoanalysis, which attempts to delve into the depth of personality, has no experimental methods which make the approach reliable. The neurotic behavior of patients can neither be measured nor predicted nor generalized for a large group of people. We have to design a new type of investigation, which uses the surface behavior, the everyday behavior, and which, penetrating into the depth, locates a center of personality. A center is a point of convergence of many manifestations; to find a center many approaches have to be made to converge. Which expressions of personality can we use to locate such a center by applying exact methods of measurement?

DIAGRAMS OF MOVEMENT

The observation that personality is revealed in a person's movements is very old. Proverbs 6:12-13 says: "A naughty person, a wicked man, walketh with a froward mouth. He winketh with his eyes, he speaketh with his feet, he teacheth with his fingers. . . ." Everybody knows the language of personality; the child jumps and runs if he is happy and withdraws and shows restricted movements if he is sad. Our immediate reactions of sympathy and antipathy are based upon our unconscious reading of expressive movements. For experimental use these expressive movements can be recorded—the voice by a phonograph and movements by means of a film. In investigating the relationships of expressive characteristics we may approach the depth of personality by experimental methods. The present author has described this approach of his experimental depth psychology in other books [466, 467]. The present volume is devoted to one specific problem, to obtaining a diagram of the unconscious. The movement patterns of our gestures are too complex to be measured; they must be reduced to diagrams just as the movements of our heart are demonstrable in a cardiogram, just as our breathing or the electrical responses of our organism can be measured by their transformation into graphs. When different people react to the same stimulus, their differences of reaction reveal their personalities. Diagrams of these different reactions to the same stimulus would allow us to measure such personal differences, as well as the inconsistencies of each individual. For the transfer of bodily movements into diagrams we do not need complicated apparatus. Writing and free drawing are a transfer of hand movements to lines made on paper. We may object that the pattern of these lines is learned and stereotyped, but we know that everybody learning to write the same letters does it differently, that no two artists draw the same object in the same way. Methods of discriminating genuine and forged handwritings have been used for a long time in criminology; however, their efficiency, which is generally accepted in this field, did not enhance graphology, whose claim to diagnose personality from handwriting is mostly rejected in scientific circles. But if handwriting identification succeeds in cases where the usual writing is purposely disguised, it follows that the writer in spite of his intention to transform his writing is not able to do so. What hinders his conscious intention? There must be unconscious trends in his personality which he cannot suppress. Thus, admitting the possibility of handwriting identification, we must also admit that handwriting expresses personal trends, or, in a wider sense, personality.

If we study graphic movements experimentally, we have to abstract the factor of learning and of content, and we must eliminate as far as possible what a person does intentionally. This can be done by an indirect method, namely, by measuring the length of movements and the position of patterns—abstract relationships which the subject produces without being conscious of them.

A Graphic Experiment on Consistency

Before I started to design an experimental series with the intention of obtaining a diagram of the unconscious, I formulated my expectations on the basis of known observations. The first experiment aimed at measuring a consistency of movement. If a subject repeats the same movement pattern, the first movement may have originated by chance and the repetitions may be imitations of this first chance movement. A consistency thus obtained would be determined rather by the factors of memory and imitation than by a structural formula of personality. Therefore, we had to exclude a stereotyped sequence; we had to alternate different movement patterns and to repeat the first one when the subject's memory image was more or less dissolved. But even so, the movement pattern might be stereotyped by learning and thus reveal conditions set by environment and not by personality. Accordingly, the subject had to make the same movement pattern under conditions he had not encountered previously—as in writing with his left hand and his eyes closed, for instance. His usual expression, produced with the right hand and open eyes, might be transferred to unusual conditions of writing.

Several studies have been made concerning a transfer of learning

[52, 64a, 310, 361, 472]. W. Preyer [333] and R. Saudek [368], claimed that the expression of handwriting, executed with the right hand or with the left hand, even with the mouth or with the toes, remains basically unchanged. An individual's movements projected upon paper could no longer be explained as the result of training of a specific muscle group (e.g. those of the right hand), rather, the different muscle groups, such as of right hand and left hand, foot, and mouth, seemed to be controlled by the same brain center. In our experiment a certain movement pattern had to be repeated with the right hand and with the left hand with eyes open and with eyes closed.

The experiment on the consistency of movement patterns was supposed to answer the following three questions:

1. If a person repeats the same graphic pattern after an interpolation of different patterns, will the repetition show characteristics identical to those of the first?

2. If a person repeats a graphic pattern with the left hand and with closed eyes, will the repetition under such unfamiliar conditions show characteristics identical to those done under familiar conditions?

3. Suppose we do not find external similarities in the patterns compared, will they show identical characteristics of *inner* relationships?

The following experiments were conducted by this writer during the years 1941 and 1942 in the Department of Psychology at Vassar College. Twenty girl students were the subjects of the experiments, which were carried out in individual sessions. Each session was repeated twice after intervals of three days. When the subject entered my office I explained to her that I wanted to make a study on the representation of simple geometrical forms. The subject, comfortably seated at my desk, had a pad of paper (6 x 12) in a horizontal position under her hand. She was told to close her eyes, to draw what I told her, tear off the page without looking at it and to place it face down when she had finished a pattern. The first direction was:

Make your choice of *one* of the following patterns: a horizontal line, a vertical line, a circle, a triangle or a square. Make one form only, whichever you like.

Next came a series of patterns, each of them put on a separate page, all with eyes closed. The subject was told:

Now make a horizontal line—now a vertical line—now a circle—now a triangle—now a square.

Next came a series of handwritings, using the signature as a person's most stereotyped graphic pattern, investigating whether consistencies appear under intentional change. The instructions were:

Now write your name—now write it smaller than usual—now bigger than usual—and now try to disguise your name.

The next series was a repetition of the first, but under changed conditions of writing. The subject had to keep her eyes closed but to take the pen in her left hand. (A few left-handed individuals had to perform the series with the right hand.)

The next series was again a repetition, but now the subject had to perform the patterns with her eyes open, right-handed, and finally with eyes open and left-handed.

The ten patterns were made first with eyes closed and the right hand; second, with eyes closed and the left hand; third with eyes open and the right hand; and fourth, with eyes open and the left hand.

The list of graphic movements is shown in Table 3.

TABLE 3

Pattern	Conditions of Writing and Number of Items			
	eyes closed, right hand No.	eyes closed, left hand No.	eyes open, right hand No.	eyes open, left hand No.
Choice of pattern*	1	11	21	31
Horizontal line	2	12	22	32
Vertical line	3	13	23	33
Circle	4	14	24	34
Triangle	5	15	25	35
Square	6	16	26	36
Writing signature as usual	7	17	27	37
Writing signature smaller than usual	8	18	28	38
Writing signature bigger than usual	9	19	29	39
Writing disguised signature	10	20	30	40

*Horizontal line, vertical line, circle, triangle, square.

From the forty graphic movements those of the same patterns made under the varying writing conditions were compared. In many cases it appeared very strikingly that the size of a pattern remained the same under the different conditions. Here we have a constancy of graphic expression under various unfamiliar conditions. Let us give an example: One subject made the following identical patterns (Fig. 2):

In the free choice of a pattern the same size circle with the right hand, eyes closed (1) and open (21); and later under instruction the same size circle with eyes closed, right-handed (4) and left-handed (14), and with

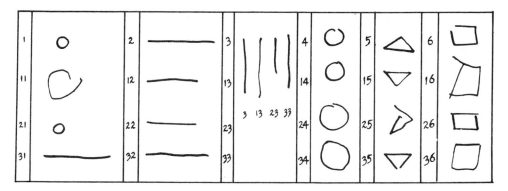

FIG. 2.—Consistency of patterns made right-handed, left-handed, eyes open and closed.

eyes open, right-handed (24) and left-handed (34); the same size horizontal line left-handed with eyes closed (12) and right-handed with eyes open (22); the same size vertical line right-handed with eyes closed (3) and left-handed with eyes open (33); the same size triangle right-handed, eyes closed (5) and open (25), and left-handed, eyes closed (15) and open (35); the same size square right-handed, eyes closed (6) and eyes open (26).

Hence, consistencies may appear under the most different conditions of writing.

Let us see what this simple observation involves. Statisticians tell us that a certain number of identical lengths is to be expected in any case. If we make similar movements at random we obtain about 10 per cent of identities simply by chance. However, the number of our identities was far above chance namely, in 54 per cent of the 20 subjects. A similar result was obtained in experiments with male students at Bard College.

The psychologist might explain the identities by habit. Everybody learns certain movement patterns and repeats them even under different conditions. But this explanation cannot stand, because in a new experimental series each subject produced other identities. Each subject may start a pattern with each series, and his memory trace condition his repetitions; thus, a consistency of behavior would be due to learning and imitation. A closer examination of the patterns, however, shows that this phenomenon is more complicated. The problem arises especially with handwriting. Here the signatures made with the right hand and with the left hand, with eyes open and closed, look very different. It seems that consistencies do not play any role, that the movements are more or less patterned by chance. However, if we measure the extent of movements, for instance, from beginning to end of the writing, we get a surprising result. The extent is in many cases exactly the same. We give an example of a male subject. There appears an intricate relationship of consistencies. The subject wrote his name, *Paul Oppenheim,* under the four experimental conditions (Fig. 3):

a. eyes closed, right-handed
b. eyes open, right-handed
c. eyes closed, left-handed
d. eyes open, left-handed

Measuring the length from beginning to end in the first name and the second name, the following relationships appear:

Paul (a) is equal to Paul (d)
Paul (b) is one half of Paul (c)
Oppenheim (a) is equal to Oppenheim (c)
Oppenheim (b) is equal to Oppenheim (d)

In our experiment with 20 subjects such hidden consistencies appeared in 28 per cent of the cases. This percentage of consistencies is above chance, as we shall explain later (see page 46 ff.). It thus appears, interestingly, that consistencies need not lie on the surface, but may be detected in the depths of the structure investigated.

We repeated our experiment with the 20 subjects after an interval of a week. The consistency of forms which in the first experiment was observed in 54 per cent of the cases, now was seen in 46 per cent; the consistency of signatures, formerly in 28 per cent of the cases, now was observed in 25 per cent. Thus, there was a slight decrease of consistency. A new surprise arose with the third series of experiments, again made after a week's interval. In this session the experimenter demonstrated to each subject the consistencies she had made. Everybody was very surprised and some could hardly believe it. The subjects admitted having performed these consistent movements without any intention; they had the feeling that an unconscious organization had directed them. Several subjects exclaimed: "I don't want to have such consistencies; you destroy my belief in freedom of the will"; and similarly others complained: "Why do I always have to do the same thing?"

In order to see how much a conscious intention and the subject's resistance influence the movement patterns, new instructions were given to the subjects:

> You have seen that your graphic movement produced a high number of consistencies. Now we shall see whether, if conscious of this fact, you will again produce such consistencies. Let us once more repeat the whole series.

The result was surprising. The consistencies did not diminish but increased slightly. Just as resistance against a suggestion or hypnosis may increase susceptibility, so resistance against the consistencies increased the subject's readiness for them. The arithmetical mean for the consistencies of forms with 20 subjects in the third series was apparent in 59.0 per cent of the cases. The arithmetical mean for the consistencies in the length of first and second name in the same series was observed in 31.0 per cent of the cases.

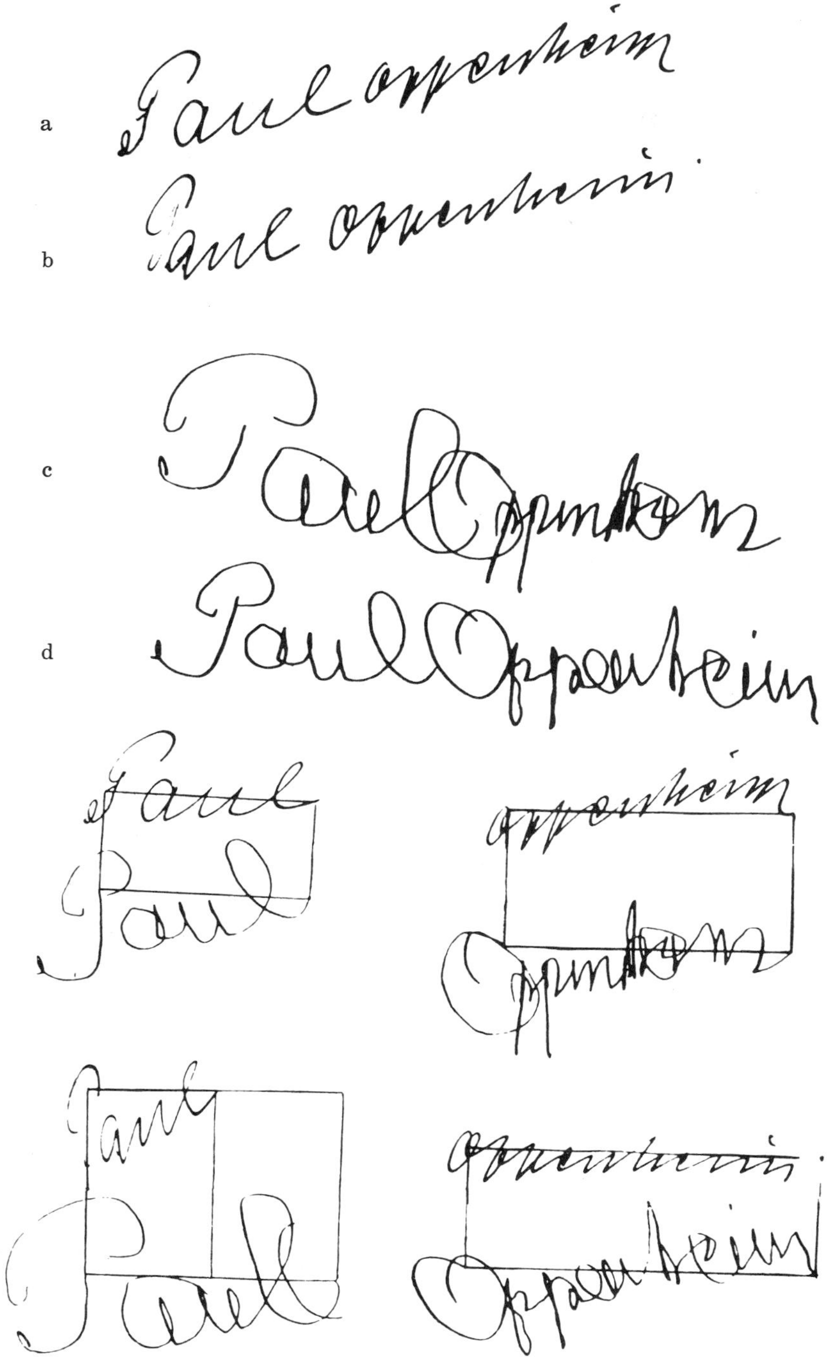

FIG. 3.—Consistency of movement in signatures, made right-handed, left-handed, eyes open and closed.

Comparing the arithmetical mean in the three series we observe:

TABLE 4

	1st series	2nd series	3rd series
A. M. of forms:	54.1 per cent	46.0 per cent	59.0 per cent
A. M. of name:	28.0 per cent	25.0 per cent	31.0 per cent

Our observations confirm the many observations made by other investigators on muscular consistency. G. W. Allport and P. E. Vernon [7, p.98] conclude from their own experiments:

> In a given task our subjects are, to a rather striking degree, constant in their performance. Single habits of gesture, as we have measured them, are stable characteristics of the individuals in our experimental group.*

But we cannot speak of "habits of gesture," since this consistency appears with habitual movements as well as with untrained movements, such as writing under visual control or without, using the trained right hand or the untrained left. Allport and Vernon, as well as other investigators [52, 289, 299, 310], also report the evidence of cross-transfer. Allport states [7, p. 177]:

> The average correlations for tasks performed with different groups of muscles are just about as high as those performed with identical muscles. This finding confirms many studies on cross-transference, and proves that the performance of single tasks is not specific to single members of the body. We have here clear evidence for intermuscle consistency.*

Our material, however, allows a further observation. If a subject repeats the same movement pattern under each of the four different conditions outlined above, we may suppose that consistencies would be higher with the movements of the right hand than with the left, or with the movements done with open eyes than with those done with eyes closed. We compared the consistencies of right movements, of left movements and the consistencies in opposite movement patterns, i.e., in those made with the right hand to those done with the left, and the performances with eyes closed to those with eyes open; these we call cross movements.

The percentages of these consistencies in our three experimental series were as shown in Table 5.

TABLE 5

Percentage of consistencies in the same movement pattern done under different conditions of writing.

	First Series	Second Series	Third Series
1. Right movements	32.0	32.0	31.0
2. Left movements	21.0	23.0	19.0
3. Cross movements right-left	47.0	45.0	50.0
4. Eyes open	32.9	39.5	32.5
5. Eyes closed	25.6	27.1	24.7
6. Cross movements eyes open-closed...	41.5	33.4	42.8

*From G. W. Allport and P. E. Vernon: "Studies in Expressive Movement." Copyright 1933 by The Macmillan Company and used with their permission.

In our cases, consistencies of movements made under normal conditions (right hand, eyes open) are higher than those made under abnormal conditions (left hand, eyes closed) ; but the highest degree of consistency appears with cross movements, namely, with the same movement made with right and left hand, as well as with eyes open and closed. We remember that Allport and other investigators concluded:

> The average correlations for tasks performed with different groups of muscles are just about as high as those performed with identical muscles.

Our indication was that the average correlation for tasks performed with different groups of muscles seems to be higher than for those performed with identical muscles. These observations have, as we shall discuss later, a correspondence in other observations of personality, all of which suggest that regularities may not appear directly but indirectly. Such regularities are not apprehended if we focus upon parallel phenomena, as is usually done by the experimental method, but they are if we focus upon interrelationships and transfer with the depth of personality in mind.

CONSISTENCY WITHIN TRANSFORMATION

Our experiment introduced an important problem, which, as we shall see, has decisive implications for our concept of psychological organization. Graphic movements reveal certain consistencies which cannot be explained by chance, nor by learning, nor by imitation of a set pattern. An inner mechanism may be at work which may determine all of our movements, whether they are projected upon paper during the act of drawing or writing or whether they become manifest in other movements, such as gestures and walking. Whether such set patterns reflect personality is another question, which we must try to approach step by step. If so, we might well be bewildered, for that would suggest that personality functions like a clockwork in definite patterns.

The fact that a person has typical gestures is known to us from daily life. We recognize a person by his typical gestures and observe that everybody has a characteristic way of walking. The measurement of graphic movements enabled us to demonstrate this constancy diagrammatically. We are therefore led to this assumption: A person's movements are not accidental, not determined by chance; rather, certain characteristics tend to remain consistent even if environmental conditions have changed; they are related to a consistent factor in the organism. But these consistencies cannot always be observed; they do not appear in everybody; they appear stronger in some subjects in one experimental session than in another, and they do not appear in each subject in the same way at different periods of time. How can we explain these contradictions of regularity and irregularity if we consider the great uniformity of man's basic reactions?

One observation led me to the belief that consistencies may be hidden. Compare a signature written with the right hand and with the left.

The results look completely different; but measuring the length of movement described from beginning to end I found an identity in several cases. This finding led me to further investigations. Perhaps these identities do not always appear in the same length of the total movement but in simple proportions of this length or in certain strokes, in certain relationships. It seemed to me that we could not apply the static consistency of a machine to organic processes, but had to look for a dynamic consistency which would include changes and transformations.

Failure to discover general laws by no means permits one to deduce that they do not exist. On the contrary, experience in physics and mathematics should lead us to believe that either these laws are not yet discovered because our attention has not been directed toward them, or that appearances which seem to be irregular have their regularity hidden. The mathematician Jean Baptiste Fourier discovered that apparently irregular periods can be reduced to simple harmonious trigonometric oscillations (Fig. 4). We had to consider the total pattern of movement and

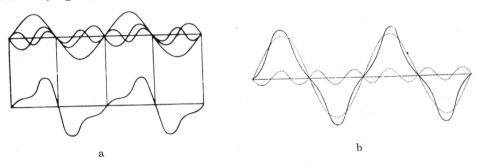

a   b

FIG. 4.—Fourier's reduction of irregular periods to simple harmonious oscillations.

to embark upon an exploration of elements and their relationship to the whole before we could decide the problem of consistency. The following chapters will give an account of this investigation.

Comparing our movement patterns with the graphs we obtain from records of nervous activity, we may consider each movement-consistency as a wave of characteristic length and shape. Although the waves recording nervous activity have a characteristic length and shape for everybody, the typical structure can easily be disturbed by outer influences. Similar disturbances may occur if a subject feels himself watched by an experimenter; it may happen if the size of paper, pen, or place of writing offers any inhibitions. We therefore tried to get material made spontaneously. In studying signatures of letters by the same person written at different times, consistencies were observed to a far higher degree than under experimental conditions. On the other hand, signatures which the same people made on their checks showed a low degree of consistency. We had some indication that the small space left for the signature on a check inhibited the consistent pattern.

In order to exclude the chance factor we searched in each group of signatures by the same writer not only for one consistency, such as the length of the name measured from beginning to end, but for a number of various consistencies. If the phenomenon of consistency appears to be multi-determined, and if a similar multi-determination appears with many samples, the probability is very high that we are in the presence of a regularity of movement patterns.

Before discussing the principles of organization in expressive movements by the following examples, some general considerations have to be mentioned.

1. The examples which we present are not rare exceptions; according to the principles of classification they are selected from a random collection ot signatures which were taken from autograph collections, from the author's private letters and from books and published manuscripts. Concerning published reproductions of signatures the question may arise as to whether these specimens were faithfully reproduced in their original size. If we have several signatures of the same writer for a comparison, measurements of many elements in a signature allow us to check upon this point.

2. In order to exclude the factor of chance, published random samples have been analyzed, such as the signatures to the Declaration of Independence and of the Constitution, entire pages of published autograph collections, and groups of signatures from advertisements.

3. The greatest limitation of the chance factor, however, lies in the very structure of many signatures which not only show one regularity of movement but many which determine each other.

4. Investigations on signatures over a person's life period show that regularities are not single phenomena but tend to remain consistent over periods of time in such intricate relationships as to be unexplainable by chance factors.

5. The regularities of graphic interrelationships are defined according to organizing principles into which most signatures seem to be classifiable.

6. The regularities of movement depend on organizing principles which sometimes are difficult to detect; and movement patterns which, at the first glance, do not show principles of organization, usually reveal them after a detailed analysis. The detection of centers of organization demands a long training to see graphic relationships.

7. In the verification of organizing principles under controlled experimental conditions several difficulties are encountered: (a) on some people the experimental situation itself has a disturbing effect; (b) regularities need not to be rigid but may shift from one configuration to another, so that signatures written in successive repetitions may present different schemes of organization.

8. Although a statistical evaluation was made with some of the phenomena demonstrated, not all data could be subjected to a rigid statis-

tical procedure because of the interrelationship of patterns in which often no single part can be considered detached from the whole.

9. For visual classification relationships are presented by means of punctuated lines, circles and squares. Since one group of regularities with various signatures of the same writer consists in equal distances from beginning to end of signatures, these consistencies are demonstrated by paralleling the lines of distance which in some cases becomes clearer by changing the position of signatures. Our first procedure to indicate relationships by means of letters was given up since they interfered with the graphic structure of the patterns.

10. The reader will visualize and "experience" the relationships with greater intensity if he repeats the measurement with the samples presented and with those of his own choice, following our directions of measurement and applying the principles of classification which we shall discuss.

Attempting to discover an unconscious organization of graphic patterns and taking signatures as examples, we asked ourselves first what kind of regularities a signature might offer because of its structure. A signature may consist of first name, middle name and last name, each of these three parts written in full, or abbreviated, or initialed. Taking each part as a graphic unit, the length of each unit may remain the same in various signatures of the same writer. Furthermore, the length of one unit may be equal to, or a simple multiple of the length of another unit.

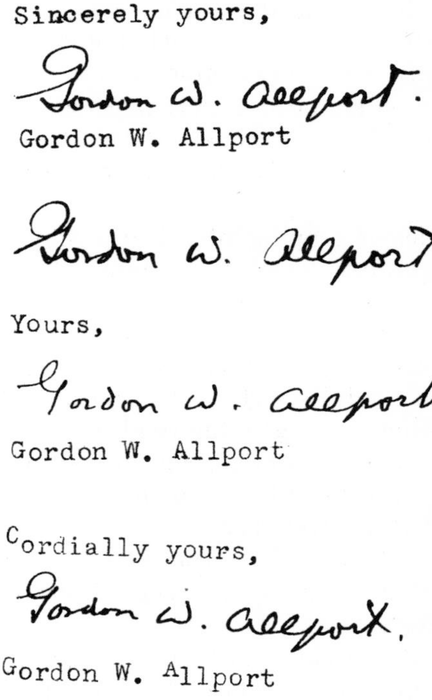

Sincerely yours,

Gordon W. Allport.

Gordon W. Allport

Gordon W. Allport.

Yours,

Gordon W. Allport

Gordon W. Allport

Cordially yours,

Gordon W. Allport.

Gordon W. Allport

FIG. 5.—Consistency of movement over four years.

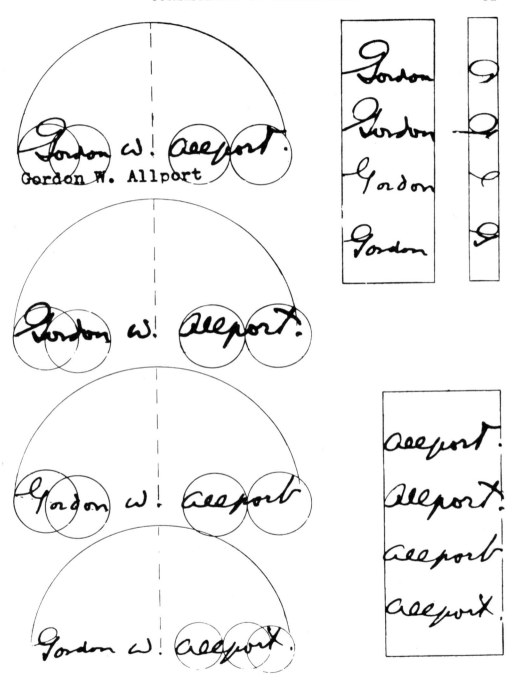

Gordon W. Allport

FIG. 5A

How do we measure a length? A signature and each of its units can be measured from the beginning to the end of the movement. However, frequently a unit is longer than its distance from start to end, since loops or additional strokes may extend its limits. Thus, the length of a unit cannot be followed only in its process of movement, but each unit can also be measured as a finished pattern from its left to its right limit. In the same signature as well as in various signatures of the same writer the length of one unit may be the same as the length of another unit or a simple multiple of it. Furthermore, a signature has many distinct elements the length, height and position of which can be measured. The length of each unit may be a multiple of the length of a significant stroke; the placing of dots may be in a fixed relationship to the length of each unit or to the whole signature.

Our first example is from *Gordon W. Allport,* to whose studies in expressive movement we have referred. The four signatures used (a-d) were written during four successive years (Fig. 5). The total length of the name measured from beginning to end is different in the four signatures. However, if we compare the constituent elements of one signature with those of the others we discover the consistencies. The following consistencies are obtained:

1. The first name is of equal length in 3 signatures.
2. The initial's loop is of equal length in 4 signatures; in 2, however, it is only the inner part, in 2 the total loop, which shows this consistency.
3. The second name is of equal length in 4 signatures.
4. The second name is one and a half times the length of the first name in 3 signatures.
5. The first name is three times the length of the last movement, i.e., the length of the letter "t" in 3 signatures.
6. The second name is four times the length of the last movement in 3 signatures (5 times this length in the 4th signature).
7. The dot after the second initial is exactly in the center of the signature so that a circle drawn around this point touches beginning and end of the signature; this happens in all 4 signatures.

These seven regularities of movement exclude the possibility of a chance factor. We observe here, however, a new characteristic of regularities. In our experiment discussed previously, we used as one example of consistency only the length of the name measured from beginning to end. We see now that regularities appear in very different ways. The first name, Gordon, shows an equal length measured from beginning to end; the second name shows an equal length if measured from the left to the right limit. Concerning the loop of the initial, there is one variation within the consistency. There are consistencies of the relationship of movements, as between first and second names, and between both names and the length of the last letter, "t." Thus, consistencies may appear in simple proportions, one movement being a multiple of the length of another

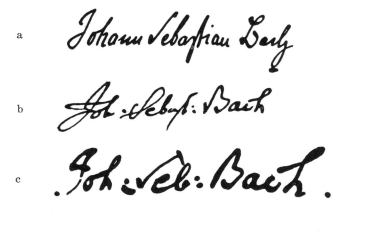

FIG. 6.—Consistency of movement at different years of life and in different forms of writing.

movement. This most important phenomenon of proportions will be discussed later.

The variation in the type of consistency indicates that we cannot apply the same measurement for each signature. Although our procedure cannot be rigid but must be flexible, the phenomenon of regularity can be demonstrated because the individual type of consistency remains stable. Sometimes it takes a long time until one discovers which part of the movement a writer has adopted for his consistency. As we shall discuss later, the various types of consistency allow a simple classification (see page 124 ff.).

We now present several historical examples of consistencies.

Johann Sebastian Bach (1685-1750) (Fig. 6):

Three signatures from different periods of Bach's life, written in three different forms: (a) Johann Sebastian Bach; (b) Joh. Seb. Bach; (c) Joh. Sebast. Bach. The following consistencies appear:

1. The length of the first name, "Johann" or "Joh," is identical in 3 signatures.

2. The length of the middle name, "Sebastian," "Sebast.," or "Seb.," is identical in three signatures.

3. Concerning the limits of the last name, "Bach," the length of signature (c) is double the length of signature (a).

4. The dots after the first and second name divide the signature into equal parts, each of which has the same length in both signatures although there are three parts in signature (a) and 4 parts in signature (b).

Benito Mussolini (1883-1944) (Fig. 7):

Three signatures, written at different periods of his life: (a) as socialist; (b) in the beginning of his dictatorship; (c) at the height of his dictatorship, written in three different forms—(a) separating first and second names, (b) connecting first and second names, (c) signing only with the second name. The following consistencies appear:

1. The length of the full name is the same in 3 signatures.

2. The length from the beginning of the first name to the end of the second initial is equal in 3 signatures.

3. The length of the initial "M" increases in simple proportions in the successive signatures; the size of "M" in signature (c) is double that of the "M" in signature (a), and the "M" in signature (c) is double the size of the "M" in signature (b).

4. Regular increase of size also appears in the first and in the second names. A scale indicates the proportional increase of size, which becomes especially significant when the length of "Mussolini" in signature (c) is double the length of "Mussolini" in signature (a).

5. The movement in each signature is characterized by three dots. In signatures (a) and (b) we find the three dots over the "i"; in signature (c) we find two dots over the "i," and the third dot appears with the beginning of the initial "M." The relationship of distance between the

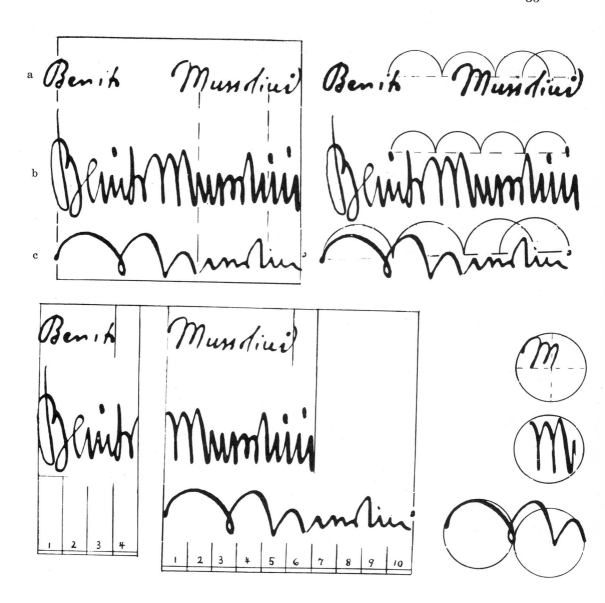

FIG. 7.—Consistency of size, position and interrelationships.

three dots remains the same in 3 signatures; the distance between the first dot and the last dot is seven times the distance between the second and third dots in signatures (a) and (c), and eight times this distance in signature (b).

These consistencies led us again to new observations. Consistencies appear not only in the length of the total name and its parts, first and second name, but also in the size of initials and in the relative position of dots. Simple proportions play a decisive part in the phenomenon of consistency.

Richard Wagner (1813-1833) (Fig. 8):

Three signatures of Wagner illustrate the phenomenon of consistency in the following respects:

1. The length of the full name, measured from left limit to end, is equal in the two signatures (a) and (b), the length of the last signature being a third of the preceding one ,(c).

2. The length of the first name, measured from left limit to end, is the same in the two signatures (b) and (c).

3. The length of the first initial is equal in the two signatures (a) and (c).

4. The starting stroke of the first initial is equal in the two signatures (a) and (c).

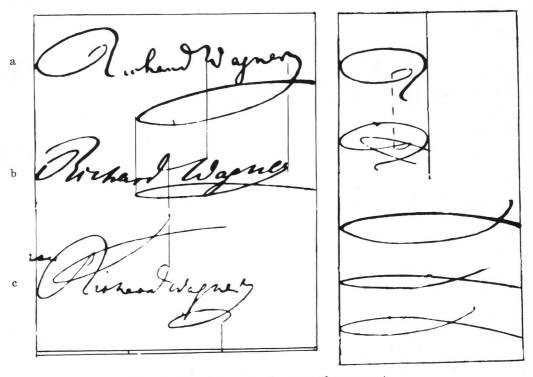

FIG. 8.—Consistency in elements of movement.

5. The length of the flourish is equal in three signatures, the additional ornamentation of the name becoming integrated into the scheme of consistencies.

Even if a signature consists only of initials, their extension may be a simple proportion of the full signature by the same writer. An example is that of two signatures from two letters written by the psychologist *Lawrence K. Frank* (Fig. 9) to the author. The following consistencies, measuring all movements from left to right limit, appear between the full signature and its abbreviation by initials:

1. The length of the first name in the full signature is equal to the length of the second name.

2. The length of the first and second names in the full signature is equal to the length of the abbreviated signature.

3. The corresponding initials in both signatures are equal or simply proportional in length to each other; letter "f" in the full signature is one and one half times the length of letter "f" in the abbreviated signature.

This example brings us new observations, i.e., that consistencies may remain stable, even if the pattern of a movement representing the same concept has changed. Accordingly, the movement pattern remains consistent whether the name is written in full or in abbreviation.

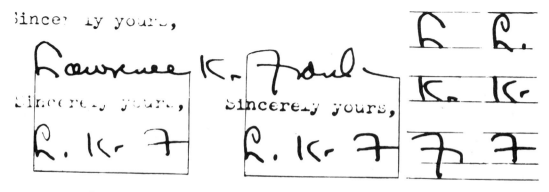

FIG. 9.—Consistency of movement between signature and initials.

That consistencies remain, even if the outer appearance of the patterns changes, can be observed in various ways. It first appears if the
same content is expressed differently, as when the same signature is written with different movements of the same hand. The phenomenon appears
also when a different content is expressed, i.e., when a different kind of
signature is written (examples: Frank, Bach, Mussolini). Finally, the
phenomenon appears when the signature is written with different muscle
groups, with the right or with the left hand. We have already mentioned
this characteristic, referring to our experiment; now we add a historical
example.

Horatio Nelson (1758-1805) (Fig. 10):
We present two signatures of Nelson,* one written with the right
hand (a), the other written about ten years later (b), after Nelson had
lost his right arm. Here he wrote Nelson H. Bronte. The following consistencies appear:
    1. The length between the limits in Horatio Nelson is five times the
length of the initial "H."
    2. The length between the limits in Nelson H. Bronte is four times
the length of the initial "H."
    3. The length of the second name, Nelson, remains the same.
    4. Comparing the remaining parts of the name in both signatures, the
length from beginning to end in Horatio is equal to the length between
the limits in H. Bronte.
    5. The lengths of the initials' starting strokes are in simple proportion
to each other. In the second signature, the lengths of the starting strokes
in both initials are equal. In the first signature, the first initial's starting
stroke is one and a half times longer.

Thus it appears that consistencies remain stable with different kinds
of transfer, transfer of movement, transfer of content, and transfer of
muscle groups. The phenomenon of transfer indicates that consistencies
may be present in the expression of personality, even if we do not immediately perceive them. These consistencies had to be detected in relationships by penetrating through the surface into the depth of movement
patterns. In a similar way different reactions of a person, even apparent
contradictions in personality, may be consistent manifestations. Allport
and Vernon remark [7, p. 134]: "Measures which do not correspond statistically may nevertheless be congruent psychologically."**

Our observations which, through considerable additional material,
will find added support in the following chapters, already suggest that
the reason for this discrepancy between "measures which do not correspond statistically" and which "nevertheless are congruent psychologically" may be found in an incongruence between measurement and

*From R. Saudek: Experiments with Handwriting. New York, William Morrow
& Company, 1928.
**From G. W. Allport and P. E. Vernon: "Studies in Expressive Movement." Copyright 1933 by The Macmillan Co. and used with their permission.

FIG. 10.—Consistency of movement in change of name and shift from right-handed to left-handed writing.

its object. We cannot measure at random, but we must find out which characteristics of the object are significant for measurement and which principles of measurement are adequate to the object. In taking bodily measurements the measurement of the length of hair is certainly insignificant and inadequate. But although the measurement of limbs is a more adequate procedure in general, it is not the absolute size of one limb but its relative size which is significant. Measurements get their value from relationships. Furthermore, for one person the size of the head, for another the size of the hand, for a third the size of the legs is significant for his bodily scheme. In a similar way general principles of measurement can be established for measuring patterns of movement, but they are modified by individual indicators which determine the individual diagram of movement. Although the measurement remains a static tool of experimentation, it is its application which must be dynamic in order to be congruent with the dynamics of personality.

CHAPTER III

SYMMETRY IN PERSONALITY

CONSISTENCY AND SYMMETRY

Our search for consistency of movement patterns by the medium of signatures led us to the discovery of strange regularities. These regularities appeared in different movement patterns of the same person, for instance, in repetitions of the same signature. This phenomenon of regularity is consistency in *repetitions*. We found furthermore that the consistency may appear if the same movement pattern is made with different muscle groups, demonstrating consistency by a *transfer of muscle groups*. In the first case the consistency was manifest and immediately visible. In the second case the manifest movement pattern had a very different appearance; however, there were hidden consistencies, which had to be detected by detailed measurements. But there was also consistency if the same content was expressed differently, if for instance a signature comprised the first and second names, or only the second name, or was written in abbreviation. This showed consistency by a *transfer of content*. Here also the consistencies were hidden. These three consistencies—of repetition, transfer of muscle group, and transfer of content—became apparent when we examined the same or corresponding movements of a person over a period of time. We observed these regularities in what we may call consistency of movement in time. Over a certain length of time certain characteristics of movement remained identical.

However, we not only observed regularities in different movement patterns of the same person, but in one and the same movement pattern as well. In one graphic expression different movements may pattern the space in the same way, in what we may call consistency of movement in space. We found, for instance, that the length of the first name was sometimes the same as the length of the second name or that both names stood in simple proportion to each other. The length of the name was in simple proportion to the length of the beginning movement (starting stroke) or to the length of the ending movement (end-stroke). A dot after the middle initial was exactly in the center of the signature, and the distances of various dots appeared in simple proportion to each other.

Thus, consistencies of the same unit of length and regularities of relationships became manifest in one movement pattern. Here the phenomenon of consistency opens a new view. If, for instance, the dot after the middle initial divides the signature into two parts of equal length, or when the length of the first name equals that of the second name, we have a characteristic of symmetry.

SYMMETRY IN NATURE

As we have pointed out, the phenomenon of consistency plays a decisive part in our life; in fact, most of our social relationships and our habits are determined by it. But symmetry plays a role no less decisive. If we look upon our own body, its right and left halves suggest symmetry; each animal, each flower, each leaf is, with slight deviations, symmetrically built. All the objects man makes, his houses, his furniture, his decorations, are patterned symmetrically. Ancient objects of art emphasize symmetry in geometrical designs, and the music of primitive peoples is characterized by repetition of the same sounds, by an emphasis on rhythm which is a special manifestation of symmetry. Modern artistic expression emphasizes rhythm but tries to avoid symmetry. The emphasis upon symmetry as well as the attempt to avoid it seems to have fundamental psychological reasons. Symmetry is a repetition of the same, and the same as a known factor gives a feeling of security. Whether modern man designs fixed mathematical, physical, chemical formulas or whether ancient man used fixed ceremonies and magical practices for a conjuration of forces, they both apply a principle of symmetry which was and is supposed to guarantee success and to give security. But this positive aspect of symmetry has its negative counterpart. The repetition of the same is the characteristic of law but also implies the concepts of necessity, unchangeableness, fate, and fatality. Modern man, with his goal of self-dependence and of independence from the forces of nature, has become very sensitive to the problem of freedom and determination. Applying symmetry to his scientific endeavors, he tries to exclude it from his daily life; he tries to exclude it from his sphere of freedom in order to enjoy that freedom. A person who emphasizes symmetry in his daily life is called a pedantic or a neurotic personality. It is characteristic that symmetries play a great role in the artistic manifestations of mentally diseased people, as if these would try to find a pattern of security in their mental disturbance. Symmetries are also emphasized by young children, who in every respect love the return of the same. The attempt to get security in the world they are beginning to explore seems here also to be the decisive factor.

Thus, we may understand why certain persons emphasize symmetries and why others try to avoid them. However, whether they actually are able to avoid them is a question, since we have seen that in graphic movements, as one expression of man, symmetries may not be apparent, but hidden. If we were to use psychoanalytical terms, we would say that symmetries may be repressed.

After our sketchy attempt to indicate the implications in the expression of symmetry we shall discuss the historical and practical use of the term. The Greek word "symmetria" signifies "right proportion, evenness, measurableness and dimension." The concept implies the meaning of a regular arrangement. Plotinus* describes symmetry as an aesthetic principle:

> Now by almost all persons it is maintained that it is the symmetry of the different parts with respect to each other, and the beautiful color, which produce beauty for visual observation; and for those as well as for the common intellect beauty is identical with symmetry and being shaped after fixed proportions.

Several studies have been made on the principle of symmetry in aesthetics. Of the more modern scientists, Ernst Mach [263] was especially interested in this problem. Mach reports from observation at the Asylum for the Blind in Lausanne that blind persons were found to take pleasure in the periodic repetition of the same forms in tangible objects, while disturbances in the symmetry of forms were unpleasant to them. In his lectures on symmetry he remarks [262]:

> The possession of a sense for symmetry by persons who are one-eyed from birth is certainly an enigma. Yet the sense for symmetry, although originally acquired by the eyes, could not have been confined exclusively to the visual organs. By thousands of years of practice it must also have been implanted in other parts of the human organism, and cannot, therefore, be immediately eliminated by the loss of an eye.

According to F. M. Jäger [194], the sense for symmetry of the blind develops in connection with their sense of touch, and Jäger therefore suggests that the preference for symmetry, and especially for vertical symmetry, is connected with the movement of the extremities. Jäger mentions that true symmetry is seldom accomplished in nature. One half of a leaf is never precisely the same as the other half and one leaf is not the same as another. In spite of these differences we immediately identify a certain leaf as that of an oak tree, another as that of a maple tree, etc. We have formed an idea-image of the perfect leaf for each species, abstracting all the deviations. All forms observed in nature are more or less perfect approximations to the ideal form. The symmetry principle is, as Jäger states, an idealistic scheme of nature to which mathematical reasonings are applied, a concept which is close to the idealism of Plato.

SYMMETRY IN PERCEPTION

A study of the preference for symmetry in our perception according to an ideal image became the subject of experimental investigations. Several studies have been made in presenting to subjects simple figures and making the visual impression somewhat unclear, either through the effect of illumination or through a short exposure of the figure. The subject was then asked to draw what he has seen and the structure of his copy was compared with that of the original stimulus. L. Hempstead [175] used 71 figures, presented under varying illumination, and he observed

---

*On Aesthetics, first Ennead, liber 6, ch. 1.

that the reproductions usually showed wrong perceptions concerning the details, but that these defects could be explained as having originated "under the guidance of the two principles of symmetry and similarity." We reproduce some examples (Fig. 11):

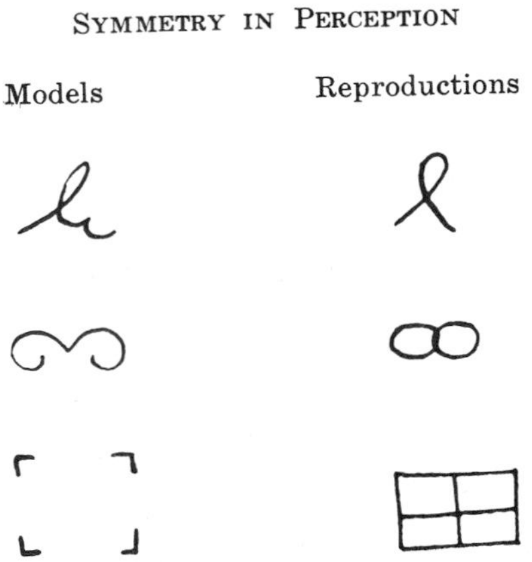

SYMMETRY IN PERCEPTION

Models   Reproductions

FIG. 11.—Symmetry in Perception. Models. Reproductions.

Similar experiments, of exposing figures for a fraction of a second (using the tachistoscope, an apparatus which exposes an object in a flash), have been made by several investigators [156, 252, 321, 457, 468]. All these authors report that the reproductions show an emphasis upon regularity, symmetry, and stability of the form perceived.

G. W. Allport [4] says, concerning the results of experiments along these lines: "Perhaps the most striking of all the results is the tendency for the figure to retain or to achieve symmetry." And Perkins [321] states: "It became evident from detached examination of the data that all changes were in the direction of some balanced or symmetrical pattern." The explanations of these changes toward symmetry were two-fold: they were either explained as due to habit and past experience [Gibson 147] or as due to the properties of the object perceived [Lindemann 252, Wulf 468].

These experiments are very important in regard to our problem, for they demonstrate that we perceive things in view of their symmetry and that we tend to transform in our memory asymmetrical objects into symmetrical ones. The pressure toward symmetry dominates perception, memory, and, as we have already discussed, the structure of objects we make. However, one characteristic of symmetry, the repetition of the same, is also inherent in the fundamental functions of our organism, in our pulse and in the rate of breathing. Another characteristic of symmetry, that of balance, guides all of our movements. Thus symmetry is a principle so inherent in our physiological being, so deeply rooted in our emotional expression and continuously emphasized by the object-world, that we should expect its manifestation in each unconscious expression of man.

If man's movements are not determined by chance but are manifestations of the organism and of its fundamental characteristics, an expression of movements upon paper might show a diagram of symmetries. This is actually what we found and what we are going to demonstrate below.

A Graphic Analysis of Symmetry

Our previous experiment on consistency has given us additional observations on symmetrical patterns in graphic movements, but these observations have not been systematized, and first of all we must establish their statistical validity. The number of several symmetrical incidences in the same movement pattern suggests that we are dealing here with a phenomenon not to be explained by chance; but it still could be objected that, looking for symmetries, we might find them everywhere. Let a machine make chance movements, recorded as strokes upon paper; a certain number of these resulting patterns will, by the laws of probability, be identical. We had to discover a method by which we could calculate statistically how often a regularity is expected to result from chance and how our results deviate from such a chance pattern. In our first exploration we encountered too many different regularities to permit application of statistical procedures. We had to limit our test to one specific regularity in order to arrive at a significant evaluation by means of statistics. We could have taken the regularity of the dot after the middle initial, when it is in the center of the signature; however, only a limited number of writers sign that way. We might have investigated statistically each of the many symmetries which we shall systematize later on; again, in each case only a certain group of signatures falls into the same category. One characteristic, however, holds for many signatures: a possible relationship of length between the first and the second name. We observed in many cases that the length of the first name, measured from beginning to end, was either identical to the equally measured length of the second name or a simple proportion of it. As an example note the signature of *Irving Stone* (Fig. 12); the length of the first name is equal to the length of the second name. There were many cases where such symmetries became apparent only if we did not make our measurements from beginning

Fig. 12.—Symmetry of movement. Equal length of first and second name.

to end but from limit to limit. Yet for statistical reasons we had to count all of these cases as having no symmetry. In other instances proportions between the lengths of first and second names were observed neither by measurement from beginning to end of the movement nor by measurement of the extreme limits of the movement pattern, but the symmetries sometimes occurred between the length of the initial and the name. All of these cases had to be discarded as negative ones, although, actually, they were not devoid of symmetry but fell into different symmetry groups.

We present now our statistical study, using 342 signatures of soldiers, 42 of the signatures on the Declaration of Independence, and 36 signatures on the Constitution of the United States. (A few signatures had to be discarded, as we shall explain later.) The measurements of the signatures were made and controlled by myself and a group of my students in psychology at Bard College. The statistical evaluation (see below) was made by Dr. Franco Modigliani of the New School for Social Research, New York. This study demonstrates that in our group of signatures, taken at random, one type of symmetry—the length of the second name as an integral multiple of the length of the first name—appears far over chance expectancy. The statistical values suggest that this one type of regularity is to be expected in 22.6 per cent of the population (see Figs. 13 and 14 below). The remaining part of the population seems to follow principles of symmetry other than those we have tested, but in order to decide this question, other statistical studies for each of the symmetries observed have to follow. However, one type of symmetry being evidenced statistically may suffice for our first endeavor in drawing attention to the phenomenon of symmetries in graphic movement.

A STATISTICAL INVESTIGATION OF ONE REGULARITY IN SIGNATURES

We investigated the following hypothesis: In a signature consisting of first and second names, the length of the second name is an integral multiple of the length of the first name. The lengths of the first and second names were measured with graph paper, measuring 400 sq. to an inch, the measurement always being made to the nearest 1/40 of an inch, i.e., half of a partition. We subtracted from the length of the second name the nearest integral multiple of the length of the first name. The remainder, which could be positive or negative, was then divided by the length of the first name, and the result of this division was labeled "R" and recorded.

Example: Suppose the second name has a length of 12/40 of an inch and the first name has a length of 10/40, the remainder would be: 12/40—10/40=2/40; R would be 2/40:10/40=.2. If on the other hand the length of the second name was 17/40, and the length of the first name again 10/40, then R would be —3/10=—.3, since the integral multiple of 10 closest to 17 is 20. The R's were rounded off to one decimal place, since usually the second decimal place would not have been significant;

they were then arranged in a frequency distribution with class interval of .1. The distribution thus has 10 remainder classes.

It is clear that if there were no systematic relationship between the lengths of the first and second names, any signature, taken at random, would have equal probability of falling into any of the 10 remainder classes; that means that the probability of an observation's falling into any specified class would be precisely 1/10, or 10 per cent.

If on the other hand the second name tends to be an integral multiple of the first, the remainder will tend to be 0 or nearly 0. Therefore, if the hypothesis that the second name tends to be an integral multiple of the length of the first name were correct, so that the remainder would be 0 or nearly 0, we would expect to find a large number of observations concentrated in the 0-remainder class.

Our first experiment was based on a sample of 342 signatures written by soldiers of an Army Specialized Training Program unit which was at Bard College during 1943-44. The signatures were made on quiz sheets, and thus were done completely spontaneously and without any knowledge that the sample was later used for our purpose. The frequency distribution of the R's computed from this sample is shown in Table 6.

TABLE 6

Class interval (Remainder classes)	Frequency	Percentage
.4	22	6.4
.3	25.5	7.4
.2	27.5	8.0
.1	31.5	9.2
0	72.5	21.2
—.1	40.5	11.9
—.2	39.5	11.6
—.3	30	8.8
—.4	29	8.5
±.5	24	7.0
	342.0	100.0

It will be noticed that the last class is labeled ±5; this is necessary since an observation for which R is exactly .5 may be recorded as +.5 or as —.5, hence the class boundaries of this class are from +.45 to —.45. The half frequencies which are found in some classes are due to observations for which the second and consecutive decimal place in the R were 500. For example, an R of .250 was recorded as a half frequency in the class .2 and as a half frequency in the class .3. It appears from this table that the 0-remainder class contains a large number of observations, representing 21.2 per cent of the total. This large frequency is in accordance with our theory. (See chart in Fig. 13.)

Although this percentage far exceeds 10 per cent, it may still be explained by those chance factors commonly denoted under the name of sampling fluctuations. In order to test the validity of our hypothesis we must therefore determine whether a percentage as large as the one observed could be explained by chance.

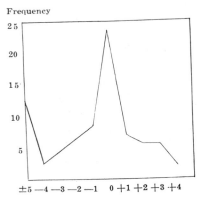

Frequency

FIG. 13.—Frequency distribution of 342 modern signatures concerning the length of first and second name.

Since the distribution of proportions from samples of the size stated above is approximately normal we proceed to compute the standard deviation of this distribution under the null hypothesis by the usual formula

$$sp=\sqrt{\frac{pq}{n}}\text{where } q=1-p. \text{ In the present case } sp\sqrt{\frac{(.1)\ (.9)}{342}}=0.162 \text{ or } 1.62\%.$$

Now we know that if the true percentage were 10 in only about one case out of 100, a percentage as large as $10+1.622(2.57)=14.17$ or as low as $10 — 1.622(2.57)=5.83$ would occur as a result of chance. The observed percentage, 21.2, is far outside these limits. We may thus conclude that the number of cases in which the length of the second name is an integral multiple of the length of the first name is much too large to be reasonably explained by chance.

Just as we took a random sample under present conditions, so we took a random sample from writers of the past. We used a historical document which had many signatures, open to everybody's control, namely the Declaration of Independence.* A photostat was taken from the original

*See L. C. Draper, "An Essay on the Autograph Collections of the Signers of the Declaration of Independence and of the Constitution," New York, 1889; L. C. Draper, "Autograph Collections of the Signers of the Declaration of Independence and of the Constitution," in: Reports and Collections of the State Historical Society of Wisconsin, vol. X, 373-447, Madison, Wisconsin, 1888.

manuscript in the Library of Congress. There are 56 signatures written in six columns. The last column, however, consisting of 13 signatures, and one signature in the fourth column (Geo. Read) have faded out and the beginning and the end of the names are not fully recognizable. We are thus left with 42 signatures. One has to be very careful concerning the authenticity of the documents used. The Declaration of Independence as reprinted in the New York *Times* on each July 4 and most of the copies reprinted in books, are taken from an engraving.* This is also the case with the reprint published by the Department of the Interior, Bureau of Education, Washington, D. C. Although the engraver copied as faithfully as possible, there occurred slight deviations, destroying the original proportions. We used also the signatures from the Constitution of the United States. From these 40 signatures 4 had to be disqualified, one being illegible (last signature), two having merely one initial and a small distance between beginning and end (J. Routledge, B. Franklin) and, with one complex name, it being uncertain what the writer considered as belonging to the first name (Dan of St. Thos. Jenifer). The Declaration of Independence (42 signatures) and the Constitution (36 signatures) together gave us a sample of 78 signatures.

The frequency distribution of the remainders is given in Table 7 and in Chart II (Fig. 14). The percentage of observations falling in the 0-remainder class is 30.13%.

TABLE 7

Frequency distribution for 78 signatures of the Declaration of Independence
and of the Constitution

Class midpoint	Frequency	Percentage
.4	2	2.5
.3	5.5	7.0
.2	5.5	7.0
.1	7.0	9.1
0	23.5	30.1
—.1	8.5	10.9
—.2	6.5	8.4
—.3	4.5	5.8
—.4	2.5	3.2
±.5	12.5	16.0
	78.0	100.0

*On May 26, 1824, Congress directed the Secretary of State to distribute certain facsimile copies of the Declaration of Independence, engraved by William J. Stone of Washington, from the original, then in the State Department.

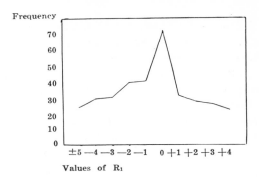

FIG. 14.—Frequency distribution of 78 signatures from the Declaration of Independence and the Constitution concerning the length of first and second name.

To test the significance of this result we follow the procedure used for the first sample. Using the formula described above, we find that the standard deviation of the distribution proportions from samples of 78 under the null hypothesis is .03397 or 3.4%. Thus the observed proportion exceeds .10 by nearly 6 standard deviations. The difference is again much too large to be reasonably explained by chance. The available evidence shows that this is definitely not the case. To illustrate this point we give (Table 8, p. 51) the number of letters and the length of the first and second name for all the signatures falling in the zero remainder class for the second of our samples. It will be seen that there is no close relationship between the length and the number of letters in each name. Only in three cases out of twenty-one is the ratio between the length of the two names equal to the ratio between the respective number of letters.

Our samples were taken from different periods, one written in our time, the other over a century and a half ago. Now we wanted to know whether it could be maintained that the same law operates under different historical conditions.

The percentage of cases falling in the 0-remainder class was $p_1 = 21.2\%$ for the soldiers' sample and $p_2 = 30.13\%$ for the sample based on the historical documents. Is the difference between these two percentages too large to be consistent with the hypothesis that the two samples "come from the same population"? Using a well known formula we find:

$$s(p_1-p_2) = \sqrt{\frac{p(1-p)}{342} + \frac{p(1-p)}{78}} = \sqrt{(.2286)(.7714)\left(\frac{1}{342} + \frac{1}{78}\right)} = .0527 \text{ or } 5.27\%$$

where $p = .2286$ is the proportion computed from the two samples taken together. Finally

$$\frac{p_1-p_2}{s(p_1-p_2)} = \frac{21.2-30.1}{5.3} = 1.68$$

Entering a normal probability table we find that under our hypothesis a difference as large as the observed one could be expected to occur by

TABLE 8

Analysis of signatures of the Declaration of Independence and the Constitution, falling in 0-remainder class.

No. of sign.	First Name	No. of letters	Length in 1/20"	Second name	No. of letters	Length in 1/20"
A. Declaration of Independence						
1	Button	6	15	Gwinnett	8	15
3	Geo	3	16	Walton	6	16
10	Arthur	6	26	Middleton	9	13
14	Thos	4	8	Stone	5	16
15	Charles Carroll	14	24.5	of Carrolton	12	24.5
19	Benj	4	10	Harrison	8	30
27	Geo	3	10	Clymer	6	20
30	James	5	10	Wilson	6	20
31	Geo	3	11	Ross	4	11
35	Wm	2	8	Floyd	5	8
37	Frans	5	12	Lewis	5	12
39	Rich	4	9	Stockton	8	18
41	Fras	4	8	Hopkinson	9	16
B. The Constitution						
4	John	4	11	Dickinson	9	22
11	James	5	5.5	Madison	7	11
27	Roger	5	10	Sherman	7	30
28	Alexander	9	22	Hamilton	8	22
29	Wil	3	7	Livingston	10	21
30	David	5	11	Brearley	8	22
31	Wm	2	6	Patterson	9	24
37	Thos	4	8	Fitzsimmons	10	24

chance in about 9 cases out of 100. The difference is therefore not significant according to the usual standards. We have no reason to reject the hypothesis that the two samples come from the same population, i.e., that the same type of regularity acts upon signatures regardless of time. Since we may suppose that the two samples come from the same population we can estimate the true proportion of cases falling in the 0-remainder class by combining the two samples. The resulting estimate is: $p = .22857$

or 22.9% with a standard error $sp = \sqrt{\dfrac{.17633}{420}} = .020489$ or 2.05%.

Having decided to accept the hypothesis that there is a definite relationship between the lengths of the first and second names, we may try to investigate the underlying probability distribution. The procedure must again consist in formulating alternative hypotheses and in testing them on the basis of our samples. At this point a large number of hypotheses could be formulated all of which seem to be equally plausible at the start. We shall confine ourselves here to testing one of them, but others will be investigated in further research and on the basis of additional evidence.

Our hypothesis is the following: Signatures can be divided into two classes—for one class which contains a certain proportion p_0 the length of the second name is an integral multiple of the length of the first name, while for the remaining class no systematic relationship exists. The members in the first class would all be concentrated in the 0-remainder class, while the members of the second class would be distributed at random among the 10 classes. Under this hypothesis the proportion which does not show the characteristic will be $1-p_0$; therefore the proportion of signatures falling in any remainder class except 0 would be: (1) $\dfrac{1-p_0}{10}$ while the total proportion of cases falling in the 0-remainder class would be

$$(2) \quad \frac{1-p_0}{10} + p_0 = \frac{1+9p_0}{10}$$

By equating expression (2) with the observed proportion of observations falling in the 0-remainder class, we obtain an estimate of p_0. Thus for the first sample we will have:

$$\frac{1+9p_0}{10} = .212 \text{ or } p_0 = .12444 \text{ or } 12.44.$$

Taking this as an estimate of p_0 we find that the proportion which does not exhibit the characteristics is $1-p_0$ or .8756. If our hypothesis that the proportion $(1-p_0)$ of the population is distributed at random among the remainder classes were correct, we would expect to find $.08756 \times 342 = 29.95$ observations in each remainder class except in the 0-remainder class. The question to be tested is whether the proportions observed in each case are consistent with the hypothesis that the true proportion is .08756.

The hypothesis can also be tested by means of the chi-square test. The computed value of chi square is 11.03, and entering the chi-square table with 8 degrees of freedom we find that the probability for a value of chi square as large as this or larger is 20%. We have therefore no reason to reject the hypothesis tested, namely, that the part of the population which does not exhibit the characteristic stated is distributed at random among the various remainder classes. Exactly the same procedure was applied to the second sample and then to the two samples combined. In this last case the estimate of the proportion of the population having the characteristic referred to is $\dfrac{60}{420}=.14286$ or 14.3%.

The computed value of chi square is 13.22 and the probability for a value as large as this or larger is between 10% and 5% and is therefore not significant at the 5% level.

This test would lead us to conclude provisionally and pending further information that an unknown proportion of the population, estimated at about 14%, shows a definite relationship between the lengths of first and second names. The remaining part of the population, estimated at about 86%, is distributed at random in all ten classes including the

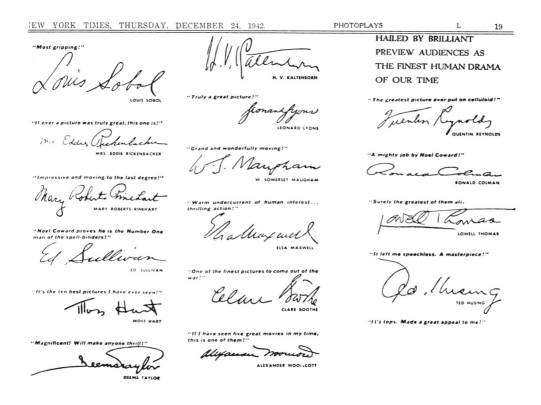

FIG. 15.—A sample of signatures from an advertisement.

0-remainder class. The percentage of the population showing the characteristic relationship between first and second names is therefore $14\%+8.6\%=22.6\%$. Whether the remaining part of the population shows other characteristics than to those tested has to be demonstrated in other statistical studies.

VARIOUS CONFIGURATIONAL RELATIONSHIPS BETWEEN FIRST AND
SECOND NAME OF SIGNATURES

Our statistical study considered only one relationship between first and second name, namely, that the length of the second name is an integral multiple of the length of the first name. Now the question arises whether all those signatures which did not fall into this category are devoid of any proportional relationship between the first and second name. Our investigation has shown that a majority of signatures has a center which divides the graphic pattern of first and second name into two equal parts or into two parts with one being a simple multiple of the other.

The centers could be classified into three distinct groups: (1) the beginning of the second name; (2) the end of the first name; (3) a dot after the middle initial.

The frame for these centers equally shows three basic varieties. The extension of the signature is considered: (1) from its beginning to its end; (2) from its left limit to its right limit; (3) from its beginning or ending to one of the limits.

In our following example we give a random selection of signatures all of which are taken from one advertisement in the New York *Times*, December 24, 1942; p. 19 (Fig. 15). This advertisement of the movie "In Which We Serve" brought the signed opinions of sixteen well known personalities. The relationships between first and second name fall into the following categories:

1. Center: beginning of second name (B)
   Frame: right and left limit of the signature
   Proportions: (a) equal parts (b) multiples

In two signatures (*Reynolds; Husing*) the distance between "B" and the right limit of the signature is equal to the distance between "B" and the left limit (Figs. 16, 17).

In two signatures (*Kaltenborn; Maugham*) the distance between "B" and the right limit is a simple multiple of the distance between "B" and the left limit (Figs. 18, 19).

2. Center: beginning of second name (B)
   Frame: beginning and ending of signature
   Proportions: (a) equal parts (b) multiples

In two signatures (*Thomas*; Hart*) the distance between "B" and the end of the signature is equal to the distance between "B" and the beginning of the signature (Figs. 20, 21).

In two signatures (*Maxwell; Sullivan*) the distance between "B" and the end of the signature is a simple multiple of the distance between "B" and the beginning (Figs. 22, 23).

---

*According to the graphic pattern the verticals seem to be made from bottom to top.

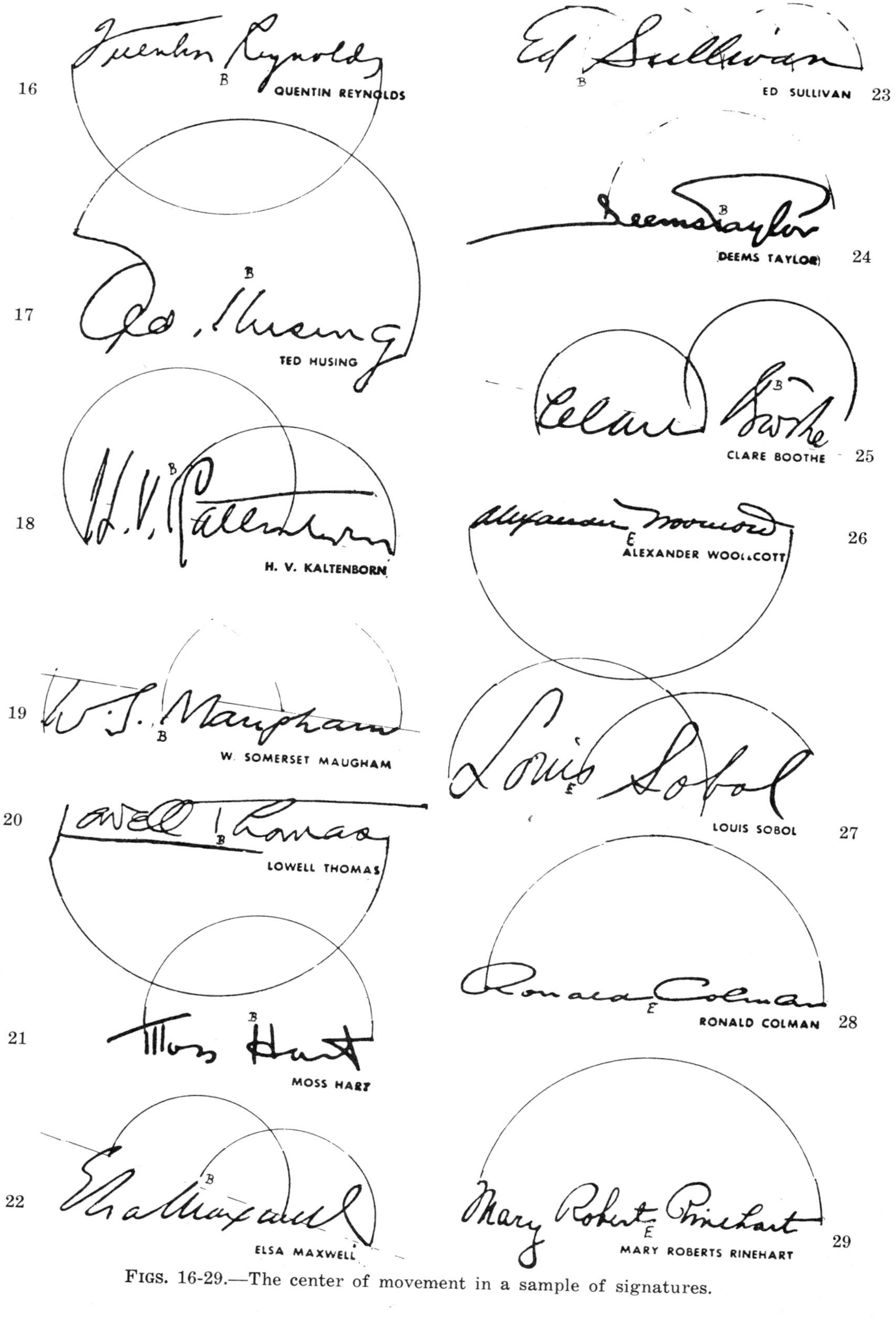

16 QUENTIN REYNOLDS

17 TED HUSING

18 H. V. KALTENBORN

19 W. SOMERSET MAUGHAM

20 LOWELL THOMAS

21 MOSS HART

22 ELSA MAXWELL

23 ED SULLIVAN

24 (DEEMS TAYLOR)

25 CLARE BOOTHE

26 ALEXANDER WOOLLCOTT

27 LOUIS SOBOL

28 RONALD COLMAN

29 MARY ROBERTS RINEHART

FIGS. 16-29.—The center of movement in a sample of signatures.

30   31

LEONARD LYONS   MRS. EDDIE RICKENBACKER

FIGS. 30-31.—Lack of center of movement in a sample of signatures.

3. Center: beginning of second name (B)
    Frame: beginning (respectively ending) and right or left limit
        of the signature
    Proportions: (a) equal parts (b) multiples

In one signature (*Taylor*) the distance between "B" and the beginning of the signature is equal to the distance between "B" and the right limit of the signature.

In one signature (*Boothe*) the length of the first name from left to right limit is a simple multiple of the distance between "B" and the end of the signature (Figs. 24, 25).

Thus in 10 cases out of 16, or in 62.5 per cent of the cases, the beginning of the second name is the center of a graphic relationship between first and second name.

4. Center: ending of first name (E)
    Frame: left and right limit of the signature
    Proportions: (a) equal parts (b) multiples

In one signature (*Woollcott*) the distance between "E" and the right limit of the signature is equal to the distance between "E" and the left limit of the signature.

In one signature (*Sobol*) the distance between "E" and the right limit of the signature is a simple proportion of the distance between "E" and the left limit of the signature (Figs. 26, 27).

5. Center: ending of first name (E)
    Frame: beginning and ending of the signature
    Proportions: (a) equal parts (b) multiples

In two signatures (*Colman; Mary Roberts Rinehart*) the distance between "E" and the end of the signature is equal to the distance between "E" and the beginning of the signature (Figs. 28, 29).

Thus in 4 cases out of 16, or in 25 per cent of the cases, the ending of the first name is the center of a graphic relationship between first and second name. Only in 2 cases (*Lyons; Rickenbacker*) out of 16, or in 12.5 per cent of the cases, no center could be discovered (Figs. 30, 31). Similar investigations have been made with other samples, indicating that a centered configuration between first and second name occurs far over chance expectancy.

SYMMETRY AND PROPORTIONS IN SIGNATURES

The ancient concept of symmetry not only means a repetition of the same but also involves simple proportions of the same unit. As we have mentioned, the Greek word "symmetria" signifies right proportion, measurableness; the adverb "symmetros" has the meaning "keeping the due medium between," a concept which French writers on the problem of

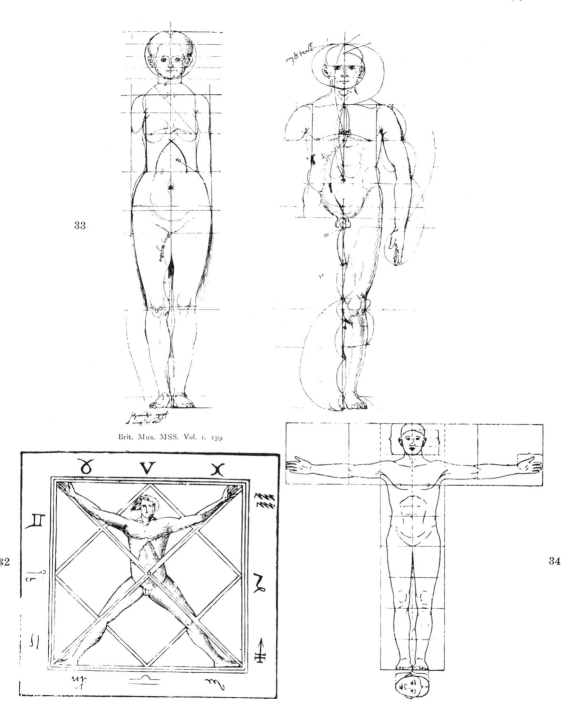

Brit. Mus. MSS. Vol. i. 159.

FIGS. 32-34.—The problem of proportion in art.

symmetry render with the expression "questions d'ordre," which illustrates the phenomenon of regular arrangements. The expression of proportions rather than of a repetition of the same is a fundamental principle in aesthetics. According to Plato "measure and proportion are everywhere identified with beauty,"* and in medieval times beauty was a "proportion of the parts,"** or a "numerable equality."*** For the Greeks the underlying concept of aesthetics was the universal principle of order, of harmonious proportions, expressed by the word "kosmos," which was applied to the world. Man's body was supposed to reflect the heavenly order, representing a microcosm in view of the macrocosm of the world. Thus, the Greeks developed a canon for the representation of the human body in art, a scheme of proportion according to which the sizes of face, trunk, legs, etc., were measured in simple proportions to each other. In medieval times the geometrical proportions of the body were brought into relationship to the cosmic system of the zodiac (Fig. 32 from Agrippa). Painters like Dürer tried to demonstrate that art is the expression of proportions (Fig. 33). Modern canons of the human figure are slight variations of those made by the ancients (Fig. 34). Several experimental investigations on the principle of proportions in aesthetics were made in the late nineteenth and twentieth centuries. G. T. Fechner [121] is credited with having been the first who tried to find experimentally an innate aesthetic law, a universal preference for a certain simple proportion, called the "golden section." In modern times, G. D. Birkhoff [40], Hambidge [164] and others have tried to revive the ancient concept of equating the aesthetic principle with simple proportions, thus achieving what Hambidge calls "dynamic symmetry." We shall devote a special book**** to the problem of measurable form principles in art as related to a new theory of aesthetics. As early as the Renaissance, artists recognized principles of proportion in the formation of letters. We give as an example "A rule for composing letter forms artistically" which originated in Italy about 1580 (Fig. 35).

In the present study we limit ourselves to graphic movements as expressed in the act of writing, centering our attention on the signature as a standardized object of investigation. Our examples illustrate not only the principle of static symmetry in a repetition of the same, but also the principle of dynamic symmetry in a repetition of simple proportions. At the end of the first part of the present book we shall try to classify the main proportions observed in more than 1000 signatures. Here we shall exemplify the principle of proportions by selecting three movement patterns—the beginning, the end, and the middle movements. In many signatures the beginning of the movement is emphasized by a long starting stroke which may be part of the letter, as in letters like "A" and "D,"

*Plato, Philebus, 64e.
**Bonaventura, Quarrachi, Ed. I, p. 544.
***St. Augustine, Nicene . . . Fathers, 1st Ser., v. II, City of God, Book XXII, Ch. XIX, p. 497.
****Art and Conflict. Psychology of Art and Imagination; in preparation.

or which may be an additional upstroke introducing the capital letter, such as may be affixed to letters like "G" and "I," or, thirdly, which represents the total length of the letter. The end of the movement is in many signatures accentuated by a long end stroke with which the last letter's end-stroke is enlarged, or by the total length of the letter, or by an additional flourish frequently put below the signature. Several signatures also show an accentuation on the middle of the written name. The up- or downstroke in the middle letter may be enlarged, for instance, the downstroke of "y" and "f."

The Measure-Unit. A signature not only has a center of movement which balances the total pattern, it also has a center of size which we call a "measure-unit." The measure-unit is one distinct stroke; its length is the norm for the signature's main sizes and distances, which are simple

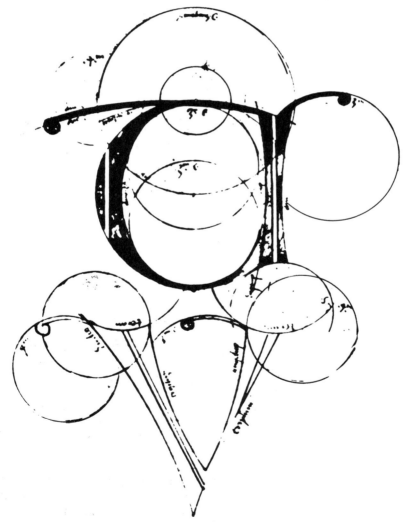

Fig. 35.—"A rule for composing letter forms artistically." Italy, about 1580.

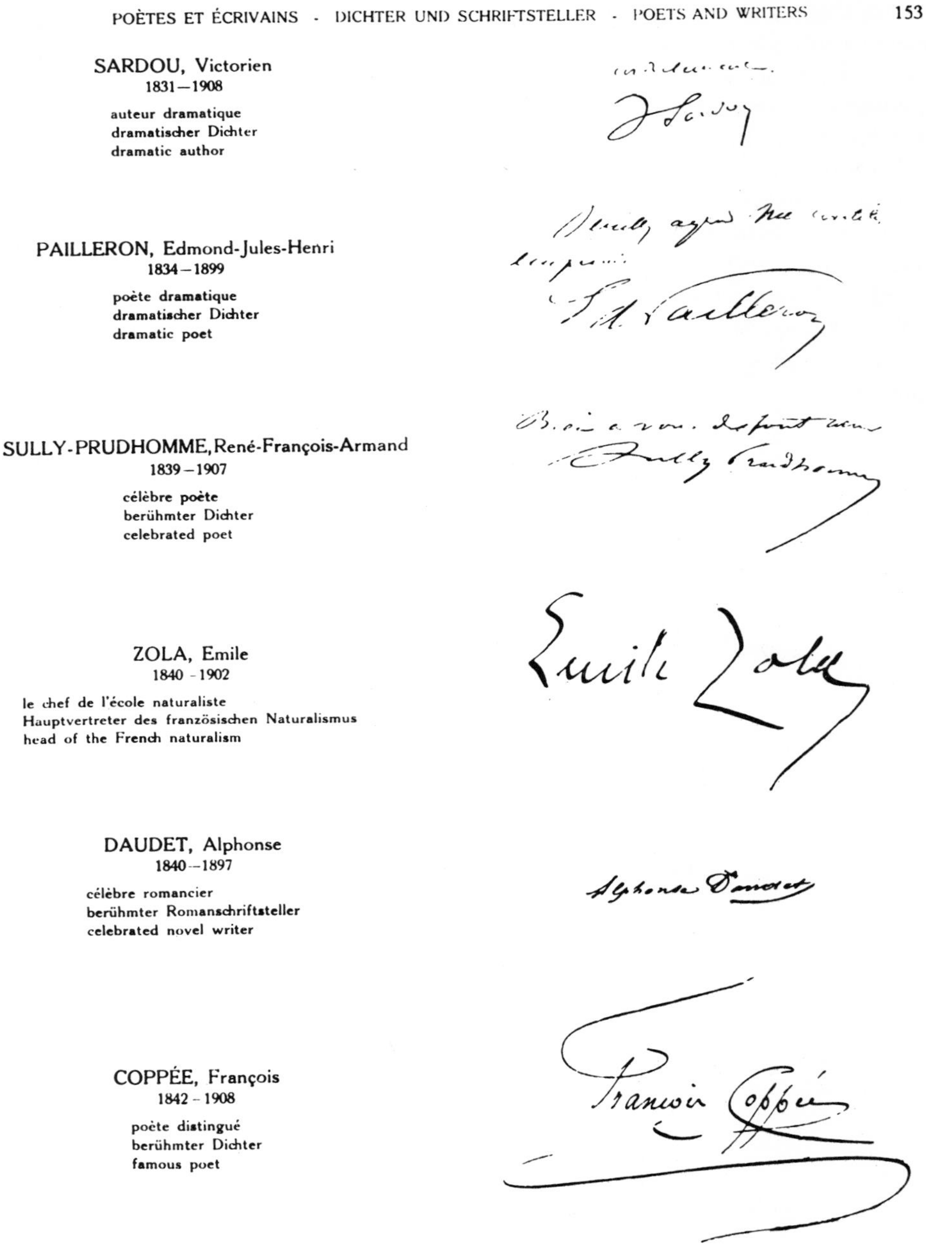

POÈTES ET ÉCRIVAINS · DICHTER UND SCHRIFTSTELLER · POETS AND WRITERS   153

SARDOU, Victorien
1831—1908

auteur dramatique
dramatischer Dichter
dramatic author

PAILLERON, Edmond-Jules-Henri
1834—1899

poète dramatique
dramatischer Dichter
dramatic poet

SULLY-PRUDHOMME, René-François-Armand
1839—1907

célèbre poète
berühmter Dichter
celebrated poet

ZOLA, Emile
1840 - 1902

le chef de l'école naturaliste
Hauptvertreter des französischen Naturalismus
head of the French naturalism

DAUDET, Alphonse
1840—1897

célèbre romancier
berühmter Romanschriftsteller
celebrated novel writer

COPPÉE, François
1842 - 1908

poète distingué
berühmter Dichter
famous poet

FIG. 36.—Sample of flourished signatures on a page from the autograph collection of Geigy Hagenbach.

multiples or simple fractions of this measure-unit. Since the measure-units vary, it is difficult to find in a random sample a majority of similar measure-units. It is, however, possible to clarify a large number of signatures, according to their measure-units, into groups in which the measure-unit is the starting, middle or end-movement. The preference for certain measure-units partly depends on "graphic fashions" and national stereo-types. For instance, at the end of the nineteenth century, the end-movement was emphasized by a final downstroke, especially in France. As a random sample of such signatures we present a page (p. 153) from the autograph collection of Geigy Hagenbach [141a], where six signa-tures of French literary celebrities are presented, all of which show this final downstroke (Fig. 36). Since the collector did not group these signa-tures according to time periods, professions and nationalities, we have for our purpose something approximating a random sample.

Victorien Sardou, dramatic author (1831-1908) (Fig. 37)

The distance from beginning to end of the signature is three times the length of the final downstroke.

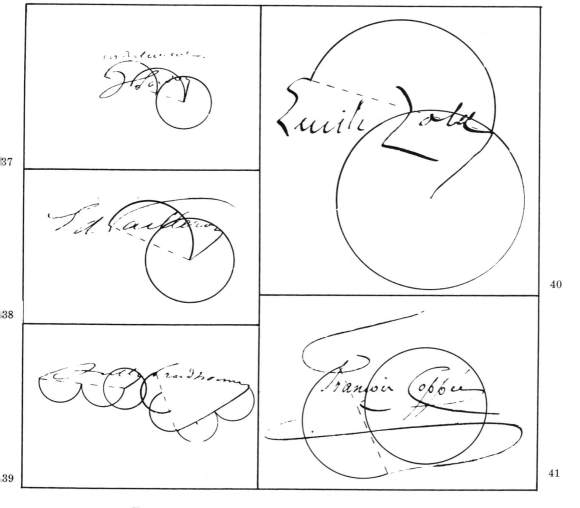

FIGS. 37-41.—The end-movement as measure unit.

Edmond-Jules-Henri Paillerou, dramatic poet (1834-1899) (Fig. 38)

The distance from beginning to end of the second name is twice the length of the final downstroke.

René-François-Armand Sully-Prudhomme, poet (1839-1907) (Fig. 39)

The distance from beginning to end of the first name is four times the length of the final downstroke. The same distance is equal to the length of the second name's final downstroke; therefore, the length of the final downstroke of the second name is four times the length of the final downstroke of the first name. The distance from beginning to end of the second name is three times the length of the first name's final downstroke.

Emile Zola, novelist (1840-1902) (Fig. 40)

The distance between beginning and right limit of the total signature is twice the length of the final downstroke.

François Coppée, poet (1842-1908) (Fig. 41)

The distance from the beginning to the end of the signature (end of flourish below the signature) is equal to the length of the final endstroke (attached to letter "e").

Thus, the end-movement in the final downstroke appears to be a measure-unit in 5 out of 6 signatures in our random sample. Lack of space prohibits giving random samples for all measure-units; but especially significant are those signatures which not only show an emphasis on one and the same measure-unit but on two or even three similar measure-units.

From our large collection of signatures of famous personalities we selected a number of those which show an emphasis on all three move-

Fig. 42.—The same proportion determining the total movement and its main single parts.

Figs. 42-48.—Starting-stroke, middle-stroke and end-stroke as measure units and the balance of movement.

ment patterns, starting-stroke, middle-stroke, and end-stroke. Our choice was limited since many signatures accentuate only one or two of these movements. We give below six examples by which we should like to demonstrate that in each single case the length of the total signature is a multiple of the length of the starting-, middle-, and end-movement, which demonstrates that the same proportion determines not only the total movement but also its main single parts.

I. *Edmund Burke, British political writer* (1729-1797) (Fig. 42):
Connecting start and end of the signature, this distance is
a. four times the length of the starting-stroke
b. twice the length of the middle-stroke
c. six times the length of the end-stroke.
The starting-stroke is 1½ times the length of the end-stroke. The middle-stroke is 3 times the length of the end-stroke.

FIG. 43.—The same proportion determining the total movement and its main single parts.

II. *Francis II, French Emperor* (1544-1560) (Fig. 43):
The signature, measured from start to end, is:
a. twice the length of the starting-stroke
b. equal to the length of the middle-stroke
c. three times the length of the end-stroke (length of letter "s")
The starting-stroke is 1½ times the length of the end-stroke. The middle-stroke is 3 times the length of the end-stroke.

FIG. 44.—The same proportion determining the total movement and its main single parts.

III. *Eugénie of France, French Empress, wife of Napoleon III* (1826-1920) (Fig. 44):
   The signature, measured from start to end, is:
   a. three times the length of the starting-stroke (length of first initial)
   b. equal to the length of the middle-stroke
   c. twice the length of the end-stroke.
   d. The position of the accent and of the dot follows the configurational scheme (see page 103).

FIG. 45.—The same proportion determining the total movement and its main single parts.

IV. *Paul Valéry, French poet* (1871-1947) (Fig. 45):
   a. The distance from start to left limit is equal to the length of the end-stroke, so that the distances between the three limits of the signature result in an equilateral triangle.
   b. The length of the end-stroke is five times the length of the starting-stroke and
   c. Seven times the length of the middle-stroke.
   d. Furthermore, the start of the second name lies in the center of the graphic configuration, which also appears in the distribution of other distances.

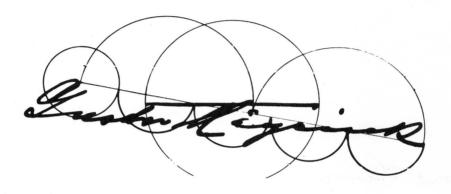

FIG. 46.—The same proportion determining the total movement and its main single parts.

V. *Gustav Meyrink, German writer* (1868-1932) (Fig. 46):
   The signature, measured from start to end, is:
   a. nine times the length of the starting-stroke
   b. two times the length of the middle-stroke
   c. twelve times the length of the end-stroke

FIG. 47.—The same proportion determining the total movement and its main single parts.

VI. *Jacques Natanson, French writer* (1901-   ) (Fig. 47):
The signature, measured from start to end, is:
a. four times the length of the starting-stroke
b. measured from left to right limit, the length of the signature is twice the length of the middle-stroke
c. seven times the length of the end-stroke

In these six examples the total signature is in proportion to the length of three defined movements. In each signature, the total length is either equal to or double the length of one of its longest part-movements; for instance, in the cases of Eugénie and Francis, the total signature is equal to the length of the middle-stroke; in the cases of Burke, Meyrink, and Natanson, the total signature is twice the length of the middle-stroke. Since all these proportions are interrelated, the movements in the signature seem to follow a principle of dynamic symmetry.

As we have already mentioned, symmetry is a form of balance. The three parts of the movement pattern, the starting-, middle- and end-movement, like a clockwork keep the entire movement in a dynamic relationship. If we visualize, with the help of circles, these movements as rotating, the starting-stroke and end-stroke frequently turn around the whole signature like the hand on a dial. In a signature of *Goethe*, for instance (Fig. 48), the end-flourish, turned downward, if turned counter-

FIG. 48.—Clockwise and counter-clockwise movement.

clockwise would touch the starting point of the signature; and the starting-stroke, if turned clockwise, would touch the end point of the signature. Thus the two-part movements encircle the whole from the beginning as well as from the end.

Encircling graphic patterns are known from primitive peoples as so-called protective lines. In many symbolic representations the symbol is surrounded by a circular line as a sign of protection against evil spirits. The Egyptians encircle the hieroglyphic name of the king as a sign of distinction and protection. Young children, the mentally diseased, and neurotic personalities have a similar tendency to encircle their graphic expressions. This tendency may be detected in many signatures as well.

We may venture the hypothesis that the regularity of our movement patterns as an expression of dynamic symmetry not only seems to be a symbol of balance, but also an expression of protective movements. The principle of symmetry, which in its static form is a repetition of the same and as such a symbol of security, may, in its dynamic form, equally be a symbol of security, which is a fundamental aim of man at all times of his existence.

CHAPTER IV

RHYTHM IN PERSONALITY

RHYTHM AND PERIODICITY

The concepts of consistency and of symmetry, even of dynamic symmetry, are too rigid to cover fully the phenomenon of graphic organization. Many investigators of such expressive movements as gait and handwriting recognize one characteristic called rhythm which Allport and Vernon describe as follows [7, p. 10]:

> Rhythm is a term frequently encountered but seldom defined in literature on expression. It seems usually to stand for an "indefinable something" which provides a refuge for those who are unwilling to surrender movement entirely to analytical and quantitative treatment. In this sense "rhythm" is something that can only be understood by "intuition"; it is a pattern too intimate and integrated and too meaningful to be studied adequately through analysis.*

In another book Allport says that the concept of rhythm is used to describe "the unanalyzable effect created by the whole pattern of movement" [5, p. 487]. Although investigators of rhythmical activity did not use measurements and did not recognize regularities of expressive patterns they sensed that expressive movements have something in common with what is called "rhythm" in art and especially in music.

One characteristic of rhythm is periodicity. The Russian scientist, M. Bechterev [27], searching for fundamental laws which govern nature as well as man's psychological reactions, believed that rhythm is such a basic principle, which "we see in all the movements of the inorganic organic, and superorganic worlds." Periodicity appears in the change of seasons, in the alternation of day and night, in phenomena of our body, such as circulation of blood, heartbeat, respiration, the periodic processes of ovulation, of sleeping and waking. Laboratory experiments show that nervous currents as well as muscular contractions are of a periodic nature appearing in graphs as regular waves.** And in mental processes, such as memory, attention and concentration, and in phases of creativeness, oscillations of periodic time-intervals may be observed. In the sphere of feeling and moods periodical alterations are known which, in the cyclo-

---

*From G. W. Allport and P. E. Vernon: "Studies in Expressive Movement." Copyright 1933 by The Macmillan Company and used with their permission.

**MacDougall [260, p. 465] remarks:

"We may conceive a periodical facilitation and inhibition of nervous activity to arise from the relation between the periodicity of its own rhythm of functioning and certain intervals in the objective series of stimulation."

thyme, show an extreme state characterized by the constant alternation of elation and depression. June E. Downey remarks [102a, pp. 122, 230]:

> Rhythm is one of those basal experiences with which even the little child has intimate acquaintance, but the scientist has difficulty in penetrating. There have been almost as many theories concerning the ultimate explanation of it as there have been theorists on the subject. That the experience of rhythm is very rooted in the physiological life would be conceded by all. But it is another matter determining the particular mode of functioning of the nervous system that issues in the awareness of rhythm.

RHYTHM AND THE GROUPING FACTOR

Periodicity is not the only characteristic of rhythm. Rhythm is not merely a regular repetition of stimuli or a regular succession of accents or tone-impulses, as in music, but also a phenomenon of grouping. Succeeding stimuli, such as the tones of music, can be perceived as a melody only if they are grouped. Different impressions of our visual perception can result in a perception of objects only if these single impressions are grouped and interrelated.*

But organic periodicity is not the same as the perception of rhythm. A coincidence between organic rhythm, e.g., that of respiration, and that of reading syllables in different rhythms could not always be found [281]. The objection was raised that our feeling of organic rhythm is too indefinite to serve as a grouping factor in perception.

The integration of several stimuli into a subjective unit, perceived as a whole, has been termed "the temporal range of consciousness." This term assumes that rhythmization is a factor of conscious perception, thus implying that a person is consciously aware of this act. But in effect, we are generally not aware of our grouping act, which takes place unconsciously.

Rhythm is a characteristic of our feelings and emotions, which Wundt [469, p. 3] described as a regular alternation of states of expectation and satisfaction. It was argued [401, p. 96] that a rhythmic grouping can occur in a state far from expectation and satisfaction, namely, in that of indifference; and, as emotions are weakened by a repetition, we should expect a weakening of the effective tone of rhythm if the rhythm is repeated. But this seems not to be true; on the contrary, the feeling of rhythm generally increases with repetition. Furthermore, emotion involves contrasted feelings, but rhythm runs in a comparatively unbroken course. Finally, rhythm cannot be a phenomenon of attention, as Squire explains, because it was observed that attention itself has fluctuations in which the subject periodically does not perceive the object observed. This holds for hearing, seeing, speaking, and every kind of mental work which is continuously done in a state of attention. On the basis of the

---

*Meumann [281, p. 271] remarked:
"The subjective holding together of the impressions in a whole is inseparably bound up with the simplest cases of rhythmic perception."

observation that persons follow stimuli with movements of some parts of the body, rhythms have been related solely to sensations of muscles called kinesthetic sensations. But the parallel phenomenon of rhythmization in sensations of smell, taste, touch, and vision runs counter to the opinion that rhythm derives solely from kinesthetic sensations.

RHYTHM OF THE OUTER AND OF THE INNER WORLD

Bolton [43, p. 234] demonstrated in experiments that subjects hearing certain rhythms felt irresistibly impelled to make certain muscular movements. He reports:

> If they attempted to restrain these movements in one muscle, they were likely to appear somewhere else. The most common forms of muscular movements were beating time with the foot, nodding the head, or swaying the body. Most subjects were unconscious of their muscular movements.

Leumann [244] and Mentz [280] found that inspiration or expiration can be regulated according to metronome beats. They found a "frequent falling together of the accented beat and the respiration summit or valley." Studies on the effect of rhythmic and antirhythmic stimuli on work-efficiency and on fatigue showed that an antirhythmic accompaniment increases weariness, and that synchronized rhythm decreases it. The immediate influence of outer rhythm upon organic changes is shown in ceremonial movements, marches, and dances that lead to ecstasy. The two rhythms, that of the outer world and that of the inner world, confront each other and are in continuous relationship. It may be observed that the most pleasurable rhythm is that in which the outer rhythm coincides with the inner one. In so-called rhythm-therapy, especially in cases of stammering caused by the fact that the subjective rhythm is not adapted to the objective one, cures have been effected by an environmental change and through treatment by adaptation.

One type of individual rhythm seems to be innate. From the moment of birth, twins frequently show marked differences in their speeds of reaction and of movements. Another type of individual rhythm originates in learning. Murphy, Murphy and Newcomb remark [300, p. 48]:

> An obvious example is the establishment in the newborn child of a feeding rhythm. The doctor prescribes three-hour intervals between feedings. Before long, the child's stomach (and hence his voice) proclaims the three-hour interval almost as effectively as an alarm-clock. A change of schedule produces only a few days' disturbance. Now we have a four-hour and later a six-hour feeding rhythm.

The authors conclude:

> The rhythm is demonstrably imposed not by the unalterable characteristics of inner tissues, but by neural patterns established in experience.*

One phenomenon of the outer rhythm is the alternation of day and night which results in our sensing of time. This time is perceived not only with our eyes; it is well known that, even during sleep, persons have

---

*Gardner Murphy, Lois B. Murphy and Theodore M. Newcombe: "Experimental Social Psychology." Copyright 1937 by Harper & Brothers and used with their permission.

such time-feeling that they can awaken exactly at a predetermined hour, even if this hour is far from the usual time of awakening. Many observers have emphasized the relation between rhythm and time.* Mach [261], who at first thought that we have a special sense for rhythm, localized in the ear, later on considered time-feeling and rhythm to be a special energy of the brain [261a]. But this relationship between rhythm and time is not always apparent, as children, primitive peoples, and the mentally diseased have a keen sense of rhythm but a very poor sense of time.

Thus, we may conclude that personal rhythm is determined by the rhythm of environment as well as by inner, organic processes; and that the degree of each of these rhythmical determinants is different, some persons being rhythmically more determined from without, others from within.

The rhythmical manifestation of periodicity has the characteristic of a repetition of the same pattern which we call consistency if it is repetition in time, and symmetry if it is repetition in spatial arrangement. But besides consistency and symmetry, rhythm has the characteristics of a definite movement pattern, just as a wave of sound or a bit of color has its definite frequency of oscillations. Every elastic body, be it a wooden beam, stretched string, glass jug, steel bridge, or a roomful of air, has its own natural period of vibration. A pendulum of a fixed length always makes the same number of swings in a second. Whether they are small or large, they have the same kind of periodic motion. Two examples may demonstrate an object's or body's own natural period of vibration. The custodian of a steel bridge is always on the lookout to see that no series of shocks appear, since he knows that these vibrations if they are timed properly and if they continue for a long time may break one thousand tons of steel girders. A powerful singer can break a glass by maintaining a certain note. In these examples rhythm as a natural period is the expression of an object's or body's central organization and thus unvariable.

If the rhythm in graphic movement were to show unvariable characteristics it might be compared to a natural period of vibration.

STABILITY AND CHANGE OF RHYTHM

The pattern of rhythm is not affected by transpositions. When we have an acoustic rhythm, say, one long and two short beats, the pattern is not affected whether the sound be loud or soft, and whether the sound be performed by sticks, waterdrops, or piano keys. However, the rhythm is affected by a change of intervals, that is, by a change of the relationship of beats. When we have a visual rhythm, say, a periodical alteration of a long and two short dashes, the pattern is not affected whether the rela-

---

*Meumann [281, p. 249] says that:
"Each sense participates more in rhythmical phenomena, the more it is an organ of time-estimation. Hearing, being the best sense for timing, is most adapted for receiving rhythmic impressions."

tive size of the dashes be long or short or whether circles and dots (or other forms) be substituted. However, the rhythm is affected by a change of grouping, that is, by a change of the relationship of elements.

We made a similar observation in patterns of graphic movements: neither the change of the relative size nor a change in the use of form-elements necessarily affects the pattern of proportions. The rhythmical pattern of movement is changed, however, if the relationship varies.

If graphic movement were an expression of personality we would expect both phenomena, stability and change of rhythmical patterns. The pattern of our personality remains stable for certain periods of time, longer for some people, shorter for others. It is through deep-reaching experiences that this pattern changes. For many years of his life a person may possess a fixed neurotic pattern of living, but through a penetrating experience or through the application of psychotherapy this pattern may suddenly change. If a person becomes unhappy his expression of personality changes; for instance, it may change from activity to passivity, from an expansion of movements to a withdrawal. Such changes appear also if a person becomes sick bodily or mentally. Changes of movement patterns produced by psychological changes have been observed experimentally.

Several investigators have demonstrated a relationship between mental processes and the contraction and relaxation of muscle groups. Measuring grip pressure, the tension of the jaw muscles, the alterations of tonus, etc., before and during a mental effort, E. Jacobson [189] found that mental effort is accompanied by contractions of muscle groups. A. G. Bills [35] found that increased muscular tension accompanies increased efficiency of learning. F. L. Golla and S. Antonovitch [150] photographed the action currents in muscle groups and found that their size increases during mental effort.

The extremes of psychic tension are elation and depression, exaggerations of the feelings of happiness and unhappiness. The word "tension," from the Latin "tensio," means "the act of stretching or straining." In elation this stretching of forces is a raising of level, and, actually, the meaning of the word "elation" is elevation of mind, while depression means "the act of pressing down, a sinking of a surface; a sinking of the spirits." Experimental observations supported this insight of language. As G. V. N. Dearborn [89, p. 70] remarks:

> In a pleasant emotional state there will be an extension rather than a contraction of muscles (to jump for joy); one will lean forward rather than recoil.

H. H. Remmers and L. A. Thompson, Jr. [346], asked students to draw lines on paper while thinking of pleasant events and of unpleasant events. The lines drawn during pleasant thoughts were longer than those during unpleasant thoughts. The involuntary tendency toward extension or contraction of movement appears to be based upon emotional stimuli. F. L. Goodenough and C. R. Brian [154], testing children who were throwing rings upon a peg, found that a child who made a "ringer" was likely to overshoot the target on the next trial. The authors remark:

> The effect of the pleasurable emotion aroused by success was shown in a decidedly greater tendency to throw beyond the mark in the case of those errors immediately following success.*

J. E. Downey [101], who was the first in this country to experiment with handwriting, reports that she and another subject wrote their signatures every day for four months, at the same time indicating their mood. When, at the end of this period, Downey compared the different signatures in relation to the moods in which they were written, she found that the total graphic movement increased when made in an energetic mood. However, an extension of movement, combined with instability and irregularity, also appeared if the writer's control of movement diminished as in states of exhaustion. Similar observations have been made in experiments on the estimation of lengths. According to H. Münsterberg [299] depressive states are related to underestimation, elated states to overestimation.

THE RHYTHM OF CONTRACTION AND EXTENSION IN GRAPHIC MOVEMENTS

All the findings on movement patterns under opposite moods demonstrate a positive relationship between emotional states and motor activity. The question which we ask now is whether even such changes of personality are determined by a subject's formula of movement, whether the increase or decrease of movement observed follows a law of proportion. Asking our subjects to write their names while imagining happy and unhappy events, we observed with some a proportional increase or decrease in the length of the name and its single graphic elements; others did not show variations, so the results were not significant statistically. However, experiments on imagination are not too reliable, because many subjects are influenced not by imagination but only by direct experience. The artificial creation of happy and unhappy moods offers difficulties for laboratory arrangements. I therefore collected a number of signatures of historical personalities, which were written at a time of highly favorable circumstances, and compared them with average signatures of the same persons. I also compared signatures written during youth, middle life, and old age of the same person. Finally, signatures were investigated at the moment of a climax, for instance at the moment of a catastrophe, and during an epileptic attack. Although these studies are still in an exploratory stage, they are already very suggestive.

The Contraction of Movement. Galileo Galilei (1564-1642) (Fig. 49):
It was in 1609 that Galileo, then at Padua, first turned a telescope towards heaven. He wrote to Belisario Vinta on January 30, 1610:**

---

*F. L. Goodenough and C. R. Brian: "Certain Factors Underlying the Acquisition of Motor Skill by Preschool Children." J. Exper. Pschychol. *12*:127-155, 1929.
**Letter to Landucci and Belisario Vinta. The Private Life of Galileo, London 1870.

FIG. 49.—Proportional contraction of movement under adverse psychological conditions.

> I am at present staying at Venice for the purpose of getting printed some observations which I have been making on the celestial bodies by means of a telescope which I have made by means of a lens, and being infinitely amazed thereat, so do I give infinite thanks to God, who has been pleased to make me the first observer of marvelous things, unrevealed to bygone ages.

In 1633, when seventy years of age, Galileo had to face a public accusation of the Inquisition. As prisoner of the Inquisition he was forced to recite a dictated abjuration, from which we quote:*

> . . . . I have been adjudged and vehemently suspected of heresy, namely, that I maintained and believed that the sun is the center of the world and immovable. . . . I with sincere heart and faith unfigured abjure, and detest the aforesaid errors and heresies . . . and I swear that I will never by any word hereafter say or assert, by speech or writing, anything through which the like suspicion may be had of me.

After this humiliation Galileo's forces began to decrease; his eyesight began to fade. On January 2, 1638, he wrote to Diotaty:

> Your dear friend and servant Galileo has been for the last month hopelessly blind; so that this heaven, this earth, this universe which I by my marvelous discoveries and clear demonstrations enlarged a hundred thousand times

---

*The accusation, condemnation and abjuration of Galileo Galilei before the Holy Inquisition at Rome 1633 by R. Carlyle, London 1819.

beyond the belief of the wise men of bygone ages, henceforward for me is shrunk into such a small space as is filled by my own bodily sensations.

If we compare a signature of Galileo written in middle life (a) and one from his prison in Arcetri (b), when he was an old man in despair, we see that his signature had decreased in regular proportions. Measuring in both signatures the extensions of first and second names from left to the end-point and taking the smallest movement, that of the second name in the late signature, as a standard of measurement, the following relationships are observed:

In the earlier signature the length of the first name Galileo equals that of the second name Galilei, both measured from left limit to end. In the late signature Galileo's eyesight was so bad that he lost the direction in writing his second name, writing it Galii, one "i" is higher, one "i" is lower than the other letters. Did Galileo write the upper "i" or the lower "i" as the last letter? Our measurements indicate that the lower "i" was the last letter:

1. In the earlier signature the dots over the first first "i" have the same position in Gal*i*leo and in Gal*i*lei. In the late signature the dot over the upper "i" has the same position as the dot over the first "i" in Gal*i*leo.

2. Furthermore, if the lower "i" is the end of the signature, the movement of Galii is half the movement of Galileo, therefore falling into the scheme of proportions.

3. In both signatures the distances between the beginning of the signature and its left limit is equal to the distance between the beginning and the end of the signature, if the lower "i" is the last letter.

4. In both signatures the distances between the three dots over the "i" are in proportional relationship to each other. The distance between first and last dot is in the earlier signature 3½ times, in the later sngnature 3 times the distance between middle and last dot.

The regular contraction of movement also becomes visible if we put the beginnings of both signatures exactly below each other; the distance between the left limits of both signatures equals the distance between the right limits as marked by the dots of the "i". We should like to mention here two further consistencies in both signatures. In both, the distance between the beginning of the signature and its left limit is equal to the distance between beginning and end of the signature. In both signatures the distances between the first three dots over the "i" are in proportional relationship to each other. In the earlier signature the distance between the first and last dots is 3½ times the distance between the middle and last dot. In the later signature the distance between the first and last dots is 3 times the distance between the middle and last dots.

Adolf Hitler (1889-1945) (Fig. 50):

When Adolf Hitler was a successful party leader he attempted to overthrow the German Republic. This first attempt failed in 1923 and he was imprisoned; his hopes were gone; the party disintegrated.

We compared two of his signatures,* one written shortly before his attempt to overthrow the government, at the time of his success (a); the other signature written in prison (b). In the latter signature the extension of his second name decreased in extent exactly by one half. Furthermore, comparing the distance from beginning to end, the signature written before his imprisonment is one and a half times the length of the later one. The decrease of movement refers only to the second name. "Hitler." The proportions of the first name, "Adolf," remain exactly the same. First and second names show two basically different expressive

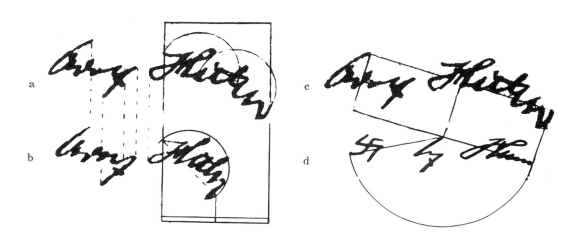

FIG. 50.—Proportional contraction of movement under adverse psychological conditions.

characteristics. The first name remains stable, the second name changes. The first name is written with Gothic letters, the second with Roman letters. The rhythm of the graphic movement represents two different patterns, that of stability and that of regular decrease.

Another signature of Hitler, written seventeen years later, in 1940 (c)**, has exactly half the length of the earlier signature (a); but in this signature Hitler includes a swastika. We observe that the distance from the beginning of the first name to the end of the second name is equal to the distance from the beginning of the first name to the end of the swastika; and so the length of the total signature in 1940 is functionally equal to that in 1923.

Signatures made in old age which usually is characterized by a decrease of motor power, frequently show a regular decrease of graphic movement.

*From: Ludecke, K. G. W.: I Knew Hitler. New York, 1937.
**From Henry O. Teltscher [413].

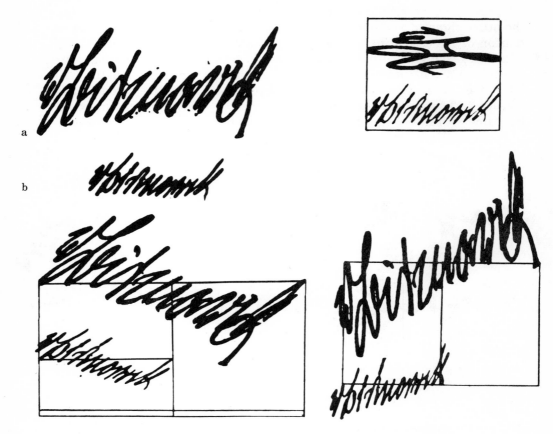

Fɪɢ. 51.—Proportional contraction of movement in old age.

Otto von Bismarck (1815-1898) (Fig. 51) :

The signature of the old Bismarck (b), compared with one from middle life (a), is exactly half the length of the former whether we measure it from beginning to end or from the left limit to the right limit. The length of the initial in the earlier signature is equal to the length of the total name in the late signature.

FIG. 52.—Proportional contraction of movement in old age.

Ferdinand Foch, French general (1851-1929) (Fig. 52):

A signature of the sixty-nine year old Maréchal Foch (b), compared with a signature from his middle years (a), shows a shrinking in extent (as expressed by the flourish) to half its former size.

FIG. 53.—Proportional contraction of movement in old age.

Joseph Haydn (1732-1809) (Fig. 53):

The signature of the old Haydn, measured from beginning to end (b), decreases to one third of that written by the young Haydn (a), and the length of his initial is halved.

FIG. 54.—Proportional contraction of movement in old age.

Franz Liszt (1811-1886) (Fig. 54):

The signature of the old and sick Liszt (b), measured from beginning to end (end of the bar of the "t"), decreases to one half of that written in his youth.

The Increase of Movement. Graphic movements increase when a person loses control of himself. It has been observed [61, 101, 365, 367] that size of letters and distance between them increase if written in a state of exhaustion and fatigue. Such an increase is especially visible in states where a person is "beyond" himself, as during a catastrophe, mental fits, and epileptic attacks. Dostoevski described the epileptic's feeling of tremendous extension of the ego when losing control during a fit.

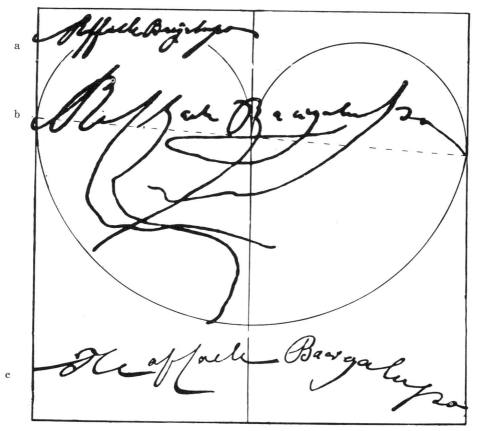

FIG. 55A.—Proportional extension of movements after epileptic seizure.

Raffaele Bargalupo, an epileptic (Fig. 55A, B) :

The Italian psychologist Cesare Lombroso in his book *Graphology* [256] published the handwriting of an epileptic (a) before, and (b, c) after an epileptic attack. Comparing the distance from beginning to end, it appears that the signatures after the attack (b, c) have increased to double the length of the normal signature (a) ; but also single elements such as the length of the first initial as well as the length of the end-stroke have doubled. Comparing the four long down-strokes in the signature after the attack (b), it appears that their length from beginning to end is the same, being in each case four times the length of the end-stroke in the same signature.

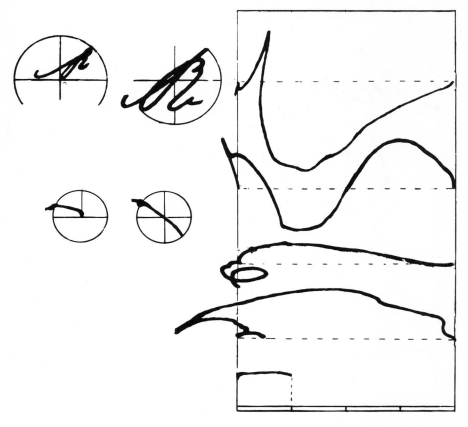

FIG. 55B.—Identities and proportions of movements after epileptic seizure.

Elizabeth, Queen of England (1533-1603) (Fig. 56):

Queen Elizabeth was said to suffer from "seizures like fits" and long attacks of unconsciousness. They seem to have been related to the deep conflict in Elizabeth's life, which she expressed by the words: "I know I have but the body of a weak and feeble woman, but I have the heart of a king."

If we compare two signatures, one written under a royal edict (a), the other written under a letter to her relative and prisoner, Mary Stuart (b), we observe that some letters end in long flourishes, branching out in a way similar to that of the epileptic in our preceding example. Although the outer shape of these flourishes is different in both signatures, their extensions remain exactly equal. The lengths of the initials in both signatures, in their horizontal as well as their vertical extension, remain exactly equal. Also the position of letters remains equal in both signatures as we demonstrate by parallels. However, the length of the longer signature, measured from beginning to end, is exactly one and a half times the

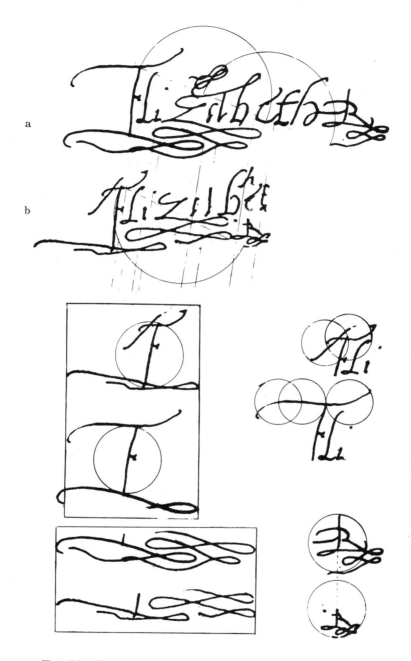

FIG. 56.—Proportional increase and stability of movement.

length of the shorter signature. The size of the initial's upper bar in the longer signature is two and a half times that in the smaller signature; and the size of the letter "R" has doubled. The shorter signature shows, in addition to the reduction of movement, a mistake in spelling. Elizabeth leaves out the letter "h" and then puts it between the letters "b" and "e." We shall later give some other examples which indicate equally clearly that mistakes in writing and spelling seem to be in relationship to the formula of movement.

Epileptic Children. That graphic movement patterns increase after an epileptic seizure and that this increase follows laws of proportion was also observed in the drawings of a man, done by epileptic children before and after seizures. Miss Florentine Hackbush, psychologist with the Bureau of Mental Health in the Commonwealth of Pennsylvania, Department of Welfare, Harrisburg, was kind enough to conduct our experiment. In her letter of June 12, 1944, Miss Hackbush gives a report of her procedure:

> On the date I went to Salinsgrove, April 1925, I had all the school children do a drawing of a man. These are not the cases at Salinsgrove, naturally, which have the most frequent attacks, but it was a supervised group in charge of intelligent persons and it seemed advisable to see what could be done with this group. I left the drawing with the teachers, who had seen the Goodenough procedure and learned it, with instructions to watch each child that had seizures, and as soon as he or she got back into the seat to give him a pencil and piece of paper and ask him to draw a man.

From my examination of the two drawings of a man, made by seven children before and after seizure, four cases are selected.*

S. A., a twelve year old boy with idiopathic epilepsy made a drawing of a man (Fig. 57) immediately after the seizure (2). The entire figure is extended to double the length of his drawing before the seizure (1) while the length of the head as well as the length of the arms remains almost exactly the same.

R. T., a fourteen year old boy suffering from petit mal attacks, shows a similar increase of graphic patterns in his drawings of a man (Fig. 58), made immediately after the seizure (2). Here the size of the total figure increases to one and a half times, and so do some single parts such as the hand on the right side of the picture; the foot on the left side of the picture increases twofold. Also other features show an increase in simple proportions, while a few remain the same as they were before the seizure, such as the size of the head (without the hat).

A. G. is a fourteen year old girl with a mental age of 6.6 and an I.Q. of 50. According to a Rorschach test she is not basically feebleminded but lives in a world of phantasy. Characteristic is a perseverance of re-

---

*See also by the same author [467, pp. 186-189].

FIGS. 57-58.—Proportional increase of movements after epileptical seizures in drawings of children.

sponses. The drawings made before and after the seizure (Fig. 59) are extremely similar, although there are significant changes in details. The drawing after the seizure has no pupils, but the hands have fingers; a further addition are "whiskers" and "clothes." In both drawings the mouth is exactly the center in the circular face. The length of the signature remains the same before and after the seizure. The drawing after the seizure shows an enlargement of all features; the proportional increase (Fig. b) is as follows:

Diameter of face (ab)	one and a half times
Distance of eyes (cd)	twice
Length of left arm on picture (ef)	one and a half times
Length of left leg on picture (gh)	about one and a half times
Length of right leg on picture (ik)	about one and a half times
Length of right arm on picture (lm)	same length
Right eye on picture (d)	twice
Nose	same length
Mouth (M)	twice

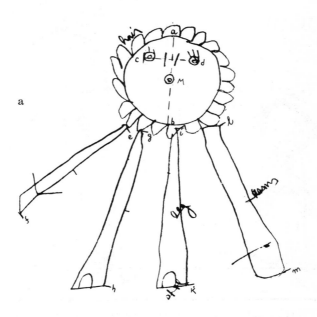

FIG. 59.—Proportional increase of movements after epileptical seizures. (a) Drawing before seizure.

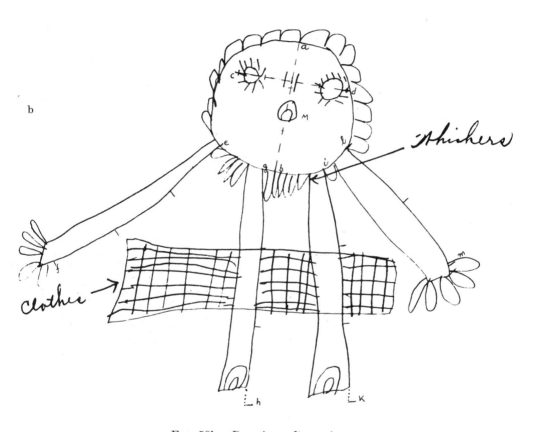

anne
may. 25, 1944

whiskers

clothes →

FIG. 59b.—Drawing after seizure.

W. K. is an eleven year old boy, showing frequent depressions; his mental age is 6.8, his I.Q. 62. His Rorschach results present a deterioration from a former better level.

In the drawing after the seizure (Fig. 60), the horizontal diameter of the head (ab) is exactly one and a half times this length in the drawing before the seizure; and the diameter of the right eye in the picture (cd) is one and a half times larger. In the picture before the seizure, the end of the ear (M) is the center of the face; in the picture after the seizure, the

FIG. 60.—Proportional increase of movements after epileptic seizure.

start of the nose is the center (M). A circle drawn around those centers, the periphery of which touches upper and lower limit of the face, has the same radius in both drawings.

In all but one case the length of features in the drawing made after the seizure increased to double or to one and a half times the length they had in the drawing before the seizure. The increase and decrease of movements keeping the same proportions indicate that graphic movements not only show consistencies and symmetries, but also a dynamic phenomenon of rhythm which, like the diastole and systole of the heart, has a pattern of expansion and contraction, of change bound by law.

FIG. 61.—Proportional increase of movement in mental disease.

Conrad Ferdinand Meyer, Swiss poet (1825-1898) (Fig. 61) :
When this poet became mentally diseased the length of his second name was double (b) the length his name had in his healthy days (a).

Friedrich Nietzsche (1844-1900) (Fig. 62) :
Two signatures, the second of which is written in one of Nietzsche's psychic exaltations (b). Although the second name falls down and shows signs of distortion, it covers exactly the same space as in the first signature (a). However, the length of the initial "F" as well as that of the initial "N" is doubled in the second signature, while the length of the initial's bar remains unchanged.

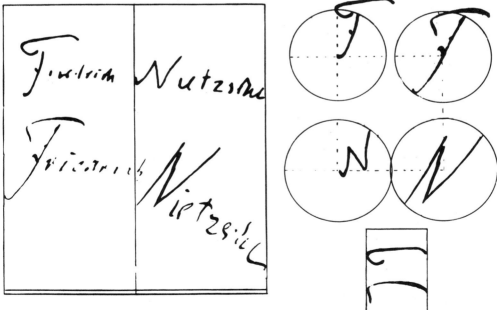

FIG. 62.—Proportional increase of movement in psychic exaltation.

a

b

c

d

FIG. 63A.—Bonaparte; Napoleon; N.

Napoleon (1769-1821) (Fig. 63):

Suddenness of disaster may graphically produce symptoms similar to those of an epileptic seizure. Such a symptom, the extension of move-

FIG. 63B.—Stability of length and position of movements.

ment, becomes apparent in Napoleon's signature after the last battle of Leipzig, which sealed his fate (d). The signature collapses completely, but the elements in the bundle of exploding strokes keep the formula of

FIG. 63C.—Proportional increase of movement during emotional shock.

movement. If we take a signature of the victorious Napoleon for comparison, the signature at the catastrophe shows the following increase of
movement:

The starting-stroke is three times enlarged.

The middle-stroke is two and a half times enlarged.

The end-stroke (flourish) is doubled.

In three signatures signed as Bonaparte (a) or as Napoleon (b, c), the
length of the flourish remains the same. The position of the starting-
stroke remains the same, while its length shows simple proportions.

CHAPTER V

CONFIGURATION IN PERSONALITY

THE THEORETICAL PROBLEM

Focusing upon constancy, symmetry, and rhythm in graphic movements, we always came to the observation that the various elements in the same movement pattern were in a harmonious relationship to each other. Such harmonious relationship existed not only in the single pattern, but also between different movements of the same person over a long period of time. These relationships became visible in the total movement pattern, exemplified by the length of the name and its parts, but they were also dependent on specific single features. We recognized the role of dots, which were like pivots around which the movement circled; we found that the length of certain strokes, such as the starting-, middle- and end-stroke, had the function of a standard of length according to which all the other elements were patterned. We could use these elements as "measure units," like an individual yardstick with which each movement pattern in the same signature could be measured, indicating that all other elements are simple multiples of the basic unit. There are many such measure units, which we shall classify in the present study. But first we wish to draw attention to the problem involved in the two observations, of harmonious relationships and of movement-centers. These relationships, dependent on the building units and arranged harmoniously around them, illuminate a phenomenon of configuration. The graphic movement appears to be built up like a piece of art, like a drawing or a musical composition, with inner aesthetic relationships. This configuration is definitely unconscious, nobody up to now having been aware of these mathematical constructions in his graphic movement. Moreover, nobody would be able to construct such an intricate scheme of harmonious relationships in graphic patterns intentionally, at least not in such a flash performance as that represented by a signature.

Such an unconscious configuration of movement patterns must be rooted in the depth of the organism, and if graphic movements reflect personality, as is suggested by their changes in elations and depressions, the configuration of movement patterns seems to reflect the configuration of personality. This concept leads us into the midst of most important problems. Many people believe that personality is simply the sum of what a person has learned, all the traits being piled up according to experiences by which they are conditioned. According to such a view there is no more in personality than what we put in from without, and everything becomes manifest in our surface behavior. For other people the personality of each individual is something completely unique for which no regularities or laws can be found; it is, in the words of William Stern [404], "the asymptote of the science that seeks laws." A third view assumes laws in each individual, but, as G. W. Allport states [5, p. 21]:

> . . . each person by himself is actually a special law of nature; so too, is any structural occurrence within the pattern of his life. . . . When the investigator turns his eyes upon the individual he finds that in him all laws are modified.*

The view toward which we are led by the present study is slightly different. The phenomena of consistency, symmetry, rhythm, and configuration appear in all manifestations of nature. The investigator now might not find that in the individual "*all* laws are modified," but that it is the manifestation of *one* general law which is modified. The general law of configuration, expressible mathematically, may become operative in each individual in a special way. This theory is not new; in fact, it is the assumption of ancient civilizations that man's personality can be expressed by a formula, by a basic numerical proportion. Such belief in a basic cipher of personality prevailed in the old civilizations of Babylon, Egypt, and Palestine and is expressed, for example, by St. John in Revelation, where he speaks of "the number of a man; and his number is six hundred threescore and six."** Number was often a symbol of a configuration of dots, as is still evident in our dice. The ancient idea of a cipher of personality has two implications: first, the assumption that personality in general follows laws as do numbers, and, second, that each individual has his special number-configuration. The idea of a general and specific formula of configuration in personality has a parallel if we consider that the shape of our body is determined by a general formula of configuration which is the same for everyone. In everyone the eyes, ears, hands, etc., are at certain places in a certain relationship to each other; this is the *general* body formula, the canon of the human figure. (See page 57, Fig. 34.) There is, furthermore, a *specific* body formula. This is the individual appearance, partly determined by heredity, by the features of father, mother, and ancestors. But the formula of the body has its reflection upon a formula of personality. Let us consider that the organism is a unity, that bodily changes have an immediate influence upon our behavior and upon our personality, and that changes in personality have an immediate influence upon body and behavior. This psychosomatic relationship is evident from findings in psychology, psychiatry, and biology. If man's organism is a unity, and if the organization of the body depends upon a general and a specific formula, we may expect that personality also follows a general and a specific formula.

Up to now science has not been able to decide whether individuality, the self, follows a formula or a law. We now have some indication that our patterns of expression do follow laws of configuration.

---

*From G. W. Allport: "Personality." Copyright 1937 by Henry Holt & Company and used with their permission.
**Revelation 13:17-18.

CONFIGURATION AND PERCEPTION

Our study of symmetry indicates similar characteristics of perception and expression. Perception is an act of unconscious configuration, and intention has not much influence upon it. If we did not possess the ability for perceptual configuration we would not be able to see any object as a whole. A house, a tree, would be a sum of patches but not the unities that they are. In certain injuries of the brain a person actually may lose the ability to recognize an object as a whole. Our configuration in perception has its parallel in our configuration of expression. The painter uses single spots of color, evoking the impression of a whole figure; the composer uses single sounds to express a musical piece perceived as a whole. The law of configuration is the cornerstone of the school of gestalt psychologists, who call the configurating principle which they find active in processes of perception a gestalt principle, and the configurated object a gestalt. K. Koffka [214, p. 682] remarks that the word "gestalt" is implied in the term "organization." W. Köhler defined "gestalt" in the following way [215, p. 192]:

> [It] has the meaning of a concrete individual and characteristic entity, existing as something detached and having shape or form as one of its attributes.*

The unifying principle is not of a kind that can be explained in atomistic terms. The gestalt, constituting the whole, is different from a mere summation or blind combination of elements. If the gestalt principle is, as its advocates believe, a general phenomenon of nature, personality also should be determined by that principle. Koffka asks: "Is personality a gestalt?" He answers in the affirmative, but with a mere assumption [214, p. 677]:

> What would it mean if personality were not a gestalt? That its different behavior units or traits were independent from each other and could be united in any combination. If, on the other hand, personality is a gestalt, then there would be interdependence between its various manifestations, and a great number of combinations of traits would be excluded.**

PRINCIPLES OF CONFIGURATION IN PERSONALITY

Up to now no experimental methods have been found that enable us to demonstrate that personality is determined by a gestalt principle.*** Our findings with graphic movements seem to be the first step in approach-

---

*Wolfgang Kohler: "Gestalt Psychology." Copyright 1943 by the Liveright Publishing Corporation and used with their permission.

**K. Koffka: "Principles of Gestalt Psychology." Copyright 1932 by Harcourt Brace & Company and used with their permission.

***Koffka remarks [214, p. 679] (ibid):

> "Gestalt theory . . . has started to approach those conditions under which personality itself enters the investigation. But since this is but the barest beginning it seems wiser to bide our time. And thus this section is unduly brief not because I underrate the importance of the personality, but because I have too high a regard for it to treat it less consistently than any other part."

ing experimental proof that personality, as reflected in graphic expression, is acting under the principle of configuration and organization, or as a gestalt. The law of proportion and configuration in expressive movement, which is visible and measurable in its graphic reflex, is largely independent of learning and training, of environment and mood, and of somatic conditions (for instance, whether we write with eyes open or closed, with the right hand or with the left, in a healthy state of mind or in mental disease). Whatever the personality trends are which determine expressive movement, they seem to become configurated just as spread iron filings are configurated by a magnet. The configuration of trends is like the grouping of elements into a figure, like a combination of letters into a word, and may be considered the formula of personality.

Personality is formed through all the experiences which a person embodies, by a phenomenon which is called "integration." Even if the personality system is modified by each influx and changes with each integration, basic configurations, expressed by proportions and relationships, seem to remain stable. Hence, from this point of view, integration is part of the gestalt principle which effectuates the embodiment of factors following the formula of personality. In the process of integration the choice and location of newly integrated parts into the system of personality are determined by the whole, or gestalt, of personality, and each integrated part determines the whole. With regard to certain psychic disturbances, no partial healing is possible if personality is not treated as a whole. Psychoanalysis especially stresses this point of interrelationship of tendencies within the whole of personality. Wertheimer describes it with regard to perception [446, p. 7]: "What happens to a part of the whole, is determined by intrinsic laws in this whole."

Graphic expression demonstrates the principle of the part's dependence upon the whole. If a person, as a result of outer or inner conditions, changes parts of his signature, he also will change all other parts in the same way so that the basic proportions and configurations will remain stable.

One of the main factors of gestalt is that it can be transposed; a melody preserves its basic structure in whatever key we play it, and a form will remain the same for our perception after it has changed its place, color, size, and brightness. Graphic expression shows us that expressive movement may completely change its place, size, and form, but that the gestalt principle of proportion and configuration is then only transposed. One of the main attributes of the principle of gestalt or organization is what Wertheimer calls "the law of Prägnanz" (structurization). Koffka formulates it as follows [214, p. 110]: " . . . psychological organization will always be as 'good' as the prevailing conditions allow. In this definition, the term 'good' is undefined. It embraces such properties as regularity, symmetry, simplicity, and others."

The law of "Prägnanz" was demonstrated in experiments on perception. If several geometrical organizations are to be perceived, that figure will be perceived which has the most stable shape. The law of configuration is stronger than the law of experience. Our experience of printed letters is certainly stronger than our experience of a figure like this, but nobody will perceive the letters A, M, V, W, X, which are inherent in the figure; everybody perceives a geometrical pattern; this is due to the law of configuration.

Our findings in graphic movements indicate that we not only *perceive* that figure which has the most stable shape, but that we also *express* that figure which offers the most stable pattern. A person can give his letters the most varied shapes and sizes, but he will select those shapes and sizes which form part of a well-structured unity. A person whose name has, for instance, a "t" in it, will be quite unaware that the length of the "t" bar may be in proportion to the length of the whole name; but the gestalt principle in graphic expression seems to determine the choice of that stroke with regard to its fitness into the whole scheme of expression.

Since graphic expression is a reflection of personality, we now ask: What implications has the gestalt principle of expressive movement for the total personality? The principle of configuration indicates that personality is not built up in an accidental way but follows an organized pattern. Just as the physical body is organized by symmetry, co-ordination of movements, and interrelationship of functions, so personality seems to be determined by forces causing symmetry, co-ordination, and interrelation of trends. The principle of balance in our body seems to correspond to the principle of balance in personality. The law of stability can be considered the basic law of personality; it is that principle which in expressive movement holds together the parts of a gestalt and which causes the inner principle of a gestalt (proportion and configuration) to remain stable even if conditions change its outer appearance. The concept of personality itself is related to that of stability because we can separate one personality from another only if personality shows a definite and relatively stable pattern. As pointed out by Ernst Mach, personality also seems to be determined by this principle—that forces give to a system of balance the most regular configuration of which this system is capable. These forces, acting in the direction of most regular configurations, become visible in the regular proportions and configurations of graphic movement.

Just as the child learns to keep his body in balance, so one is tempted to conclude that the phenomenon of balance and symmetry in expressive movements also is due to training and learning. The fact that the symmetry and balance of graphic movement was never trained nor learned nor is even known to a person speaks against such a supposition; neither is this function conditioned by environment, nor its basis an adaption of the organism. However, this problem leads us to inquire whether the principle of configuration in graphic movements is active in young children before they have learned to draw or to write; and whether it would appear in a blind person, who does not perceive a configuration with his eyes.

CONFIGURATION OF EXPRESSIVE MOVEMENTS

A configuration of movements appears in early infancy, as K. Lewin [245] and others [3] have shown in photographs and films. The movements of six-month-old infants are predominantly those of unified muscle action, and not specific action; they react with their entire bodies, reach for objects with both hands and feet, later with both hands, and finally one. The originally simultaneous action of movements becomes differentiated in the course of human development. This can be observed both in child development [75, 332] and in cultural development. Movements of primitive peoples also show a high degree of unification. Speech, gesture and thought form an inseparable unity. Westermann [447] reports that, when repeating to natives one of their own recorded narratives they failed to recognize it as their own, because he omitted the gestures. It appears that a normal adult regresses during emotional excitement to this original unity of expression, using voice, gestures, and thought at the same time. The specializing forces of our civilization abolish more and more the overt expression of "symbolic" gestures. But on the other hand, where the unity of movements seems to have disappeared, detailed investigation shows that only the amplitude of such movements has sometimes decreased beyond our capacity to recognize it, but that the pattern itself has not entirely vanished. Where the child expresses its dislike by screaming, crying, and trampling, the adult may only lift his eyebrows. Where the primitive manifests his joy by an outburst of shouting, dancing, and reciting, the adult in our civilization may show only a smile and a gleam in his eyes. Holt [184], among others, has demonstrated that vestigial infantile movements persist throughout life.

Thus, the intensity of unified expression decreases with the development of personality, but the phenomenon itself seems not to vanish. If we could attach a magnifier to that decreased expression, we would get the same effect as in its primitive form. In different cultures, the expression of unification shifts from one manifestation to another.

Such a shift of unification appears also in the development of the single individual, and not only over a longer period of time, but at every moment of his life. Just as an artist may express the same concept by variations of one characteristic theme, everybody expresses his individual pattern of life by various means. If we analyze them, these various manifestations appear as different symbols of the same configuration. Observations in psychotherapy make this phenomenon especially clear. W. Stern [405] emphasized this concept of configuration in personality, demonstrating how the integration of personality is determined by the basic principle of congruence, of configurating different reactions and actions to a whole.

Not only are our conscious activities configurated under a unifying goal, but also, as discovered by psychoanalysis, our unconscious trends follow the principle of configuration. Studies in expressive movements find the same phenomenon in our expressive acts. Allport and Vernon's studies [7], analyzing a subject's speed in various manifestations such as reading, counting, walking and comparing estimation of sizes such as distances, angles, and weights, as well as preferences in drawing figures, etc., indicate, in the words of the authors [7, p. 121]:

> . . . unambiguously interrelations between motor performances which cannot be accounted for by chance, nor in terms of the specificity of habit; but which obviously evince the tendency of expressive movement in one sphere of activity to correspond to expressive movement in other spheres of activity.*

The authors' observations, based upon statistical evidence, led them to the conclusion [7, p. 171]

> that there is some degree of unity in personality, that this unity is reflected in expression, and that, for this reason, acts and habits of expression draw a certain consistency among themselves.*

Allport and Vernon's studies, which found much support in successive studies of other investigators, continued some of the present author's experimental researches, published from 1929 on.** That the same pattern is expressed by the most different media becomes especially visible by "matching" experiments which the present author helped to introduce.*** Several forms of expression were recorded from each subject: (a) his vocal expression, (b) a profile picture of the subject's face, (c) a picture of his hands, (d) a film of his gait, (e) his manner of retelling a folk story, stenographically recorded, (f) a specimen of his handwriting. The matching experiments consisted of the presentation of two different forms of expression made by three subjects. The judge was asked to match the specimens made by the same person. Three voice records and three handwriting specimens, for instance, were matched correctly about one and a half times as frequently as would be expected by chance. R. Arnheim [13] made matchings of photographs with quotations, handwritings with sketches of personality, and so on, giving results which far exceed chance.

J. E. Downey's experimental studies of subjects' handwriting, gait, gestures, and carriage tested the proposition that "graphic individuality is but a specific example of a pattern that is impressed upon all the expressive movements of a given person." [101, p. 97.] The reason that her results are only "slightly in favor of an agreement between graphic and expressive movement" seems to stem from the many variables of

---

*G. W. Allport and P. E. Vernon: "Studies in Expressive Movement." Copyright 1933 by The Macmillan Company and used with their permission.

**Allport and Vernon introduce their studies with the following remark (*ibid.*, p. 13): "Wolff has made a definite experimental attack upon the problem of intra-individual consistency in expressive movement. With the aid not of impression but of correlation we hope in the present study to improve upon Wolff's method, if not upon his clear-cut perception of the problem."

***W. Wolff [460, 466].

experimentation she employed, such as the selection of the material tested, the training of the judges, the manner of presentation. She used ten characteristics and got 60.5 per cent of positive correlations, while chance would allow 50 per cent; if we eliminate the three unmatchable characteristics out of the ten the value with the seven other characteristics yields positive correlations above 70 per cent; that is, about one and a half times more than chance.

All these experiments indicate that favorable experimental conditions allow us to demonstrate that a person's expressive movements are interrelated under the same common denominator; or, from our present point of view, that a person's patterns of movement are configurated by the scheme of his personality. In the words of Allport and Vernon [7, p. 248], a person's

> expressive activities seem not to be dissociated and unrelated to one another, but rather to be organized and well patterned. Furthermore, the evidence indicates that there is congruence between expressive movement and the attitudes, traits, values, and other dispositions of the inner personality.*

CONFIGURATION OF GRAPHIC MOVEMENTS

Our preceding study has pointed out that the principle of configuration of our perception in response to impressions has its correspondence in our form of expressions. It is through our method of measurement that we can demonstrate diagrams of configuration in graphic movements. We have already observed the relationship of lengths between the total pattern of movement and the length of certain measure-units. But the fixed extension of movement alone does not prove the principle of configuration. Everybody might have a certain rhythm of movement, either innate or developed by conditioning in his early youth. However, the relationship of movement patterns to each other, the form of elements and their position change continuously in a person's expression. If this distribution of graphic elements is equally determined by fixed relationships, the concepts of consistency, rhythm, and symmetry are no longer sufficient as an explanation of this phenomenon. In this case we would require a new principle, that of configuration.

A. The Dot

The simplest graphic element in a signature is a dot. Such dots appear at the beginning of a movement (example: Mussolini), over the "i," after the first or middle initial, and after the signature. Below we give some examples of the fact that the position of the dot is not selected arbitrarily, but is frequently in a fixed relationship to beginning and end of the name and in a proportional relationship to other dots of the graphic pattern. This indicates that the position of the dot is determined by the whole pattern of movement, that it is not an isolated unity but part of a total configuration.

Op. cit.

We have already seen some examples of such configuration of dots. In the signatures of G. W. Allport (Fig. 5), the dot after the second inital was equidistant from beinning and end of the signature. In the signatures of Joh. Seb. Bach (Fig. 6) the dots after the abbreviated names have in both signatures the same position, dividing the total signature into equal parts. In the signatures of Benito Mussolini (Fig. 7), as well as in those of Galileo Galilei (Fig. 49), the distances between the three dots were in proportional relationship to each other.

We now give a few examples in which the dot over the "i" is the center of the signature. This can be demonstrated by drawing a circle around this point, with a radius of the point's distance to the beginning of the signature. The periphery of such a circle touches the end or limit of the signature.

FIG. 64.—The dot as center of movement.

Raymond Poincaré, French statesman (1860-1934) (Fig. 64) :
The dot over the "i" is the central point of a circle the periphery of which touches the left limit, right limit, and end-point. The end-stroke is interrupted by the date and afterwards enlarged; this enlarged stroke is not a comma, since this is not customary in the French writing of the date. It appears almost as if it were used in compulsion to complete the law of configuration. Some writers told me of observing during writing that they felt a compulsion to make a dot or a finishing stroke in order to complete their signatures. In the signature of Poincaré the distance

FIG. 65—The dot as center of movement.

between the interruption and the enlarged end-stroke is equal to the length of the accent, situated exactly over the end-stroke. Later, we shall give other examples of the determination of corrections. (See page 131 ff).

Mary Queen of Scots (1542-1587) (Fig. 65) :
The dot over the "i" is the center of a circle the periphery of which touches left and right limits of the signature.

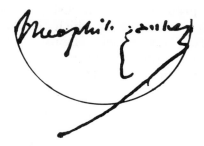

FIG. 66.—The dot as center of movement.

Théophile Gautier, French writer (1811-1872) (Fig. 66) :
The dot over the "i" in "Théophile" is the center of a circle the periphery of which touches left and right limits of the signature.

If the dot is not in the center its position is frequently, as we have seen, in a definite proportion to beginning and end of the signature, and if a signature has several dots the first dot has a proportional position within the scheme.

We give some further examples of the relationship of dots.

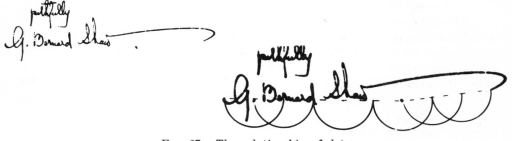

FIG. 67.—The relationship of dots.

George Bernard Shaw (1856-   ) (Fig. 67) :
Dots appear after the first initial and after the complete signature.

The distance between both dots is five times the distance between starting-point and first dot.

The distance between the last dot and the starting-point of the signature is six times the distance between first dot and starting-point.

The distance between last dot and end-point of the signature is three times the distance between first dot and starting-point.

George Washington (1732-1799) (Fig. 68) :

An upper and a lower dot.

Distance from upper dot to end of signature is three times the distance from upper dot to start of signature.

The distance from lower dot to end of signature is four times the distance from lower dot to start of signature.

FIG. 68.—Dots as proportional centers of movement.

Louis Philippe, French king (1773-1850) (Fig. 69) :

Four dots; one at the beginning of the second initial (1), the second after name "Philippe" (2), the third before the upper part of the flourish below the signature (3), and the fourth at the end of this flourish (4).

a. The first dot, at the start of the second initial, is the center of a circle the periphery of which touches the starting-point of the signature and the dot after "Philippe" (2). This dot is also the proportional center for the entire signature.

b. The distance from the first to the last dot at the end of the flourish is three times the distance between the first dot and the third dot.

c. The distance between the starting point and end point (end of the flourish) of the whole name equals the distance between beginning and ending of the second name and equals the length of the flourish.

In the signature of Eugénie of France (Fig. 44) we have observed that middle- and end-strokes have the same proportions, the middle-stroke being twice the length of the end-stroke and equal to the distance between beginning and end of the signature. The position of the two dots now follows the same unit of measurement. The distance between the two

FIG. 69.—Dots as proportional centers of movement.

dots is half the length of the end-stroke. The distance from the beginning of the signature to the last dot is four times the distance between both dots. The distance from the end of the signature to the last dot is twice the distance between both dots. The distance from the extreme lower limit of the signature to the last dot is six times the distance between both dots.

B. The Position of Starting-, Middle-, and End-Movements

We have had several examples of the interrelationship of the length between the three basic movements of a signature. We have seen that the proportional relationship of the distance between beginning and end of the signature determines the position of each stroke, thus involving the principle of configuration. Focusing now upon this problem of configuration, we give further examples.

L. W. Sontag, psychologist (Fig. 70):

In this example from my personal letters the length of the end-movement (letter "g") is the measure-unit. The length of starting-movements (initials "L" and "S") is double the length of the end-movement (letter "g"); the middle movement (bar of "t") is four times the

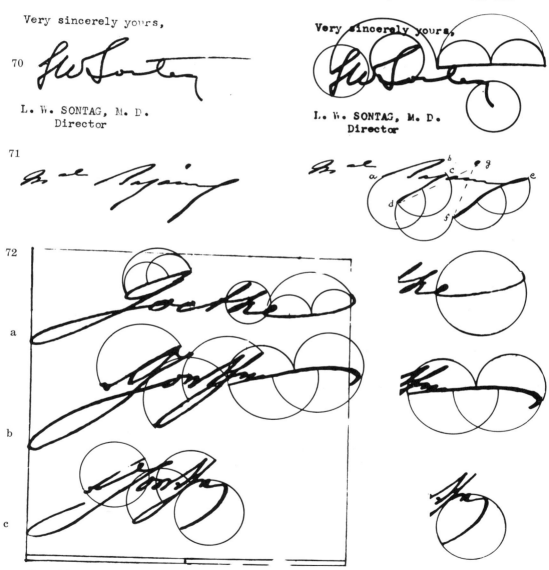

FIGS. 70-72.—Position and interrelationship of basic horizontal and vertical movements.

length of the end-movement. The position of these three movement patterns is interdependent: The distance between the beginning of the starting movement (initial "L") and the beginning of the middle-movement
(t-bar) equals the length of the middle-movement; the end-movement
(letter "g") starts below the center of the middle-movement.

A. Bazaine, French general (1811-1888) (Fig. 71):

This signature, taken from Geigy-Hagenbach's collection (page 57),
shows starting-, middle- and end-movements as vertical strokes. The
middle-movement is the "measure-unit," the length of strokes and the
distance between significant points being a simple proportion of the
measure-unit's length. Significant points are beginnings and endings of
the three vertical strokes and the distances between them and the dot
over the "i." We denote each movement by letters: starting-movement,
a-b; middle-movement, c-d; end-movement, e-f; and the dot, g. The following regularities of position may be observed: the distance between beginning and end of one movement to beginning and end of the next movement
is a simple proportion of the length of the middle-stroke c-d, namely:
a-d $= \frac{1}{2}$ c-d; d-f $=$ c-d; e-f $= 1\frac{1}{2}$ c-d; g-f $= 1\frac{1}{2}$ c-d; d-g $= 1\frac{1}{2}$ c-d.

The interrelationships of the three basic movements and their consistency become beautifully apparent in two signatures of *Goethe*. The
extension of both signatures (a, b) is the same; that of the third (c) is
half the former. The letter "h" is the measure-unit of the middle-movement
in both signatures. Signature (a). The length of the initial is four times
the length of the middle-movement. The end-movement is twice the length
of the middle-movement. Signature (b). The length of the starting-movement is one third of the length of the middle-movement. The end-movement is equal to the length of the middle-movement. Signature (c). The
length of the starting-movement is one third the length of the middle-
movement; the end-movement is equal to the length of the starting-movement. The length of the three basic movements shows the following interrelationships among the three signatures:

The length of the starting-movement in signature (a) is equal to
the length of the starting-movement in signature (c).

The length of the end-movement in signature (b) is one and a
half times that length in signature (a).

The length of the end-movement in signature (c) is half that length
in signature (b).

The middle-movement does not show interrelationships in three signatures.

C. The Flourish

In a great number of cases the length of the flourish is equal to or
a simple proportion of the length between the beginning and end of the
signature. However, not only the size but also the position of the flourish
seems to be determined by a scheme of configuration. In many cases, the

FIGS. 73-77.—The configuration of graphic patterns by flourishes.

distance between the beginning of the signature and the beginning of the flourish is in a definite relationship to the distance between the end of the signature and the end of the flourish.

Richard Wagner (1813-1883) (Fig. 73):

The signature has a flourish at the end of the name and a flourish above the name. The distance between the beginning of the name and the beginning of the upper flourish is equal to the length between the end of the name and the end of the upper flourish.

Friedrich von Schiller (1759-1805) (Fig. 74):

There is a flourish above the name. The length between the beginning of the name and the end of the flourish is equal to the length between the end of the name and the beginning of the flourish.

Wolfgang Amadeus Mozart (1756-1791) (Fig. 75) :
The distance from the beginning of the signature to the end of the flourish is equal to the distance between the end of the signature and the beginning of the flourish.

Napoleon (Fig. 76) (See Fig. 63) :
Napoleon surrounds one of his signatures with four flourishes. One is put at the starting stroke of his initial, a second one is put over his entire signature, a third one at the end of his name which is divided by a fourth flourish. The distance between start of the first and end of the third flourish is equal to the distance between start of the third and end of the second flourish. The end of the fourth flourish is at equal distance from the start of the first and from the end of the second flourish. We demonstrate the equal distances by punctuated lines.

Elizabeth, Queen of England (1533-1603) (Fig. 77) :
A flourish is made at the end of the letter "z"; a second flourish at the beginning of the letter "b"; and a third flourish at the end of the name. The distance between the beginning of the name and the end of the first flourish (letter "z") is equal to the distance between the end of the name (letter "h") and the beginning of the flourish (letter "b"). The distance between the ends of all three flourishes are equal to each other, thus forming an equilateral triangle. The flourish has, in these cases, the function of a balancing element.

D.   The Determination of Curves

Not only the position of dots and flourishes but also the diameter and the shape of curves seem to be determined by a unit of graphic movement.

John Calvin (1509-1564) (Fig. 78) :
The first part of the signature is the letter "J," which is limited above by three strokes and by a fourth stroke below. It appears that the second stroke is twice the length of the third; the first and second strokes together are three times the length of the third, and the fourth stroke is four times the length of the third. Thus the third stroke appears as a measure-unit. The curve of the initial "C" is part of a circular movement the radius of which is equal to the length of the third stroke. The center of the circle lies on a line which would connect the basis line of the initial with the last movement appearing in the two dots. The circular movement of the second initial starts on this imaginary line.

Hélène Vacaresco, Rumanian poetess (1866-   ) (Fig. 79) :
The measure-unit which enables us to reconstruct the large curve of the initial "V" (compare with the original signature) lies in the middle movement, the down-stroke of initial "V." The beginning of this initial is the center of the name. The end of the down-stroke coincides

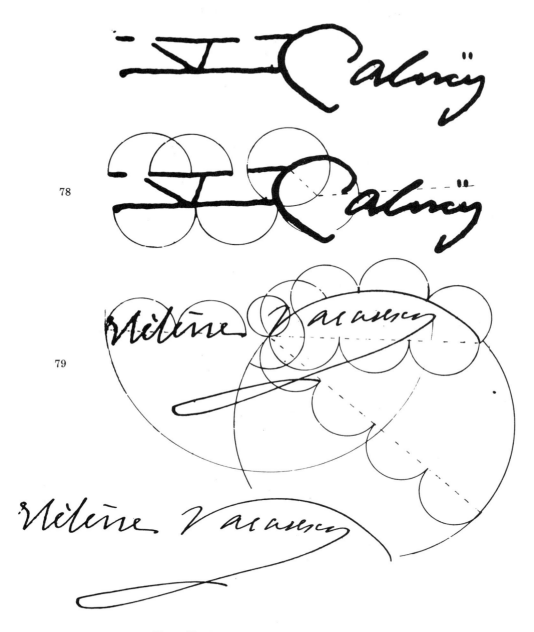

FIGS. 78-79.—The determination of curves.

with the beginning of the initial's long curve. The diameter of the curve from its beginning to its end is six times the length of the down-stroke. The periphery of the circle is seven times the length of the down-stroke. The distance from the end of the down-stroke to the end of the signature is six times the length of the down-stroke. The length of the first name from left to right limit is four times the length of the down-stroke of initial "V." The center of a circle, the periphery of which coincides exactly with the curve of initial "V," has a radius of four times the length of the down-stroke (the same length as the first name).

FIG. 80.—The determination of curves.

Rembrandt (1609-1669) (Fig. 80):
     Two signatures of Rembrandt, one showing a circular (a), the other an elliptical curve, of the initial (b). The diameters of the circular and of the elliptical curves in both initials are equal. The diameter is in the first case one fourth of the length of the end-movement as described with the bar of the "t"; in the second case one half the length of the "t"-bar. The remaining name is in the first as well as in the second case twice the curve's diameter. The distance between beginning and end of the curve is in both cases half the diameter's length. In the first case the initial consists of two parts, beginning (a) and end (b) of the curve and a hook. The distance between the beginning (a) and the end (b) of the curve equals the distance between the end of the curve (b) and the end of the hook (c). Thus the curves as well as the other features of both signatures are simple multiples of the same basic movement-unit of the "t"-bar.

Richard Wagner (Fig. 81):
     A letter which Wagner wrote in 1879, and of which we reproduce the second half in Fig. 92, shows an emphasized curve in the letter "z" of "aimez." The radius of this curve is double the length of the dash after

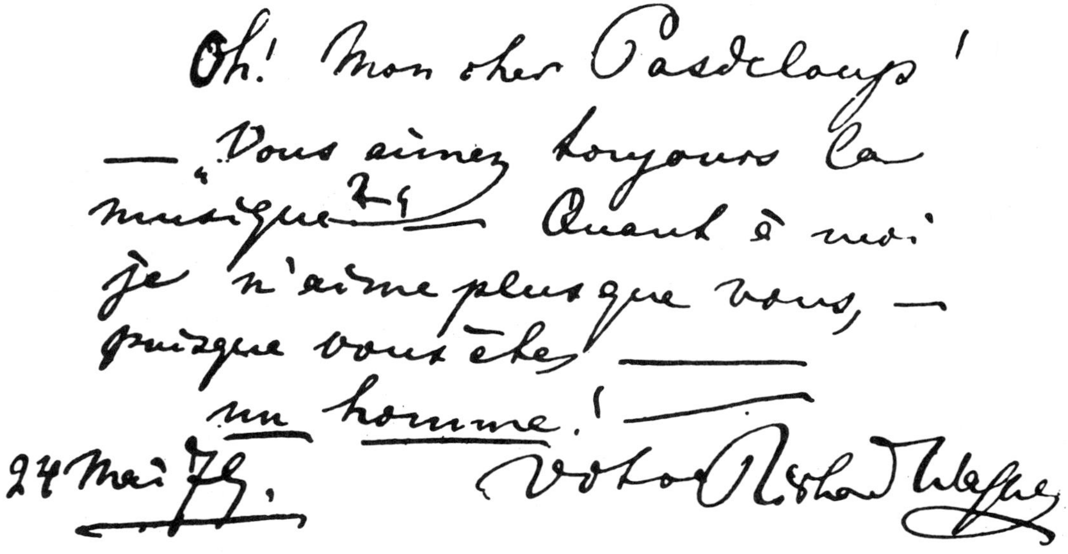

a

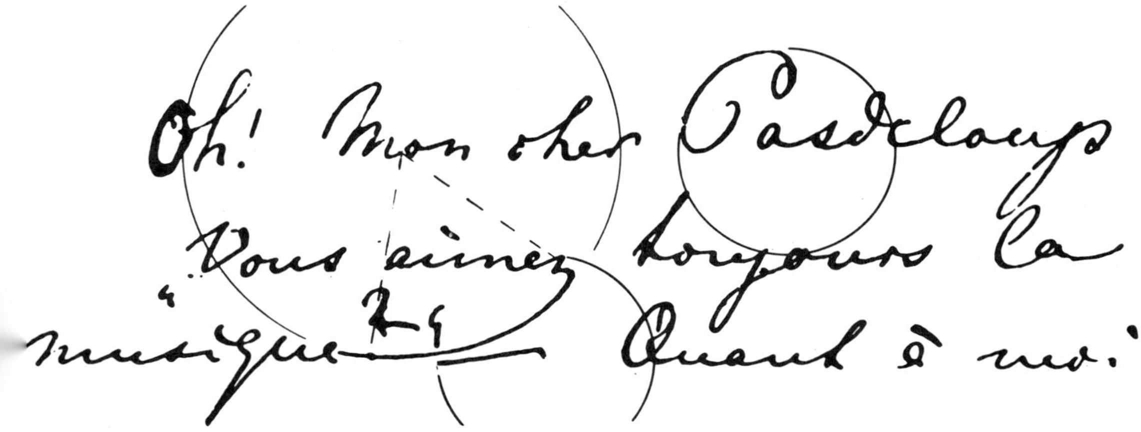

b

FIG. 81.—The determination of curves.

the sentence. The radius of the curve in the initial "P" of the addressee's name is equal to the length of the dash.

John Hawkyns, English Admiral (1532-1595) (Fig. 82):

This end of a letter is characterized by many circular curves. The measure unit for all these curves is the end-movement of the flourish. The circular movement at the beginning as well as at the upper end of the

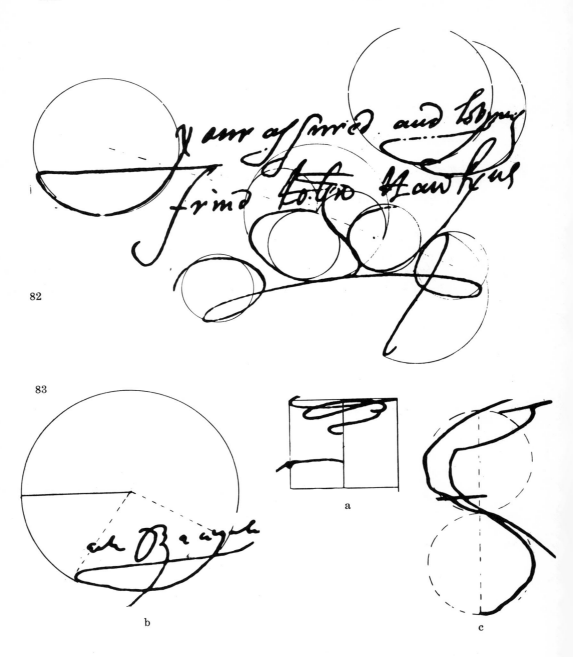

FIGS. 82-83.—The determination of curves.

flourish has a diameter which is half the length of the end-movement. The circular curve in the name "Hawkyns" has the same diameter, and the vertical diameter of the elliptical curve in the "h" of John again has the same length. Moreover, the periphery of this curve coincides with that of a circle drawn around the end-point of the "h," and the radius of this circle has the length of the diameter mentioned. The curve of the "y" in the word "your" again is part of a circle with the same radius, and the end of the same line with the word "lovyng" again shows a curve in the "y" with the same radius. Finally, the curve of the "g" in the word "lovyng" has the same radius. Thus the seven curves appearing in this writing are all part of the same unit of movement.

Raffaele Bargalupo (Fig. 83):

The principle of configuration does not seem to be destroyed during mental disturbances such as epileptic attacks. We have already demonstrated units of movement in the signature of an epileptic (Fig. 55). Referring now to the same signature, we searched for the formula of movement which produced the curves in the letter "g" (Fig. b) and in the letter "f" (Fig. c) in this writing. The diameter of these curves is a simple multiple of the length of the starting-stroke, which is double the length of the end-stroke (Fig. a). The radius of the curves in the letters "f" is equal to the length of the end-stroke, and the radius of the curve in letter "g" is equal to the length of the starting-stroke.

Thus, the configuration of movements not only allows us to apprehend the given position of a dot, but also the shape of letters as it appears, for instance, in the structure of curves.

E. Signature and Text

Since a configuration of movement patterns appears not only in the length of movements but also in their relative position and finally in the shape of graphic elements, as in the form of curves, we cannot deal with the factor of configuration as with an isolated phenomenon attached to single characteristics of movement; rather, we must consider the configuration as an act working in the depth of the organism and radiating simultaneously upon the various manifestations of movement such as size, position, and form.

Now there arises the question whether the configuration determines graphic movement only when the writer expresses his personality in graphic movement, or whether this phenomenon is constantly present. The signature, which stands for the person himself, might have for the writer the value of a symbol, of a mark, as was actually the case in medieval manuscripts and printers' marks. It might be that only in this case does graphic movement become a "crystallized gesture" [7].

May we expect to find the principle of configuration in graphic movements other than those related to a signature? Several outer factors such as the length of words used in a text and the size of paper we have to deal with might hamper the graphic movement in a written text and destroy the principle of configuration. If, on the other hand, the same principle of configuration were to appear not only in the signature, but also in the text under which the name is signed, the principle of configuration would appear as a very strong one, overcoming the outer inhibiting factors. Of course, we cannot always expect to find the principle of configuration, which is frequently hidden even in a signature and which would be even more hidden in the complex pattern of a text. Furthermore, certain factors of regularity, such as rhythm, are easily affected in all bio-rhythmical manifestations such as pulse, breathing, and brainwaves. Therefore we cannot expect configuration to be always manifest. But if we should find many instances of a total configuration, including signature and text, we would have to assume that the configurating principle is always *potentially* present.

For this crucial question we investigated some written texts, including signatures. In order to reduce the degree of arbitrariness in selecting such specimens as objects of investigation we used all specimens of the same publication, namely, texts and signatures published by the French journal *Les Annales* in its inquiry for "The Dream of My Life." Here our material of investigation was limited and, being published, is accessible for objective control. We again limited the choice of specimens in that we considered only those texts consisting of one line, and actually we found in such writings six cases out of ten (60 per cent) in which the length of the written text from beginning to end was a simple proportion of the signature's length. Below we demonstrate these six cases:

Each writer's sentence was an answer to the inquiry: "What is the dream of your life?" The following answers were given:

1. Paul Valéry (Fig. 84). Me réveiller. (To wake up.)

2. Jacques Natanson (Fig. 85). Vivre. Et ne plus rêver. (To live. And not to dream any more.)

3. Henri Béraud (Fig. 86). Avoir des ennemis. (To have enemies.)

4. Lucien Descaves (Fig. 88). Qu'on me fisse la paix. (That one leaves me alone.)

5. Pierre Brisson (Fig. 87). L'amitié d'un auteur dramatique. (The friendship of a playwright.)

6. André Lang (Fig. 89). Ne pas engraisser trop rapidement. (Not to become fat too quickly.)

In five cases the length of the total signature was measured from beginning to end; in one case (Descaves) the second name only involved the measure unit. In all cases the text was measured from beginning to end in multiples of the signature's length. The following relationships appeared between signature and text:

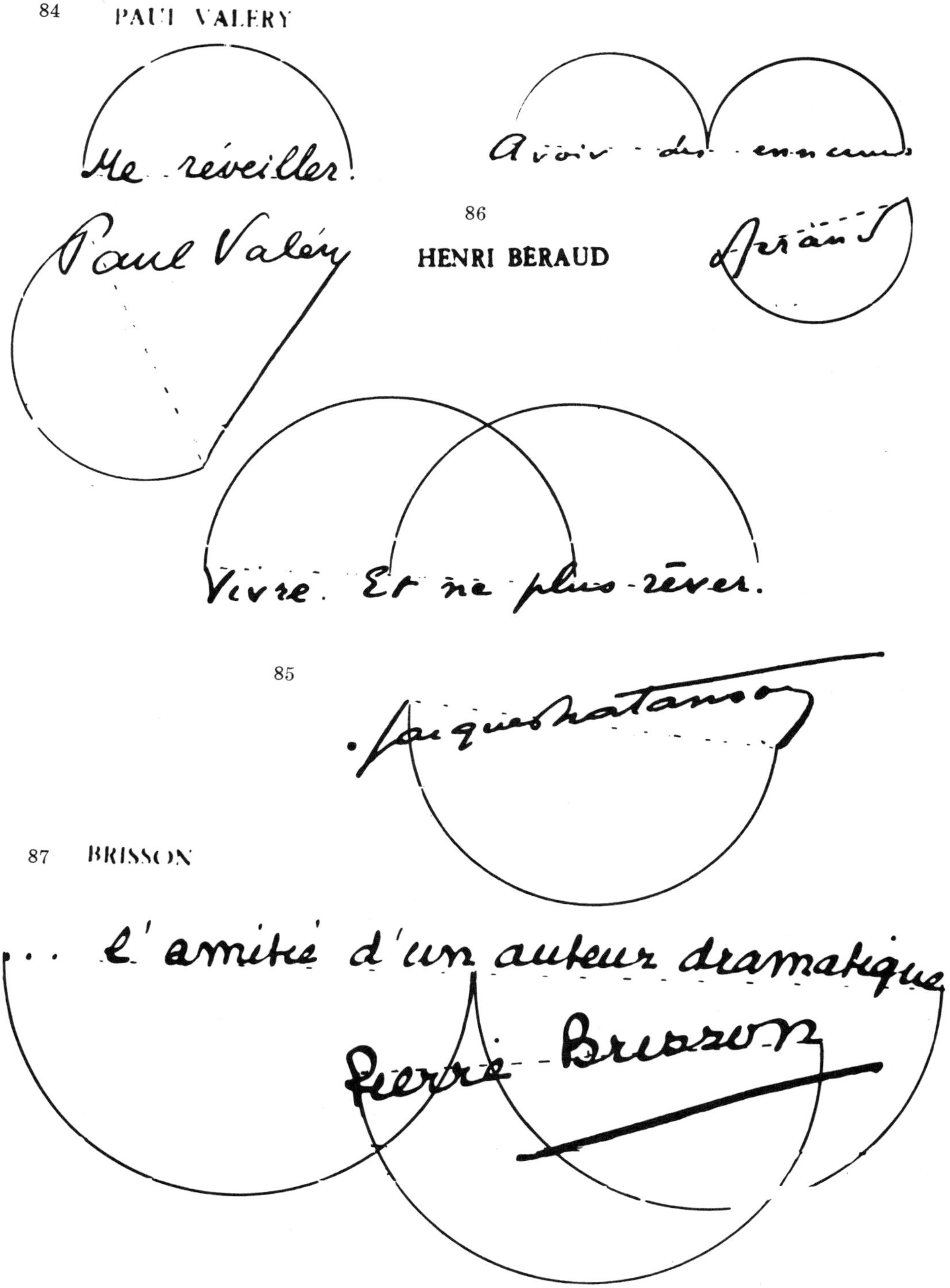

84 PAUL VALÉRY

Me réveiller!

Paul Valéry

86

HENRI BÉRAUD

Avoir des ennemis

Béraud

Vivre. Et ne plus rêver.

85

Jacques Natanson

87 BRISSON

... l'amitié d'un auteur dramatique

Pierre Brisson

FIGS. 84-87.—The unit of movement in text and signature.

Name	Number of times that unit of name appears in the length of the sentence:
1. Paul Valéry	1
2. Jacques Natanson	1½
3. Henri Béraud	2
4. Lucien Descaves	3
5. Pierre Brisson	2
6. André Lang	3½

F. Horizontal Lines

The indication that the unit of movement, as expressed in a signature, reappears in the corresponding text found its support in many cases to which we cannot refer here because of lack of space. We shall now make some explanatory investigations to determine whether certain patterns of movement in a letter text, such as the length of underlinings and long dashes, represent the same units which we have discovered in the corresponding signature.

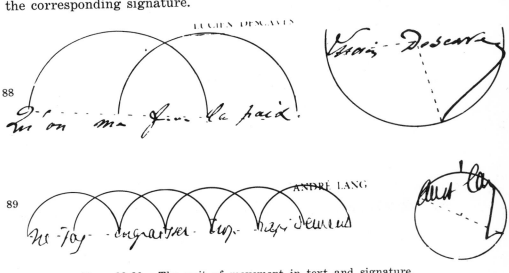

FIGS. 88-89.—The unit of movement in text and signature.

Piotr Ilyich Tchaikovsky (1840-1893) (Fig. 90):
Our first example is part of a letter written by Tchaikovsky to Francesco Berger on March 7, 1888. This letter, written in German, shows many underlinings and long bars of the "t" (Fig. a). We compared the length of each of these horizontals and, as our Figure shows, observed that they were simple proportions of that unit of length which was established with the first underlining (Fig. b).

90

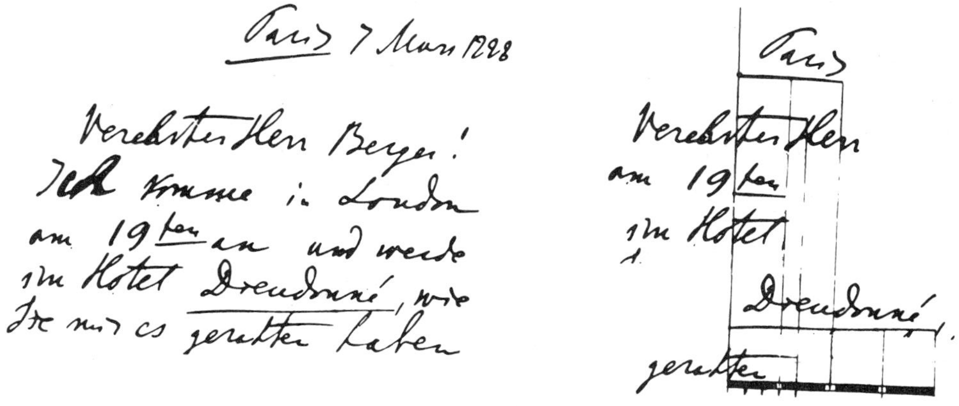

91

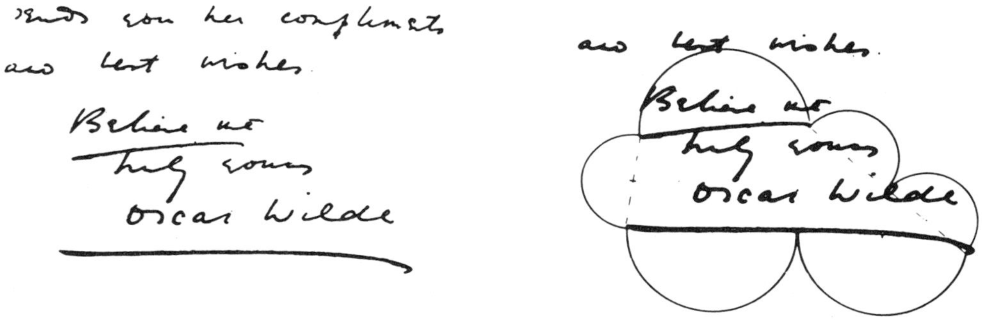

92

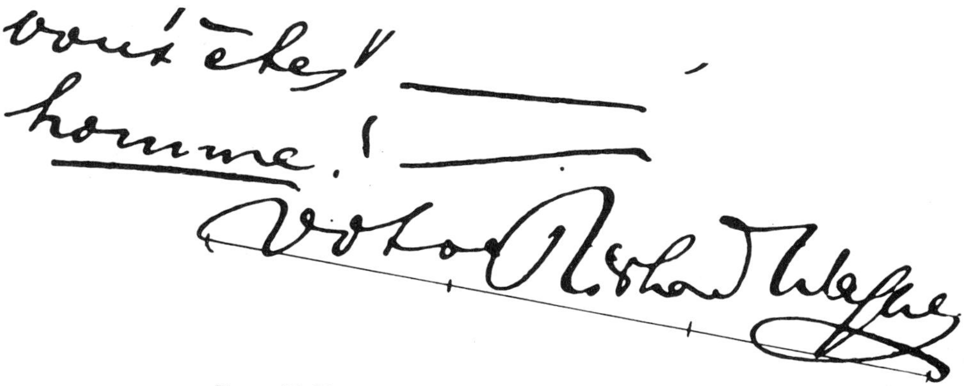

FIGS. 90-92.—Horizontal lines as movement units.

Oscar Wilde (1856-1900) (Fig. 91):

Oscar Wilde makes, under his name, a horizontal line (Fig. a) which is exactly double the length of his letter "T" in the closing word "Truly" (Fig. b).

For the sake of brevity we add only one more example.

Richard Wagner (Fig. 92) :

From the last two lines of a letter written by Wagner on May 24, 1879* (from the sentence "je n'aime plus que vous, puisque vous êtes un homme" (I love only you because you are human), "votre" (yours) "Richard Wagner"), we reproduce a cut, showing three horizontal lines above the signature, an underlining of "homme," a dash after "êtes" and a dash after "homme." All three of these horizontals have the same length, and each horizontal is one-third the length of the signature "votre Richard Wagner" written as one unit (measured from beginning to end).

The phenomenon of configuration includes all the principles we have discussed: those of consistency, of symmetry, of rhythm, and the characteristic of interrelationship which patterns distances, positions, and shapes of graphic elements.

G.   The Total Configuration

One example demonstrates the relationship of all these characteristics especially well.

Matthew Vassar, founder of Vassar College (1792-1868) (Fig. 93) :

We used the only two printed signatures of Vassar, one printed in the Seventy-Fifth Anniversary catalogue of Vassar College (Fig. a), the other in the Alumnae Magazine of December 1938 (Fig. b).

Signature (b) is made without any flourish. It appears that a great number of main movements, such as the end-points of all down-strokes, beginnings and ends of the bars, and the end-points of the first and second names have exactly the same position as they have in the unflourished signature. The flourishes are thus an addition to the basic structure of the name without changing its fixed movements. But these flourishes again follow the basic scheme. The name Vassar from the beginning to the right limit of the name is, with the flourishes, double the length of the name in the latter signature without flourishes.

The middle movement, appearing in the bar of the "t," is the measure-unit which determines most of the proportions and configurations. If we draw circles with a radius of the bar's length, beginning at the starting point of the signature and continuing to the points where the circle touches the periphery of the writing, the beginning and the end of the dominating graphic movements coincide with beginning and end of our successive circles' arc. Such beginnings and ends are the beginning of the first initial, beginning of the bar, beginning of the flourish of the second initial, end of the flourish of the second initial, end of the flourish below the signature, and, returning to the beginning, the starting-point of the signature. The distance between beginning and end of the second initial is three times the length of the bar. The curves at the beginning of the first initial and the end of the second initial coincide with the peri-

---

*See the first part of this letter in Fig. 81.

FIG. 93.—Configuration of the total pattern.

phery of a circle with the same radius, drawn around the beginning and end of the name, respectively.

The signature of Vassar shows further proportions. The right dot over the "a" is at the center of the name "Vassar." A circle drawn around this dot embraces the name. Vassar's signature has five flourishes: one at the beginning of the first initial (A) ; one at the beginning of the second initial (B) ; one at the beginning of the second initial (C) ; one at the end of the name (D) ; and one below the signature, start (E)-end (F). There appear the following identities of distances:

A-B equal to C-F

C-D equal to E-F

C-E equal to D-F

The vertical length of the flourish below the signature is half the vertical length of the signature.

Configuration is a special characteristic of proportion. This is defined by Plato in the "Timaeus" (31c) :

> It is not possible for two things to be fairly united without a third, for they need a bond between them, which shall join them both. The best of the bonds is that which makes itself and those which it binds as complete a unity as possible, and the nature of proportion is to accomplish this most perfectly.

Configuration means the integration of proportions into a unity.*

---

*G. L. Raymond [342] thus defines proportion (p. 9):
   "A part is said to be in proportion because of the relationship which its measurements sustain to the measurements of other parts or to the whole of a product. Proportion includes the ideas, both of ratios or relationships, as in 1:2, and also of likeness or equality in ratios, as in 1:2::3:6. . . . Proportion is to effects in sight what rhythm is to effects in sound."

CHAPTER VI

DIAGRAMS OF PERSONALITY

MOVEMENT AND PERSONALITY

Our finding of formulas of configuration in movement patterns has not only the widest theoretical implication, but also many practical implications. The exactness of correlations and interrelationships of graphic patterns might lead us to think of these diagrams as a scheme in which all properties could be predicted from the laws of its construction. But the difference between a supposed construction of personality and a mechanical construction lies in the fact that personality is not static like a mechanism but grows, and changes with its growth. It is continuously transformed by environmental conditions, to which it responds, not rigidly, but by adaptation, elimination and organization. These variables alone would make it impossible to predict exact results from a given formula. What we call "dynamic" vs. "static"—organization vs. construction—holds not only for personality but for the human organism as a whole. The self-regulation of functions, regenerations, adaptations, and integrations suggest a basic difference between machine and organism.

In spite of this general difference, there are so many fixed reactions of our organisms that frequently a physician can make his predictions with as much certainty as if he were dealing with the static elements of a machine. Our sense organs are so similar to a mechanical construction that their functions can be described in diagrams as if they were the products of an engineer. Since, as modern observations indicate, body and personality form a unity as two stereoscopic pictures of one fundamental system, we may assume that personality follows the same principles as the body.

Although the system of personality may show certain invariables, the question is whether we can isolate such invariables in personality as we have succeeded in doing with invariables of the physiologic system. Our present investigation seems to give an approach to such an enterprise. It took medicine centuries to achieve the certainties of prediction of physiological processes which are commonplaces today. The study of personality, which is still in its beginnings, needs at least as much time to arrive at formulas for the definition and prediction of psychological phenomena, as was necessary for medicine and biology to arrive at somatic formulas. Within these limits the following attempts to use the observed configurations of movements for a diagnosis of personality are exploratory suggestions.

The idea of using movement patterns to diagnose personality has been formulated since the days of the Bible (see page 19) and since

121

Aristotle stated the first known system of psychology. Experimental investigations, however, are of recent date. A Russian study [315] proposes to classify types of expressive movements, to measure, and to record them. This study is mainly devoted to determining the motor maturity of children. Several investigators [220, 390] have demonstrated a rather fixed relationship between bodily features, temperaments, and activities. W. Enke's study of psychomotor types [113] tries to relate characteristics of speed to such bodily types as are supposed to go with certain behavior characteristics. The broad and round-featured pyknics, who usually are adaptable to their environment, show, according to Enke, more "soft, rounded and uninhibited movements," while the more narrow and angular-featured leptosomes, who usually are less adaptable to their environment than the pyknics, show more a "stiff and angular" pattern of movement. E. Mira [291] used a test of simple graphic movements (not handwriting) as one of the techniques to diagnose mental disturbances. As chief psychiatrist during the Spanish Civil War, he found this test an invaluable aid in screening personnel. He remarks [292, p. 142]:

> Psychological space is not neutral; all movements executed by the individual—either purposefully or not—acquire a peculiar meaning according to the direction in which they are performed. . . . All mental activity may be considered as a succession of acts implying a succession of postural changes; whenever the mental equilibrium is distorted, such distortion must in some way be detectable in the individual's movements.*

Mira measured the accuracy of a subject's retracing simple lines and forms without visual aid by the degree of his deviations. Of earlier experiments, when using a kind of monotometer as a measuring device, Mira remarks [292, p. 135]:

> I was impressed by the fact that the length of movements tended throughout to decrease in the inhibited subjects and to increase in the excited subjects, irrespective of the content or the nature of the verbal reply.*

According to several observers [101], expansive movements seem to go with a "general freedom of impulse" while restricted movements seem to indicate "the presence of inhibitory tendencies." Contractions of muscle groups also accompany mental effort, which is related to self-control and so to inhibitory tendencies [189]. Expansions of muscle groups indicate a lessening of control which might result in emotional instability [365].

These observations are supported by studies on recorded tapping movements, in which the variability in tapping speeds seems to have some correspondence with criteria of emotionality [196, 230, 391].

Upon the whole, all these studies on the characteristics and qualities of movements did not yield results that were too significant because either the movement investigated (tapping) was not expressive enough of personality, or expressive movements such as handwriting have not been investigated by adequate procedures.

---

*Reprinted from "Psychiatry in War," by Emilio Mira, by permission of W. W. Norton & Company, Inc. Copyright 1943 by the publishers.

Experiments with movements under the imaginative influence of pleasant and unpleasant events (see page 73 ff.) indicate the dependence of movement patterns on mental activities.

The influence of thought and imagination upon movement patterns becomes especially visible in experiments in hypnosis. A hypnotized subject told to be Napoleon assumed those movements which according to familiar pictures are characteristic of Napoleon, and he tried to imitate Napoleon's handwriting [367]. Experiments in hypnosis also show the symbolic value of movements [458], a phenomenon which originally was emphasized by S. Freud [131, 132].

The concept of an integration of movements has been taken up by Allport and Vernon [7]. Integration, which has been defined as the correspondence of various habit systems in the individual [138] or as the unifying function of the individual [199], has been interpreted as indicative of moral qualities, a high integration indicating "good character," that is, desirable qualities such as honesty and intelligence [168]. However, without taking exact measurements it seems to be very difficult to determine any degree of integration, especially since integration, working in the depth of personality, cannot be apprehended in surface behavior.

A few studies have been made on hereditary characteristics of movements. Movement patterns of twins [218] and siblings [407] show a high degree of similarity, especially in their handwriting; also, the resemblance of graphic patterns in families has been noticed [99, 144].

Summarizing those various observations on graphic movements which led to diagnostic statements in quantitative terms, the following agreements have been obtained in a majority of cases:

1. Graphic movements are related to those processes which we attribute to "personality."

2. Certain classifications of graphic movements seem to be possible according to stereotyped features, characteristic of certain personality types.

3. Expansion and reduction movements are significantly related to certain mental and emotional characteristics.

4. Graphic movements are influenced by mental activity.

5. There seems to be some evidence of family patterns in graphic movements.

MEASUREMENT AND DIAGNOSIS

The phenomena of consistency, symmetry (proportion), and configurations, demonstrate in a measurable way that graphic movements are not accidental but a fundamental expression of the organism. The configurational pattern in graphic movement suggests that it is made spontaneously, since the writer is unable to make such a pattern with premeditation; furthermore, up to now nobody has been aware of the presence of such configurations. Diagnostically, our finding has several implications:

1. A consistency of configuration in several similar patterns suggests that these patterns were made by the same person; on the other hand, several patterns claimed to be made by the same person can be discovered as being of different origin if the configurational scheme is completely different in each case.

2. The pattern of configuration is based upon certain elements, the length of which is the yardstick for the measurement. It may be diagnostically significant which elements of his movement pattern a writer uses as such a measure-unit.

3. There are different parts of a graphic pattern in which the effect of the measurements determining length, position, and form of graphic elements becomes especially manifest. It may be diagnostically significant which parts of the graphic pattern are selected for main configurations.

Before attempting to apply these observations we must be clear about the principles of configuration and the principles of measurement. The following is an elementary classification, applicable to signatures:

The Constitutive Elements of a Signature

A. The Movement

(a) A signature may consist of what we call *total movement*. Such a signature consists either of the last name only, or first and last names are written as one unit without interruption.

(b) A signature may consist of *part-movements*. The first and second names, and in some cases first, middle, and last names, are each written as a special unit of movement. This holds true whether the names are written in full, abbreviated, or with initials.

B. The Elements

Besides the movement which is characterized by its beginning and end or by its limits, there appear the main elements. Of these we distinguish:

(a) The starting-stroke or the total length of the initial;

(b) The middle-stroke or the total length of the middle letter;

(c) The end-stroke or another end movement such as a flourish.

C. The Centers

The center of a signature is that part which divides a signature into equal or proportionally equal parts, by means of corresponding length of elements or by distances. Such centers are a dot, a horizontal, or a vertical line.

(a) The dot. It may appear after the first or middle initial, at the end of the name, as part of a flourish, or as a dot over letters. Several dots frequently appear in simple relationships to each other.

(b) The horizontal. It may appear as a bar on letters (e.g., "t"), as an ornamental annex, or as underlining.

(c) The vertical. It may appear as an emphasized up- or down-stroke, or as part of a flourish. Several vertical or horizontal lines frequently appear with their lengths and distances in simple relationships to each other.

D. The Forms

(a) Measure-units determine the shape of curves, such as circles and ellipses.

(b) Measure-units determine the size of curves.

E. The Extension

The most usual measurement is applied from the beginning to the end of a movement. However, some people do not express a length by motor-extension of movement, but by its visual extension. In these cases the measurement is applied between the visible limits of movements, between the left and right limits. Some writers are a mixture of the motor type and the visual type; the measurement of their signatures follows from beginning to the right limit or from the left limit to the end of a movement.

Thus, the measurement is applied:

(a) From beginning to end;

(b) From left limit to right limit;

(c) From beginning to right limit;

(d) From left limit to end.

Regarding the proportion between measure-unit and extension of the signature, the distribution as obtained with the signatures of 70 famous persons chosen at random is shown in Table 9.

TABLE 9

Extension of the Signature Distance from:	Proportion of Measure-Unit in Percentage
Left limit to end	12
Beginning to right limit	17
Left limit to right limit	24
Beginning to end	47

The most frequent proportion between the extension of graphic movement and measure-unit appears with the measurement of the signature from beginning to end.

Comparing the relative frequency of the basic measure units in signatures of 70 persons we obtained the distribution in Table 10.

TABLE 10

Measure Unit	Percentage of its Appearance
Middle-Stroke	12
Bar	14
End-Stroke (or flourish)	19
Initial	25
Dots (all kinds)	30

The use of initials and dots as measure-units appears twice as frequently as the use of middle-strokes and bars.

The measurement is applied to the distance between significant points as well as to the length of graphic elements. For the measurements it is advisable to use graph paper (40 squares to an inch), calipers, and compasses in which the distances can be fixed. Hypothetical lines, squares, and circles make the relationships especially visible for demonstration.

DISTURBANCE AND CONSERVATION OF THE FORMULA OF CONFIGURATION

For measurement, graphic material must originate as spontaneously as possible. Laboratory conditions are unfavorable for the best configurations, since these are disturbable. A limitation of paper size is an inhibiting factor for the free expressive movement. So are unfavorable conditions of writing, such as awkward position of the writer, insufficient ink, etc. The influence of outer factors upon the genuine graphic movement has been stressed by R. Saudek, who also emphasized [367, 368]: "The value of a handwriting for research material is the greater the more the attention is distracted from the writing." However, the degree of disturbability varies with different subjects. I have not yet found out what the degrees of disturbability mean with reference to certain personality traits; in any case, the absence of disturbability of graphic movement patterns indicates the strength of the formula of configuration.

Harry S. Truman (a mosaic signature) (Fig. 94):

The conservation of the individual formula of movement in spite of outer disturbances appears with especial clarity when the writing act is interrupted. As an example, we give President Harry S. Truman's signature under the British loan, on July 15, 1946 (c). The signature was reproduced in *Life* magazine of July 29, 1946. The president, who likes to create souvenirs of pens with which he signs important bills, used twenty-six wooden pens to write the word "Approved," the date and his signature, continuously interrupting the writing in a fifteen minute process. Since the text consists of 30 letters or numbers, the use of 26 pens indicates that almost each letter or number element has been written separately. Investigating whether the formula of configuration has been lost in this mosaic-signature, I compared it with two others of his

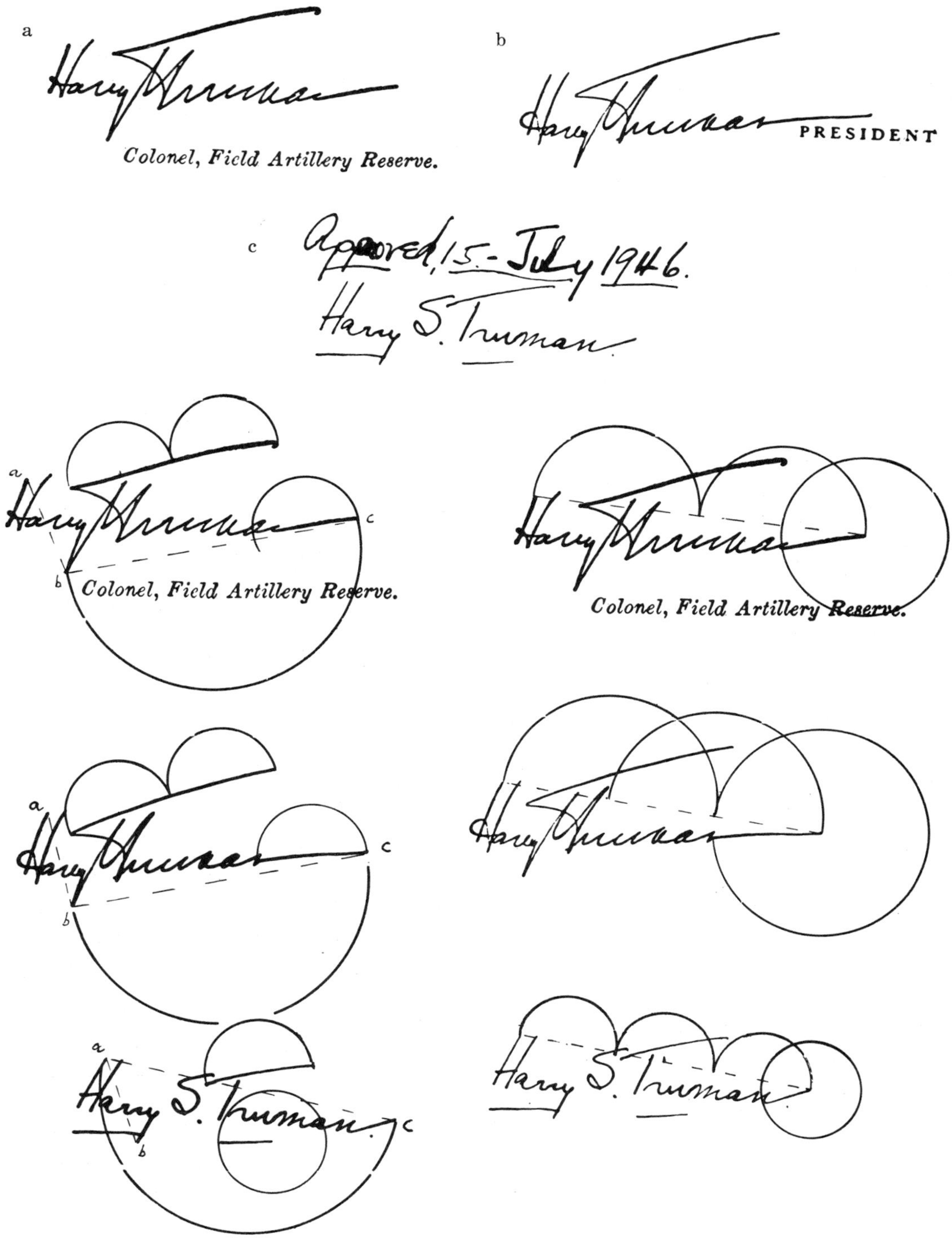
a
Colonel, Field Artillery Reserve.
b
PRESIDENT
c
Approved, 15 - July 1946.
Harry S. Truman
a
b
c
Colonel, Field Artillery Reserve.
Colonel, Field Artillery Reserve.
a
b
c
a
b
c
Harry S. Truman
Harry S. Truman

FIG. 94.—Conservation of the formula of configuration during interrupted movements.

signatures. In order to limit the principle of possible arbitrary selection, I used the two signatures which have been published in Teltscher's book on handwriting [413]. Teltscher, in his study of Truman's handwriting, reproduces one signature of Truman as Colonel, Field Artillery Reserve (a) and another of Truman as President (b). In Fig. A we present these two signatures comparing them with the mosaic signature. The following constancies of proportions may be seen:

Figure B

The Colonel (a)	The President (b)	Mosaic signature (c)
1. The length from beginning to end of the first name (ab)	is equal (ab)	is equal (ab)
2. The length from beginning of the second name to the end of the second name (bc)	is equal (bc)	is equal (bc)
3. The length of the t-bar	is equal	is half that length in the two other signatures
4. The length of the t-bar is half the length of the end-movement which combines the end-stroke of letter "a" and letter "n" (we distinguish this from the "end-stroke," no. 5)	the length of the t-bar is half the length of the end-movement (letter "n")	the length of the t-bar is half the length of the end-movement which is the underlining under the letters "Tru"

Figure C

5. The length from beginning to end of the total signature is 4 times the length of the end-stroke	the length from beginning to end of the total signature is 3 times the length of the end-stroke	the length from beginning to end of the total signature is 6 times the length of the end-stroke

We thus have five interrelated criteria indicating the consistency of the formula of configuration which, in this case, persisted even during interruptions of the writing movement.

Our movement pattern follows the law of configuration, whether we are young or old, sick or healthy. An inner psychological configuration seems to be present as long as our bodily configuration exists; life is configuration. But if there is no real absence of configuration, how can we use our discovery for diagnostic purposes? Configuration and unification are not the same. A dancer's movements are configurated and unified in a steady flow. The movements of a mentally diseased person may be configurated but they may lack an inner coherence. Handwritings show the difference between configuration and unification. Both are, for instance, present in the following signature.

Christopher Morley, American poet (1890-   ) (Fig. 95):

Two signatures of Christopher Morley, one (a) from Georges Schreiber's collection: Portraits and Self-Portraits,* another one (b) from a catalogue of the Columbia University Press. In signature (a) the length of the first name equals the length of the second name, both names measured from start to end. The length of the bar of the "t" equals the length

*Boston, 1936, p. 109.

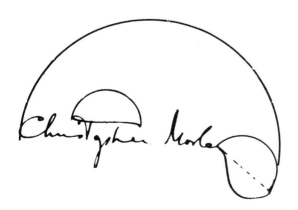

FIG. 95.—Balance and configuration.

of the flourish, measured from start to end. Signature (b) falls into three rhythmical units: "Chris"—"topher"—"Morley", each of them determined by the same unit which appears with the length of the end-stroke. Although both signatures show a different organization, one being divided into two, the other into three units, in both signatures first and second name as well as length of t-bar and the length of end-stroke are in simple proportions to

FIG. 96.—Unbalance and configuration.

each other. Both signatures of Christopher Morley show the principle of unification and balance in an especially high degree.

An opposite example is that of a schizophrenic murderer,* Eugen Reiss (Fig. 96).

---

*His case is described in the author's book "The Expression of Personality" [466].

We demonstrate by added lines how all letter movements are counteracting (a). Before our discovery of proportions many people believed that outer conditions of writing were the cause of a lack of movement co-ordination, supposing that patterns of movement were conditioned either by chance, by learning, or by conditions of writing. Our formula of configuration allows us to distinguish between outer and inner factors of movements. In the present case, a configuration can be observed. The length of the signature, measured from beginning to end (ad), is twice the length of the large vertical "s" (cd). The beginning of the second initial (b) is the center of the whole signature (b) ; the dot over the "i" is the center for the second name (c). Thus it appears that the lack of outer organization is not a matter of chance but is rooted in an inner formula.

THE MEANING OF THE MEANINGLESS, AND THE DIAGNOSIS OF PSYCHOLOGICAL DISTURBANCES

The relationship between "outer" and "inner" patterns leads us to the problem of chance and determination. We have mentioned before that outer factors such as paper size, attention, etc., may disturb the configuration. However, not only outer but also inner disturbances may be present, such as sudden inhibiting thoughts and rising emotions. But such inner disturbances are part of the total organic activity and if they eliminated the configuration we would have no criteria for a diagnosis based upon our measurements. We observed, however, that even grave inner disturbances such as epileptic attacks, mental disease, and catastrophic experiences, do not destroy the formula of movement but only modify it in characteristic ways.

A corresponding observation has been decisive for modern psychiatry. The abnormal is no longer considered unique, wholly different from the normal, but only as an exaggeration of traits and behavioral characteristics which are also present in a normal person. Abnormality is not a destruction of psychological laws of the normal but a modification and exaggeration of them. On the other hand, since Freud's exposition of a "psychopathology of everyday life" it has been recognized increasingly that the threshold between normal and abnormal fades; certain reactions of normal people have all the characteristics of disturbed behavior. But these disturbances, as can be demonstrated, are just as "meaningful" as intentional acts; the difference is only that they follow an unconscious and not a conscious pattern of configuration.

We now have the possibility of demonstrating such patterns in our "diagrams of the unconscious." In contrast to disturbances enforced upon the organism from without, disturbances originating in the depth of personality and visible in the graphic pattern seem to become integrated into the formula of movement. Looking for graphic disturbances in signatures, written spontaneously and present in historical documents, we give the following examples from our selection.

Galileo Galilei (Fig. 97, see also Fig. 49) :

We observe one distortion in a signature of Galileo when he was almost blind. Not being able to write his name properly, he wrote "Galii," and the last "i" fell down from the line of writing. However, the distance of the three dots over the "i" remains in the same proportional relationship to each other as in his normal writing (Fig. 49), and, putting one letter "i" on top of the other, as if they formed one letter, these two signs have the same slant as all the preceding letters.

Elizabeth of England (see Fig. 56) :

Another distortion appears in a signature of Elizabeth, who, signing a letter to her prisoner, Mary, Queen of Scots, left out the letter "h" which she later put above the signature, having apparently miscalculated the space left for the signing. It is in this way, however, that the shortened signature in the arrangement of the single letters corresponds exactly to the letter position in another signature, having at the same time one third of the former's extension.

A disturbance in graphic movements frequently becomes visible in a break of the movement. Such a break results either in a gap or in a patch of the stroke. We give below a few examples of such breaks.

John Hawkyns (Fig. 98; see also Fig. 82) :

We again refer to the letter of John Hawkyns. The curve of the letter "y" in "your" is broken in two. The diameter of the right half of the "y" is equal to the length of "f" in the word "friend" which is written beneath this letter. The curve of this "f" is like a mirror image of the "y." The left part of the curve has a diameter equal to the radius of the circle the periphery of which coincides with the total curve of the letter.

Giuseppe Verdi (1813-1901) (Fig. 99) :

The signature shows a break in the flourish surrounding the name. This break divides the signature into two equal parts. The distance between the left break and the signature's left limit is equal to the distance between the right break and the signature's right limit.

Friedrich von Schiller (Fig. 100; see also Fig. 74) :

The initial is broken; the length of that breach in the continuity of movement is exactly the same as the length between the beginning and end of this initial.

"Yo el rey," signature of Philip of Spain (Fig. 101) :

This signature shows a break in the end-stroke of the flourish. At the breaking point the flourish is patched up by an additional stroke. The measurement reveals that the breaking point lies exactly in the middle of the total stroke. The length of the thus enlarged end-stroke is the same as the length of the formula "Yo el rey" from left to right limit.

FIGS. 97-101.—The meaning of the meaningless in the disturbance of movements.

Mary Todd Lincoln (1818-1892) (Figs. 102, 103):

Just as psychoanalysis is able to use a person's so-called faulty acts, such as mistakes in spelling, speaking, and acting, as clues in personality diagnosis, so our mistakes in writing may become important if we can prove that they are not accidental but are rooted in inner disturbances. Such is the case when the disturbance is integrated into the usual formula

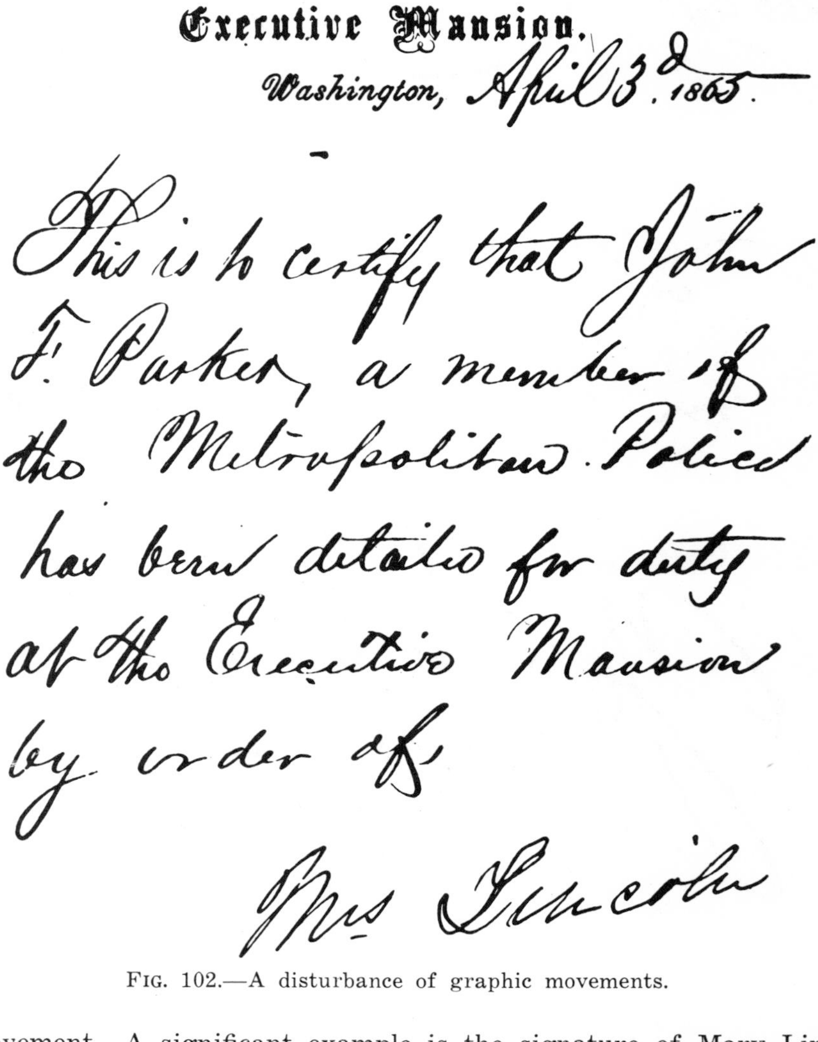

Executive Mansion.
Washington, April 3d. 1865.

This is to certify that John F. Parker, a member of the Metropolitan Police has been detailed for duty at the Executive Mansion by order of

Mrs Lincoln

FIG. 102.—A disturbance of graphic movements.

of movement. A significant example is the signature of Mary Lincoln in that letter in which she determined the bodyguard for the President (Fig. 102). This guard was known as "exceedingly violent and disrespectful."* Shortly before the time when the murderer entered the box

*Otto Eisenschiml: "Why Was Lincoln Murdered?" Boston, Little, Brown & Company, 1937. Fig. 102 used by permission of the publisher.

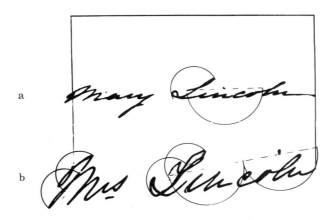

FIG. 103.—The meaning of the meaningless in the diagnosis of personality.

where Lincoln was sitting, the only protector of the President had left his post of duty.

Three years before Lincoln's death, Mary Lincoln showed schizophrenic symptoms. Elizabeth Keckley* reports that "Mary Lincoln had hallucinations, seeing persons that did not exist and hearing sounds that were not." In 1863 she made an attempt to commit suicide. Thus the schizophrenia appeared three years before Lincoln's death, and nine years later she became definitely insane. She then said that she had been admonished by her husband to die in a few days.

In her signature in the fateful letter (Fig. 103b), Mrs. Lincoln makes a correction of her initial "L." The first movement is afterwards enlarged; by this enlargement the initial obtains the same length as the initial "M" in "Mrs." Comparing both signatures, the former written "Mary Lincoln," both show the same length from beginning to end. The initial of the second signature is one and a half times the length of the former. The dot belonging to the "i" is near the end in the second signature, while it is near the beginning of the name "Lincoln" in the first signature. The distance between dot and beginning of the name in the first signature is equal to the distance between dot and end of the name in the second signature. The distance between the beginning of the initial and the dot over the "i" in the second signature is three times the same distance in the first signature. Thus the distortion of the "L" by enlarging the letter, as well as the distorting additional stroke, form part of the configurative scheme so that the distortion is not due to chance but seems to stem from an inner psychological disturbance.

The common explanation of all these symptoms is that the graphic movement, which is a direct reflection of brain activity expressed in the written words, is disturbed. This inhibition seems to have the same origin

*"Behind the Scenes," New York, 1868.

as that which Freud discovered for mistakes in speaking or spelling. Let us give an example from our own experience. A person wrote a formal letter: "I shall never forget the days I spent in your *lice* house." The analysis revealed a strong hidden aggression. The misspelling originated in the phenomenon that one intention, suggesting a positive emphasis (+) of the idea expressed, is blocked by another intention, suggesting a negative emphasis (—) of the same idea. The negative intention had to be suppressed and the inhibited energy caused a "disease" of the word. We may generalize: A symptom appears from a conflict of acceptable and nonacceptable or "plus" and "minus" factors. The origin of this symptom lies in associations connected with this word.

Similarly "graphic diseases" may be explained. If one letter is distorted in a word, such a word may be a "complex-word" related to an affective association. If the distortion appears in the initial of this word, the emotional tone becomes operative at the start of the word; but if the distortion appears in the body of the word, certain affective associations may be connected with this special letter. In this way graphic patterns may furnish a key for discovering psychological disturbances.

Thus the principle of configuration in apparent distortions demonstrates the "psychopathology of writing" just as Freud showed it in "faulty acts" such as mistakes of speaking or spelling, forgetting names, and losing objects. Such disturbances in everyday-life reactions are not meaningless but configurated by unconscious processes. Our measurements of graphic distortions allow us to demonstrate the meaning of the apparently meaningless as a diagram of the unconscious.

DIAGNOSIS OF ADAPTATION

It has frequently been observed that the writings of husbands and wives and of parents and children show patterns of similarity. In one experiment, conducted by the present author, twenty subjects were asked to match handwriting specimens (text: The United States of America) of three students (group A) to that of their mothers (group B) and fathers (group C). Only the matching of the students' writing to that of their mothers was correct above chance (41 per cent), but frequently the parents were matched correctly though matched with the wrong student. A correct matching of the parents appeared in 70 per cent of the cases.*

In another experiment simple graphic patterns (horizontal lines, triangles, circles), made by students and their parents were compared regarding length of lines and size of patterns. The students' lines were smaller than those of both parents in every case, and their size of patterns was smaller in a majority of cases (80 per cent as compared with father's, 75 cent as compared with mother's pattern). However, the lengths of lines showed a greater degree of similarity between father and mother in a majority of cases (88 per cent) than between one parent and the stu-

*Described in: Werner Wolff, "What is Psychology?" Grune & Stratton, New York, 1947. P. 304.

dent, and also a similarity of size of design was apparent (60 per cent).

As an example of graphic adaptation of husband and wife we give a sample of the handwritings of Abraham Lincoln and his wife, both written on the same page (Fig. 104).* The length of both signatures, A. Lincoln,

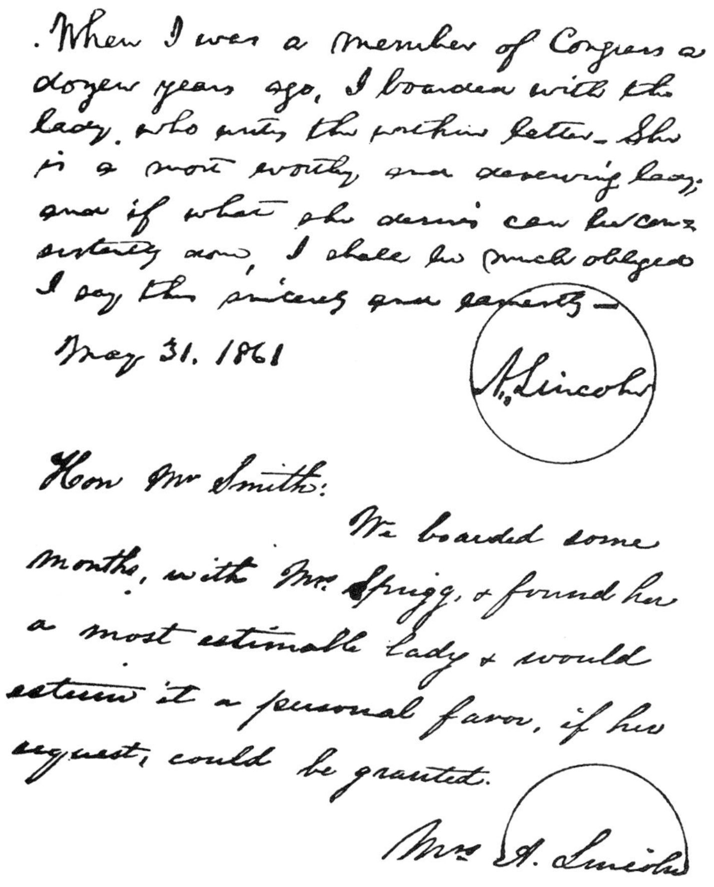

a

When I was a member of Congress a dozen years ago, I boarded with the lady who writes the within letter. She is a most worthy and deserving lady; and if what she desires can be consistently done, I shall be much obliged. I say this sincerely and earnestly—
May 31, 1861
A. Lincoln

b

Hon Mr Smith:
We boarded some months, with Mrs Sprigg, & found her a most estimable lady & would esteem it a personal favor, if her request, could be granted.
Mrs A. Lincoln

FIG. 104.—The adaptation of graphic movements.

is almost equal, although Abraham Lincoln writes his signature without interruption while Mary Lincoln separates the initial of the first name from the second name.

If several persons sign the same document, measurements may reveal whether the signers adapt to each other, distinguishing between those who set the pattern of adaptation, the leaders, and those who follow. We give as an example signatures on the Declaration by the United Nations, signed

*From Carl Sandburg: "Mary Lincoln, Wife and Widow." Harcourt-Brace, New York, 1932; pp. 88. Fig. 104 used by permission of the publisher.

on January 1, 1942 (Fig. 105), of the Appendix to the Declaration by the United Nations (Fig. 106), of the Agreement in the Crimea (Fig. 107) and of the Atlantic Charter (Fig. 108). In the Declaration by the United Nations the first signer is Franklin D. Roosevelt; the next, Winston Churchill. Measuring the extension of movement from beginning to end in the signatures of both signers, it appears that it is equal (Fig. 107a). This phenomenon could be due to chance, but it reappears with the first signature of Roosevelt and Churchill in their mutual understanding about the Atlan-

The foregoing declaration may be adhered to by other nations which are, or which may be, rendering material assistance and contributions in the struggle for victory over Hitlerism.

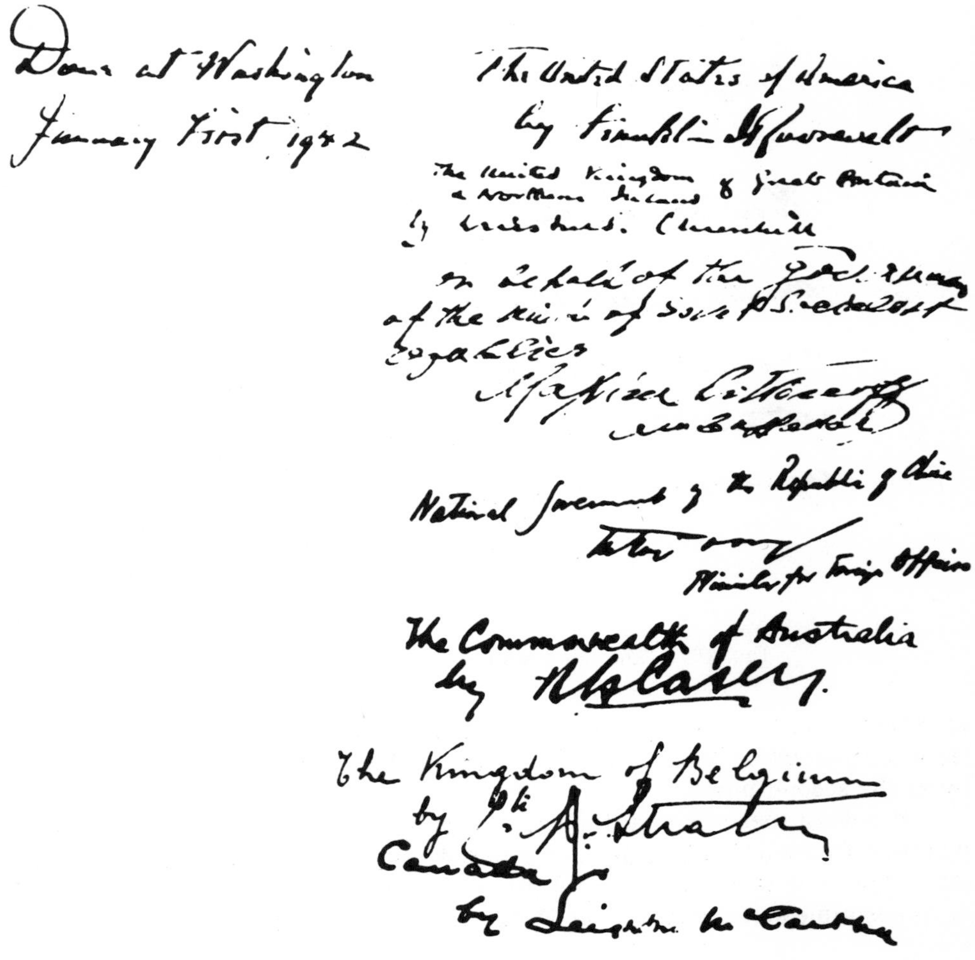

FIG. 105.—Signatures of the Declaration by the United Nations.

tic Charter. Here also the extension of both signatures is equal (Fig. 108). Also, both signatures to the agreement in the Crimea in 1945 (Fig. 108) have an equal length (Fig. 109b). The repetition of this phenomenon indicates that it cannot be explained by chance; however, it could be that Roosevelt and Churchill have always the same extension of movement in their signatures so that the present phenomenon could not be explained by the factor of adaptation. We therefore studied other signatures of both statesmen, knowing that they were not written jointly. In these signatures we do not perceive an identity of extension. As an example we reproduce a signature of Churchill, published by Teltscher [413] and a signa-

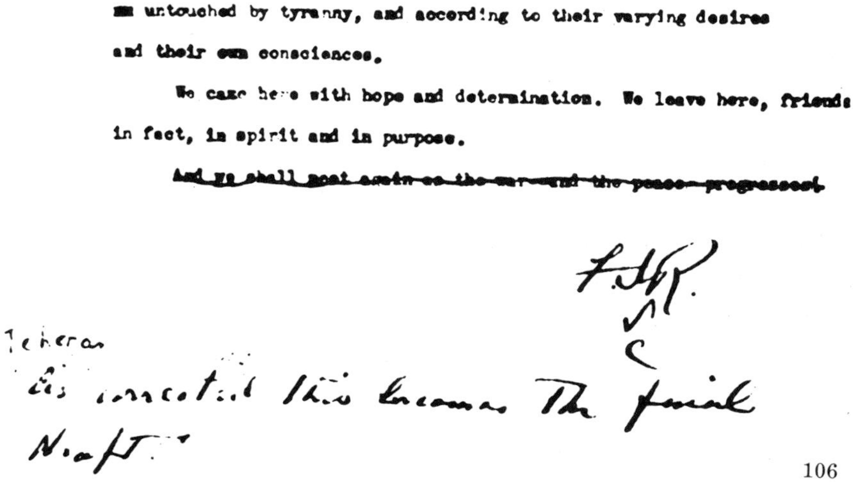

untouched by tyranny, and according to their varying desires
and their own consciences.

We came here with hope and determination. We leave here, friends
in fact, in spirit and in purpose.

And we shall meet again on the sea and the peace progressed.

106

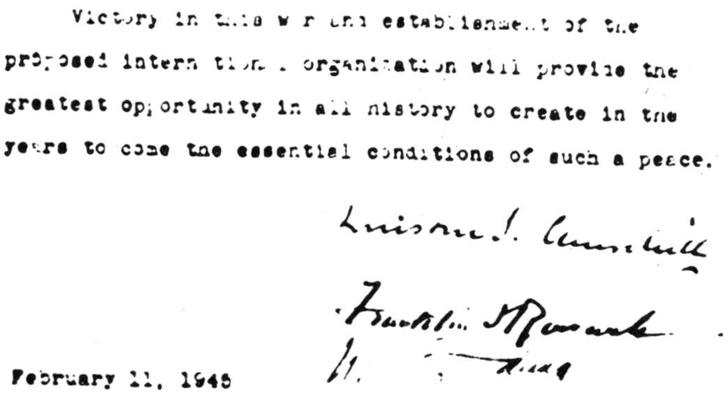

Victory in this war and establishment of the
proposed international organization will provide the
greatest opportunity in all history to create in the
years to come the essential conditions of such a peace.

February 11, 1945

107

FIG. 106.—Signatures of the Appendix to the Declaration by the United Nations.
FIG. 107.—Signatures of the Agreement in the Crimea.

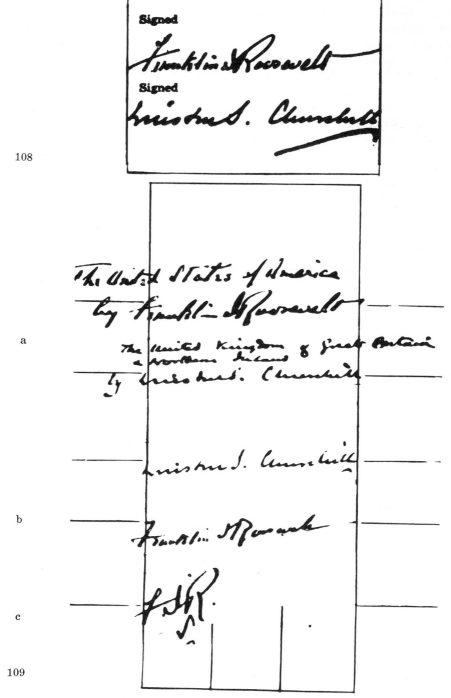

FIG. 108.—Signatures of the Atlantic Charter.
FIG. 109a-c.—A diagnosis of adaptation.

ture of Roosevelt from the White House (Fig. 109d). Also other signatures of Roosevelt (Figs. 130 a-q, p. 162) do not show an extension which is identical with that of Churchill. The signature to the appendix of the Declaration by the United Nations (Fig. 109c) consists only of

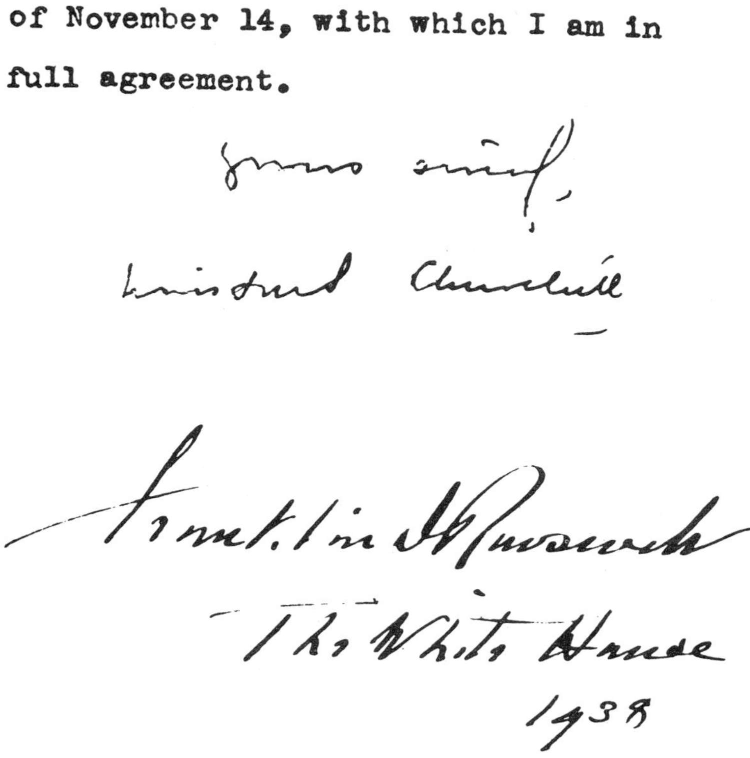

FIG. 109d-e

Roosevelt's initials. The length from beginning to end, which is the dot after the last initial, is exactly one third of the preceding signatures. When the extension of movement in Churchill's signature follows the extension of movement set by the preceding signature of Roosevelt, we can diagnose the adaptation of the second signer. Our diagnosis of Churchill's adaptation to Roosevelt's pattern seems to get some support by the observations of Elliott Roosevelt, who in his book, "As He Saw It,"* describes the meeting of both statesmen on the occasion of the signing of the Atlantic Charter. Churchill, in his characteristically emphatic manner on such occasions, addressed Mr. Roosevelt with these words, according to the President's son: "Mr. President, I believe you are trying to do away with the British Empire. Every idea you entertain about the structure of the

*Published by Duell, Sloan & Pearce, New York, 1946. P. 41.

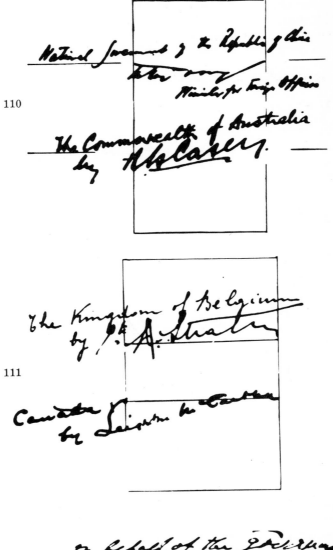

FIGS. 110-112.—A diagnosis of adaptation.

postwar world demonstrates it. But in spite of that, we know that you con-
stitute our only hope. And—*you* know that *we* know that without America,
the Empire won't stand." It was a revealing acknowledgment of the primary importance of the United States in the winning of the war.

The principle of adaptation is demonstrated by the other signers of
the Charter. The extension of the signature by the signer for the Republic of Chile equals the extension of movement by the following signer
for the Commonwealth of Australia (Fig. 110). The extension of the
next signer for the Kingdom of Belgium sets the size for the signature of
the following signer, Canada (Fig. 111). The only exception in these
groups of mutual adaptation is the signature of Maxim Litvinoff, for
Russia, which in extension neither follows its predecessors nor is followed
by the next signers (Fig. 112).

DIAGNOSIS OF INSTABILITY

We have observed that a contraction of movements goes with an
act of self-control which appears, positively, as mental discipline, negatively as inhibition. An expansion of movements goes with a loss of self-
control which appears, positively, as spontaneity, negatively as nervous
excitation. The distinction between the positive and negative qualities of
movement is usually based upon the detection of motor distortions. Such
distortions in the expansion of movements are immediately visible in our
examples of the epileptic (Fig. 55), in one signature of Nietzsche (Fig.
62), one of C. F. Meyer (Fig. 61), and one of Napoleon (Fig. 63). Here
I give an example from my personal letters. The distortion appears immediately in the rigidity of letters and especially in the last down-stroke
with the strangled end.

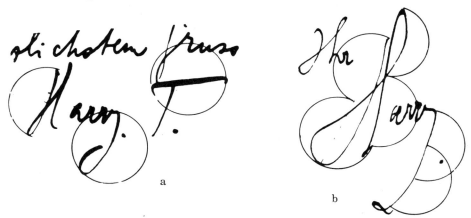

Fig. 113.—Diagnosis of Instability.

Harry, 19-year-old student (Fig. 113. See Fig. 153.) :
Intense fear of not passing an examination was expressed in a letter
written by the young friend whose signature we show (b). The starting-

stroke of the initial has twice the length, and the end-stroke one and a half times the length of the corresponding stroke in a preceding letter (a).

When *Life* magazine* reproduced some signatures from the Nuremberg trials, I looked for the signatures of the accused in their times of success. The German Encyclopedia Brockhaus gave the signatures of Hermann Göring, and Franz von Papen, which we also find in the *Life* publication.

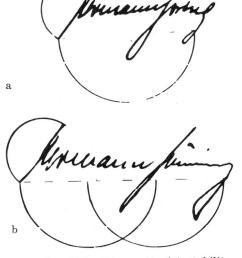

FIG. 114.—Diagnosis of instability.

Hermann Göring (1893-1946) (Fig. 114):

This signature from the time of the trial (b) shows signs of distortion, each of the single letters having lost its shape and distinction. Compared with an earlier signature (a), taken from the German Encyclopedia Brockhaus, the extension from beginning to end has increased one and a half times. The length of the starting-stroke remains the same.

Franz von Papen (1879-   ) (Fig. 115):

While Göring's signature shows a disturbed expansion, von Papen's signature at the time of the trial (b) does not change much from that published in the Encyclopedia (a). The length of the covering flourish remains equal, and so does the extension of the second name, Papen.

THE DETECTION OF FORGERIES

If each individual has a typical formula of proportions and configuration, such a finding should enable us to determine authenticity of signatures as part of the forensic investigation in disputed cases [31, 88, 126, 229, 234, 266, 314, 341, 375]. Configuration and proportions are unconscious processes of which nobody is aware; and since these phenomena are of a

---

Life, December 10, 1945, p. 27.

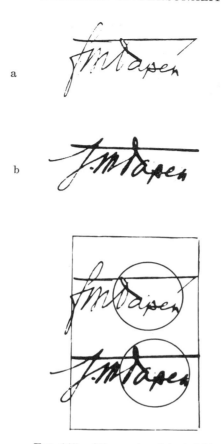

a

b

FIG. 115.—Diagnosis of instability.

very complex kind it would be extremely difficult to construct them intentionally. Even if the law of configuration and proportion might become
known and if reconstruction were technically possible, such a reconstruction would destroy the spontaneous fluidity of writing and thus make it
possible to detect a forgery. The coincidence between the law of configuration and proportion and the spontaneous fluidity of movement is a characteristic of organic activity, and it seems to be impossible to replace it me-
chanically. With several signatures of the same person, the formula of
organization may be detected, and each forgery would show a deviation
from this organizing principle.

An example of this is shown in three signatures (Fig. 116) published
by Muriel Stafford in the New York *Post* of December 4, 1941, p. 10.
There it was stated: "The jury's verdict in the trial of Isaac Brown for
attempted murder of Mathilde Le Boyer may hinge on these three signatures." One of these three signatures, the specimen on the right, was
conceded to be genuine. The authenticity of the other two was first denied
by Miss Le Boyer. Later she admitted that they might be genuine. But
Muriel Stafford states: "Whether or not the reproductions . . . are

the signature of Le Boyer is not decided." Our method of measuring, the "graphometrical" method, reveals (Fig. 117) that the length of "Mathilde" has equal proportions in all three signatures. The longest size (c) is double the smallest (a); the middle size (b) is one and a half times the smallest. Regarding the second name, "Le Boyer," the third writing is exactly one and a half times the first; the second shows a small deviation. Since most of the initials also show the same proportions we may conclude that the three signatures were made by the same person.

In July 1946, a quiet 17 year old student, who had entered the University of Chicago when he was only 16, was accused of three murders.

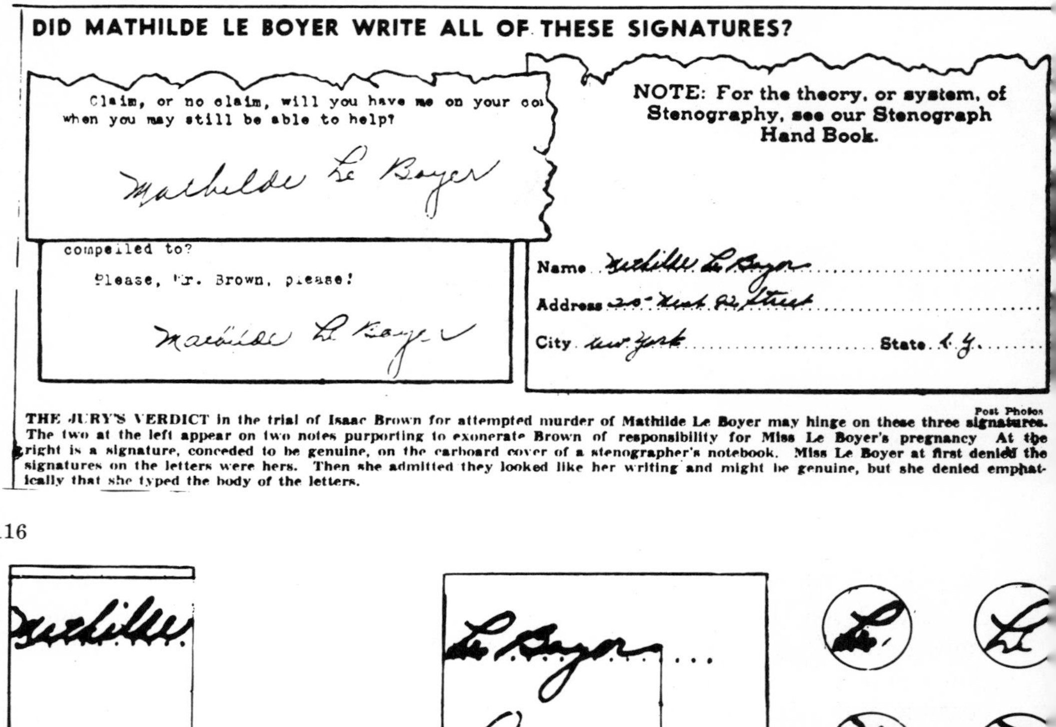

116

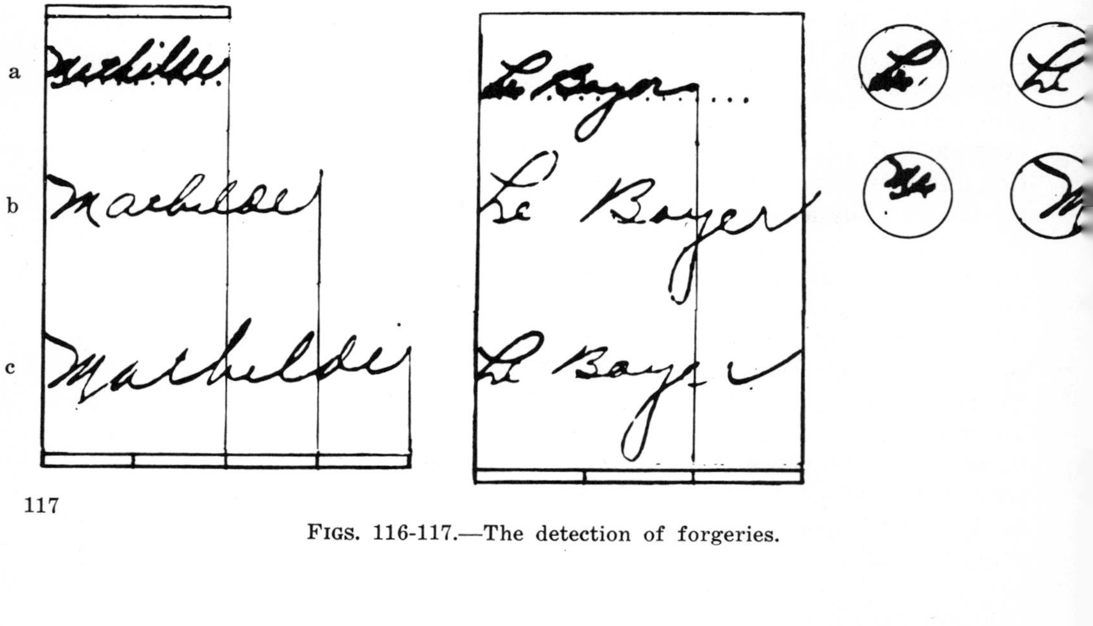

117

FIGS. 116-117.—The detection of forgeries.

Life magazine (July 29, 1946) reproduced the handwriting of the student (Fig. 118) together with a different handwriting of a kidnap-note, supposed also to have been written by him (b). The case is described as follows: Young William Heirens, like many a lonely child with a vivid imagination, invented an imaginary companion, "George Murmans." "Murmans" was the youthful hoodlum type, wild and fast in speech and action, an opposite to Heirens himself. William Heirens did not outgrow his companion; as he grew older and more studious and retiring, "Murments, stabbed a housewife and shot an ex-Wave, at the same time that his scholarly inventor was studying at the university. The two seemed to grow

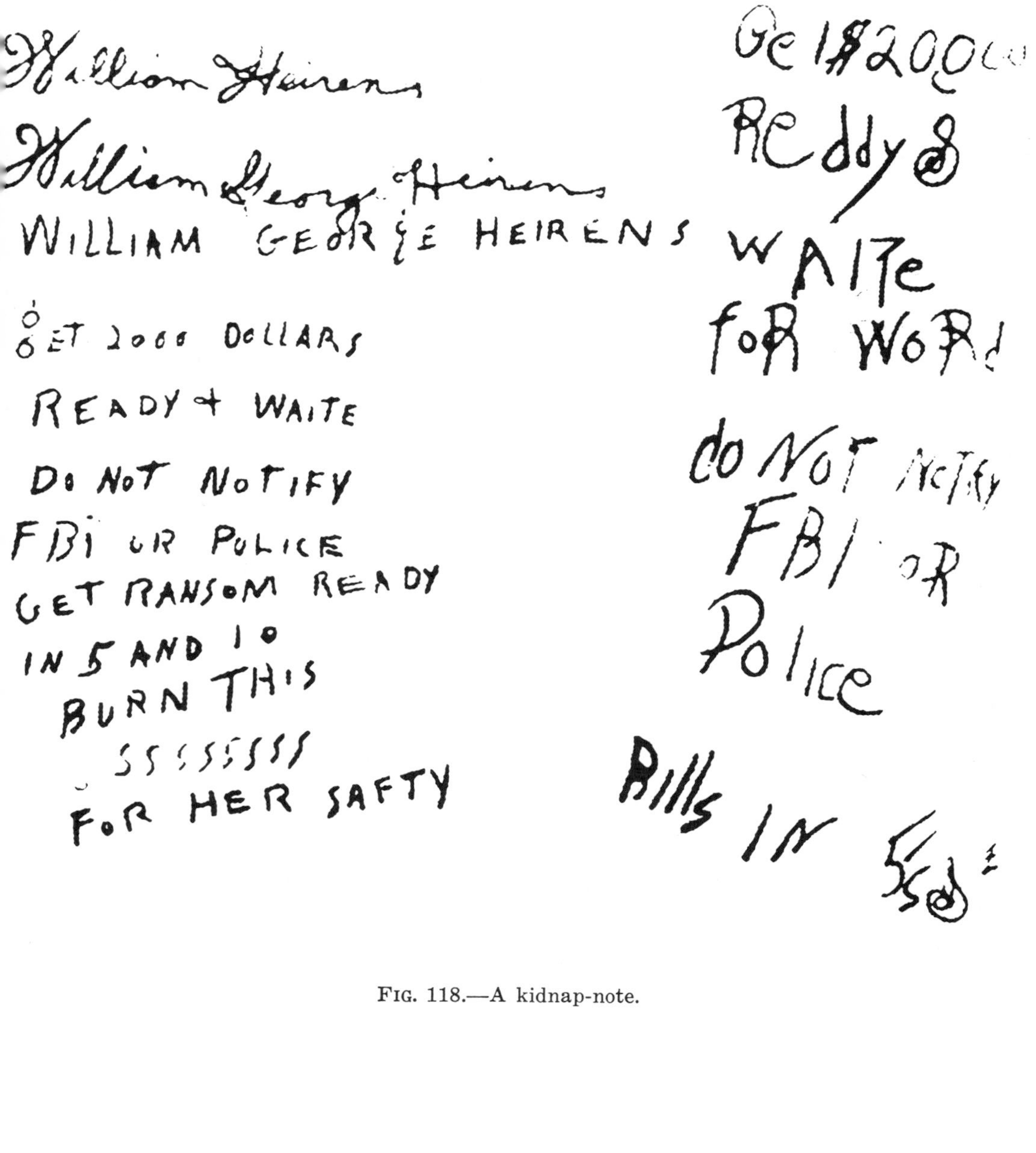

FIG. 118.—A kidnap-note.

FIG. 119.—Identification of a kidnap note.

closer together, even exchanging letters, and then evidently merged. Little 6-year-old Suzanne Degnan was to be the victim of this final mingling of personalities. William Heirens left his friends after a movie one evening, and an hour later George Murmans kidnapped, killed and dismembered the unfortunate child. The following morning, Heirens attended his customary classes untroubled by his deed of the night before. As he lay strapped to his bed in the police hospital awaiting trial, he is reported to have said: "George did it. I told him not to be such a bad boy."

The normal signatures of Heirens, written with interconnected letters or with printed letters, show consistencies in the first name and last name (Fig. 119); the length of each name, measured from beginning to end, is the same in both types of handwriting (a) the name George, however, the name of his second personality (George Murmans), does not show consistencies (b). Comparing the same words of the kidnap-note with Heirens' handwriting, the following consistencies can be found:

In the kidnap-note the word WAITE is double the length, the words POLICE and FBI are one and a half times the length of the corresponding words in the normal handwriting. The size of the letters FBI in the kidnap-note is double their size in the normal handwriting. No consistencies are found with the words "Ready &" and "Do Not Notify."

The detection of forgeries has not only a great importance in criminal cases, but it also serves to discover whether in a collection of precious autographs all are genuine. As I shall demonstrate in a special study, several autographs in a most precious collection in the British Museum are not genuine, while a few others claimed to be fakes can, by measurements, be proven to be genuine. This, of course, changes the actual and hypothetical value of this priceless collection.

CHAPTER VII

ON THE ORIGIN OF CONFIGURATION

CHARACTERISTICS OF CONFIGURATION

The principle of configuration is almost synonymous with personality. The characteristic configuration of traits in personality distinguishes one individual from another, and the configuration of movements creates what we call the co-ordination of our activities. It is the configurating principle of our senses which enables us to perceive, and only the configuration of thoughts makes our thinking possible. The first fundamental question is whether this ability of configuration is acquired in the development of each individual through the processes of learning and conditioning or whether this ability is an innate property of our organism transmitted to us by heredity. The co-operation of our bodily functions is certainly not acquired. Nobody learns the co-operation of inner organs such as heart, lungs, stomach; nobody learns the organization of the nervous system and the interrelationship of glandular functions. If the ability to configurate lies within us, implanted by heredity, the material for configuration must come from without, from the environment. We now ask: Does every stimulus become configurated? This is certainly not the case. We do not accept everything that the environment offers; we accept some stimuli and neglect others, we resist and modify, in short, we select the environmental factors. This forms the problem of the development of personality. Does personality develop by chance, or does it follow an inner law, which causates *that* we act and react and patterns *what* impressions we receive and what expressions we produce.

As the first characteristic of a configuration is the relative stability, we started with a search for *consistency* in personality. Experimental investigations have shown such a consistency in two dimensions. One consistency, which we may call consistency in space, indicated that an individual patterns his graphic space with different features which, however, have one factor in common, namely, the same proportions. As matching experiments indicate (see page 185 ff.) common factors also appear in a person's different forms of expression. A person's expression of handwriting shows certain characteristics which we may also find in his voice and his facial patterns. The other consistency, which we may call the consistency in time, indicates that characteristic features remain consistent over a length of time.

Another characteristic of configuration is the relative *symmetry* of its parts. We observed a trend toward symmetry in our perception, which reflects impressions, and in our movements, which reflect expressions. It is a general trend toward balance and symmetrical arrangement which governs our lives. Our form of balance appears with the spatial arrangement and in the rhythm of patterns.

A third characteristic of configuration is the significant *relationship* between all of its parts. Such an inner relationship of all parts to each other, and between each part and the whole, is the characteristic of an organization. Until the discoveries of psychoanalysis, it was assumed that the organization of behavior depended on our consciousness. When it was recognized that the apparent chaos of our dreams follows organized patterns, and that disturbances in the activities of the normal and abnormal personality follow definite rules, the configurating principle of the unconscious became evident. If the apparently disorganized is organized, the concept of chaos seems not to exist for any human process. We can speak only of different forms and various degrees of configuration. Although Freud originated the concept of an unconscious organization, he made a statement in which he contradicts himself. Dividing personality into a conscious and an unconscious region, Sigmund Freud described the unconscious region as the domain of chaos and boiling energies opposed to the conscious reign of order. The mechanism of these unconscious trends was considered to be very different from the conscious ones. Here was supposed to reign another mode of expression, another concept of time, another handling of space.

The expressive movement in writing is made chiefly in a state of unawareness, automatically and impulsively; the expression is unconsciously directed. Now our findings indicate that these unconscious movements represent a reign of order, proportion, and configuration, appearing in the same exact way as if they had been consciously calculated, measured, and constructed. The unconscious expression appears to be determined by the same concepts of order, premediation, and organization as the conscious expression. There seems to be no gap between the two kinds of manifestations; personality appears as a unity, it is directed by some organizing principle. And even in cases where graphic expression reflects "boiling energies" of the unconscious, as in phases of an epileptic attack, mental disturbance, etc., these tendencies become integrated into a total harmonious pattern.

THE PROBLEM OF INNATE CONFIGURATIONS

Although we never learned the configuration of graphic movements and are not aware of it, the configuration of movements into a harmonious pattern might have been learned unconsciously, by adapting our form of expression to the organized patterns of nature.

There are two ways to answer the question whether or not the configuration of movements depends on our visual experience. One is an investigation of movement patterns at the earliest age of life, when the infant has not yet been exposed to many observations, or to training. Such an inquiry of mine has indicated that children, even the first time they hold a pencil in their hands, frequently make a scribbling in which the lines show simple patterns of configuration. These investigations are still in an exploratory stage, but we give a few examples. For reasons of objectivity we use as the first example reproductions of drawings which were published by other authors who were unaware of the problem in question. Helga Eng [112], for instance, published drawings by the same child from ten months up to eight years of age. The first scribbling of this child (Fig. 120), made at the age of ten months, consisted of two

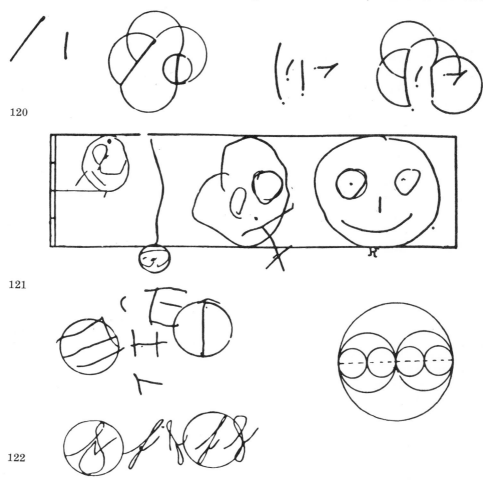

120

121

122

FIGS. 120-122.—Configuration of movement in early childhood.

strokes. These two strokes are in definite proportion to each other, not only with regard to their size but also with regard to their distance from each other. The longer stroke has double the length of the shorter. The upper distance between both strokes is equal to the length of the shorter stroke. The lower distance between the two strokes is equal to the length of the longer stroke. The two strokes are thus determined three times by the same unit, a coincidence which seems to exclude any possibility of chance. Moreover, the same or corresponding movements appear in 35 per cent of the other drawings, of which Helga Eng gives 112 examples. At one year of age this same child repeats a figure which is extremely similar to her first drawing: the longer stroke has the same size as that in the first drawing and again is double the size of the shorter stroke (Fig. 121). The upper distance between the long and short stroke is almost equal to the size of the short stroke. Other drawings by the same child show the most varied repetitions of the unit of movement previously discussed. This unit reappears at all ages at which drawings are given. The diameter of heads (c), the length of lines in the scribbling of letters (d), the size of eyes, etc., frequently show a movement the size of which is either the same as or several times that established with the first stroke. (Fig. 122).

a

b

c

FIG. 123.—Consistency of movement in early childhood.

Some children are able to write their names at a very early age, as for instance, a four-year-old boy of the Vassar Nursery School (Fig. 123). Three signatures of this boy were at my disposal, and the sizes of all three signatures are in simple proportion to each other. Whether the signature "Jan," is written normally (a), partly mirrored (c), or totally

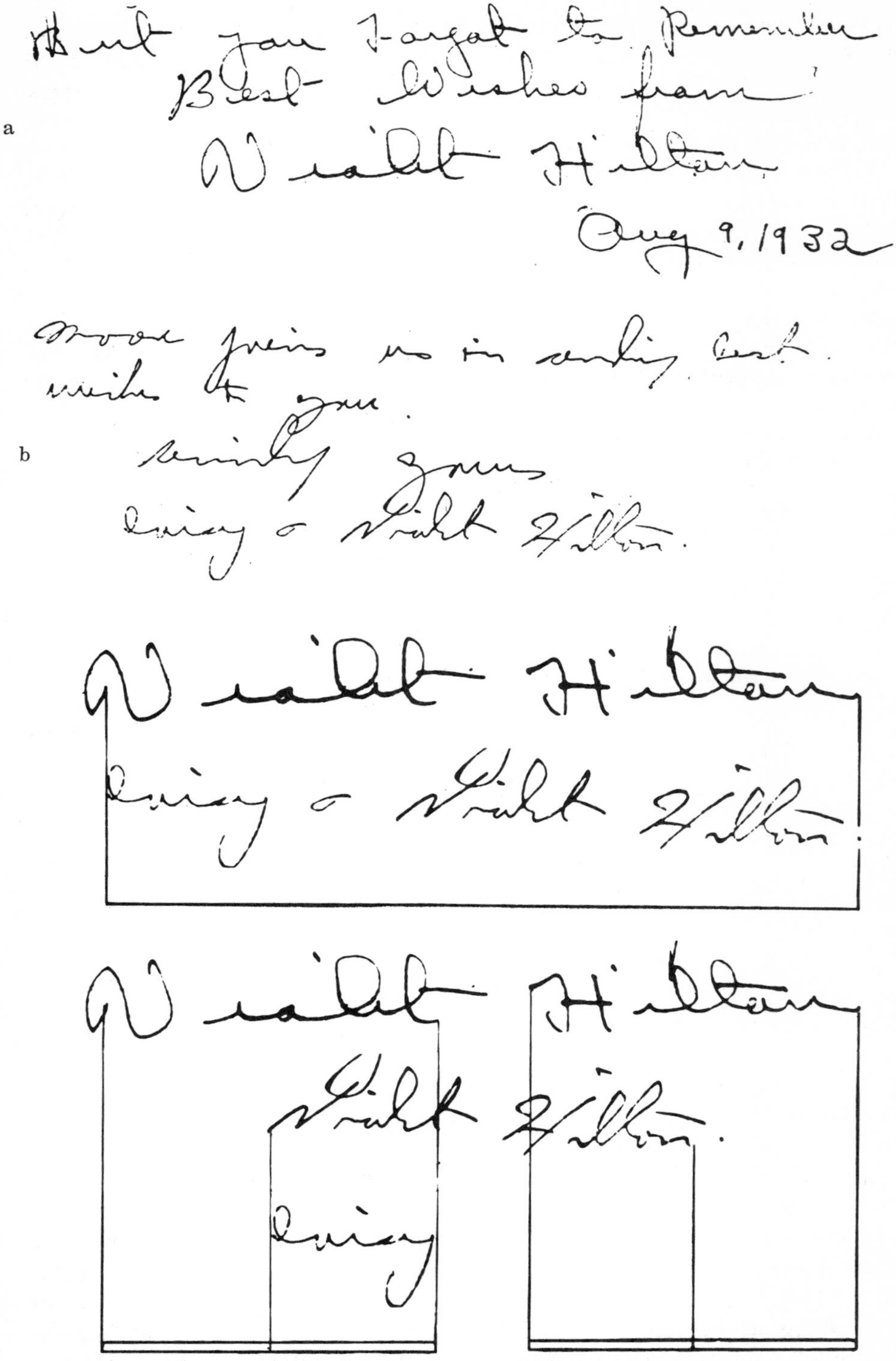

Fig. 124.—Consistency of movement in Siamese twins.

mirrored (b), simple proportions appear in the horizontal as well as in the diagonal extension from left to right limit. The largest signature, measured horizontally from left limit to the right limit (a), is double the corresponding measure of the smallest signature (c), while the middle signature is a third longer than the smaller (b).

Our investigation throws a new light upon the research on twins. Most observers found that the majority of handwritings by twins are, against any expectation, dissimilar to each other. Since twins, especially identical ones, show many striking similarities in their appearance and their expression, the conclusion was drawn that the dissimilarity in handwritings of twins proves that handwriting characteristics are accidental and thus not significant for any personality investigation. The differences of expressive characteristics even appear in the handwriting of "Siamese twins" whose bodies are conjoined. Seeman and Saudek [386] present the handwritings of the Siamese twins Violet and Daisy. Although these twins show great similarities of behavior they have some characteristic differences in their likes and dislikes [386, p. 115].

> Violet loves blue and Daisy pink. But as they must wear the same dress and as a costume half blue and half pink would make them appear ridiculous, they compromise on a daily alternation of their favorite color schemes. In literature and drama Daisy likes romanticism, she likes to be carried away by the imaginative adventure stories of Conrad and Sabatini.—Violet doesn't like romanticism at all—her interest is in the reality of things, in attaining a philosophical understanding of life.—Daisy sews, she delights in designing and making little pieces of needlecraft, Violet is not particularly fond of sewing, rather, she likes to concern herself with the arrangement of things—furniture, bric-a-brac, pictures. Violet likes to cook.*

Violet is the more active, more realistic and more extravert person, Daisy the more passive, more imaginative and more introvert individual. These characteristics seem to go together with their graphic movements, Violet writing with her right, Daisy with her left hand. The twins' diagram of the unconscious reflects in the most instructive way their difference within their identity. Seeman and Saudek [386] published two letters of the sisters Violet and Daisy Hilton (Fig. 124). One twin signs "Violet Hilton" (a) ; the other, Daisy, signs for herself and in the name of her sister "Daisy and Violet Hilton" (b). It appears that the length of this signature, "Daisy and Violet Hilton," written by Daisy (b), is exactly the same as the length of the name "Violet Hilton," written by Violet (a). If we now investigate the first and second names in both signatures, it appears that, if measured from beginning to end, the name "Violet," written by Daisy, has half the length of the name "Violet" written by Violet. The length of the name "Daisy," from beginning to right limit, is the same as the length in Daisy's writing of the name "Violet" from beginning to end. The name "Hilton" is half the length of Violet's writing of this name. There appear similar proportions in other signatures of the twins.

Thus, it appears that in spite of their different graphic expression the

---

*E. Seemann and R. Saudek: "The Self-expression of Identical Twins." Character and Personality (Duke University Press) 1:115, 1932.

formula of configuration is the same with both twins. But furthermore, the proportional relationship of both signatures coincides with their different behavior pattern. The signature of the active, more extravert Violet is double the signature of the more passive and more introvert Daisy. This observation confirms what we had with signatures written in a state of elation and of depression and with signatures written during the activity of youth and the resignation of old age. The outgoing and active behavior coincides with an extension of the movement, while an introspective and passive behavior coincides with a contraction of movement.

Our observation shows again that manifest dissimiliarities may be underlayed by latent similarities or identities. The dissimilar appearance of handwritings by identical twins does not allow the conclusion that handwriting characteristics are accidental, or a product of learning; on the contrary, the fusion of difference and identity seems to reflect the fusion of individual differentiation and hereditary factors. Manifest similarities could not prove this point. As J. M. Reinhardt remarks [344, p. 319]:

> Personality analyses, however, whether by the use of graphological materials or by the somewhat more familiar methods of personality testing, do not as yet provide a basis for determining the relative importance of heredity and environments as determinants of personality qualities. It is observed that identical twins reared together tend to acquire a unique "type of social structure" which may be both casual and effectual in relation to the development of identical native potentialities.*

Our observation of latent identities, underlying manifest dissimilarities indicates that the identities are not stimulated by the environment from without, but that they are the reflection of the individual's basic structure.

Another support for our supposition that the law of configuration does not originate in experience is given by studies with graphic movements of the blind. Signatures and a few drawings which I obtained through the courtesy of the New York Institute for the Education of the Blind and from The Lighthouse, New York Association for the Blind, indicate that blind persons are moved by the principle of rhythm and of configuration, although they show it in a lower degree than the person with normal sight. I quote from the first letter I received from The Lighthouse (May 9, 1944):

> We were not able to obtain drawings made by blind people as this would be a very unnatural and unnecessary thing for a blind person to do. On the other hand, it is important that a blind person learn to write in order to sign his name and for other purposes. Accordingly, I am submitting two examples. Sample A: Ruth Askenas, blind since childhood (Fig. 125). Sample B: Albert Mayhew lost his sight in 1938 (Fig. 126a). Sample C: Signature of Albert Mayhew before he lost his sight, in 1937 (Fig. 126b).

Examples A and B show proportions between first and second names. In the case of Ruth Askenas (Fig. 125) the length of the first name is equal to that of the second, both measured from beginning to end. In Albert Mayhew's signature (Fig. 126) before and after blindness, the

---

*J. M. Reinhardt: "Heredity and Environment." Character and Personality (Duke University Press) 5:319, 1937.

length of the total name is a simple multiple of the length of the first name, both measured from beginning to end. After blindness (a) the length of the second name shrinks to $\frac{1}{3}$ of its former size (b). When I asked for samples in which blind people had been instructed to write their names repeatedly, I got ninety-six signatures made by twenty-one blind persons. Ten subjects showed regularities about one and a half times over probabil-

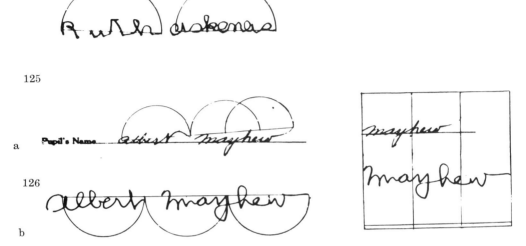

125

a   126

b

FIGS. 125-126.—Configuration of movements with blind people.

ity. The other subjects fall below probability. Although the total was statistically not significant, the positive group seems to indicate that blindness need not destroy the principle of configuration. In this connection, a note I received from The Lighthouse is interesting. I quote:

> One of our very able and devoted volunteer workers, Madame Ferdinand Pisart, has been giving script lessons to the blind at The Lighthouse for the past season. The additional samples I am submitting were prepared by her pupils. She wrote me the following:
> "Some of the earlier sheets made by my pupils show the wonderful efforts they made to become what they are now. Although taught in the same way, by the same method, the pupils have a very definite and personal way of writing even though starting from scratch. A few of these blind people, who have written before they lost their sight, to some extent write by remembering. Teaching to write by rhythm helped wonderfully with almost all of the students."
> Madame Pisart told me that she usually used a definite rhythm in speaking to the pupil while describing the motion required for each letter: such as, "L—up, loop, down, straight."

Although the role which heredity plays in the phenomenon of configuration is not yet decided, our observations suggest that the consistency and symmetry of expressive movements in terms of proportions, etc., depends on a basic organizing factor within the individual which predetermines the configuration of movement of that personality. However, it seems that environmental factors may sometimes prevent the configuration from being actualized. Therefore, many blind people show an absence or a

T HE signature given in facsimile below is probably the earliest specimen of the handwriting of her present Majesty the Queen. It was penned

a

when she was but four years old. Her first signature as Queen is taken from the original appended to the coronation oath.

b

FIG. 127.—Consistency of movement in childhood and adulthood.

low degree of this function, while others are unaffected.* In other words, it seems that graphic movements are influenced by nurture, by training, and by experience, but that they are also determined by nature, by a formula of personality which remains stable within all variations. It is thus out of the dynamics between nature and nurture that personality gets its configuration.

*I refer to drawings of the blind in another publication [467, pp. 185-186].

Consistency of Configurations in Childhood and Adulthood

The individual extension of movements which is one fundamental factor in the scheme of configuration seems to be either inherited or adopted at an early age. We present some signatures from famous personalities made at an early age and compare them with their signatures made in adulthood.

Victoria, Queen of England (1819-1901):

A publication on the *Handwriting of the Kings and Queens of England* gives probably the earliest specimen of the Queen's handwriting: "It was penned when she was but four years old." We compare this signature with the following given right below, taken from the original appended

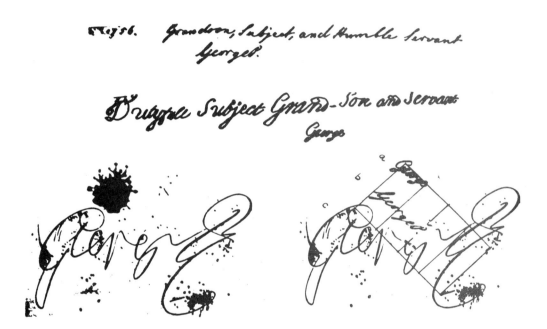

Fig. 130.—Consistency of movement in childhood and adulthood.

to the coronation oath (Fig. 127). The extension of the name written by the four year old princess remains almost the same with the Queen. The length of the starting-movement as well as the length of the end-movement made by the four year old are exactly half these lengths made by the Queen. The length of the middle-stroke, appearing in the bar of the "t," remains equal.

George III, King of England (1738-1820) (Fig. 128):

The work on the *Handwriting of the Kings and Queens of England* also gives three reproductions of George's signature: one made when

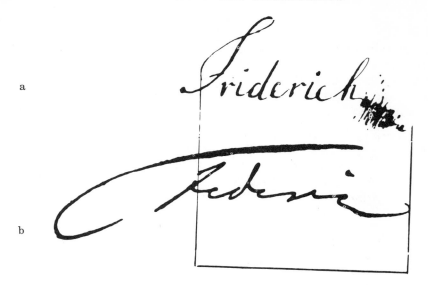

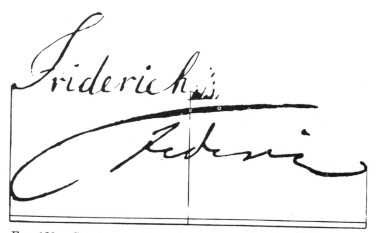

FIG. 129.—Consistency of movement in childhood and adulthood.

eleven years of age (a), one when eighteen years of age (b), and one when seventy-two years of age (c), during his last attack of insanity. Measuring the three signatures from beginning to end, the length of the eighteen year old's signature (b) is double the length of the eleven year old's (a) and the length of the seventy-two year old's signature (c) is double the length of that written at eighteen (b).

Frederick the Great, King of Prussia (1712-1786) (Fig. 129):
Comparing a signature of the eleven year old prince, signing "Friderich" (a) with a signature of the kind, signing "Federic" (b), the length

from beginning to right limit is exactly equal in both signatures. Comparing the limits of both signatures and excluding the flourish from the earlier signature, the latter is exactly double the former.

It is not easy to obtain significant samples for demonstrating a consistency of configuration over a person's life period. On October 24, 1947 I went to the Franklin D. Roosevelt Library and asked the librarian to give me an at random sample of twenty signatures of the late President, covering periods of his life from the first signatures in the Library's possession up to the last. In order to get a uniformity of samples, I took autographs from Roosevelt's personal books and a few letters from his childhood. The footnote lists the books from which the autographs reproduced as Fig. 130, were taken.*

The date of the earliest signature in the Library is 1889 (Fig. 130a), when the seven year old Franklin wrote down his Christmas wishes. I took the distance from beginning to end of the signature "Franklin" as a measure-unit, investigating whether the same measure-unit or a simple proportion of it would appear in the President's later signatures of his first name, covering various periods of his life. In 16 out of 20 signatures from the year 1889, 1892, 1895, 1913, 1915, 1916, 1920, 1925, 1929, 1934, 1936, 1938, and 1945 the distance between beginning and end of the first names was either equal to the distance of the first signature (1889) or half its length. The last name "D. Roosevelt" was first measurable in a signature from 1895 (c); two other early signatures

---

*   (a) 1889. Glass plate Christmas card.

    (b) Roosevelt, Franklin D. [Notebook] 1892.

    (c) Jan. 8, 1895. Letter to his mother.

    (d) Montieth, James. New Physical Geography for Grammar and High Schools, and Colleges.

    (e) Navy Dept. Regulations for the Government of the United States Navy, 1870.

    (f) Scharf, J. Thomas. History of the Confederate States Navy from its Organization to the Surrender of its Last Vessel.

    (g) Navy Dept. Regulations of the Government of the Navy of the United States. 1893.

    (h) Navy Dept. Regulations for the Government of the Navy of the United States. 1905.

    (i) Preble, George Henry. A Chronological History of the Origin and Development of Steam Navigation.

    (k) Davis, Charles G. Ship Models: How to Build Them.

    (l) Around the World with the Fleet, 1907-1909; a Pictorial Log of the Cruise.

    (m) Roosevelt, Franklin D. Public Addresses of Franklin Delano Roosevelt. Compiled by Merwin W. Hunt.

    (n) Pollard, Josephine. Our Naval Heroes: in Words of Easy Syllables.

    (o) Howe, Octavius Thorndike. Beverly Privateers in the American Revolution.

    (p) Bunkley, Joel W. Military and Naval Recognition Book.

    (q) Fourth Inaugural Address, Jan. 20, 1945.

    (r) Vergilius Maro, Publius. . . . The Greater Poems of Virgil. Vol. 1.

    (s) Truxtun, Thomas. Remarks, Instructions, and Examples Relating to the Latitude & Longitude.

    (t) Meissner, Mme. Sophie (Radford) de. Old Navy Days.

    (u) Mackenzie, Compton. Mr. Roosevelt.

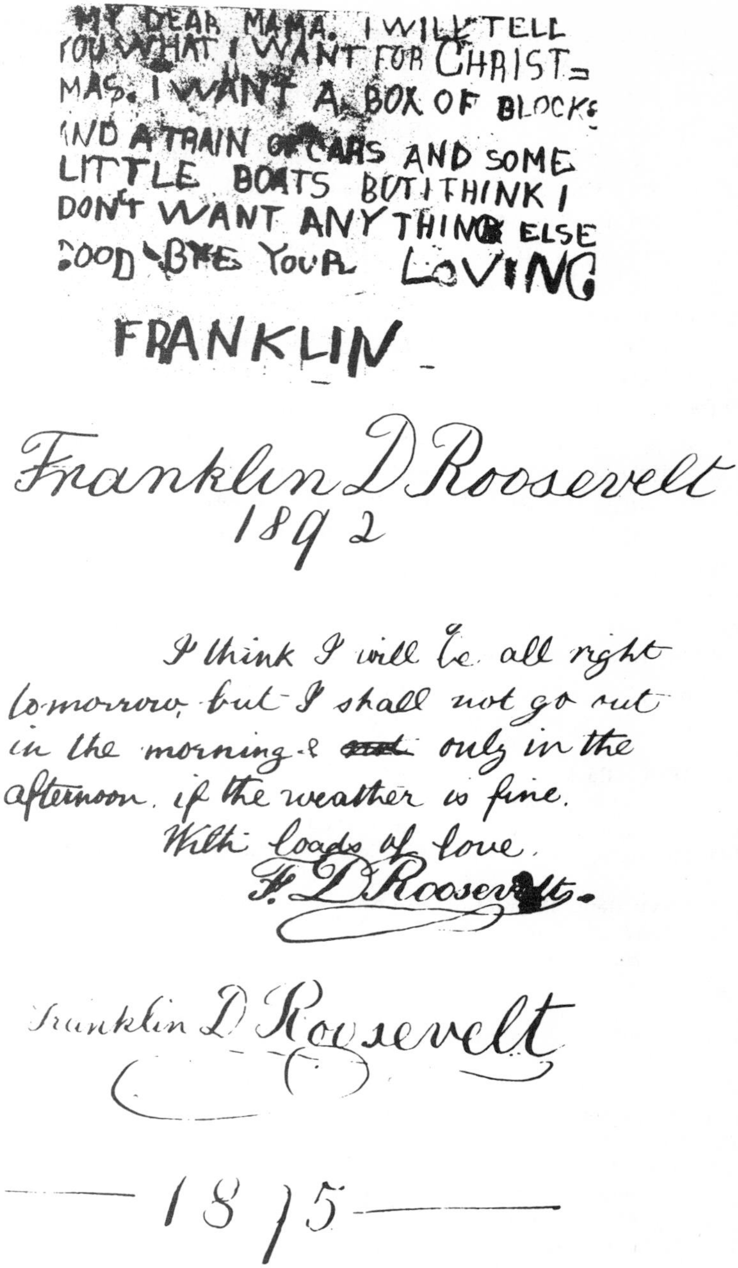

a

MY DEAR MAMA. I WILL TELL
YOU WHAT I WANT FOR CHRIST=
MAS. I WANT A BOX OF BLOCKS
AND A TRAIN OF CARS AND SOME
LITTLE BOATS BUT I THINK I
DON'T WANT ANYTHING ELSE
GOOD BYE YOUR LOVING

FRANKLIN

b

Franklin D Roosevelt
1892

c

I think I will be all right
to-morrow, but I shall not go out
in the morning & ~~~~ only in the
afternoon, if the weather is fine.
With loads of love.
F. D. Roosevelt.

d

Franklin D Roosevelt

1895

FIG. 130.—Random sample of signatures over a person's life period.

with the last name (b, d) could not be measured since the margin of
the book cover had cut the movement; however, according to the measure-
unit of movement we can determine where the movement presumably

e

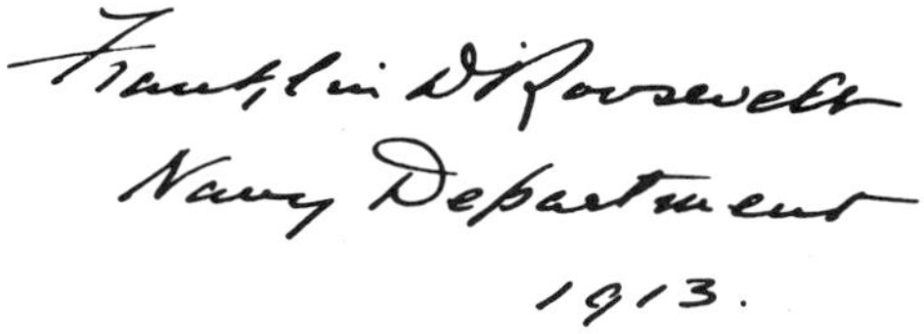

Franklin D Roosevelt
Navy Department
1913.

f

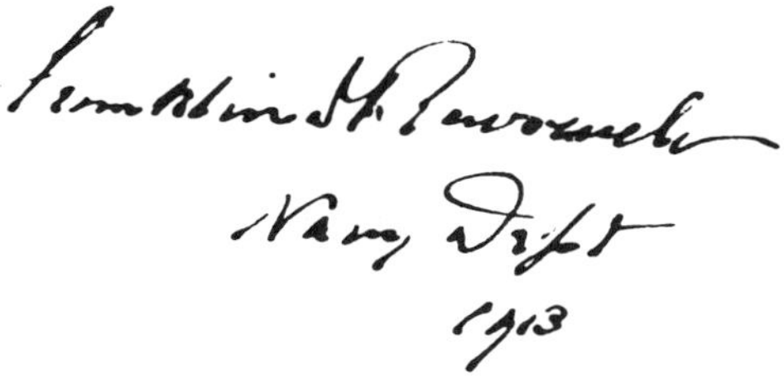

Franklin D. Roosevelt
Navy Dept
1913

g

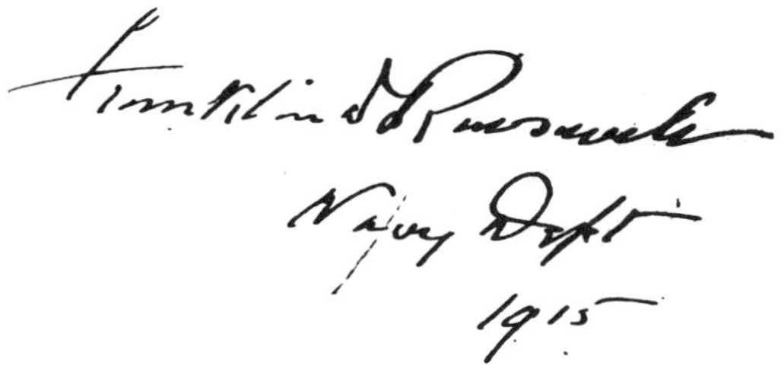

Franklin D Roosevelt
Navy Dept
1915

h

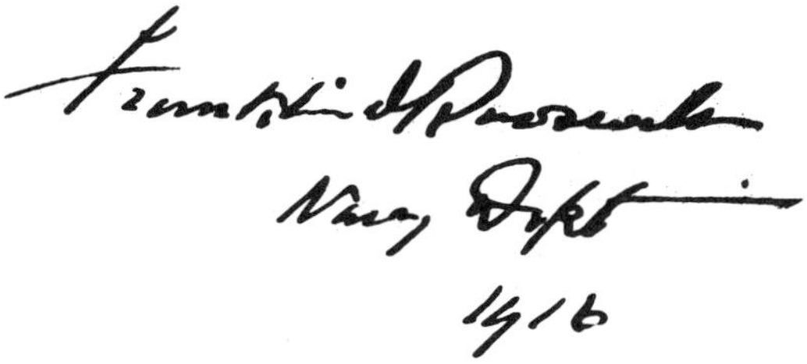

Franklin D Roosevelt
Navy Dept
1916

i

Franklin D Roosevelt
1920

FIG. 130.—Continued.

would have ended. Taking the length between beginning and end of "D. Roosevelt," written in 1895 (c), as a measure-unit, the same length appears in 13 out of 16 signatures, 3 being discarded because they either do not show the last name (a) or because the movement is cut by the

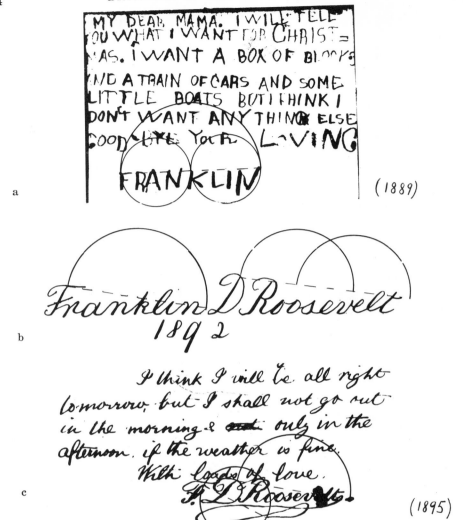

a

(1889)

b

c

(1895)

FIG. 130A.—Consistency of movement over a person's life period.

book margin (b, d). This length appears with the name "D. Roosevelt" in 7 cases (c, e, h, m, n, o, p); with the name "Roosevelt" in 4 cases (f, g, i, l); and in 2 cases (k, q) the length includes the distance from the end of the first name to the end of the last name. Thus, the consistencies appear in a large majority of cases, but they are subjected to certain variations within the units of the signature. The *same* unit of movement concerning the first name appears with 20 signatures in 13 cases (d, e, f, g, h, i, k, l, m, n, o, p, q), or in 65 per cent of the cases. The same unit of movement concerning the last name "D. Roosevelt" appears in 7 out of 16 cases, or in 44 per cent of the cases; and, if admitting the variation of using for measurement the last name "Roosevelt" exclusively, in 11

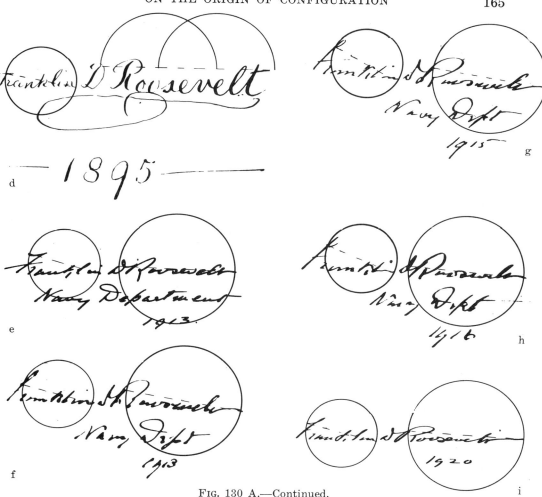

FIG. 130 A.—Continued.

cases, or 69 per cent of the cases. Hence, a unit of movement manifested at an early age may reappear frequently throughout a person's lifetime.

Since units of movement and configurations appear as early as in infancy, and since these movements are carried over from childhood to adult life without changing in spite of continuously new experiences, we suppose that the configuration is not conditioned by experience but is an innate pattern.

THE DEGREE OF CONFIGURATION

Although everybody seems to possess the capacity of configuration, just as normal man possesses intelligence, the degree of this as of other capacities is different in various individuals. If we attempt to measure the individual degree of configuration, we have to establish a standard test as it was done for the measurement of intelligence. The signature may serve as one standard, but it is relative since everybody has a different

k

n

l

o

m

p

We pray now to Him for the vision to see our way

clearly -- to see the way that leads to a better life

for ourselves and for all our fellow men -- to the

achievement of His will to peace on earth.

q

FIG. 130 A.—Continued.

configuration of letters. A standardized sentence cannot be international-ized for different languages, and neutral words are not apt to evoke the inner participation of the writer which seems to be necessary for obtain-ing natural movements. On the basis of the observation that the same law of configuration appears in any graphic movement, whether it is a signature, a scribbling, or a drawing, we used the drawing of a man as an item to be standardized.

A statistical standardization is not yet completed. The average ap-pearance of proportions between features in the drawing of a man can easily be standardized. We distinguish three kinds of proportions covering length and position of graphic elements:

I. Figural Proportions.

The lengths of head, trunk, legs and arms are measured, investigating whether each of these single parts is a simple multiple of the smallest unit.

II. Featural Proportions.

The relative positions of features, such as dots for the eyes and nose, strokes for the mouth and ears, and the limbs of features, such as the ends of the arms and feet, are measured in their proportional distance re-lationship.

III. Accessory Proportions.

Taking the very basic elements in the drawing of a man as a standard of measurement, additional features such as hair, buttons, hats, and shoes are considered as accessory elements; what is considered as accessory depends on the age group investigated. The evaluation of the degree of proportions is twofold. We distinguish an "objective" degree in taking as a norm the average number of proportions for a certain age group from a "subjective" degree in taking as a frame of reference the number of graphic elements in the drawing of each individual. The quotient of pro-portions can be found by dividing the number of average proportions in an age group by the number of individual proportions. This gives us the "Objective Rhythmical Quotient," which we call O.R.Q. Combining further the number of graphic elements in each drawing and dividing it by the number of proportions observed, we obtain the "Subjective Rhythmical Quotient," or S.R.Q.

A comparison between the Rhythmical Quotient (R.Q.) and the In-telligence Quotient (I.Q.) may give us some indication of the relationship between a person's conscious and unconscious organization. Examples of this procedure for nursery school children are given in the author's book, *The Personality of the Preschool Child* [467].

Configuration in Drawings of Preschool Children

Our observations up to now suggest that the Rhythmical Quotient is in no positive relationship either to the intelligence or to the health of an individual [467]. On the contrary, the unconscious organization frequently increases when conscious controls are lowered. However, a strong discrepancy between I.Q. and R.Q. seems to be significant. If the I.Q. is far above the R.Q., the unconscious emotional organization seems to be handicapped; if the R.Q. is far above the I.Q., the mental capacities seem not to have reached their potentiality of development.

We give as examples a few drawings of young children, taken from F. Goodenough's book, *Measurement of Intelligence by Drawings*, to which we have referred elsewhere [467] in greater detail (Figs. 131, 132). The indication of a relationship between the degree of configuration and

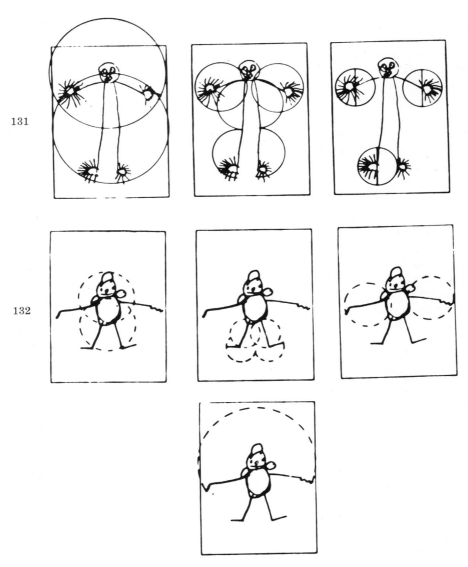

131

132

FIGS. 131-132.—Configuration in drawings of preschool children.

the development of the personality suggests that the origin of configuration depends on the relationship between innate structure, environmental limitations and the development of personality in relationship to the interacting forces.

CONFIGURATION, INTUITION AND INSIGHT

Our examples of configuration were not produced by means of a calculating intelligence, by premeditation, or by deduction; the writer made just the right length for his main strokes and put each into just the right position. The writer *intuitively* did the right thing, if the right thing for a movement is the same as it is for other psychological manifestations, namely, the integration of elements into a whole. Intuition is a preconscious process, frequently described by philosophers as a faculty for grasping the essentials, the "truth" of reality (cf. Fichte, Schelling). Some philosophers consider this arranging and penetrating faculty of intuition as inherent in man's psychic structure. Some modern philosophers identify intuition with feelings which, opposed to logic and science, penetrate reality (Bergson) and which find their highest expression in art (Croce). We shall undertake elsewhere an analysis of intuition, but in the present context we wish to point out that the main characteristic of intuition is the ability to establish relationships *immediately,* without premeditation; it is the capacity for spontaneous configuration. Psychologists use the word "insight" for describing this process of creative thinking. The main characteristic of insight is that processes which would demand a long time by intellectual operation are accomplished in an instant. Insight in perception allows one to see immediately main characteristics which by an intellectual procedure would be obtained only by a complicated deduction. A similar process in expression allows one to produce instantly organized patterns. If a writer is able to produce instantly a complicated mathematical proportion in his graphic movement, he would be obliged intellectually—if at all able to do it—to use instruments and to spend much time with the construction. Processes of insight overcome the obstacles of space. This phenomenon is characteristic of perception and of expression. Calculations do not allow us to conceive different space relations and their interrelationships at a glance, but demand the forming of space relations successively. Insight produces a simultaneous perception and expression of spatial relationships. Hence, a characteristic phenomenon of insight in expression and perception is the different reaction to the laws of time and space.

In order to study the ability to perceive and inter-relate patterns at a glance, the author made the following experiment with fifteen subjects, students of Columbia University in the Guidance Laboratory of Teachers College.* Each subject, in a single experiment, was seated before a tachistoscope and was to perceive objects which were exposed by a camera shutter at rapidities of 1 second to 1/300 of a second. Some days before

_____

*Cf., 466, pp. 124-130.

starting this experiment on perception, the subject had to fill out a card, writing two lines: (1) "Teachers College, Columbia University"; (2) his own signature. The experimenter separated the text of the first line, which was the same for all subjects, from their signatures, and in the actual experiment he gave each subject the first lines of three persons and, separately, the signatures of these three persons, one specimen at a time. Among these three specimens of the text and among the three specimens of the signatures were his own. Now he was instructed to tell what he perceived and asked to give a judgment about its expressive value. All of our subjects were able to do so. A preliminary exposure of a writing, not used for the experimental evaluation, served to demonstrate the procedure, and, further, the speed with which the subject was able to perceive the object was standardized. The maximum speed used for perception and characterization was different with different subjects. With the same subject the speed was in a majority of cases stable for different writings exposed on the same day. Repeating the experiment with the same subject and the same specimen exposed, it was found that the speed remains consistent only for each experiment, and not for the different experimental series. In a majority of cases the speed increased in successive experimental series.

For our present purpose it is only significant that 40 per cent of our subjects were able to perceive and to characterize the expressive values of a writing by exposures of $1/200$-$1/300$ of a second; but even with lower speeds of $\frac{1}{3}$ of a second, the subjects were not able to grasp single features or to read the words. Thus the ability to judge an expression remained when perception was limited. We present an example of a subject's perceiving and characterizing the writings of another person (speed $1/200$ of a second):

> I can't read the words but I see a clear, very distinct writing; not bold; fine pen; belongs probably to a person who has achieved something; feels secure; positive sort of writing.

Exposing the subject's own writing, it was observed that in most of the cases the subject did not recognize his own text and in some cases not even his signature; but in spite of his lack of identification, he was fully able to characterize his own writing, though unaware that it was his own. We give an example of the same subject just referred to:

Text:
(Speed had to be decreased to $\frac{1}{3}$ of a second)

> Calling card; cannot describe the writing; very tiny writing; very delicate; not very bold; very perfect and nice, like Arabic writing.

Signature:
(Speed $1/200$ of a second)

> Very long line of writing; it does not look like Latinized script; like Arabic script; strokes from top to bottom are more distinct than the other ones; intelligent; fine; sympathetic; makes me curious who it is.

The writing of the same subject was judged by others:

> (a) Very fine handwriting; backhand, slanting to the right; not distinguished, not attractive.
> (b) Fluently; intelligent but not so sympathetic.

In the self-characterization some main features are diagnosed in spite of an absence of self-recognition. Here we had the opportunity to verify the significance of the judgment. Later on when asked what "Arabic" meant to her, our subject said:

> I do not like our usual Latinized script; I have been in the East, I think very often of that time. For the last years my concern is more with the Mohammedan world than with our civilization. My emotions are with the Arabs. I have been there three times, and I am thinking of going back to the East.

Thus we may conclude that during a rapid exposure of graphic expression, where the subject is not able to recognize the words or even the letters and is not able to identify his own handwriting, he is, notwithstanding, able to grasp instantly characteristic expressive features. Hence it was demonstrated that an extreme reduction of the time factor does not affect the process of insight in perception.

Not only complicated relationships of perception but also those of expression are made in a flash. In the act of insight the individual seems to jump over the usual determination by time, and, as in a dream, an instant has the characteristics of long duration. Thus, one factor of configuration seems to be insight and intuition, which we admire in artists and inventors, but which, as we could demonstrate, is a property not only of genius but of everybody. The genius, however, makes use of his potential configuration, transferring it from the unconscious into the realm of consciousness.

As already mentioned, the configurative principle, which leads the graphic movement in its three dimensions, determines the position of graphic elements in its relations to space and time. If we draw a geometrical figure, showing simple proportions, we must first establish a unit and then measure each additional element in relation to the unit. This measurement follows successively: we establish element "a," then element "b," and so forth. We are not able by conscious calculation to establish complicated relationships of elements simultaneously. With the unconscious configuration of graphic movements, however, such a simultaneous configuration takes place. When the starting-stroke is a simple proportion of the end-stroke, we must have anticipated the structure of the latter, when making the former stroke. Our *future* intention must be operative in a present act. As graphic movements show the degree of consistency which we found, so that, for instance, the starting-stroke is equal to or a simple proportion of the corresponding movement made months or even years before, we must have retained the structure of the previous stroke when making the present one. Our *past* accomplishment must be operative in the present act. Thus, in explaining the con-

sistency of graphic movement, which in a present movement bears relationships to past and future, we may say that in the configurative principle
factors of past, present, and future are united. As rays are united in a
prism and spread out in their projection upon a surface, we may imagine
that the dimensional differentiation does not appear in the origin but only
in the projection of our expressions. While our conscious construction
is accomplished by successive steps, our unconscious configuration is accomplished by simultaneous acts—a sort of bird's-eye view as against our
partial one. Thus we might compare the configurative principle with a
factor acting behind the scene of the dimensions of space and time. The
configurative principle is like a pivot around which the elements are moved,
but it is not possible to visualize this pivot itself. The structure of the
organism seems to prevent our entering behind the scene.

Configuration and Brain Processes

The phenomenon of configuration has more and more become the
basic problem for all sciences; it seems to be the phenomenon in which
the most different manifestations of nature have a common root. The
manifest and the latent configuration of the forces of nature is the basic
problem of physics, chemistry, and biology, of all the natural sciences
which aim to detect causes and to predict effects. For the social sciences,
as well, configuration is the basic object of investigation. Sociology and
economics study the configurational forces of the environment; anthropology tries to reconstruct configurational patterns of culture; philosophy
and religion offer hypotheses to interpret the world from a configurational aspect. Now, the most different psychological schools, indepen-
dently of each other, have discovered the problem of configuration. Gestalt
theory found it in the phenomena of perception, psycho-analysis in the
manifestations of unconscious organization, the study of personality in
the patterns of expressive movements.

The phenomenon of configuration has deep implications for all matters of psychological approach. If each single element derives its value
only from the configuration of which it forms a part, the validity of
measuring single functions, detached from their context, is limited in
usefulness. All tests which measure single traits, such as intelligence, or
single aptitudes, neglect the configuration of the individual; and all statistics, based solely upon number of occurrences, neglect the configuration
of environment. The problem of configuration also determines the use of
terms in defining psychological data, because each term gets its validity
from related phenomena. Configuration modifies our view of the organism, in which psychological phenomena no longer can be separated wholly
from biological ones, since every human manifestation seems to be a
psychosomatic pattern, in which what we call psyche influences bodily
reactions, and vice versa.

The concept of configuration has certain consequences for a theory
of brain mechanism. Personality was formerly considered as the summation of millions of independent specific habits which have their origin

in millions of corresponding brain processes. E. L. Thorndike states [417, p. 248]:

> Training the mind means the development of thousands of particular *independent capacities*, the formation of countless particular habits. . . .

But Thorndike also states:

> Improvement in any one mental function or activity will improve others only in so far as they possess elements common to it also.

Thorndike's assumption of partly identical elements, originating in "the same cell action in the brain," is categorically rejected by Lashley, who says [232, p. 172]:

> There is no evidence to support this belief in the identity of nervous elements. On the contrary, it is doubtful if the same neurons or synapses are involved even in two similar reactions to the same stimulus.*

These two views on the brain organization involve two main problems concerning the structure of personality:

1. Do personality traits correspond to brain activities independent of each other, or does interrelationship of personality traits exist, suggesting interrelationship of brain processes?

2. Do different expressive movements of a person show identical elements which lead us to suppose an identity of nervous elements? Or do all expressive movements of a person, differing from each other, lead to belief in innumerable independent brain processes?

The expression of movements on paper in the graphic patterns of writing and drawing allowed us to show diagrams of unconscious activities and to demonstrate their hidden patterns of configuration. If these diagrams reflect personality, which is indicated by their relationship to psychological changes, we are inclined to assume that those inner-psychological processes which we call personality follow unified configurational patterns. These patterns being an organization and interrelationship of many elements, it would seem that corresponding brain processes do not work in isolation from each other. The assumption of independent capacities becomes improbable. On the other hand, a certain identity of nervous elements is suggested. Future investigations may indicate whether the graphic formulas of configuration correspond to definite formulas of personality patterns. But even if we became able to give a real diagram of the unconscious, illuminating the total personality, we cannot hope to make definite predictions. For, supposing that the individual follows his formula and the environment follows its own, it is the unpredictable interrelationship of both forces which is reflected in the diagram of the unconscious.

Configuration and Balance

The determination of graphic movement became manifest in the phenomenon of balance, which demands that length and position of strokes be distributed as if premeditated in order to obtain an equilibrium.

---

*K. S. Lashley: "Brain Mechanism and Intelligence." Chicago, University of Chicago Press, 1929.

Balance is known physiologically; each step in walking seems premeditated, so that we do not fall. Here balance has a very practical
reason and our regulating tendency might have been developed by the
constant unconscious stimulus: "Keep balance, otherwise you will fall
down." Such a stimulus does not seem to be evident in graphic expression,
and while we are aware of the existence of such balance in the movement
of walking, we are not aware of the corresponding phenomenon in the
movement of writing. Observations of gestalt psychologists [214] indicate that our perception is directed by a tendency to perceive symmetrical
and balanced patterns. O. B. Cannon* emphasized for the body as a whole
the principle of balance, of the best possible equilibrium, a phenomenon
which he described as physiological homeostasis.

With the unconscious configuration of movements into "figures,"
which become visible in graphic expression, the "figures of perception"
have their correlate in "figures of expression." In both cases different
stimuli are brought into a fixed relationship to each other like spread
iron filings by a magnet. The supposition that electrical energies are
the basis of organic and inorganic matter makes a comparison of "psychic
figures" with magnetic and electric figures** and sound figures*** more
than a metaphorical approach. Just as magnetic force, electric force, and
sound waves form symmetrical figures, so our psychic figures seem to be
determined by proportion and configuration. The configurating principle
which appears in the inorganic world (in crystallization, etc.) as well as in
the organic world (e.g., integration and interrelationships of functions in
the organism) seems to be rooted in basic processes of matter and, ulti-
mately, of energy. Personality, as part of the living organism, which
itself is part of nature, is a receiver and transformer of energy.

At the basis of nervous processes lies the nervous current. The
nervous current is an energy and, as brain waves indicate, is related to
electrical processes. Thus we might consider the psychic figures as corresponding to a magnetic or electric field, in which the expressive movements of personality are configurated like iron filings. If, on the other
hand, the configurational principles of expression were determined by
psychological factors, we might bring it into relationship to man's fundamental drive toward stability, security and balance which each self realizes
according to his "individual proportions." The configurational principle in
expressive behavior may reflect the probable basic manifestation of personality: the balance of self.

---

*The Wisdom of the Body. New York, Norton, 1932.
**The so-called "Lichtenberg's Figures," which are formed by sprinkling a
dielectric surface with some powdered substance after having brought it in contact
with a charged body.
***The so-called "Chladni's Figures," which are formed by sand settling upon the
nodal lines of metallic plates, when the latter are made to vibrate by a violin-bow.

PART II

EXPRESSION AND MOVEMENT

CHAPTER VIII

UNITY OF EXPRESSIVENESS

The first part of our investigation has indicated that the form of graphic patterns cannot be explained by environmental conditions influencing the act of writing, such as quality of paper and pen, position and circumstances of writing. The form of graphic patterns can not be considered only a product of learning and of cultural stereotypes, because graphic forms determine each other in a unique configuration, characteristic of the individual. We have demonstrated by measurements that size, form and position of graphic patterns originate neither in chance nor in conscious intention, but that they reflect unconscious principles of organization. Thus, graphic movements are "diagrams of the unconscious." Since these unconscious patterns are modified by psychosomatic changes of the organism, such as elations, depressions, and seizures, graphic movements are evidenced as a reflection of psychosomatic processes.

Having established a scientific basis for a positive relationship between graphic movement and processes which involve that psychological factor which we call "personality," we are prepared for the next step of our investigation, namely, to search systematically for definite indicators of personality, so that graphic movements can be used as a diagnostic tool.

Personality does not only become manifest in certain form-principles. If a certain facial pattern of several people indicates that they are happy and another facial pattern that they are sad, the same forms may have a different expressive value for each individual. Although the emotions of different people may have the same basic form, their degree and their structure is so manifold as to produce a great variety of expressions of personality. Each movement pattern consists of form and expression. We first dealt with the principles of form and are now concerned with the principles of expression. Expression has no spatial dimensions allowing measurements similar to those of forms. Expression involves a discharge of emotional and mental phenomena and for their investigation we must know how a majority of people express themselves and how the individual modifies the general expressive principle. This modification may be revealed by mental processes which accompany the act of expression, by the individual's associations.

For an investigation of expression we designed experiments involving the principles of stimulus-response and association. A series of experiments was destined to give general results concerning four basic problems: those of individual expressiveness, of collectively analogous expressiveness, of the origin of expressiveness, and of the various manifestations of expressiveness. The experiments were made with 20 female students in the Department of Psychology at Vassar College in 1941-42 and with 20 male students in the Department of Psychology at Bard College in 1943-44. Some single experiments had been conducted by the author in the Psychological Institute of the University of Berlin in 1930-32, some in the Psychological Institute of the University of Barcelona in 1933-1935, as well as some in mental hospitals near Berlin and Barcelona. The experiments were carried out with each subject alone in several sessions, separated from each other by an interval of half a week or a week. The experimenter introduced the experimental series with the following remarks: "We are making experiments concerned with expressive movements as they appear graphically. We only search for general trends; problems of the individual personality such as might be revealed through any kind of handwriting diagnosis are completely excluded."

In the following we give the results of the Vassar experiments; those made in other institutions were not fundamentally of such difference as to warrant their presentation. Our first experiment dealt with the question: *Is the expressiveness of handwriting an individual one?* Perhaps graphic features are simply a reflection of an individual's habits acquired through imitation, learning, and training. If so, the individual would not express himself but copy some pattern set by the school or by chance. If, on the other hand, graphic movements of the same person exhibit persistent features in his various ways of writing, even in an attempt to disguise his own writing, these persistent features can be considered as personal characteristics. Each subject received the following instructions: "Write the words 'The United States of America' in your ordinary handwriting; then in printed capital letters; and then try to disguise your handwriting." This experiment was continued in the second session, where each subject was given the handwriting samples, "The United States of America," written in triple form (normal writing, printed capitals, and disguised writing) by three other subjects. Now the subject received the following instructions:

> We will start today by making some experiments in judging graphic movements. The specimens are made by students; some of the handwritings may be known to you. If you recognize a handwriting please let me know immediately.
>
> (a) Here you see the words "The United States of America" written in the usual way, written entirely with printed capital letters, and written in a disguised way. From these nine specimens try to match those which are made by the same writer.
>
> (b) Try to distinguish between the original writing and the disguised writing.

Results (Fig. 133):

(a) The subjects made correct matchings of unrecognized handwriting specimens in 83 per cent of the cases.

(b) The subjects succeeded in distinguishing the original writings from the disguised ones in 70 per cent of the cases.

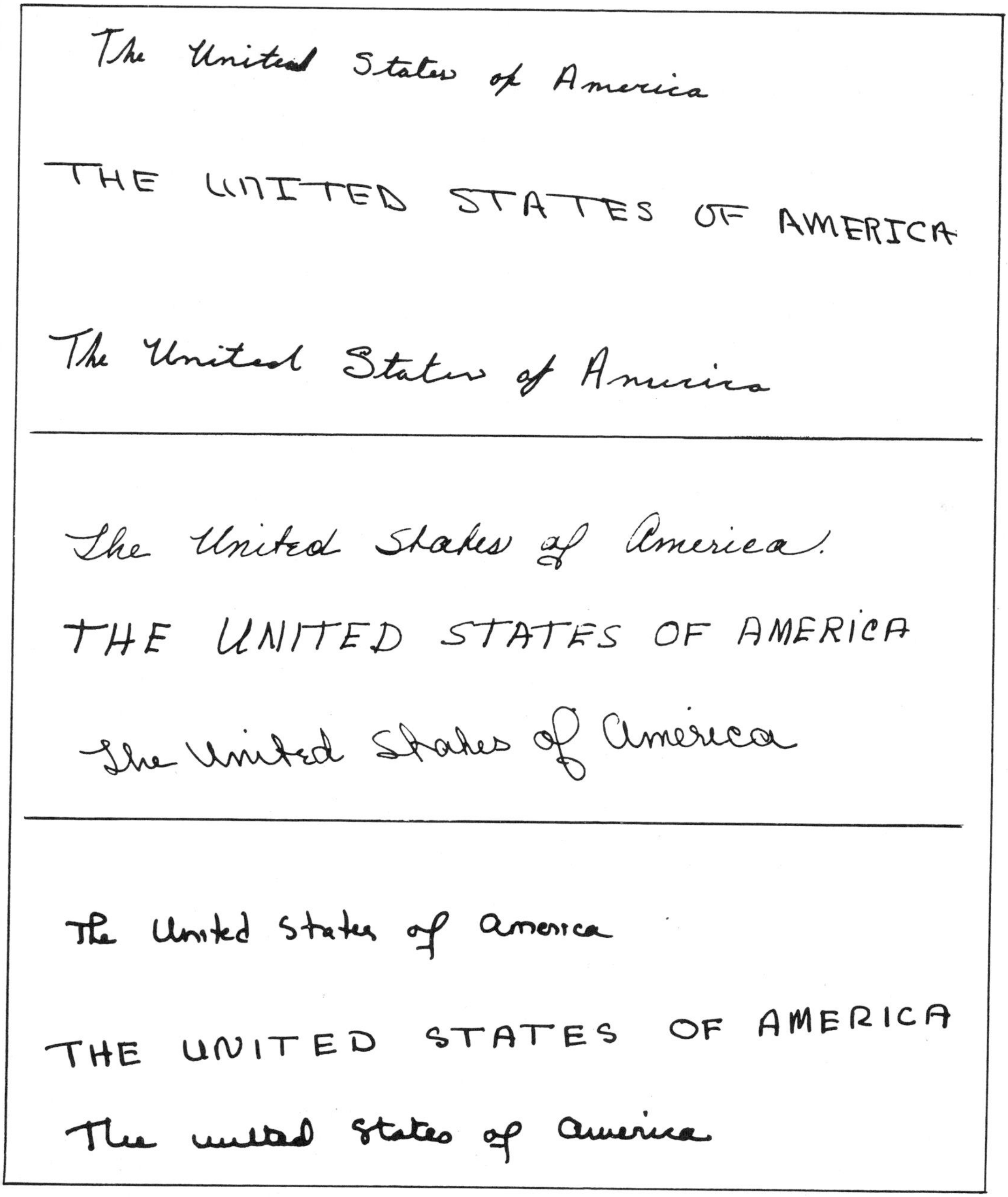

FIG. 133.—Unity of expression in different ways of writing.

These results suggest an affirmative answer to our first question: Do graphic movements reveal a personal expression at all? The high percentage of correct matchings indicates that graphic movements, in whatever form they are made, have an individual pattern which allows the layman to recognize the individual basis in different appearances. The high percentage of successful distinction between original writing and disguised writing seems to indicate that graphic movements have a uniformity of individual pattern which is distorted in the disguised sample. However, there seem to be different degrees in the expression of personal characteristics, and the untrained observer is not always able to distinguish them.

ANALOGY OF EXPRESSION

The following question deals with what we call "analogy." This means: *Do different people have a similar or analogous concept of expressive principles?* Although the preceding experiment indicates that graphic movements show the expression of an individual characteristic, we would be able to diagnose personality from graphic movements only if different people have certain similar concepts of expression.

In this series of experiments the subject received the following instructions:

> Write the letter "g" the way that you imagine a very *aggressive* person might do it. Then write the letter "g" the way a *submissive* person might do it. And then write the letter "g" the way an *unstable* person might do it.

The same instructions followed for the letter "f."

In the second session the writings of the letter "g" done by three other persons were shuffled, and these nine specimens were presented to the subject. The instructions were:

> Here you have the letter "g," upon which three persons tried to project their ideas of aggression, submission, and instability. Try to match the letters written by the same person, and try to indicate which represent aggression, which submission, and which instability (Fig. 134).

The subjects recognized the graphic expression of aggression, submission, and instability as expressed in the letter "g" in 81.6 per cent of the cases, and in the letter "f" in 79.6 per cent of the cases. When we analyzed the errors we found that the concept "aggression" was correctly matched with the corresponding letter in all but one case. The errors referred to a confusion between the concepts of "submission" and "instability."

Our experiment indicates that there is a commonly accepted convention for certain graphic characteristics such as the expression of aggression and submission. However, we cannot follow from this artificial experimental condition that a layman would be able to interpret a natural handwriting equally well. In the early work in the expression of emotions, when an actor posed for certain emotional expressions such as "mirth," "disgust," and "fear," subjects succeeded quite well in identifying these staged emotions; but when they were shown pictures of real unposed emotions, identification decreased considerably. For our purpose, however, the ability to express emotions by letters indicates that

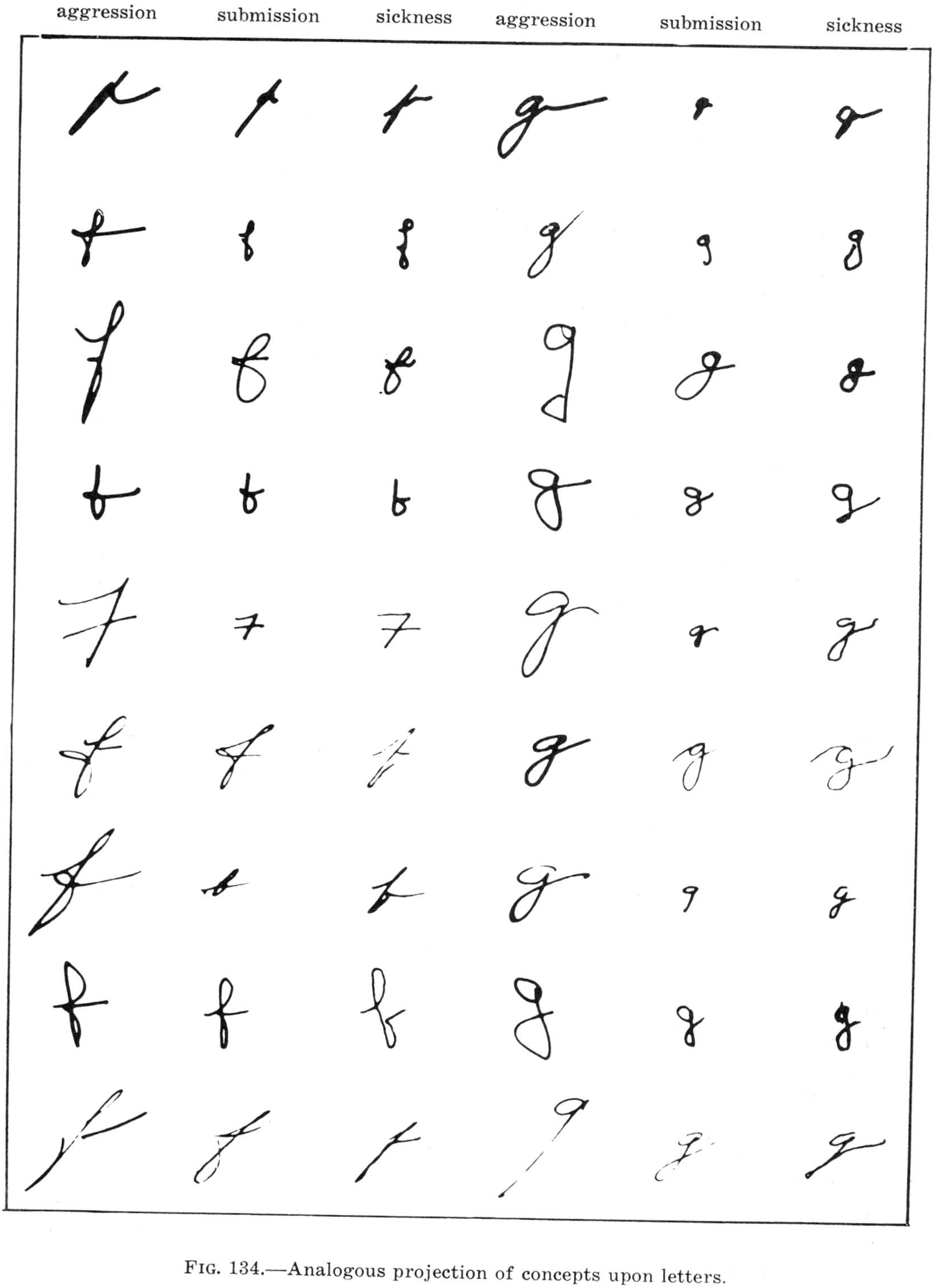

aggression	submission	sickness	aggression	submission	sickness

FIG. 134.—Analogous projection of concepts upon letters.

graphic movement may be expressive of certain emotions and associations, and that agreement exists to represent certain emotions graphically in a certain way.

FAMILIARITY OF EXPRESSION

Our two observations are somewhat contradictory. The first suggests that handwriting reflects a personal expression, different for everybody but consistent in the same individual. The second observation indicates that handwriting may reflect concepts with which many people are familiar. If familiarity is such an important point an individual could adopt at will each form of expression, and thus a supposed expressiveness would not necessarily be genuine but might be a copy of familiar patterns. We thus come to the question of the origin of expressiveness. The first thesis—that factors of learning, training, and familiarity may play a decisive part in an individual writing—had to be tested. If a person is so aware of other people's expressive movements that he is able to imitate single features, he must be especially aware of his own patterns, which he has the frequent opportunity to see and study; thus, confronted with his own letters and words, he should recognize them immediately.

In order to decide this question our subjects were given their own letters "f" mixed with those of three other writers. We used the letters "f" written with the expressions of aggression, submission, and instability, and the subject was asked to match the twelve specimens to four writers. One's own letter was not recognized in 64 per cent of the cases. Hence, familiarity with one's own form of writing seems to be rather low. One example illustrates that even the suspicion of finding one's own specimen among the letters need not increase ability to recognize. One subject said: "I suspect that one series of these letters is my own." When the experimenter asked: "Which letters do you suppose to be your own?" the subject pointed to letters made by another person.

Another experiment of self-recognition of one's own writing had a similar result. If the factors of familiarity, training, and learning were very important we should recognize our writing even if it were slightly distorted. We asked a subject to write the name "New York" on a slip of paper; then the paper was folded so as to make a blotted mirror image. In the next session the subject was given three such writings, one of them his own, two of two other persons. These inkblot images, in which the name "New York" could be clearly recognized, were presented in such a way that "New York" appeared in a vertical position, the letter "N" on top. The subject received the following instructions:

> Here you see three inkblot pictures. Please tell me which one you like best, which least, and which one takes the middle position; state the reason for your scaling (Fig. 135).

The subjects did not recognize their own writings in 85 per cent of the cases. The experiment was repeated with the same inkblots, and in the second series a lack of self-recognition appeared in 60 per cent of the cases. From these observations we might conclude that the factor of familiarity is not decisive for the judgment of graphic expression. This, however, would be a premature conclusion. Remembering our postulate that each observation gets its significance only from several observations to which it is related, we investigated the emotional attitudes the subject had to the expressiveness of his own unrecognized specimen, to that of his own recognized specimen, and to that of the specimens of other people. A lack of familiarity with one's own expressiveness of writing would cause chance distribution of preferences. Thus, asking the subject

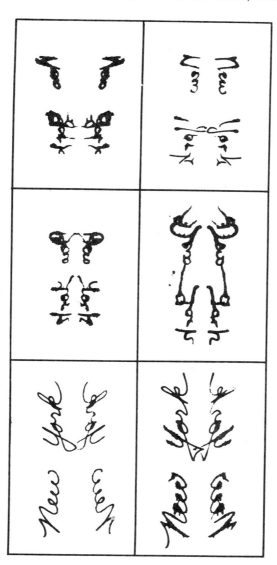

FIG. 135.—An experiment of familiarity with one's own handwriting.

to scale the writings according to his preference, a statistical expectation would be that preferences—likes, and dislikes—would appear in equal proportion for one's own handwriting (recognized and unrecognized) and for that of other people. Such a probability distribution, however, did not occur.

We compare how the subjects scaled their own specimen in the case of self-recognition and of non-recognition (Table 11).

TABLE 11

Place of preference of one's own graphic specimen in per cent:

	Cases of self-recognition	Cases of non-recognition
First Place	0	58.8
Middle place	66.0	11.7
Last place	34.0	29.5

In the case of nonrecognition, where the majority of subjects put their own writing in the first place, they gave as reasons for their preference that this specimen was smoother, clearer, and simpler. One's own writing seems to have a special appeal to one's unconscious. In the case of recognition when the subject's own specimen was never preferred, modesty seems to have inhibited this appeal.

The present author studied, in other experiments described elsewhere [466], a subject's reaction toward his own writing presented under conditions not experienced before. The experimenter showed the subject's own handwriting and specimens of other persons in a mirror, and he got more emotional response to the subject's own unrecognized pattern than to those of other persons. The same thing happened if the subject's own handwriting (not mirrored) was shown in a tachistocope, an apparatus which exposes the object for a split second. It was found that one's own handwriting was harder to recognize than that of other persons, and again that one's own unrecognized pattern evokes a higher emotional response than the writing of other persons (see p. 170 ff.).

Thus, lack of recognition does not solve the problem of familiarity. The lack of recognition, linked up with the high evaluation of one's own pattern, either raises the question of familiarity in the unconscious, as if we were familiar with and attracted by our own pattern but didn't remember it consciously; or the lack of recognition is based upon an unconscious resistance against identification. We shall not dwell here on interpretations of these phenomena, which we have discussed elsewhere [466]. In any case, it appears that a supposed factor of familiarity does not work consciously, but that if it is present it implies unconscious roots of expressiveness.

THE COMMON DENOMINATOR OF EXPRESSION

The factor of familiarity can also be attacked from another point of view. If our expressiveness in handwriting is a copy of expressions by other people we have been familiar with, our expressiveness in other manifestations, such as the voice, gesture, gait, should similarly be a copy of familiar expressions. Since our experiences and associations related to our development of speech are different from those which influenced our gestures or gait and different from those which had a bearing upon our handwriting, the expressiveness of our various media of expression should be completely different, without any relationship to each other. If, on the other hand, an individual's basic expression is equally apparent in various manifestations, we must conclude that the expressiveness is not only patterned by learning, training, and familiarity, but that it has its origin in the unique personal pattern, called individuality. This individuality would be impressed upon whatever medium a person expresses himself.

The experiments with which we shall deal in the following did not form part of the Vassar series, the description of which we interrupt for a moment for methodological reasons. The experiments were carried out in the Psychological Laboratory of the University of Berlin and are described elsewhere [466] in detail. Allport and Vernon [7] report results of various experiments in terms of the coefficient of contingency. Our procedure was based upon the matching technique, introduced by Arnheim [13] and by the present author [460, 461, 466] and developed by several students of personality [7, 331, 416, 432, 433, 434]. We presented our subjects with six samples of expression for instance, three voices recorded on disks and three handwriting specimens of the same persons. The instruction was to match handwriting and voice of the same person. The chance expectancy for correct matchings would be one out of three; the number of correct matchings obtained in our experiments was from one and a half to twice the chance numbers.

In another experiment styles in retelling a story and specimens of handwriting had to be matched. A number of persons had to retell a story that was first read to them. Each version was then typewritten, and the three versions and three handwritings were presented to the subject. The number of correct matchings was one and one half times greater than might be expected if chance had operated.

Another experiment was made in presenting a moving picture of walking persons and their handwriting. The gait was filmed while each of these subjects performed the same task. Each of them wore the same clothing (a ski suit), and their faces were not visible in the movie. The matching of gait and handwriting was successful in double the number of cases that chance would allow.

Actually, graphic movement and gait have one common denominator, that of movement. A sure or timid, harmonious or tense, expanding or contracting movement could be recognized in both forms of expression. When a person's outer movements are similar in his various forms of expression, each of which is based upon different factors of learning and training, we must conclude that the outer movements are reflections of what we might call the inner movements of personality. Some cases show us such a reflection directly. One of my subjects started each task very timidly, but during her action she became more and more confident and displayed increasingly an aggressive decisiveness. After the accomplishment, however, she was exhausted to the point of a breakdown. The gait of this subject had similar characteristics; in the beginning she walked hesitantly, but increasingly her movements became tense and straightforward until she almost ran to the goal. This walking movement had

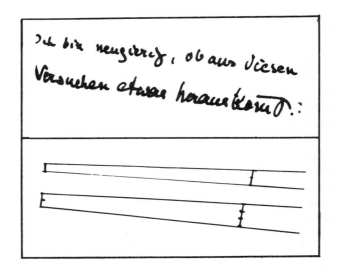

FIG. 136.—Gait and graphic movement.

its correspondence in her handwriting (Fig. 136). The subject was asked to write the following sentence in German: "Ich bin neugierig, ob aus diesen Versuchen etwas heraus kommt." (I wonder whether these experiments will yield any results). The subject wrote the sentence in two lines, and it was characteristic that the writing started with letters of very small size, which, however, gradually increased. If we draw a line through the extreme upper and lower points of the letters, we get two lines which increase proportionally in the same way, like rays of a projector. The projection of this increasing dimension becomes especially apparent through the fact that this movement continues similarly in the second line. Thus at the end the height of the first letter is triple that of the first. The bar of the "t" emphasizes this movement, but its sinking end indicates that this exaggerated movement breaks down at the end. Each movement pattern of this subject showed the same characteristics: a timid start, characterized by a contraction of movement, an increasing confidence, characterized by an increasing expansion of movement, and a final breakdown. This indicates that "inner movement of personality" is projected upon both the bodily and the graphic expressions. In this case projections of personality upon graphic movement could readily be recognized; in other cases it is more difficult, because the personality may not show such definite trends, or some people's personality may be more strongly expressed in the gait and others' more strongly in handwriting. A dancer is apt to be more expressive in the movements of his body, a writer more in his graphic movements. Each person seems to have certain preferred channels of expression. Thus we should not wonder that certain forms of expression may be revealing in some cases,

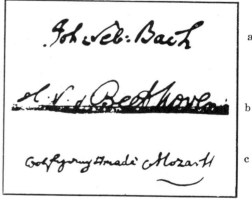

FIG. 137.—Matching of handwritings with musical notations and musical expression.

and not in others (see p. 249); that judges vary in their ability to interpret forms of expression, according to their degree of identification with certain media of expression; and that matchings of different forms of expression of the same person vary in their significance (see p. 185).

Since the layman usually does not have an opportunity to make matching experiments, we present the following two examples of matching experiments with graphic expressions. Almost everybody connects certain expressive characteristics with the music of Bach, Beethoven, and Mozart. We present specimens of the handwritten musical notations of the three composers and ask the reader to match the musical notations to the composers' handwritings (Fig. 137). Successful matchings indicate that two different forms of expression such as musical notation and handwriting have expressive traces in common. Such common graphic characteristics in different graphic forms also can be demonstrated by matching a person's handwriting with his doodlings.

One group of ten subjects received the handwriting specimens of three persons with instructions to describe their expressive qualities; another group of ten subjects got the doodlings of the same three persons for an analysis; and a third group got the judgments on the doodlings and the judgments on the handwriting with instructions to match the judgments belonging to each of the three persons. In 70 per cent of the cases these matchings were correct. Thus, the same expressive qualities were recognized by different observers on the basis of different graphic representations. The following are examples of judgments about the doodlings and handwritings of three persons, to whom we shall refer again later (Fig. 138).

Handwriting of Subject L (Fig. 138):
   "Nervous handwriting, restless, jolting, has the tendency to unite opposite trends; lonesome, uneven and aggressive, psychically in danger, neurotic."
Corresponding doodling (III):
   "Abrupt and cramped lines expressing fear, darkness, isolation and aggression; opposite tendencies, uneven."
Handwriting of Subject G:
   "The writing climbs slowly, sinking suddenly. This indicates a depressive nature, brooding and lonely; love of nature, tender and girlish."
Corresponding doodling (I):
   "Tender; musical, which is visible in the harmonious curves. The close forms seem to hint at a closed and lonesome personality."
Handwriting of Subject M:
   "Very rounded, very self-confident, but at the same time somewhat weak and broken, which is indicated by the spaces within the words. This weakness is compensated by an attempt at graphic composition; very young."
Corresponding doodling (II):
   "Childlike images, motifs of nature; attempts formation and exactness and avoidance of all abstract or mobile lines which derive from intrapersonal tendencies."

However, the successful matchings of two different graphic expressions of the same person such as doodlings and handwriting may be based upon similarities of graphic *forms* and not upon similarities of *expres-*

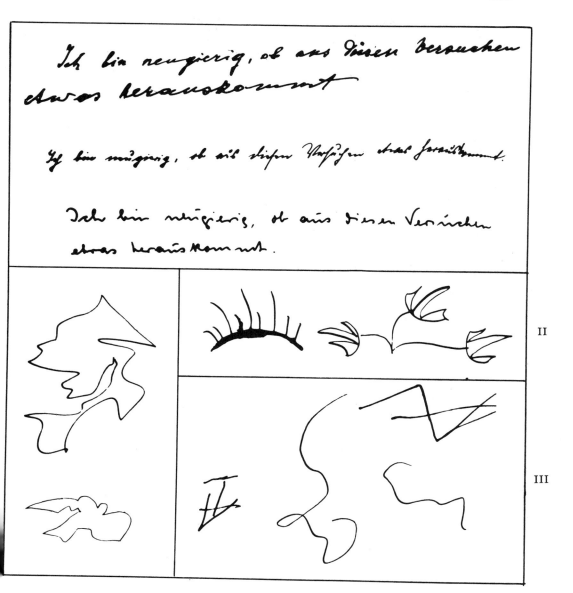

FIG. 138.—Handwriting and doodling.

sion. We must distinguish between the two. A similarity of form appears
for instance, if a subject has round movement patterns in his doodlings,
his musical notation, and the letters of his handwriting. A similarity of
expression may appear even if the forms used are completely different;
for instance, aggression may appear in the distorted forms of a doodling,
in a heavy pressure in musical notation, and in vehement strokes in handwriting. We know that the same expressive content—for instance, joy—

may be expressed by laughing, jumping, singing, and so forth. The expression of music may be similar to the graphic expression of the composer. We now ask the reader to match the composers to their notations on the basis of expressive characteristics attributable to the music of each of them.

Many readers will be surprised that their matching is correct namely, concerning the musical notations: I—Beethoven, II—Mozart, III —Bach, and concerning the handwriting samples: A—Bach, B—Beethoven, C—Mozart. We have obtained correct matchings in 80 per cent of the cases. Some of my subjects explained their matchings in the following way: "Bach's music is architectonic, and so are his musical notation and his handwriting. Beethoven is explosive and so too is his graphic expression. Mozart has balance and ease, and this is shown in his graphic forms."

Our results seem to answer the basic problem of graphic expression, namely, whether the expressive value is caused by outer factors such as training, choice of paper and pen, or by the inner factors of personality. They indicate that graphic expression is not only patterned by *some* factors of personality, but by the *unity of personality*. This observation leads us to the final question, the answer to which forms an essential part of the present work: What are these factors of expressiveness?

CHAPTER IX

EMPATHY AND PROJECTION

EMPATHY AND FORM

The word "expressiveness" is used with very different connotations. We may express our feelings by sounds such as cries of pain and of joy, by bodily and facial movements and gestures, by thoughts verbalized or unverbalized, and by our overt activities. The verbal-minded person may express his feelings in a poem, the color-minded in a painting, the movement-minded in a dance. But the transfer of expression need not be realized in artistic activities. Many an angry woman will express her feeling by scrubbing the floor in fury. We may submerge ourselves in work in order to forget our unhappiness, whereas a happy mood may stimulate us to decorate our room and to sing. Expressiveness may find a direct reflection in thought and movement and in indirect reflection in symbols. However, the structure of symbols may have different characteristics. If we are angry with a friend and break a glass in anger, we symbolize our feeling by a substitute object, breaking the glass instead of the friend. One characteristic of transfer of expressiveness is *symbolization*. If unhappy feelings stimulate us to remember the more beautiful past, perhaps our childhood, or to have daydreams of a wonderful future, we project our feelings backward or forward. If some persons invest all their energy and interests in collections of objects, they project their feelings upon them. Thus, another characteristic of transferring expressiveness is *projection*. Watching a fire, almost everybody feels some excitement; observing a race, we may feel our muscles move as if we were taking the place of the runner. Here the expression of the object evokes a corresponding expression in us. On the other hand, if we call a rainy day "a sad day," if we speak of a "lonely tree," we attribute human feelings to the object. In a similar way we may speak of running lines, resting forms, thus "feeling into" the things we perceive. According to the philosopher Theodor Lipps [253], aesthetic pleasure is a transfer of human feelings upon lines and forms, experiencing their narrowness, width, height, balance, as if we were in their place. Lipps and Titchener called this phenomenon "empathy," meaning "a feeling into" an object. *Empathy* is a third characteristic of expressiveness. If graphic movements are expressive movements, we may expect to find in them these three general characteristics of expressiveness: substitution, projection, and empathy.

If we ask persons to draw lines which express happiness and lines which express sadness, the majority of lines for happiness will point upward and the majority of lines for sadness will point downward. We give an updrawn mouth to a smiling face and a down-drawn mouth to a sad face. The words "elation" (going upward) and "depression" (sinking down) express a verbal empathy into movement patterns, which even the young child makes. Experiments [219, 259] show that many expressive words, such as "sad," "quiet," "lazy," "merry," and "agitating," are represented by a majority of people by characteristic lines and forms.

As the author has demonstrated, the capacity for graphic empathy starts at a very early age. The author presented three pieces of phonograph music to children in a nursery school. Each child was asked to draw how the music sounded. We played (1) a march, (2) a waltz, and (3) a cowboy song. Most of the children were able to express the musical impressions graphically. Although the kind of transposition depended on each child's individual association, certain characteristics were uniform. In a majority of cases the accentuated rhythm of the march was represented by accentuated angular lines, the swinging curves of the waltz were graphically expressed by an emphasis on curves, the cowboy song by patterns related to objects in nature.*

Our empathy works with a great number of concepts, and a simple experiment demonstrates not only that a majority of people are capable of empathy, but that their empathy is of the same nature. Usnadze [425a] in an experiment, presented two graphic forms and two nonsense syllables, asking his subjects to match the supposed names to the graphic forms. The present author enlarged this idea in the following experiment.

Two graphic forms were presented to the subject: one angular pattern, A, and one roundish pattern, B (Fig. 139). The instructions were to match A and B to the following concepts:

To words:	1. loll	2. tick
To music:	3. march	4. waltz
To colors:	5. blue	6. red
To tastes:	7. acid	8. sweet
To smells:	9. chloride	10. rose
To temperatures:	11. lukewarm	12. hot
To feelings:	13. aggression	14. love
To elements:	15. fire	16. water

Repeated with different groups of subjects (totalling 60 subjects), the matchings were on the average uniform in about 80 per cent of the cases, while we would expect 50 per cent according to chance. The greatest disagreement appeared with the matchings to 'music" and to "colors."

---

*Reported in detail in: [467].

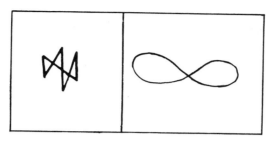

FIG. 139—Empathy in graphic forms.

The following concepts were matched most frequently to the angular Figure A and to the round figure B:

A	B
tick	loll
march	waltz
red	blue
acid	sweet
chloride	rose
hot	lukewarm
aggression	love
fire	water

The characteristic elements of pattern A are the verticals, angles, and points suggesting sharp and hard qualities, while the characteristic elements of pattern B are the horizontal position and the harmonious curves suggesting soft and balanced qualities. These elemental qualities are characteristic of the different sensual impressions and expressions to which the matchings were made.

The subject in matching experiments is frequently not aware of the reasons determining his selections. He may explain them by chance or by some unexplainable "intuitive feeling." A visual-minded subject may explain the matching of "fire" to figure A by its flame-like pattern and see a similarity to billows in the curves of figure B, thus evoking the association "water." He may try similarly to translate the other concepts. For an acoustic-minded person the round sound "loll" and the sharp "tick" are more evident reasons for his matching. Whatever the reasons for the matchings are, each figure evokes complex associations, directed by its basic characteristic of roundness or angularity. These associations allow us to "feel into" the structure of the pattern. The capacity of empathy varies with different people, but everybody must possess it to a certain degree, otherwise he would not be able to understand his fellow men, he would not enjoy works of art. Empathy into the things which impress us leads us to use similar forms to express ourselves. Thus, empathy is one of the basic factors determining the qualities of impressions and expressions.

EMPATHY AND CONTENT

Since people vary in their degrees of empathy, it is difficult to design a graphic experiment which demonstrates the general principle of empathy in graphic movements by statistically significant results. Persons who have a high degree of graphic empathy can be detected by the "Same-Initial-Experiment." When I prepared a list of words starting with the same initial, or better, which have the first two letters in common and select one word in this group with a meaning which might easily be expressed graphically, I observed that empathetic subjects project their graphic expression upon the letter-formation of this word. We give an example of the expressiveness of the word "Introversion." Introversion describes a person who lives for himself in a shell, withdrawn from his environment, contracting his energies. Fifty subjects were asked to write down the following words, all of them with a capital initial letter: Introduction — Introversion — Intuition — Interest. Empathetic subjects contracted the initial of the word "Introversion" in correspondence with the idea of contraction related to this concept (Fig. 140 a, b). Statis-

a
b

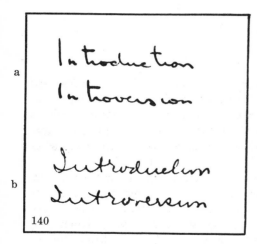
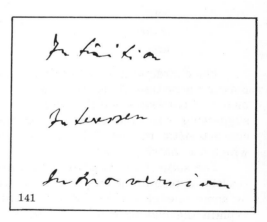

Figs. 140-141.—Empathy and word content.

tically, these data are not significant; however, they are better if we use spontaneous rather than experimental material. We collected written notes of one subject, cut out words beginning with the same capital letters, and used them for the matching experiment described above.

To test the objection that expressive principles vary in different environments and different nations, graphic specimens of German and Spanish writers were judged by our American students. The results suggest that the expressive qualities do not vary considerably in different environments. We give some examples cut from the notes of a German graphologist, showing three words with the same initial letter. The words were cut from the following text, referring to a graphological analysis:

> This is a person of a high *I*ntuition. His *I*nterests are directed towards many things, but he is knotted in himself and considers his *I*ntroversion as a burden.

We gave our subjects the three "I's" belonging to "Intuition," "Interests," and "Introversion,' to match with the corresponding concepts (Fig. 141). Asking for the motives of these matchings, we got such explanations as the following:

> The "I" of "Intuition" reaches farther up, and the high degree of "Intuition" is expressed by the largest form of the "I."

The 'I" of "Interests . . . directed towards many things" was seen in the starting line of the "I," which is turned outward like a feeler. The self-knotted "Introversion" was apparent in its knotted and restrained "I."

Potentially, the function of empathy seems to play some role in graphic expression. However, with many subjects the experimental situation destroys the principles of expression which may find their manifestation in spontaneous acts of graphic movement. In an experiment I carried out with several groups of 20 subjects each, I tried to compare how a subject writes nonsense words with his writing of emotional words, consisting of the same letters. I selected the following words which are likely to arouse some emotional responses in the subject: active, death, father, love, hate, mother, myself, passive. The letters composing each word were used to form a nonsense word which had the same initial as the corresponding emotional words. The nonsense words were: avicte, dathe, ferath, levo, heta, meroth, melfys, pevissa. These words were written on the blackboard, memorized by the subjects and then written down. Immediately afterwards the emotional words were dictated. Comparing the length of a nonsense word with its corresponding emotional word, we got with 20 subjects an equal length in 45 per cent of the cases, while the emotional words were longer in 20 per cent, and shorter in 35 per cent of the cases. The cases of a distinct difference in length between nonsense words and emotional words were not scattered according to words or subjects, but some subjects showed a general tendency to shorten the graphic movement of all or most emotional words. Other subjects showed a general increase of movement; and a third group remained unaffected by the emotional content. Thus, half of our subjects did not react expressively under experimental conditions, while the other half reacted either with symptoms of stimulation or of inhibition. Principles of expressiveness therefore should be investigated with specimens written spontaneously, under the conditions of daily life.

Life magazine,* when publishing a report about the convention of "International Business Machines" under their president Thomas J.

---

*September 15, 1947.

Watson, reproduced the words Mr. Watson wrote down as requirements for success (Fig. 142). One group of words are "the five C's that we must possess if we want to do our full share"; the sequence of words is: Conception, Consistency, Cooperation, Courage, Confidence. According to the degree of graphic expressiveness however, the sequence of concepts is different. "Courage," the fourth word, has the largest initial and the greatest extension; next comes the first word, "Conception"; then the fifth word, "Confidence"; the third word, "Cooperation"; and last the second word "Consistency." Courage and conception, or imagination, actually are IBM's sales philosophy. In almost every room in every building owned by the company hangs the motto, "Aim High and Think in Big Figures." The concepts of "cooperation" and "consistency" are graphically subordinated under the first three.

Empathy can often be observed in the relationship between a writer and the addressee. Though we have not made such experiments, we have

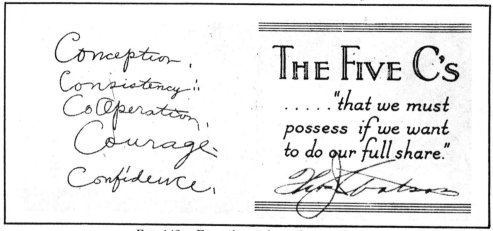

FIG. 142.—Empathy and word content.

sometimes observed that the writer adapts his handwriting to the pattern of expressive movement which the addressee has. Such an adaptation is only another instance of associations accompanying the act of writing determining our form of expression. If we think vividly of the receiver while we are writing to him we may unconsciously imitate him. Similar adaptations also appear if we write in a letter about another person who impresses us very much. We give as an example a letter written by Friedrich Schiller, in which he refers to Goethe (Fig. 143 a). Writing the name "Goethe" (line 3), Schiller uses Goethe's own shape of the letter "G" (Fig. 143 b). This "G" is not typical of Schiller's writing, as we see it in some other lines where the same letter is used in the word "Gemüthe" (line 1).

This feeling into the content of a word can be observed especially in persons with a high degree of imagination. Children are very good subjects in this respect. But children also show different degrees of this

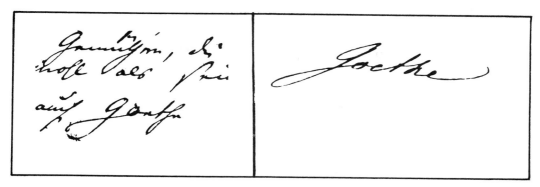

FIG. 143.—Empathy and imitation.

capacity of empathy. Since I have not repeated these experiments in this country, I give an example from my German collection; the sentences are taken out of various compositions of a 12-year-old German girl, made in the course of one school year (Fig. 144). Here again we can match the graphic expression with the story. The coincidence in content and writing of such different kinds of description reveals the chameleon-like adaptability of this child. The writings differ so much in expressive value from each other that they appear to belong to different persons. Comparing the different writings with each other, we note that Fig. d is written very close and inclined to the right while Fig. g is written spaced, inclined to the left, and with much more pressure than the preceding one. Fig. c is written with very small, broken letters, while Fig. b is written in an extremely thin manner. Fig. a is written with pressure and with very large letters, emphasizing the vertical stroke, whereas in e the horizontal extension is more emphasized.

If we try to relate the content of the stories to the expressive way of writing we note the projection upon the graphic expression. The writing carried out with pressure, with hard letters, and with a sling in the first loop of the Gothic "H," gives an aggressive impression (Fig. a). In this story the child is writing about a bad stepmother who secretly kills the child of the king and his wife, and who smears the lips of the queen with blood to make her look as if she has devoured her child. The stepmother brings the young queen into the hunger-tower. The writing specimen shows the words: "Fressen" (devour), "Hung (er-turm)" (hunger-tower). As the writing in this specimen seems more aggressive than in the other specimens, the aggressive and sadistic content of this story seems to be projected upon the letter formation.

In Fig. b, which is very pale and almost transparent, the same girl is telling a story about heaven, God, and the angels. The transparence of heaven seems to be projected in this writing. The specimen shows the word "Engel" (angel).

Specimen c, written in a rather broken and trembling way, tells about a grandmother. The idea of old age seems to be projected upon these letters. The specimen shows the word "Grossmutter" (grand-mother).

Specimen d, written in a compressed way and without any ornamental elements, is taken from a description of the autumn wind and the fear of the children. The feeling of fear is visible in the compressed letters. The specimen shows the words "Wind" (wind) and "bange" (afraid).

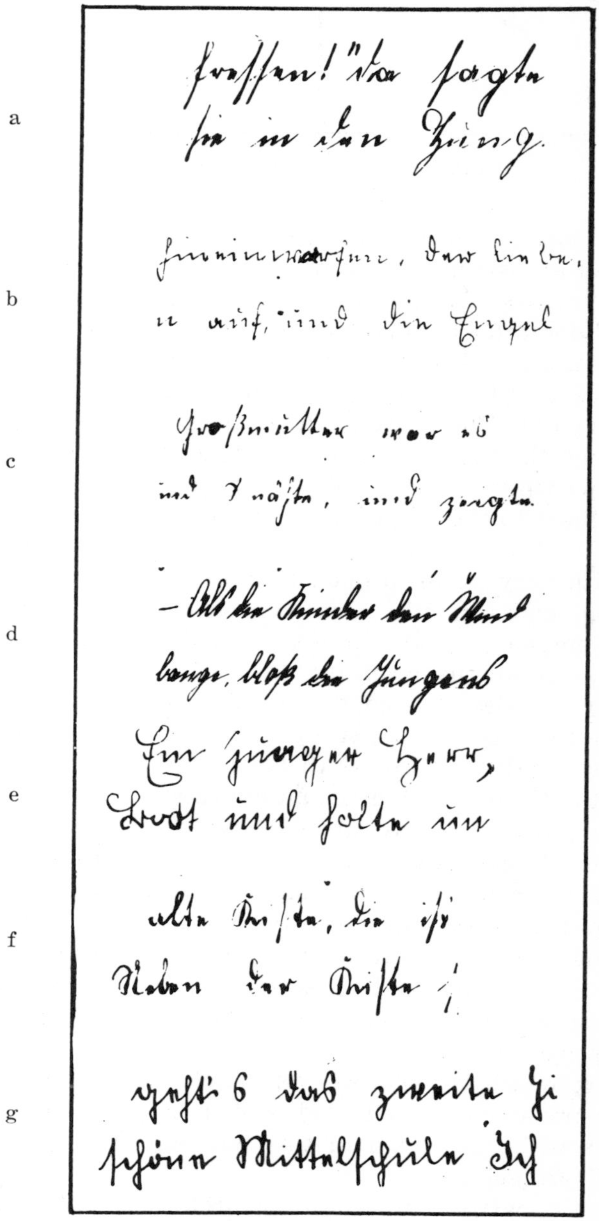

Fig. 144.—Graphic expression and empathy in childhood.

In Fig. e, the letters are very broad and steep, but insecure, as shown by broken and trembling lines. The child describes an experience of hers on the sea in a small boat which overturns. A young man comes to save her. With the idea of the young man's strength the letters become enlarged, but the fear related to the situation makes the letter formation insecure. The specimen shows the words "Ein junger Herr" (a young gentleman) and "Boot" (boat).

Specimen f, written with difference of pressure and thin lines, gives a rather architectural impression. The child describes an old chest. The chronicle-like description seems to be projected upon the letters. The specimen shows the word "Kiste" (chest) twice.

In specimen g the writing is forced and the inclination is changed. Especially is the word "ich" (I) written in an unnatural and affected way. In the description the child tells how much she likes her school. This was not the case in reality. A mask seems to be projected upon this letter formation. The specimen shows the words "schöne Mittelschule" (fine school) and "Ich" (I).

Besides a general empathy which evokes similarities of expressiveness in many people, there is an individual empathy which is based upon specific emotional reactions due to individual experiences. Everybody has certain concepts which play a special role only for him, and, corresponding to our preceding observations, we may expect that their written form will accordingly show an expressive emphasis. If we ask subjects to write down their associations relating to colors we often see that certain of these written associations are over- or underemphasized. Later explorations usually indicate that these words, written in a special way, have an emotional connotation for the writer. We give some examples of experiments carried out at Brooklyn College, Brooklyn, New York, where subjects were asked to write down their associations to the four colors: blue, red, green, and yellow.

In one example (Fig. 145) there are the words "cold" and "sad" (third line), which are written with more emphasis, and the subject asserted that she most disliked the color blue to which these associations referred.

The next example (Fig. 146) shows an entirely different expression in the word "timidity" (third line), which also stands out because the subject has written this word with printed letters.

In the third example (Fig. 147) it is the word "tumultuous" (first line) which is written with more emphasis.

An analysis by means of questionnaires indicated that these concepts which were written with a special letter formation were in effect troubling the subject. Thus, the expressiveness of empathy is related to an individual's associations linked up with the specific words he is writing. If we only detect empathy in extreme cases we can, however, not assume its absence when unnoted. Our instruments of investigation

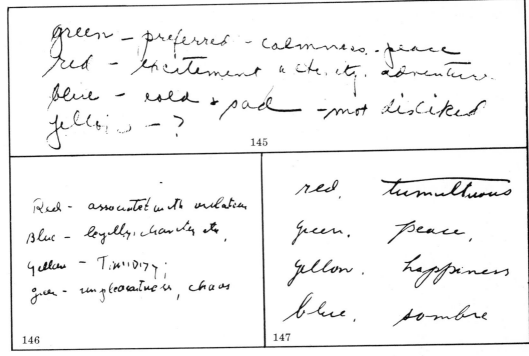

FIGS. 145-147.—Empathy and graphic expression in associations to color.

are not yet sufficiently developed for discovering traces which are too feeble to be observed by the naked eye.

PROJECTION OF FAMILY RELATIONSHIPS

If the expressiveness of a graphic specimen is determined by the content of the written word, this reveals the writer's empathy. Such an empathy appears only if the object plays a great role in our thinking. The expression of empathy is like a dialogue between observer and observed.

Projection, like empathy, is a transfer of thoughts upon our movements, which becomes visible in graphic expression. However, projection is not a dialogue between observer and observed, but a mere discharge of the observer's ideas without concern for any object. Projection, we may say, has the characteristics of a monologue. If for a child a plain piece of wood represents the mother and the same piece a short while later stands for an animal, it becomes clear that the wood itself has no characteristics which evoke in the child the image of the mother; it serves, rather, like the silver screen in the movie, as an object upon which to project an image. Thus, the structure of the object need not have anything to do with its representation. If an expressionist painter transfers his feeling of uproar and tension to his painted flowers, he does not feel into the flower as would an impressionist; he imposes his own feeling on the object.

Although empathy and projection are both transfers of expression, in the former the object, the outer world and the impression are dominant, while in the latter the subject, his inner world, and the expression predominate. The diagnostic values of empathy and of projection are, therefore, very different; in fact they have opposite qualities. Everybody has the ability to feel into another person or object and also to discharge his subjective feelings, but the degrees of empathy and projection and the dominance of one over the other are different in various personalities. Just as we are able to detect empathy only in extreme cases, so we may expect to find traces of projection only in those instances where the projecting forces are especially strong.

We now give some examples of how forces of projection can be detected in graphic expression by means of experimental methods.

Projection, as already mentioned, plays a great role in the activities of the young child. Children's scribblings and drawings are, in the first stage, merely projections of their feelings, and no other person can recognize any empathy into an object. Gradually, when the child discovers the world around him, he tries to represent the objects themselves, becoming what we call more "objective."

One of the most revealing means of demonstrating a child's projections consists in his drawings of his family. According to the author's experiments with preschool children [467], the order in which the child draws the members of his family, the size he gives to each figure, and the attributes which distinguish them are of a revealing nature. A child projects likes and dislikes, wishes and fears, by the sequence, size, position, shape, and pressure used when drawing the figures of his environment. Some children, for instance, first draw a figure which represents the child himself and then father and mother; others first draw the father, others the mother, and it has been observed that the emphasis put on the first figure indicated the child's attitude to his family. The accentuation of size, the distance between figures, and so forth have a similar value.

Projections appear both in what a child emphasizes and in what he omits. A four-year-old, for instance, when drawing his family, said: "There's my sister, isn't she a dummy? My sister isn't gonna have two arms, I don't wanna make her two arms." It is with the intentional defect of the drawing, depriving the sister of her arms, that the child projects his aggression upon his drawing.

The adult's attitude to his family was tested by the following experiment, first carried out in the Vassar series, mentioned before (see p. 178). Each subject was asked to write the words "I myself," "I mother," and "I father" on separate slips, once with eyes open and once with eyes closed. The experiment was repeated in another session, in which, however, the sequence of these concepts was changed. For the

third session the experimenter put the three concepts written in the
first series, with eyes open and with eyes closed, one below the other and
covered all but the letters "I." The same was done with the words written
in the second series. The subject then received the instructions: "Tell me
the emotional degree expressed by the different letters 'I' and make a
scale from the highest to the lowest degree of expression." When the
subject made this scale with the concepts written in the first and second
series, once with eyes open and once with eyes closed, the experimenter
could investigate whether or not the subject attributed the same degree
of expressiveness to the same concepts. The same degree of expression
apportioned to the same concept appeared in 58.8 per cent of the
cases, while chance would allow 33.3 per cent. If the graphic emphasis appears with several characteristics or remains consistent in

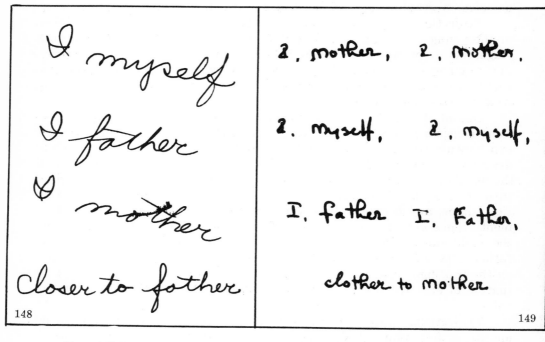

FIGS. 148-149.—Projection of family relationships upon graphic expression.

various trials, a person's attitude toward himself, toward his father and
toward his mother may be diagnosed. The subjects were asked to make a
personal statement about their relationship to their parents. Although the
value of such statements is questionable, since a subject would not be
aware of his unconscious motivations, they may reveal facts which support the graphic indications. In our first example (Fig. 148) the "I" of
"I-mother" is highly contracted, the distance between "I" and "mother"
is greater than between "I" and 'father," and the word "mother" is falling

down. The subject reported a closer relationship to her father due to a complicated family situation. Another subject (Fig. 149) writes the "I" related to "mother" in the same way as the "I" related to "myself," but writes a different "I" related to "father," thus expressing an identification with the mother and singling out the father. Repetitions showed that this variation was not due to chance. Another subject (Fig. 150) was

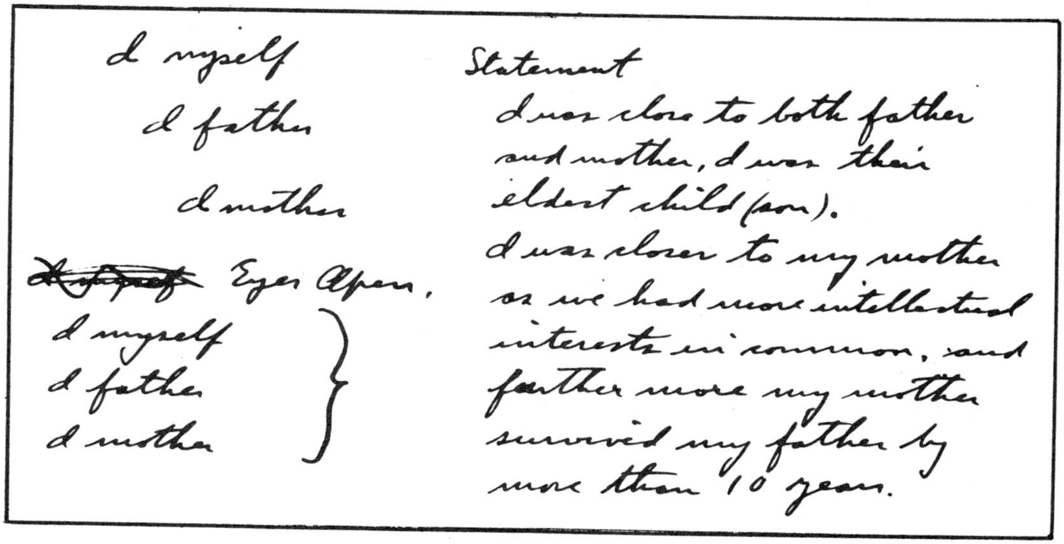

FIG. 150.—Projection of family relationships upon graphic expression.

inhibited to write the words "I-myself." While first writing with eyes closed, he later wrote "myself" with eyes open, omitting the "I" in my-self" and crossing the word out. The distance between "I" and "mother" is closer than that between "I" and "father"; the subject commented: "I was close to both father and mother, I was their eldest child (son). I was closer to my mother as we had more intellectual interests in common; and furthermore my mother survived my father by more than 10 years." Another subject (Fig. 151) emphasized the relationship to her "father" by the size of the loop of the "I" and its closeness to the word father; she stated: "Family recognition would say closer genetic relationship with father; personal feeling suggests closer contact with mother. Not very close to either. My husband is only 6 months younger than my father." The last statement suggests that the subject had a father-fixation, at least unconsciously.

PROJECTION AND EMOTIONS

Our attitudes to the environment are related to our feeling of se-curity. If we feel insecure in a strange environment we try not to draw attention to ourselves; we may speak in a low voice, sit on the edge of

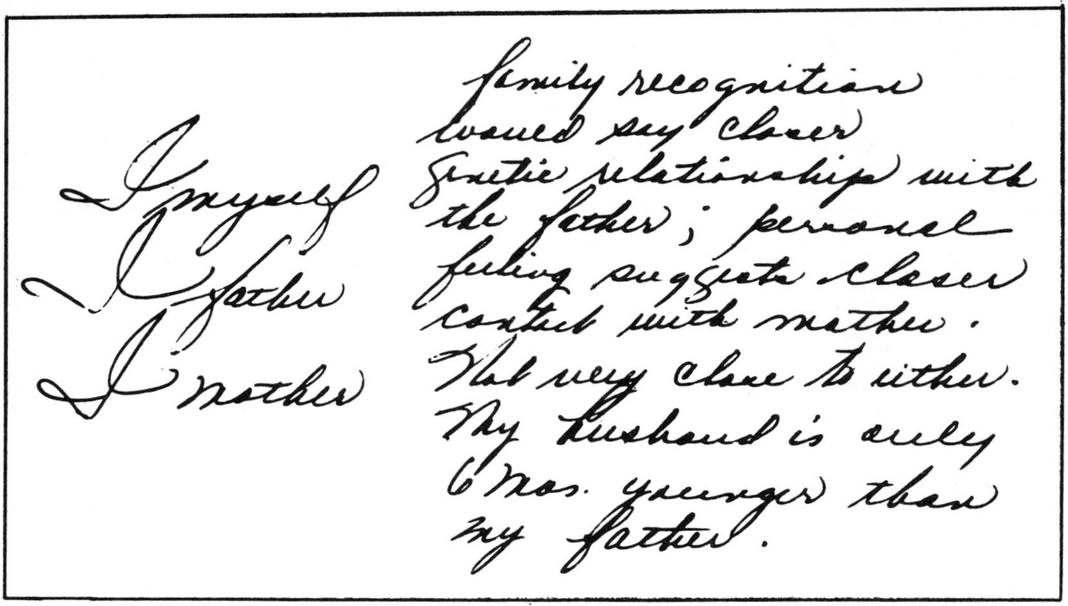

FIG. 151.—Projection of family relationships upon graphic expression.

a chair, or go around cautiously without putting much pressure in our walking and other movements. Similarly, in graphic expression a sudden withholding of pressure may be a sign of insecurity. The degree of pressure used in writing certain words can be investigated by giving a subject a pad of paper which has carbon paper concealed between its single sheets. Many subjects, asked to write certain words with a pencil—for instance, "father," "mother," "myself"—will use a different degree of pressure in writing the various words. This pressure becomes manifest in the number of copies obtained.

In other experiments which I performed in German schools, I had a group of thirteen-year-old children describe in writing a recent experience and, immediately thereafter, a dream for their future (Fig. 152 a. b.). There were children who wrote on both matters in a very dry way without subjective participation. These children did not show differences in the expressive form of letters when writing about their experience and when writing about their future. Other children, however, who displayed their emotions, showed graphic differences in both compositions. One difference in the graphic expression of both specimens was characteristic of several children: the description of their experiences was frequently written in letters which seem to be much more secure and solid than the letters used in the imaginative description, which appear to be written with insecurity. In our example we have cut apart lines with the same words in each of both compositions and underlined the corresponding

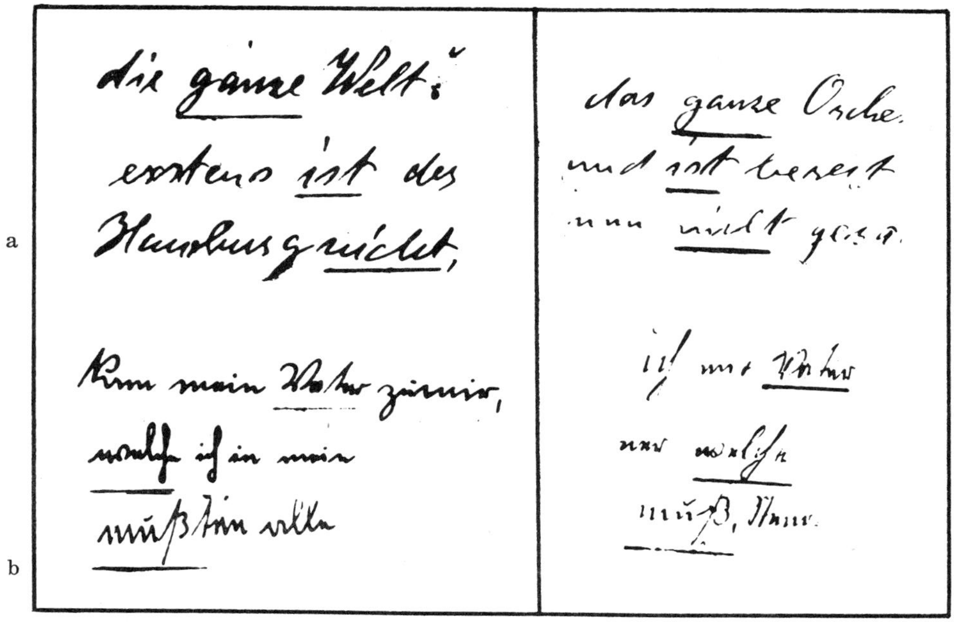

Fig. 152.—Experience and daydream.

words. The words in the description of the future, compared with the same words in the description of a recent experience, are smaller, less formed, and the direction of strokes changes. The associations related to an insecure future seem to evoke a general mood of insecurity which influences the graphic movement.

The projection of personal tendencies often becomes apparent when we compare a writer's different headings or addresses of letters directed to the same person. In Fig. 153, a, b, c, we see three letter headings written in various successive months. Comparing the initial letters of "Lieber" (dear) and "Werner," we observe that in the three specimens the "L" of "Lieber" is written in an increasingly loose manner, and the end curve of the "W" in "Werner" successively becomes enlarged. The first heading is written at the time of the first acquaintance of the writer with the addressee, the second letter at the time of beginning friendship, and the third one when writer and receiver had a closer relationship. The changing relationship becomes manifest in an increased loosening of letters and expanding movement which indicates the affection toward the receiver. The signatures correspond to the letter headings. The writer was a young man who, in the letter with signatures "b" and "c" was communicating his fears of being unable to take his B.A. degree. His emotion is seen in the suddenly increased and distorted curve of the "Y." A doodling, made at that time, shows the same characteristic (Fig. e). The writer's associations to this doodling were: "Letters 'H,' begun and

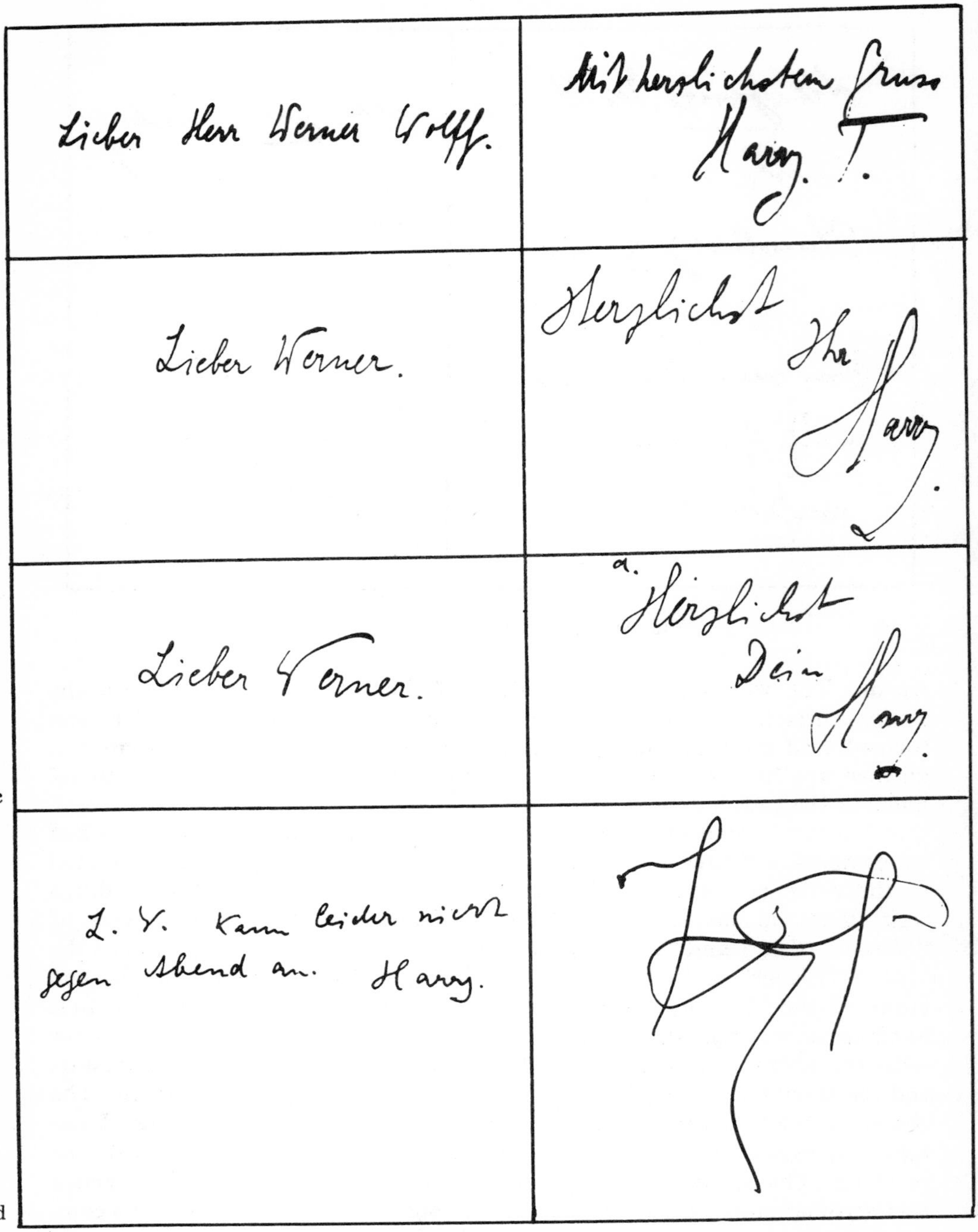

FIG. 153.—Projection of personal relationships upon graphic expression.

not accomplished, terribly destructive, unbalanced and whip-like." These characteristics of distortions were not present before his fear started (Fig. a) and when his fear had vanished (Fig. d).

An inhibition of movement in organic activity generally produces a disturbance which may, for instance, result in stuttering. Freud showed that an inhibition of associations brings about those disturbances which appear as mistakes in speaking, reading, writing and acting. An analysis usually reveals that here one association has been blocked by another association (see p. 131 ff.).

Graphic distortions may be explained in a similar way [63]. If one letter is distorted in a word, this word seems to be a "complex word," related to an affective association. Several studies in this direction have been made [203, 294, 295, 357, 363, 448]. If the distortion appears in the first letter of this word, the emotional tone becomes operative at the start of this word; but if the distortion appears with some letter in the body of the word, certain affective associations may be connected with that special letter. If our graphic movement is accompanied by associations, a break of movement seems to indicate a contrary association which stopped or interrupted the movement.

Disturbances of writing appear not only in broken letters; letters may also be badly written, and pressure may become noticeably weaker. It appears frequently that the beginning of a letter, for instance, "Dear Sir," is written with much hesitancy, as we notice it in smaller graphic strokes or even in a broken graphic movement. An exploration reveals in most such cases that the letter was written with displeasure. In the letter text the writer may overcome his inhibition which, however, often reappears in the signature. In the body of the letter we sometimes distinguish a very different shape of the same letter. Relating such a letter to the content of the word, we may be able to detect which emotional associations accompanied the written concept.

Fig. 154 shows part of a girl's letter to a young man who is hopeful about his relation to her. The girl excuses her refusal of an invitation. The receiver could guess that this refusal is more than a casual one if he considered the beginning and the end of the letter. The word "Lieber" (dear) (line 1) and the word "Herzlichst" (cordially) (line 2) are both written with inhibitions and distortions (see the "L" and "b" of "Lieber" and the "z" of "Herzlichst"). In another specimen (Fig. 155) a writer says "herzlichste Glückwünsche (congratulations) and alles Gute (and best wishes), möge Dir das so gut bestandene Examen recht bald eine Existenz bringen (I hope that the successful examination will enable you to make a living)." If we compare the words written with the same initial "G" "Glückwünsche" and "Gute" we notice a difference in the graphic form of both initials. There also appears a graphic difference with the next two "E" in the words "Examen" and "Existenz." The word "Existenz" (living) shows an error of writing and its initial is more poorly written (showing only one loop) than the corresponding initial in "Examen." Also the initial "G" in "Gute" is written more poorly than the corresponding initial in "Glückwünsche." This is the letter of a father to his son, and a knowledge of the circumstances reveals that the father did not believe that the successful "examination" of his son would give him any possibilities for making a living ("Existenz"). Thus he sends his congratulations ("Glückwünsche"), not expecting the best ("alles Gute").

Subject G (cf. Fig. 138, Ib and Fig. 173), in a state of undesired pregnancy, wrote a letter to her family in which she tried to hide her real condition. But the handwriting reveals what the words try to hide. In the address (Fig. 156 a) all letters are written with undue energy, which also appears in the underlining of the city and in the initial of "Adolf." Some time later she wrote again to her family without emotional tension, and we note that the emotional expression has disappeared (Fig. 156 b).

Freud, the discoverer of emotional motivations in the expression of personality, was himself not free from them and he gives many examples of his own experience; the following is a graphic example. In 1934 I wrote Freud and asked him whether he would care to read a manuscript of mine in which I attempted to subject psychoanalytical concepts to experimental procedures. I should have guessed that Freud was very sensitive to the word "experimental," since it easily implied a criticism of his method. In his "New Introductory Lectures of Psychoanalysis," written not long before I wrote my letter, Freud had remarked: "Not long ago, medical men of an American university refused to consider psychoanalysis as a science because it did not permit experimental proof." Thus, naturally, my letter was likely to evoke in Freud some resentment and a critical attitude. Freud answered my letter as follows (Fig. 157): "Dear Sir: I certainly shall read your studies with attention, but I customarily avoid making any criticism in such cases. . . ." While in the large handwriting of Freud the lower parts of letters frequently touch the upper part of letters in the following line, there is still enough spacing so that consecutive lines of writing do not become entangled; except in one instance: The word "attention" is deeply penetrated by the vertical downstroke of the "h" in "Ihre" (your). This stroke is longer than any other vertical stroke and is written with more than usual pressure. Relating this emphasized movement to the words in which it appears (your) and to which it is related (attention). we may deduce that attention is anticipated to involve sharp and penetrating criticism, which as such necessarily involves an aggressive note. Freud actually read the manuscript with attention, since at the same time his journal *Imago* published a summary of my work [462].

Thus, emotions may be expressed graphically by an over- and under-emphasis of graphic patterns.

THE EXPRESSION OF FEELINGS

The projections we referred to had their origin in sudden psychological tensions, producing sporadic graphic symptoms. There are, how-

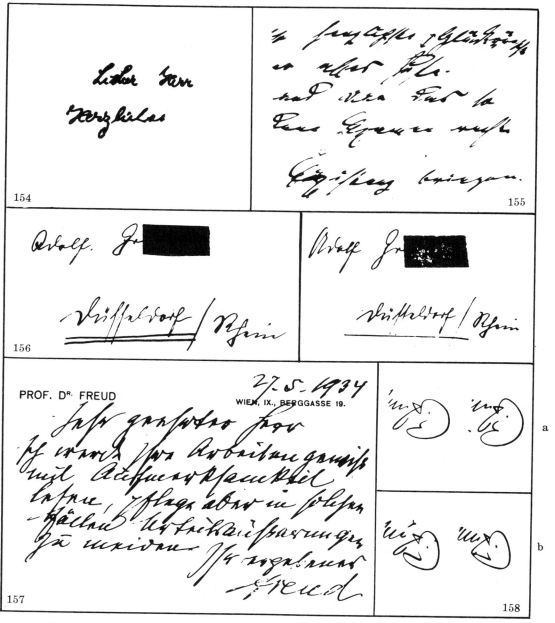

FIGS. 154-158.—The expression of emotions in over- and underemphasis of graphic expression.

ever, many symptoms which pattern our expression for a long time. A person may show constitutionally longer periods of happiness or sadness, which may prevail for months and not vanish in the flash of a discharge, such as smashing a glass in an attack of anger. These moods of longer

duration characterize our total disposition at a time when everything
seems to us gay or dark or indifferent. Moods of longer duration can
hardly be produced in experimental situations, but they originate spontaneously under life conditions, and to study their reflection in graphic
expression we have to use specimens written spontaneously in different
moods. A few examples from the author's collection may illustrate this
point.

The secretary of a businessman who was subject to periodical moods
suddenly became conscious of the fact that his employer's signature seemed
to change according to his happy or unhappy feelings. The author detected
a strange phenomenon in the end stroke of this man's signature, upon
which the man projected his varying moods. The last letter of his name
is a "g," ending in a flourish (Fig. 158). Omitting the whole name, for
reasons of identification, it appears that these flourishes seem to form
a face, some faces having a happy (a) and some a sad expression (b).
An exploration indicated that the businessman himself was not conscious
of this phenomenon, but the subjects of the letters gave ample evidence
of the coincidence between expressiveness and prevailing mood.

Next we show (Fig. 159) two compositions by Franz Schubert, one

a

b

FIG. 159.—The expression of feelings in changes of graphic patterns.

entitled "Pilgrim's Night Song" (a), the other entitled "Belief in Spring" (b). The graphic forms of the night song are written more slowly and with more pressure than those of the spring song.

While Beethoven's music usually is as explosive as his musical notation (a), the soft music of the Moonlight Sonata (b) was written with corresponding graphic movements (Fig. 160).

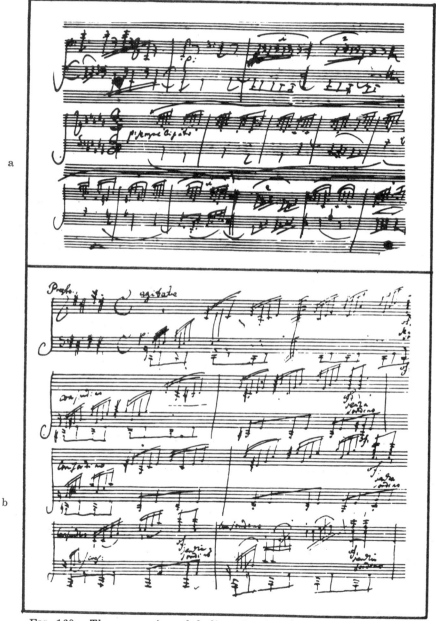

FIG. 160.—The expression of feelings in changes of graphic patterns.

The influence of mood upon handwriting may also be noticed if we
compare an author's original manuscript with his final copy. We give an
example of the German poet Wilhelm von Scholz (Fig. 161). Choosing
a part of a poem which refers to a churchbell, it says in translation:

> Push me that I swing,
> Then my sound grows,
> Sounding over clouds and lands.

The first manuscript (a) shows a high swing which appears especially in
the first line, where the poet says: "Push me that I swing." This expression has disappeared in the final copy (b). It is significant that the author
chose Gothic letters for his private notes and for the final copy Roman
letters, separating by this use of different alphabets two kinds of projections: one related to his own personality, the other to the environment.
The private note is written with much more emphasis, more speed, and
higher curves, which also appear in letters whose basic structure is
identical in the Gothic and the Roman letters of both writings as "i,"
"o," and "l."

Mahatma Gandhi had the peculiarity of writing all official papers with
his right hand (Fig. 162 a) and all private papers with his left hand
(Fig. 162 b). It seems that the change of projective ideas not only
changed his graphic expression but also the choice of his organ of writing.
The right-handed writing is inclined toward the right and written fluently;
the left-handed one is inclined toward the left and written with compressed
letters.

Reynaldo Hahn's "official answer" to the inquiry of the French
magazine *Les Annales* for "The Dream of My Life" is written very differently from his postscript; so are the ideas described in both statements (Fig. 163). The artificial and expansive movements of the "official
answer" seem to be less genuine than the fluently written postscript.
The "official answer" was: "The dream of my life: to be lighthearted," the
postscript: "to be able to eat good food without becoming fat; but one
might have thought that I am not a poet."

Handwriting may reflect a person's feelings in diagrams of his
unconscious thus projected upon the paper-screen.

THE EXPRESSION OF THE PAST

What we call the atmosphere of our present life situation is the
product of our personality and the forces of environment. But our environment is not only the present situation we live in, but also the scenery
of our past, which influences us so that we perceive the environment in
a certain way. Of three people led into the artistic setting of a castle,
one of them might perceive it as a historic document, the other as an
aesthetic experience, and the third as a matter of high financial value.
The impression of a present situation receives its expressive value from
the observer's past experiences, and each observer who tried to express
his reaction would do so differently, expressing the present in terms of the

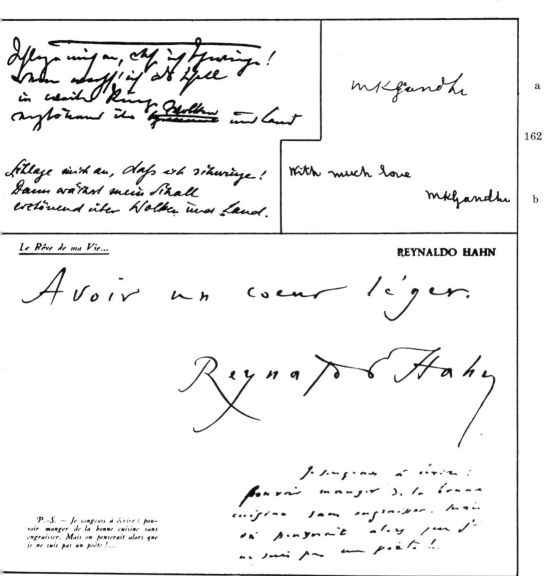

FIGS. 161-163.—The expression of feelings in changes of graphic patterns.

past. Whatever we express is determined by our remembrances of the past. Studies in psychoanalysis have revealed that many of our reactions and expressions have their roots in early experiences. Taking up our descriptive term "projection," we might describe it now as a projection of superimposed pictures. In the foreground is the projection of the present, in the background is the projection of the past, and the color and shape of the foreground picture are modified, distorted, and emphasized by the arrangement of the background. Art dealers know that many precious pictures have been painted over for many reasons: to hide the original, or to correct it according to more recent standards, or simply to make another use of the canvas. In psychological terms, the past picture is hidden or suppressed, changed or corrected, or transformed for new uses. Art dealers discover the original picture by an X-ray procedure, and psychologists excavate the buried traces of psychological pictures of the past by removing the layers of associations. Our observations indicate that associations pattern our graphic expression, and the question arises whether this expression is patterned unconsciously not only by experiences of the present but also by experiences of the past. The attempt to discover such possible traces is made by a procedure which proved useful in the interpretation of dreams. There, the individual is asked to concentrate upon each dream element and to produce associations to it. It was found that these associations actually reveal the expression of each detail, and that the interrelationship of all details enables the analyst to reconstruct a picture of the past which underlies the images of the dream. If all expressions of an individual are a unity, as was suggested by our previous observations (see p. 185 ff.), the pictures of his unconscious may not only appear in a dream, but they may pattern each form of expression, and thus also the handwriting. The characteristic way in which each individual transforms the model of letters he has learned to write may be a diagram of his associations. To test this hypothesis the author performed the following experiment.

From a subject's personal notes the small and capital letters of the alphabet were cut out. Each letter was fixed on a separate slip. Then these letters were submitted to the writer, each letter separately, irrespective of alphabetic order. The experimenter instructed the writer to imagine each letter as a drawing and to tell the associations he connected with it. The subject often did not recognize that the letters were his own. In the first session the experimenter submitted only the capital letters; in a second session, three weeks later, the experiment was repeated with small letters. Again, after an interval of two weeks, a third experiment was made, giving the subject the letters only phonetically without showing him the graphic forms. In each experiment the succession of given letters was a different one. With some letters a constancy of associations was observed in all three experimental series, although frequently the subject did not remember what he had said during the previous experiment. Lack of space forces us to give only some significant examples from this material.

One of our subjects, a physician and surgeon, responded with the following associations to his letters (Fig. 164):

Capitals

B: Raven—a cowering bird—a serpent and a sling.
R: A kitchen spoon—an African beak-like war hatchet—a raven.
P: A flag—a swung whip—a grapnel.
G: Somebody who puffs out his chest—a congenial sign, I have copied it from my uncle.

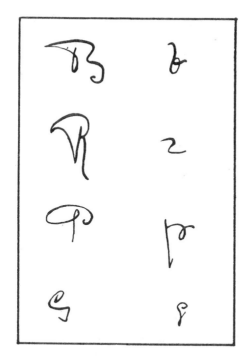

FIG. 164.—The expression of the past.

Small Letters

b: An erect snake.

r: A cowering man.

p: Flag and whip.

g: A short underlength and a swollen head—a gnome-like man—my uncle—
weapon of the South Africans, tap curry, that is a stone on an elastic stick
that has an enormous force.

Letters Given Phonetically

B: Ibis—a bird of Egypt—magic.

R: Death *r*attle (in German: *r*öcheln)—sound of death—Crown Prince *R*udolph,
whose murder was an important memory of my childhood.

P: To *p*ress (in German: *p*ressen)—oppression.

G: Go (in German: *g*eh)—the gnome-like man—my uncle A. His wife was
stabbed with a bread knife by the nephew of her cook.

We analyzed these projected ideas further by giving them as stimulus
words for new associations. These were as follows:

Raven: The raven is the bird with the big beak. It is my big nose, for which
I always have been teased. He reminds me of the ibis. In ancient Egypt the
magic power belonged to ibis and serpent. I, too, am somewhat telepathic.
My hand, too, has the Mongol line, the rare line of the Orientals. I design
very badly, but I often design the ibis and the serpent.

Whip: Whip, sling, served in my fantasies of association to catch disagreeable
people and to torture them.

Uncle: My uncle had much misfortune and was a symbol of inferiority feelings. I, too, have inferiority feelings and am afraid of disaster.

Serpent: The serpent of Aesculapius is the symbol of the medical profession, symbol of magic power and healing.

As will be noted, each alphabetic symbol, whether written as a capital or a small letter or produced as a letter sound, is connected with the same group of associations. Since these experiments with capitals, small letters, and letter sounds were made at different times, the author was able to establish that this relation was not accidental but fixed.

Comparison of the different associations reveals their relationship. We find, on the one hand, fantasies of aggression; on the other hand, the fantasies of oppression, as represented by the picture of the uncle. The oppressing inferiority feeling seems to be the motive for the subject's aggressive tendencies, and this inferiority feeling refers, as the subject states, to his big nose. He compares his big nose with the beak of the ibis, the magic bird, thus compensating the representation of inferiority with that of magic power. Our subject adds to the image of the ibis that of the serpent, which combines the concepts of danger and aggression with those of magic and healing.

The graphic expression of this subject shows us three dominating forms: that of the beak, that of the whip, and that of the swollen head. The whip is for him the symbol of aggression (letters B, P, p) ; the swollen head is the symbol of oppression (letters G, g) ; and the beak is a symbol in which aggression and oppression are united (letters R, v).

In general it is difficult to obtain an insight into the relationship of experience, image, and graphic expression, because subjects are seldom trained to make unrestricted associations. Our example indicates the possibility that basic letter forms are diagrams for projections of past experiences.

The Expression of the Future

Our inquiry into the traces which time leaves upon our expression must include the search for patterns of expectation which express anticipation of the future. Our life is shaped by the past as well as by the present, but it is also directed by goals which lie in the future. Take the expressiveness of courtship, which is directed by the expectation of winning love, and the expressiveness patterned by our studies, which are determined by the profession we seek. Take each single movement we are making, holding the pen in our hand or reaching for an object, or making a friendly gesture to our neighbor. The determination of the movement lies ahead of us, in the immediate or later goal we expect to achieve. From this point of view, there exists no expression which does not have traces of expectation or expressiveness of the future. It is difficult to estimate which determine our actions in a higher degree: the causes lying in the immediate or remote past or the expectations concerned with the immediate or remote future. Two schools of depth psychology have variously emphasized both of the determinants. Sigmund Freud in his psychoanalysis revealed the importance of past experiences; he followed a neurotic disturbance to its roots, which usually lay in early childhood. Alfred Adler in his individual psychology, which grew out of psychoanalysis, stressed the importance of expectations and goals. He discovered that neurotic disturbances may be misguided goals, that the neurotic tries to achieve by means of abnormal behavior something that he was unable to achieve by normal approach.

From immediate observation it is sometimes difficult to judge whether an expression is unconsciously determined more by the past or by the future. Usually both trends are fused, since a person expressing happiness not only has a positive reason for it in a past experience but also a positive expectation because otherwise the expression would become frustrated. When we asked subjects to express by lines concepts such as future and expectation, a large majority made rising lines. On the other hand, concepts of disappointment and lost expectations were represented by falling lines. We have sometimes opportunity to observe both directions of movement in correspondence to the expression of thoughts of expectation or disappointment.

Fig. 165 shows seven specimens of writing, always with the same content—"I am very healthy"—written by a patient during a morphine withdrawal treatment. Each line is written after different hours of the sleep treatment: the first line after 3 hours, the second after 19 hours, the third after 96, and the seventh after 120 hours of sleeping. All these lines, except the last two, are recorded in a state of exhaustion, but of expectation to be cured. In the first five lines the writing rises. However, when the patient regains the normal state his writing sinks. Many addicts report that they were looking forward to being cured; but when cured, they felt that they had lost a great value out of life. As Cocteau, an opium addict, puts it: "Healed, I feel myself void, poor, exhausted and sick. I am floating, tomorrow I shall leave the clinic. To leave—whereto?"* Such observations are frequently reported from morphine and opium addicts. We also find in last letters written before a person has committed suicide that the lines are rising. The expectation of death seems here to be related to that of redemption (Fig. 28).

When the French magazine *Les Annales* sent out inquiries for "The Dream of My Life," it received two similar answers which show similar graphic movements. One answer, from Charles Nordmann, was, "The dream of my life: not to dream any longer" (Fig. 166); the other answer, from Jacques Natanson, "To live and not to dream any longer" (Fig. 167). In both cases the phrase "not to dream any longer" is written with a falling movement, while in both cases the signature has a rising movement. From all our observations we may infer that the association of living in dreams and missing life is a source of disappointment, which the

*"Opium. The Diary of an Addict" (transl. by E. Boyd) New York, 1932.

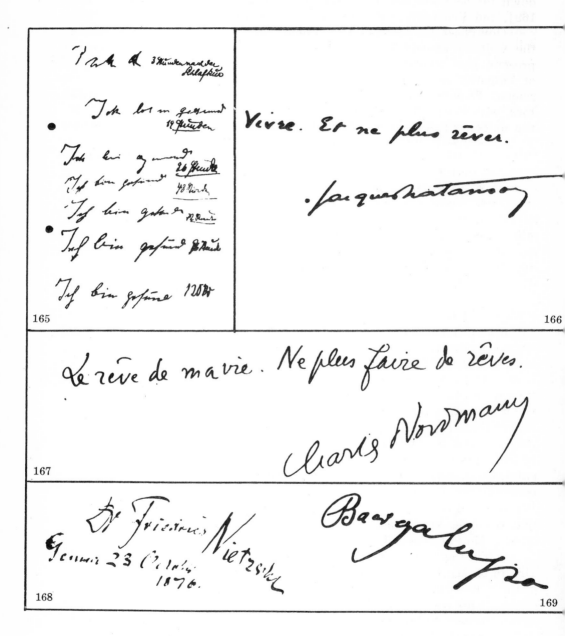

FIGS. 165-169.—The expression of expectations.

writer hopes to overcome by those expectations which accompanied the signing of his signature. The sinking movement appears especially strong in cases of mental breakdown, where, correspondingly, the signature breaks down to the lower sphere of writing (Cf. Bargalupo, an epileptic [Fig. 169], and Friedrich Nietzsche during a nervous breakdown [Fig. 168]).

Our observations suggest that graphic movements are patterned by the writer's associations, which necessarily involve the time factor of present, past, and future. These various projections as well as patterns of empathy are fused with each other in the diagram of the unconscious. Experimental approaches allow us to analyze these various factors, which actually form a unity. As we shall see in the next chapter, the unifying act itself can be studied in the process of symbolization.

CHAPTER X

SYMBOLIZATION

MOVEMENT AND SYMBOL

Acts of empathy and of projection are achieved by a process which we call symbolization. If we "feel into" the expressive value of a line—for instance, experiencing a falling line as a representation of depression—this line becomes a symbol of a certain behavior characteristic. If we project our aggressive impulse upon a movement pattern, such a projection is a symbol of a psychological process. However, for a finer distinction of expressive values the term "symbolization" should be reserved for certain characteristics which are not involved in empathy and projection. Certain movements are a direct projection of psychological reactions and aims. If something itches us we have the direct reaction of scratching our skin. If we reach for an object we make a direct and purposeful movement for getting it. Certain expressions are direct expressions of empathy, as when my face appears sad when I see an accident. Empathies and projections which are immediately expressed or interpreted uniformly should not be called symbolizations.

A symbolization is a complex representation of inner psychological processes or thoughts, the meaning of which is not revealed directly but must be analyzed for its constituents. A dream image is a symbol like a sign in an unknown language which has to be deciphered, a content which has to be translated. Everybody makes many movements, the meaning of which is not related to an immediate empathy or an immediate projection. If we ask the subject why he did it he usually will not be able to give us a full explanation. The subject frequently is not conscious of the movement, and even if he is, he does not know why he was compelled to make it. There are the many "purposeless" movements of one's hands and face, "playing" with objects such as pencils and matches, scribbling or doodling while listening or talking, apparently purposeless biting of nails, smoothing of hair or adjusting of glasses, necktie, coat, over and over again. These movements betray loss of their apparent purposes and stand for something else which usually is unknown to the performer and to the observer. Such movements are symbolizations of inner psychological processes. Why a person doodles in a certain way, with a stereotype of patterns, why he uses the substitute of biting his nails, can be explained only by delving into his unconscious. Psychoanalytic observations have made such an approach to the unconscious possible, by an analysis of a subject's associations. Many psychiatrists and psychologists have been interested in the symbolic value of gestures, which speak the language of personality [5, 131, 352]. The characteristics of symbolization have been studied in dreams, in hypnosis, and in analyses of ceremonies and customs of primitive tribes and ancient civilizations. The symbolic meaning of gestures which played a great role in the magic and religious ceremonies of the ancients is still preserved in a few of our gestural movements, as those of greeting, praying, swearing.

Graphic symbols are known from art; to a certain degree each element in a drawing is a symbol, suggesting representation or expression. Most of these symbols are "objective," that is, they are stereotyped and recognized immediately by the members of the same culture. Other symbols are "subjective," having a value only for the artist himself, and are a symbolic expression of his ideas. Such subjective symbols already appear in the drawings of preschool children. Direct questioning may reveal the subjective meaning of these symbols; the meaning of another group of graphic symbols, however, is unknown to the artist himself, and direct questioning would not elicit their significance. Here indirect methods of approach have to be used to decipher these hieroglyphics of expression.

GRAPHIC SYMBOLIZATION IN HYPNOSIS

The phenomenon of hypnosis, the hypnotist's apparent ability to direct a person's behavior, allows us to eliminate considerably the conscious intentions of the hypnotized subject and with this his attempts to disguise. A person's hidden impulses can be brought out, and, as shown by experiments [229, 458], his conscious behavior can be compared with his unconscious behavior. To illustrate, we start with a report of my own experimental investigation, carried out in Berlin in 1932 [see also 466, pp. 168-172]. Our subject was a patient under the psychological investigation of Dr. Alexander Hertzberg, of the University of Berlin. She was a woman about 50 years of age and had often been hypnotized. Her husband had been killed in the first World War and now she lived with her daughter. All her imaginings were related to her dead husband, to her daughter, and to her little grandchild. She did not like her son-in-law, a drunkard, whose vice she hated extremely.

Exploration revealed that the concepts "little grandchild—drunkard—husband" were emphasized emotionally, and so these words could be used as complex words. First we had this subject in a normal state write some sentences in which these complex words were represented. These sentences were:

(1) "I enjoy my little grandchild the most."
(2) "I don't like men to be drunkards."
(3) "I very often think of my dead husband, who fell in the World War."

It appears at first glance (Fig. 170 a) that the words "Enkelkind" (grandchild), second line; "Mannes" (husband), sixth line; and "Trinker" (drunkard), fourth line, are written with greater spacing than other

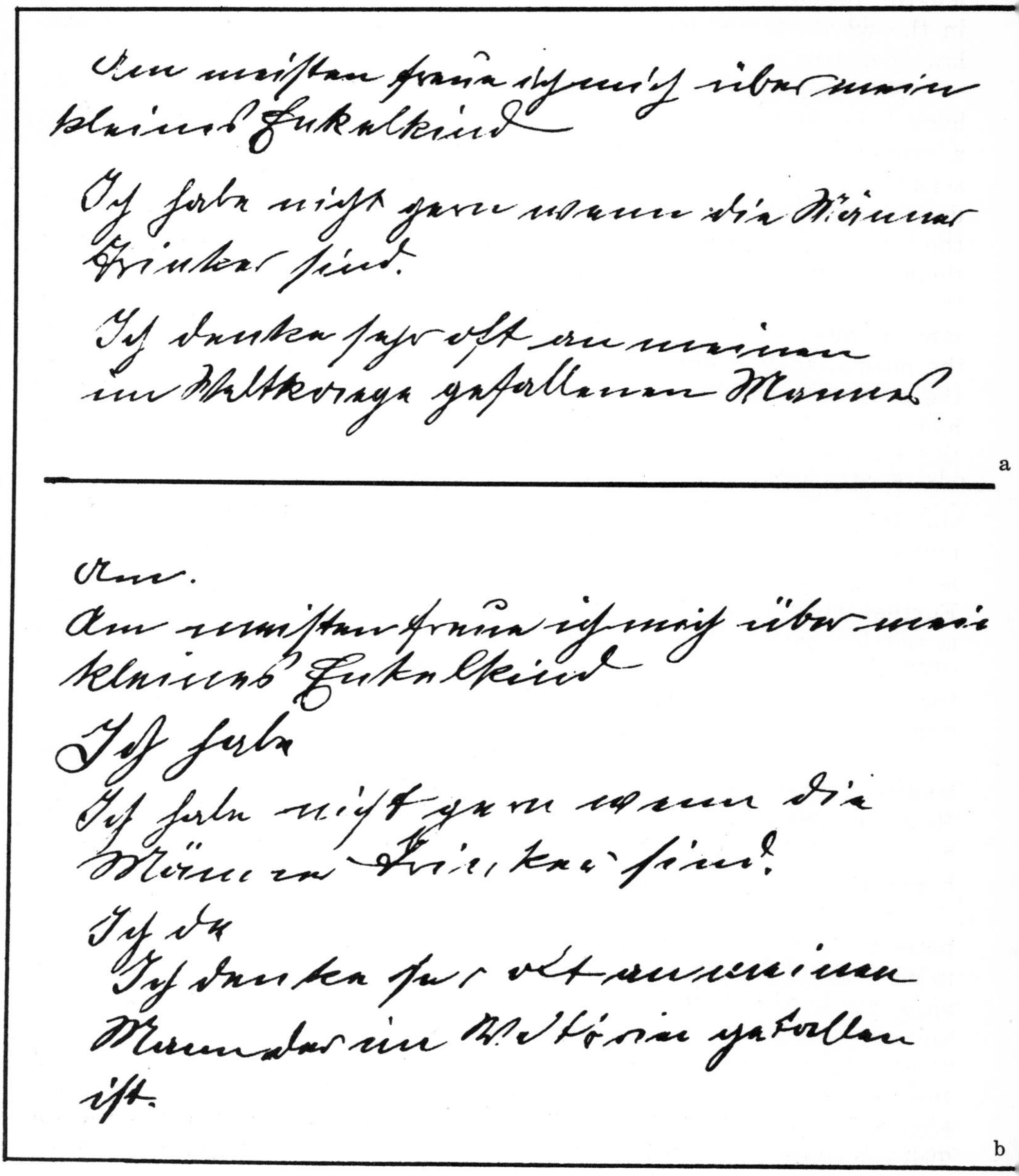

FIG. 170.—Graphic expression in hypnosis.

words. If we measure the length of these words and that of neutral words with the same number of letters, we can determine how much larger each complex word is than the average size of a neutral word. Thus we may detect the emotional degree of each word by its relative length. In our three complex words the highest emotional degree appears in the word "Enkelkind," the next is "Mannes," and the comparatively lowest degree in the emotional word group belongs to "Trinker"

Now this subject was put under a deep hypnosis. She lost her physiological sensitivity, remaining absolutely insensible when she was burnt by a candle; but as we shall see in the sequel she kept her psychological sensitivity. First she was asked to write the same sentences as she had done in the normal state (Fig. 170 b). Again measuring the length of the complex words and that of the average neutral words, and comparing them with those of the normal state, we made three observations: (1) In the hypnotic state complex words are longer than neutral words of the same number of letters. (2) However, these differences are greater in the normal state than under hypnosis. (3) The emotional degree within the group of complex words changed; the word for "grandchild," which had the highest emotional degree in the normal state, under hypnosis had the lowest degree of the three complex words.

It is interesting to note that the emotional expression of the positive statements has considerably decreased in the hypnotic state. We also notice a general decrease of pressure which in the writing under hypnosis is sometimes so low that the ink does not flow out of the fountain pen. Furthermore, we observe a decrease in the differentiation of letters, which is particularly manifest in the letters "M" and "W." Every "M" and "W" written in the normal state shows a difference in height between the first and second vertical stroke. This difference has disappeared in hypnosis.

Hypnosis thus produced in this case a lower emotional degree in the length of words, a decrease of pressure, and a decrease of differentiation. However, the general decrease of expressiveness under hypnosis appears only in positive statements; it does not appear, as we shall see, when the hypnotized person is brought into conflict.

An additional experiment gave us the following surprise. While the patient was in hypnosis we began dictating opposite statements, dictating first: "Am wenigsten freue ich mich über mein kleines Enkelkind" (I enjoy my little grandchild least) (Fig. 170 b). Our subject began to write and wrote "Am," but suddenly she began to tremble and, exclaiming "No!" she made a dot after "Am." The original positive sentence was then dictated and written without any hesitation. Now we dictated the second sentence in the opposite sense: "Ich habe gern, wenn die Männer Trinker sind" (I like men to be drunkards). The subject wrote the words "Ich habe" with a very visible emotion. But then she cried *"nicht* gern" (*don't* like) and broke down completely. Again the original negative sentence was dictated and was written without resistance. Now we dictated the third sentence in a negative sense: "Ich denke nicht oft an meinen im Weltkriege gefallenen Mann" (I don't think often of my husband, fallen in the World War). The subject wrote "Ich de——," and suddenly stopped on the "e." It was impossible to induce her to continue this sentence. Then, again, the positive sentence was written fluently and without restraint.

Thus, the graphic expression of this one subject suggests the following explanation. In general, her expressiveness decreased under hypnosis; however, her reaction to a conflict situation increased. This observation parallels other experiments with hypnosis. The hypnotized subject carries out all instructions of the hypnotist with emotional in-

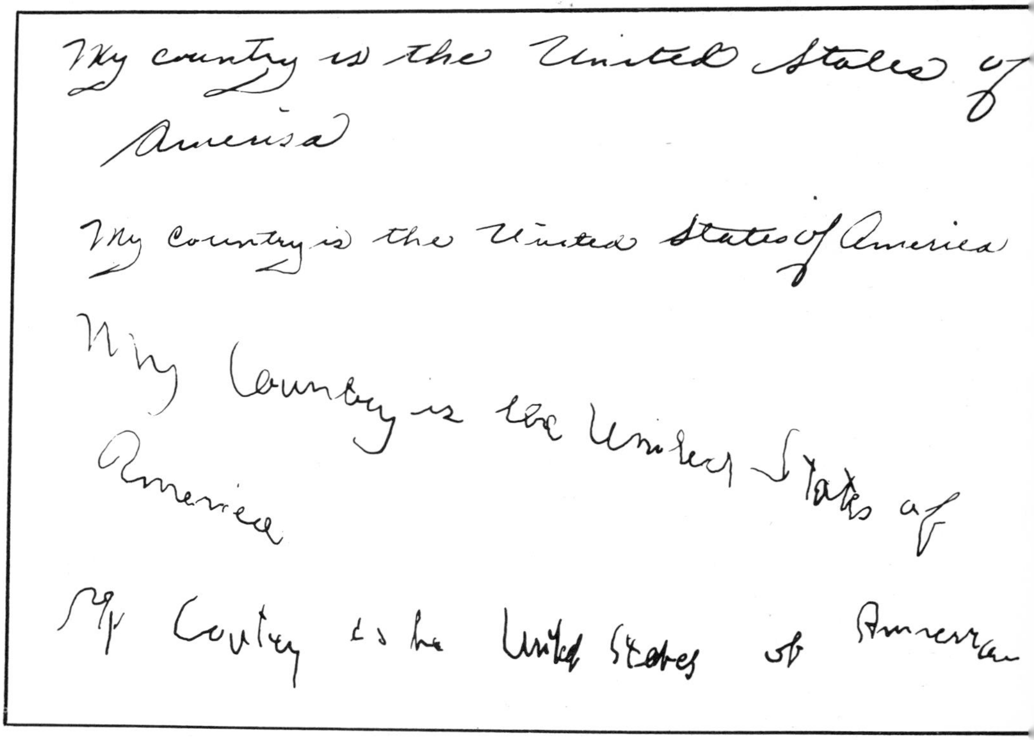

FIG. 171—Symbolization in doodlings.

difference, even if he has to perform silly acts. However, if he is asked to do something which brings him into moral conflicts, he usually reacts violently; the expressiveness is related to moral evaluations.

The decrease of differentiation under hypnosis also appears when a subject is asked to write the same sentence with his right hand and with his left hand. In the normal state the recordings of the right hand (Fig. 171 a) and those of the left (Fig. 171 b) show a considerable difference of expressiveness. In the hypnotic state, however, this difference between right (c) and left (d) decreases. This may indicate that hypnosis causes a fusion of different forms of expression, that is, a fusion of centers in personality, perhaps a fusion of conscious and unconscious reactions, making the organism react as a whole.

Symbolization in graphic expression has, as we shall see later, similarities to symbolization in dreams. This is not surprising because graphic movements are patterned by the unconscious, and the manifestations of the unconscious are the same in all media of expression. These similarities can be demonstrated by a comparison of dream images with drawings made in a state of total or partial unconsciousness. Total unconsciousness can be investigated with the help of hypnosis, as we shall discuss in the following; partial unconsciousness is present in those "absent-minded" states in which scribblings and doodlings originate. The process of symbolization can be verified if a hypnotized subject is asked to develop a dream on the basis of a stimulus given by the hypnotist. L. R. Wolberg [458, p. 185] gives a very significant example of such an experimental dream. The hypnotized subject was asked to dream about the number 65398801. Upon awakening from the hypnosis he told of the following dream, which appeared to him very ridiculous: "There was an old fellow smoking a *pipe*,* a long, old-fashioned one. It had a large porcelain bowl, German style. On it was a painted *star*. This was on the bowl. He said that meant astronomy. He said that is easy to study. He kind of banged the pipe and *broke it in half*. Then he turned it up and it turned into a *golf club*. He said this is an example of what you can do. He said that is astronomy, which *stretches into eternity in this direction* and *stretches into eternity in the opposite direction*. He made the sign of infinity vertically, not horizontally as one usually does. Then he said, 'After all the whole thing is *nothing*. There is nothing except one thing, which is *unity*'."

As Wolberg reports, the subject did not produce any significant waking associations to his dream, except that the pipe of the dream had been on the wall of the subject's room in his childhood. Under a new hypnosis, however, the subject was able to interpret the dream, and he did it exactly in terms of the stimulus number. We quote again from Wolberg:

'Under hypnosis he revealed that the *pipe* in the dream was shaped like a figure *6*, and that the *star* on the pipe had five points and therefore represented the numeral *5*. *Breaking the pipe in half* split the number 6 in *3*'s, one of which was discarded. The *golf-club* was shaped like the figure *9*. *The sign of infinity* made vertically gave the figure *8*. (There were two infinity signs, symbolizing the extensions of infinity into opposite directions.) 'The whole thing is *nothing*' signified by *zero*, and 'There is nothing except one thing which is *unity*' signified by the numeral 1. The entire dream represented to him the number 65398801."

This report shows in a significant way the process of symbolization, the first characteristic of which is that its motivation is unconscious. The dreamer is unable to reconstruct consciously the meaning of his expressiveness, as is possible with empathy and projection. The symbolization is an answer to a sudden stimulus and the material of symbolization gets its nucleus from an impression or experience in the dreamer's childhood. The mechanism of symbolization is the transformation of abstract

---

*The present author has put the significant words in italics.

elements such as numbers into concrete images and the transformation of a meaningless relationship, as the scrambling of numbers, into a meaningful pattern. This is possible by processes of elaboration, substitution of values, condensation (the two directions of infinity), transformation, union, and explanation (astronomy). These complicated processes of symbolization seem to appear in a flash, but removed from consciousness. If the subject had drawn the dream images, nobody could have recognized them as symbolizations of a number.

Several studies have been made which show that spontaneous drawings and dreams have many elements in common [467]. Spontaneous drawings, especially those made in hypnosis, are projections of associations, symbolized into a unity which also appears in dreams. During hypnosis many patients are able to explain the symbolic meaning of their drawings. Doodlings and drawings are used by psychiatrists as a diagnostic aid [125, 135, 199, 250, 250a, 303, 402]. Psychiatrists also use drawings made under hypnosis or automatic drawings [115, 116, 225, 298, 458] which originate while the subject is completely occupied otherwise, to uncover the patients' conflicts. A relationship between the unconscious expression of drawings and of handwriting appears in so-called automatic writing, which may be trained under hypnosis. We quote Wolberg's instructions for automatic writing under hypnosis [458, p. 194].

"As you sit here you will continue to be fast asleep. The arm and hand with which you write will now begin to experience a peculiar sensation. They will feel as though they are no longer a part of you. They will feel comfortable but detached. I am going to place a pencil in your hand, and as soon as I do this you will begin to write as if your hand were moving along without any effort or concentration on your part. Your hand will move along as if it were pushed by some force from the outside. As your hand moves along, you will not be aware of what it is writing."

When a pencil is placed in the hand of the hypnotized subject, his hand will move and either write incoherent words slowly or make an undecipherable scrawl, sometimes only waves similar to the diagrams of electrical organic activity. Automatic writing may be perfected to such a state that the patient can read a book, study its contents, and describe them to the analyst while he is writing. As Wolberg says [458, p. 196]: "Automatic writing is subject to the same distortions and disguises as dreams. . . . Unconscious mentation is manifest in automatic writing. The symbolisms employed, though inscrutable to the conscious mind, are less complex than conscious symbolism. Thus the cryptic automatic writing of one subject may sometimes be translated correctly by another subject in a trance, whereas the meaning will be hazy to both in the waking state."

Symbolization in Doodlings

Our next problem was to demonstrate experimentally that symbolization in graphic expression is not only a phenomenon of an abnormal state of mind, as under hypnosis. But since neither the writer nor the observer is able to recognize these processes directly we had to use an indirect approach. One hint was given by our experiments in matching doodlings or scribblings to handwritings (see page 188). It appeared that even untrained observers were able to recognize identities of expression in both kinds of graphic movements. If we mixed the doodlings and hand-writings of several persons, an observer easily found out which two specimens were made by the same person, and if handwriting and doodling were given separately for a description of their expression, both were judged similarly. This observation is important for an approach to the process of symbolization in handwriting, because the symbolic mean-ing of even abstract doodlings can, with the help of the subject's associa-

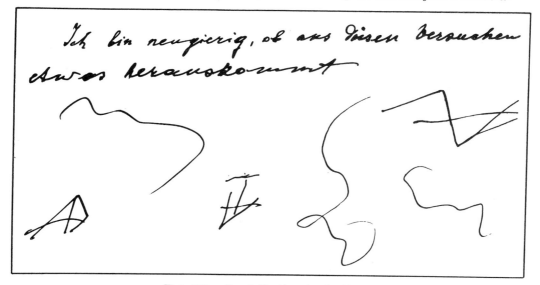

FIG. 172.—Symbolization in doodlings.

tions, be identified more easily than that of handwriting in which the content of the writing predominates over its hidden graphic symbols. Thus, an approach to these hidden symbols in handwriting is indicated by means of scribblings and doodlings in which they can be made mani-fest. Below we shall describe a few of our experiments with doodlings of normal and abnormal people. One may believe that doodlings are rather accidental; however, repetitions of doodlings of the same person show that in a majority of cases basic features remain unchanged for a longer period of time. We investigated this essential problem by two types of approach. In our Vassar experiments (see page 178) each subject was asked to make a doodling in each of the three experimental series. The three doodlings of several subjects were shuffled and presented to a neutral observer, who was asked to determine which doodlings were made by the same person.

After having been presented with the specimens in groups, namely, the nine doodlings made by three subjects, our judges were correct in 80 per cent of the cases.

If doodling symbolizes certain associations, we may conclude that these associations are dominating ones, governing the thought of the doodler. The experiments we are going to describe consisted in asking the subject immediately after the doodling was made to give associations about its meaning. We shall refer in the following to our German experiments concerning the doodlings of the subjects L., G. and M., mentioned before (cf. Figs. 138, 156). The experiments were carried out in two sessions separated by an interval of a week. In each session the subject made a doodling and immediately afterward gave his associations about it. The associations in both sessions referred to the same basic content.

Subject L. had the following associations in session 1 (Fig. 172, cf. Fig. 138 IIIa).

"Crossed lines, a lamp, the light may come into my life."

In session 2:

"A lamp, this is like a distorted letter 'L,' the initial of my husband's name, restless and entangled lines."

The associations "lamp" and "crossed or entangled lines" are the same in both sessions. The corresponding graphic elements are equally very

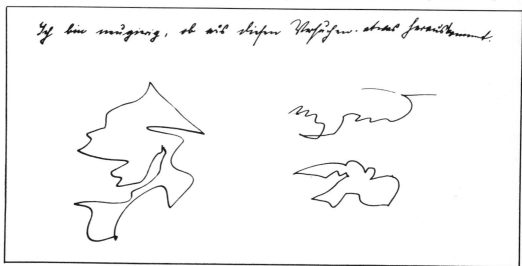

Fig. 173.—Symbolization in doodlings.

similar. The entangled line, however, shows a deeper significance only in session 2, namely, as the distorted letter "L," the initial of the husband's name. Interrelating the different associations, one may easily conclude that the restlessness is related to the husband. The life of the subject is entangled through the husband. The lamp, symbolizing—in the words of the subject—that "the light may come into my life," expresses the subject's wish to clarify the situation of her marriage. The interpretation of the associations can be verified by knowledge of the actual situation. The subject was an older woman, loving her husband but living in a very unhappy marriage. Her dominating association for years had been to bring light and rest into her entangled life.

Subject G.'s associations in session I were (Fig. 173, cf. Fig. 138 Ib and Fig. 156):

"A flying bird, something flaming up, or like the embryo of a bird."

In session 2:

"A flying bird, yet this has nothing to do with me. I would better have drawn crosses hinting at my early death. I wish I could live free like a bird."

The association of "bird" and the corresponding pictures are similar in sessions 1 and 2. The idea of "bird" is related to two associations: "embryo" and "freedom." The knowledge of the actual situation gives us a clue to the understanding of these associations. The subject was pregnant, but she wanted to be without a child, to be free like a bird.

Fig. 174.—Symbolization in doodlings.

Subject M. had the following associations in session I (Fig. 174, cf. Fig. 138, IIc):

"Sun, flower, sunflower, Helianthus, Christ."

In session 2:

"Sunflower, eyelashes, caterpillar, metamorphosis, renewal."

In both sessions the same element, graphically and verbally, is sunflower. The associations "Christ, renewal, caterpillar" seem to be related to each other. The actual situation of this subject again gives us a clue to the meaning of the associations. The subject was worried about her eyes (see the association "eyelashes") ; she suffered from squinting, loved beautiful eyes more than anything else, and dreamed of how she might be metamorphosed and change her eyes. The sunflower, which for her is a symbol of an eye with eyelashes and an old symbol for Christ (Helianthus), and therefore of renewal, becomes a representation of her dominating associations.

It appears that the doodlings of our subjects were symbolizations of their dominant associations. They were, like the experimental dreams in hypnosis, diagrams of their unconscious in which the same principles became manifest which operate in dreams: transformations of abstract thoughts, condensations of many thoughts into one image, and substitutions of thought patterns by symbols.

Although the experiments mentioned above indicated an identity of expression in doodling and handwriting, such identity could be based upon extraneous features of superficial similarities. We needed an approach to the depth of expression, demonstrating that not only the pattern of movement but the symbolic principle itself is similar in both modes of

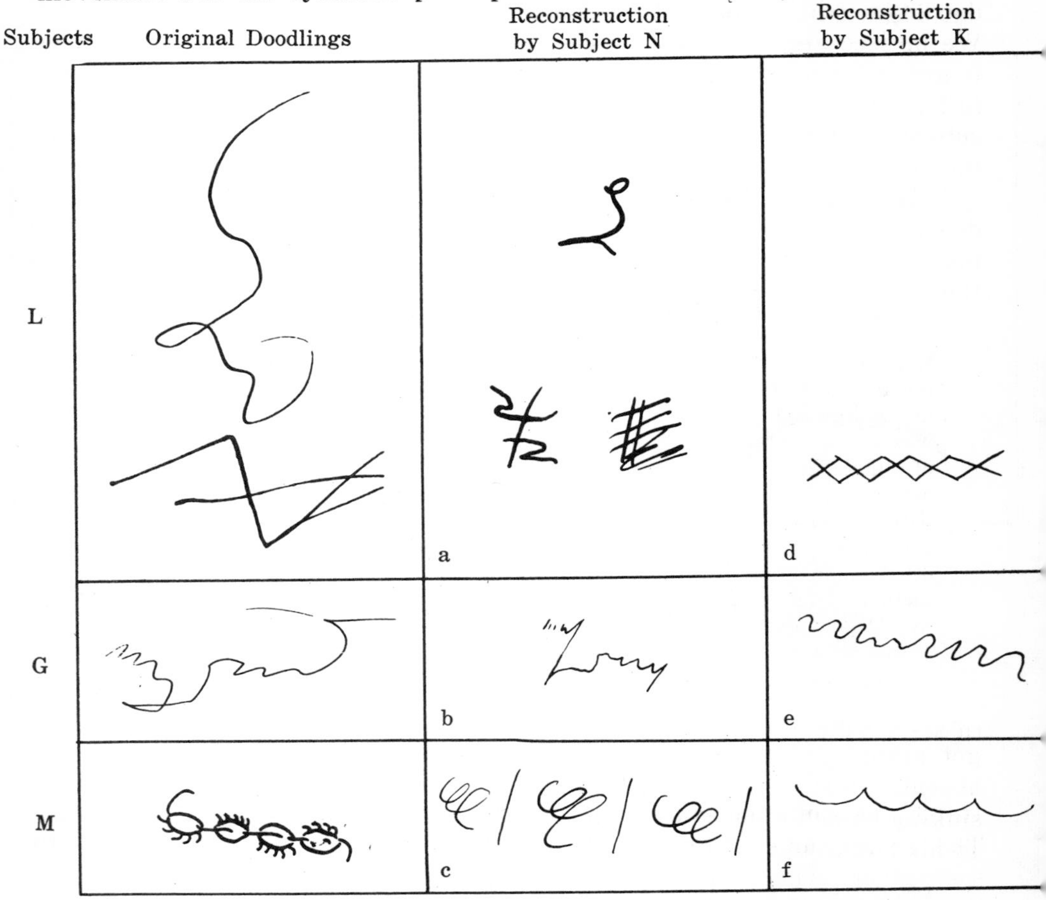

FIG. 175.—Reconstruction of doodlings from handwriting.

expression. We used a subject's ability for empathy to predict a certain type of doodling from a certain type of handwriting.

We submitted to some of our subjects who took part in the preceding experiments three handwritings which they had not seen before. The instructions were: "Try to enter into the expressive value of these handwritings and try to reconstruct a doodling of the kind these writers might have done."

Most of the subjects asserted at first their absolute inability to make such reconstructions. Some of them attempted it and did not succeed. Several subjects, however, made doodlings which actually showed a striking resemblance to those of the original writer. We selected the best ones and submitted three reconstructions to the three original writers, asking each of them to describe these doodlings (Fig. 175). When author L saw the reconstruction of her own doodlings (a) she exclaimed: "But I have made this one!" Author G pointing at the reconstruction of her doodling (b), remarked: "This drawing is rather similar to mine, but on the whole it is too relaxed." When author M saw the reconstruction of her doodlings (c), she said: "That's strange—my figure was very similar." We noticed also that other subjects who made reconstructions were able to grasp essential elements of graphic movement, elements which appeared in handwriting as well as in doodlings (Figs. d, e, f). Although not every subject had the ability for empathy necessary for the reconstructions, the successful cases indicate the potentiality of the phenomenon.

The relationship between the symbols in a doodling and those hidden in handwriting sometimes appears spontaneously in the subject who makes the doodling. Subject O.B., for instance explained his doodling in the following way (Fig. 176a):

> This is a sinking battleship. I was always afraid of this idea. I remember that in one of my children's books there was represented in dark colors a scene where a lifeboat was floating on the high seas. This high sea troubled me in such a way that I always tried to avoid this page in my book. But there was also a secret longing always to see this picture again. Fear and longing, of course, are a couple.* The ship is sinking. One person proposes to take action for life saving. He says, "Let us anchor against the action of the waves." Another person answers, "You are crazy, it is impossible to anchor in this depth of sea." One person wants an explanation of the anchor, and another one explains it to him. There were two or perhaps three persons in the picture. I identified myself with the one who was explaining. Once, I looked over these pictures with my brother while we were waiting for our mother. I was afraid when my mother was out. With the smokestacks I associate sexual symbolism.

Further comments of the subject revealed that this young fellow got sexual explanations from his older brother while the mother was absent. During the absence of his mother he felt, he said, "as if on a sinking ship." Certainly more than two or three persons were represented in his picture book; but our subject symbolizing his own experience in this

---

*This subject had studied psychology.

scene, only remembered "two or perhaps three persons," symbolizing himself, his brother, and his mother. As he remarked, he identified himself with the person who explains the significance of the anchor against the force of the waves. It is the anchor of security against the sexual impulses. And in his imagination it was not his brother who had the superiority of knowledge in this matter, but it was he himself. When our subject was looking over his doodling he exclaimed, "But this is my name!" His name was "Otto" and he pointed to the circle representing the first and last "O" and the two smoke-stacks representing the two "t's." He was

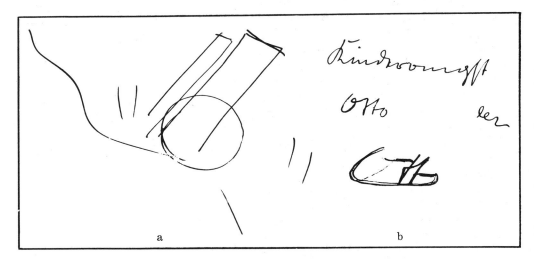

a   b

FIG. 176.—Doodling, signature and early remembrance.

asked to write his name and, on another day, he was shown in mirrored view this specimen which was preceded by specimens written by other persons, in order to make a characterization of each handwriting. Our subject, when seeing his signature in mirrored view, remarked, "This is my name, Otto; but it's strange, I suddenly see a quickly driving ship with two beautiful smokestacks, and in my second name I see curves of waves. I remember the scene of my children's book." Our subject took paper and pencil and shaped out of the written name "Otto" the outline of a ship (Fig. 176 b).

The subject was a neurotic young man, nineteen years of age; since his childhood he had had the fear of failing in life, of living on a sinking ship. In his opinion his brother was the great sailor of life. The idea of the ship of life, a concept which also plays an important role in folklore, determined even the profession of the subject. At the time our experiment was carried out he had decided to attend a school of navigation.

In this case we note that a certain image which appeared in the doodling reappears in the writing, namely, in the signature which thus represents an image of personality.

GRAPHIC SYMBOLIZATION OF INSANES

The observation of symbolization may be important for diagnostic purposes. We conducted some experiments with doodling in mental hospitals, and we shall describe the cases of two schizophrenic murderers. There follows the life history of the first case, subject S. [466, p. 179], as recorded in 1932:

> The patient is a male thirty years of age. The diagnosis is schizophrenia. He was always the first in his class at school. After his one year of military service he worked in a bank for eleven years; then he became an insurance agent. Eight years ago he suddenly felt, while reading the Bible, that the spirit of God had fallen upon him. From that day on he was a devout Christian. He met his fiancée in a religious sect; after a year they separated. He had not had any sexual intercourse up to that time. He wanted to force the girl to accept his religious ideas. After having broken with her he asked her for a last interview and went with her to the "Grünewald," a forest near Berlin. He had the feeling that he must blow up the world and then stand by, smiling diabolically. He wanted to run amuck; but then, with his remaining faculties he said to himself that if he had to kill he should only kill the girl. He felt that he had to kill her because, unless he did so, separated from him, she would have fallen a prey to world-lust and decadence.
>
> Now he knows that this thought was the devil in the shape of an angel, and that he had acted out of hate, born of rejected love. The devil could get hold of him only because, owing to his love for the girl, he had gone too far away from God. When committing the murder he first made the girl think pious thoughts; then he shot her in the back, cold-bloodedly.

When asked for a doodling this subject made a jagged line (Fig. 177b). When asked for his associations he said: "It is a trellis. I passed such a trellis when I walked with my fiancée to Nikolassee on the last day.

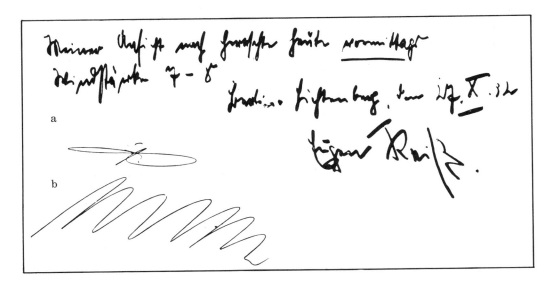

FIG. 177.—Doodling and handwriting of an insane murderer.

It is also a tight spiral. And then there are lots of bullets." This bullet-form also forms a part of his initial "R" in his signature (Fig. 177a). All these associations circulated around his leading idea of murder.

Now for the life history of subject R. [466, p. 168] as recorded in 1932:

> The patient is a male, thirty-five years of age, diagnosed as schizophrenic. He was a student at a Talmudic school. Later on he was a tutor, then a businessman. Even as a child he was distrustful. Beggars had frightened him once, and for years he lived in constant terror. At school he was the best pupil, but without friends. His father treated him well, his mother was severe. He started early to think about mending the world. He fasted two days a week. He has been married three times and was very jealous of his third wife. Psychosis began at the age of thirty-one. He began to think that his wife had given him an illness out of sadism, sending electric rays against his brain and eyes. Thereupon he received the "order" to kill her, and finally he constantly heard the evil voices shouting the name of his wife, so that he attacked her with a knife. He was put in an institution, but was released again to live with relatives. Here again he heard the voices. They told him this time that his wife had the powers of a witch, that she would kill him, that she was sucking out his blood from a distance. "At midnight the helpers of the head-devil, Lilith, came to me and wanted to tear out my soul. After a desperate battle which lasted up to four o'clock my soul was victorious. The fact that it was four o'clock when this happened means that I should take over the leadership of suffering humanity and bring redemption to it." After the call of Lilith's helpers he continued to hear the voices; he knew that he was ill, but he could not help following their advice and he killed his wife. Whereas before killing her he had heard only evil voices, after her death he heard only good ones. He thought that the murder had made him 99 per cent normal. He fulfilled the idea of an old proverb: "Destruction—Completion." "If I never had anything in life, I had one great moment: It was when my enemy fell."

When asked to make a doodling our subject first made a spiral and, beside the spiral, a waved line (Fig. 178 a). In his associations about the two lines he remarked of the spiral, "This is youth, where everybody still has imagination, that is, vividness and creative ability." As to the waved line he said, "This is the realization" (Fig. 178 b). In his signature

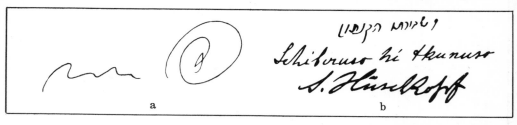

FIG. 178.—Doodling and signature of an insane murderer.

the murderer put over his name his motto written in Hebrew letters: "Destruction : Completion." His doodling was also done from right to left like Hebrew lettering. The first figure, the spiral, was for him the symbol of youth. In youth all possibilities are compressed and still bound together. The second figure, the waved line, indicated to him disillusion and decomposition, hence "destruction."

Our experiments with graphic expression seem to yield one basic result, i.e., that graphic movement is accompanied by associations which with empathy, projection and symbolization seem to influence the graphic pattern.

SYMBOLS IN SIGNATURES

The symbolic value of doodling and its relationship to handwriting suggests that the individual patterns of a person's signature may have a symbolic significance. If we ask a subject directly to give us an association to these patterns, he usually is not able to do so but insists that they have no significance at all; or that they simply are forms pleasing to him; or that they were merely rapid connections of strokes.

I, therefore, developed an indirect approach to a subject's conceptual graphic symbols by giving the following instructions: "You will get a list of concepts which I am going to dictate to you in alphabetical order. Try to symbolize each concept by the simplest graphic pattern, like a thread which you can put into different shapes and directions." The subject was asked to make his symbolization after each concept was dictated; the following concepts were given to thirty subjects:

1. action	9. future	17. present
2. death	10. happiness	18. reality
3. depression	11. introversion	19. sex
4. discouragement	12. masculine	20. sibling
5. dominating	13. mother	21. strength
6. extraversion	14. neurosis	22. unpleasant
7. father	15. past	23. wish
8. feminine	16. pleasant	24. yielding
		25. yourself

The shape of these simple patterns is likely to become repetitious and the subject's use of the same or similar patterns to different concepts becomes indicative of his symbolic relationship of concepts. Some of these patterns usually resemble a conspicuous pattern of the subject's signature which thus is interpreted indirectly by the subject himself. The pattern relationship is supported by an additional experiment in which the subject again gets the list of concepts and is now asked to match each concept with one of the primary colors. If various concepts receive the same color matching, we may deduce that these concepts, interrelated in the subject's associations, have an emotional factor in common.

The dominating pattern in the initial of one female subject's signature (Fig. 179) is the angle pointing toward the left side. The subject symbolizes "extraversion" with the same, "introversion" with a reversed pattern. The lower part of the initial shows a pattern which reappears in her symbolization of "future." The concepts "masculine" and "your-self" also show the angular pattern.—Thus, this subject's graphic symbol seems to combine her associations of extraversion, future and masculinity and she also matched these concepts with the same color, red.

One of the male subjects, Richard W.—(Fig. 180), makes a distinct adjusting stroke—that is, an extra stroke to commence a letter—

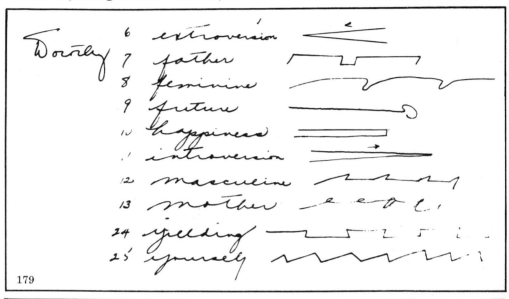

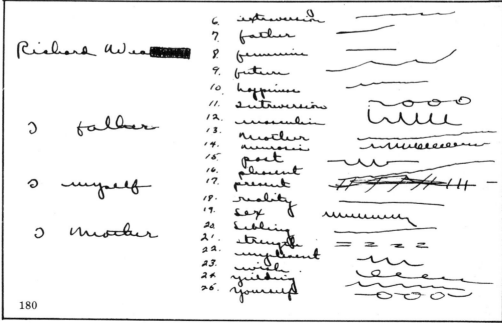

FIGS. 179-180.—Detection of symbols in signatures.

at the beginning of his second initial "W." A similar sign appears in his letter "m," however, only when he writes the word "mother." In his writing of the words "I myself, I mother, I father" (cf. page 202) we notice that the sign appears with the "m" of "mother," but not with the "m" of "myself." In his symbolization of concepts the sign also appears with the letter "n" of "neurosis," and the concept of neurosis is expressed by a similar symbol. A similar symbol also appears with the

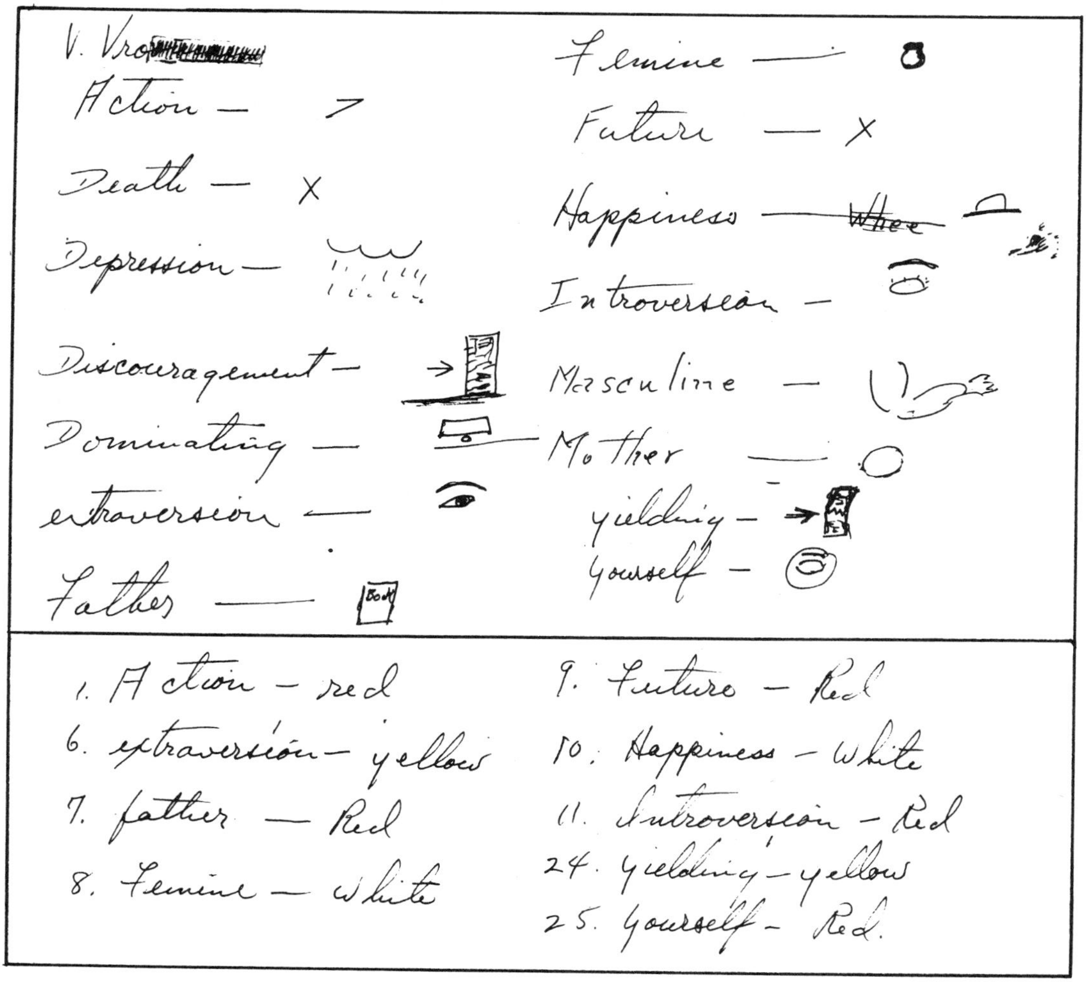

FIG. 181.—Detection of symbols in signatures.

subject's concepts of "masculine," "past," "sex," and "unpleasant." The adjusting stroke is a superfluous movement which retards the beginning of the letter and usually is a symptom of resistance. This resistance does not appear with the concept "myself," but with "mother" and his family name. The concepts of masculine, past, sex, unpleasant, neurosis, also evoke such a resistance.

The male subject V. Vro—(Fig. 181) makes sharp angles with his two initials, patterns which deviate from the otherwise rounded handwriting. In the subject's symbolization of concepts a similar sign appears only with one concept, that of "action." For the concept of "yourself" the subject draws a closed eye, the same sign with which he expresses the concept of "introversion," while "extraversion" is expressed by an open eye. In the concept of "yourself" the subject surrounds the sign of the eye with a circle, a symbol he uses for expressing the concept of "mother." The concept of "feminine" is expressed by a circular vessel; that of "masculine" by a hand in action. In the symbolization of "yourself" the subject combines the concepts of "introversion," "mother" and "feminine," which seem to be opposite to those of "action" and "masculine." We therefore might interpret the angular symbol as expressing the writer's wish-image to be different from what he is. The color matching elaborates this relationship. The color red is equally matched to the concepts of action, yourself, father, masculine, introversion, and future, suggesting that the subject wishes to realize action and masculinity in the future, without relinquishing his 'introversion."

The female subject Lucille Ed—(Fig. 182) makes a spiral in the initial of her first name, a sign which reappears with the subject's symbolization of "introversion." The second initial shows loops which reappear in the symbolization of "feminine" by the picture of a flower. The subject uses the same symbol for "yourself" and for "action," thus apparently expressing a wish-image similar to that of the subject discussed before (Fig. 181).

The four subjects discussed show two characteristically different ways of symbolizing concepts graphically. Subject Dorothy (Fig. 179) and subject Richard (Fig. 180) both express concepts in an abstract way by means of simple lines; while subject V. Vro (Fig. 181) and subject Lucille (Fig. 182) use concrete pictures for their symbolization. We shall later discuss these two types of graphic expression, calling them the oscillographic and the pictographic type (see p. 251).

These symbols of expression may be represented in concrete or in abstract pictures. Some people who think in concrete images also express such concrete images in their writing. Other people who think more abstractly express their associations in personal signs. If we ask different people to draw a man, the abstract and concrete types of representation become clearly visible, as early as in the drawings of nursery school children [467] (see Fig. 192). Galton [137] was one of the first to study experimentally such types of imagination.

However, further penetration into the process of imagination and symbolization in graphic expression demands better equipment for observing details of expression. There does not yet exist equipment with which processes of symbolic expression can be standardized, thus yielding general results applicable to everybody. Symbolic expression is so complex that our first task must be to collect empirical data, and to find certain characteristics based upon individual case material. But just as psychiatric observations of individual cases allow a hypothetical construction of systems such as those of psychoanalysis and of certain diagnostic systems such as the Rorschach test, so comparative studies of handwriting allow the formulation of a working hypothesis for explaining the structure of graphic expression.

FIG. 182.—Detection of symbols in signatures.

Here, however, we leave the laboratory atmosphere and enter the field of interpretation. Such interpretation is based upon three main factors of expressiveness: empathy, projection, and symbolization. However, the author does not agree with the advocates of interpretative psychology that experimental procedures are unnecessary or are even detrimental for approaching the processes of expressive behavior. He admits a present insufficiency of methods to accomplish this, but he visualizes it as a goal and is eager to return to the more objective field of experimentation when the data found by interpretation give us new points of view and some indications for an experimental handling of the phenomena observed. Thus our present study, which suggests methods for an experimental investigation of graphic expression, turns now to an interpretative theoretical approach in which the reader may find suggestions for an understanding of the graphic language of expression.

CHAPTER XI

INTERPRETATION OF GRAPHIC EXPRESSION

PATTERNS OF EXPRESSION AND PATTERNS OF PERSONALITY

Our study on graphic movement has dealt principally with general factors determining form and expression of graphic patterns. We have attempted to show by measurements and reaction experiments that graphic movements get their individual pattern neither by chance nor by learning and practice, but by unconscious factors. Through an analysis of these principles we seem to approach a formulation of laws which determine form, size, position and movements. These formulas of configuration of patterns and the main principles of expression determine what we call "diagrams of the unconscious."

Until this point, however, I have hesitated to interpret these diagrams in terms of an individual organization of personality. The traditional use of handwriting as a diagnostic instrument of personality has, especially in this country, come into a strong disrepute. The reason for this has been the lack of any experimental verification of the basic assumption that expressive movements in general and handwriting in particular reflect inner psychological processes. To establish such a basis is the aim of the present investigation. But a further reason for psychologists' rejection of dealing with this subject is its abuse by persons who may be successful in its application, but are unwilling or unable to use scientific methods for dealing with the diagnostic criteria. Such criteria, however, can only be developed if the basic assumption is verified, and furthermore, if the principles of interpretation are based upon an interrelated theory of expression. Our following investigation will be an approach in this direction.

Personality is an interrelated system of biophysical patterns; it is this interrelationship which makes it so difficult to subject individual expressions of personality to experimental procedures. The experiment tries to isolate one principle from the others, but since in personality the part has its meaning only within the whole, our conditions are different from those with which we have approached the single factors determining form and expression of movement. However, some general experiments have been carried out to demonstrate that an individual pattern of expression is positively related to an individual pattern of personality, and some single characteristics of expression could successfully be isolated and correlated with certain personality trends.

Professor Edwin Powers [329, 330] from Dartmouth College used matching experiments to demonstrate the unity between patterns of personality and patterns of graphic expression. Ten specimens of hand-

241

writing and case-studies, describing the personality of the ten subjects, were submitted for matchings carried out by 185 judges. The average results were only 1.77 against a chance expectancy of 1.0. However, some individual judges did very well, namely, making 6 correct matchings out of 10, so that the occurrence of chance success would be only 1 in 1920 times.

I had a number of persons retell a story that was first read to them, and I wrote down their different versions [466]. Three of these versions and the corresponding handwriting specimens were given for matchings and I obtained results that were one and a half times higher than would be expected according to the coefficient of chance expectancy.

These results, similarly reported by other investigators, indicate a relationship between patterns of expression and patterns of personality; but since the results are poor in absolute terms, the hope for using a total graphic expression for a total diagnosis of personality was not encouraging. Now the attempt was made to judge specific, not general behavior.

The Harvard Study on Personal History, Handwriting and Specific Behavior

From 1939-1941 the Department of Hygiene of Harvard University conducted a large experimental investigation on the expressiveness of handwriting within "a research focussed on the normal personality." The comparative data of 108 cases, between "blind diagnoses" of handwriting (that is, without any information other than that based upon the graphic specimen) and the diagnosis of a psychiatrist from personal experience, led to the following statements [443, p. 301]:

> . . . handwriting and history agreed about twice as often as they disagreed; agreement occurred, that is, in about 70 per cent of the judgments made. A special finding appears in respect to traits; the best agreeing would agree in something over 80 per cent of the judgments; the least agreeing trait would show not over 50 per cent or chance agreement.*

About specific traits, rated by graphological standards, the following is reported: "A neurotic script was unlikely to be associated with a 'sound' personality." Concerning various traits the diagnostic agreement was as follows: with the diagnosis of "persistence" in 87 per cent; of "energy" in 76 per cent; of "practicality" in 80 per cent; of "emotionality and calmness" in 89 per cent; of "extraversion" in 73 per cent. "Egocentrism appears to have been estimated by the graphologist in some two thirds of the cases where it was found by the psychiatrist."

Another report of the Harvard Studies is given by G. R. Pascal [319]. The handwriting of 22 college students, each of them "subjected to several hundred hours of study by the staff of the Harvard Psychological Clinic" was analyzed in terms of 36 personality variables. Graphic correlations were found for the following of Murray's [301, p. 142 ff] terms, which are explained as follows:

---

*F. L. Wells: "Personal History, Handwriting and Specific Behavior." Character and Personality (Duke University Press) 14:301, 1946.

Abasement. To surrender. To comply and accept punishment. To apologize, confess, atone. Self-depreciation. Masochism.

Defendance. To defend oneself against blame or belittlement. To justify one's actions. . . .

Exocathection. (The positive cathexis of practical action and cooperative undertakings.) Occupation with outer events . . . inclination to participate in the contemporary world of affairs.

Harmavoidance. To avoid pain . . . illness, and death. To escape from dangerous situations. To take precautionary measures.

Infavoidance. To avoid failure, shame, humiliation, ridicule. To refrain from attempting to do something that is beyond one's powers. . . .

Play. To relax, amuse oneself, seek diversion and entertainment. To "have fun." . . . To avoid serious tension.

Projectivity. (The disposition to project unconsciously one's wish-engendered or anxiety-evoked beliefs.) Mild forms of the delusions of self-reference, persecution, omnipotence, etc.*

The graphic indications were found by measuring letters according to size, distance, inclination, width, upper-, middle- and lower projections, connectedness, adjustments, and so forth. The following experimental results are reported:

At the 1 per cent level of confidence nine significant first order correlation coefficients were found . . . we find that
Upper Projection is related to Play,
Mid-Zone Ratio to Projectivity,
Distance Between Words to Play,
Width of Stroke to Exocathection and Harmavoidance,
Distance of I Dot to Infavoidance, and
Balance of Projection to Abasement, Defendance, and Dominance.*

G. R. Pascal adds further graphic characteristics and their correlation to personality traits. Curvature of the t-bar seems to be related negatively to Anxiety and positively to Play. Disconnectedness was related positively to Sentience, initial adjustment positively to Conjunctivity, left movement positively to Achievement and negatively to Emotionality, right movement positively to Conjunctivity.

The author summarizes [319, p. 140]:

This experiment, designed to test the significance of handwriting variables for personality, is completed. Hundreds of quantitative estimates of relationship were calculated. Of these, sixteen were found to be significant, nine first-order correlation coefficients, and seven multiple correlation coefficients. . . .**

And the author concludes that a null hypothesis, an absence of relationship between any variable of handwriting and any variable of personality is untenable. ". . . for our population, certain aspects of handwriting are significantly related to certain aspects of personality."

Thus the Harvard experimental study has demonstrated a positive relationship between certain factors of graphic expression and certain variables of personality. The specific correlations mentioned are sup-

---

*H. A. Murray: "Explorations in Personality." Copyright 1944 by the Oxford University Press, New York.

**G. R. Pascal: "The Analysis of Handwriting; A Test of Significance." Character and Personality. (Duke University Press) *12*:140, 1943.

ported by observations made by the present author. Although such experimental correlations should be enlarged by future investigations, our present aim was now to find a psychological frame of reference for these and other correlations. The phenomena of expression as signs for specific characteristics had to be explained in terms of a unifying theory of personality.

Since the axis of personality is supposed to unite the various manifestations of the individual, we would expect to discover the axis by analyzing various manifestations, following them up to a point where they may converge. Some graphologists believe that such a point of convergence can be understood intuitively. Ludwig Klages calls it "the level of form" which underlies all the details of handwriting. Different investigators judge forms of expression according to different frames of reference; Klages focuses upon the dynamics between emotional and rational factors, Max Pulver upon psychoanalytical principles, Jacoby upon sexual factors, Anja Mendelsohn follows Jung's concepts.

Our approach attempts to start from a subject's own frame of reference, indicated by his formula of configuration and his symbols of expression.

THE AXIS OF PERSONALITY

In trying to systematize approaches toward an apprehension of graphic expression, I am aware that the systematization can be considered only as a working hypothesis. The main task of such an hypothesis is that of a unification of the variety of factors which, if considered separately, remain meaningless. If, however, methodological reasons oblige us to describe one factor after another separately, we should never forget that each factor can be seen only as part of the whole and that it is impossible to make any definite diagnosis from one feature alone. Thus we want to put strong emphasis on the fact that the present study can be used, not like a cookbook to concoct personality diagnosis, but only as a guide for comprehending those characteristics of graphic expression which seem to be indicative of certain personality structures. As we have emphasized, the structure of personality is not a summation of isolated traits but a pattern of relationships, and these relationships are neither accidental nor a reflection of an arbitrary adaptation to the environment. The relationships are organized following principles of selection, order, and integration. This organizing factor certainly has one root in our innate structure which becomes manifest in the build and development of the organism. An analysis of personality also suggests the presence of a center to which all attitudes and reactions are related in such a way that, knowing the center, certain reactions can be deduced and predicted. We call this center of personality the *axis of personality*. The greatest danger of traditional graphology is a doctrine of fixed signs. We emphasize throughout the present study that graphic movement is a reflection of the total organization of the biopsychological personality. The analysis of these movements must always consider patterns, and an element becomes significant only in relation to the whole expression. Traditional graphology emphasized three main characteristics of graphic movement: the *size* of movement, especially the vertical length of letters, the degree of *inclination* of movement, and the kind of *patterning* of the movement, which appears, not only in the quickness and slowness of the writing act but also in the kind of spacing and the characteristic way of connecting letters. Let us take the small letter "m" as an example. Its size may vary from 1/64th of an inch when the letter is extended to a wavy line to 16/64ths of an inch and over. The medium varies as well as according to different national alphabets and periods of life. Traditional graphology believed that the size of the letter is related to degrees of self-estimation from inferiority feeling, modesty, conformity to the drive for dominance, and megalomania. The inclination of letters was measured by graphometers which indicate the degree of the angles used (Fig. 183). Traditional

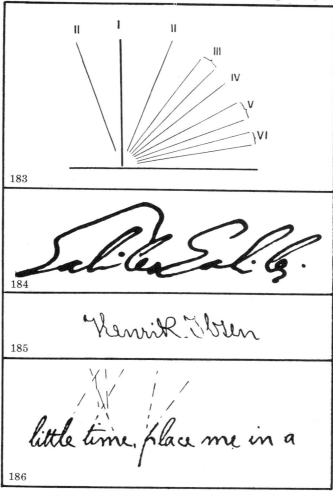

FIGS. 183-186.—Inclination of movement.

graphology correlated the degree of 90 with a rigid and cold character the degree of about 70 toward left with self-denial and dissimulation, the degree of about 70 toward right with warm-heartedness, the degree of about 60 toward right with passion up to vehemence, the degree of 45 with sensibility, and the degree of 30 with irritability. The corresponding degrees toward left were supposed to indicate degrees of resistance and coldness. In our examples the signature of Galilei (Fig. 184) has a degree of 30 toward right and the signature of Ibsen (Fig. 185) a degree of 45 toward left. A continuous change of inclinations appears in the handwriting of Robert Burns (Fig. 186). These observations also can be valid

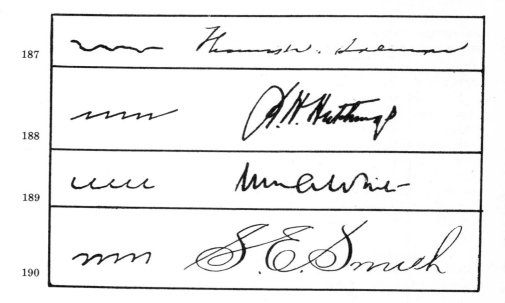

FIGS. 187-190.—Graphic connections.

only in relationship to other characteristics. Concerning the progression of movement, quickness and slowness were considered as indicators of temperament, and spacing as a reflection of psychological distance to other persons. The characteristic connections of strokes were divided into four main groups which we illustrate by signatures of presidents of the American Psychiatric Association.* There is the so-called thread formation (Fig. 187), the angular writing (Fig. 188), garlands with their curved connections (Fig. 189) and arcades with the arcade-like form (Fig. 190). The thread formation was considered as a sign of indistinctness and indecision, the angular form as an expression of will and determination, the garlands as a characteristic of obligation and feeling, the arcades as a characteristic of reserve and formality.

---

*From G. Zilboorg and J. K. Hall, editors: One Hundred Years of American Psychiatry. New York, Columbia University Press, 1944. Pp. 585-589.

The validity of these various graphic characteristics as indicators of certain personality trends has not yet been established on a statistically significant basis. If we, however, interpret graphic patterns in terms of movements the significance of many characteristics can be understood by the observation of movement patterns in gestures. We observe, for instance, a correlation of wide movements with expansion, of narrow movements with contraction, of big movements with overemphasis and small movements with underemphasis, of angular movements with tension and of round movements with adaptation. Such movement patterns become especially evident in drawings, and here some investigators were able to find a significant relationship between dominant movement patterns and certain dominant personality trends. Schmidl-Waehner [437] found that "many curved forms and few edges were used by the well-adjusted, slightly passive introversive productive types," while "few curved forms and many edges were used by those described as overtly aggressive, with low adjustment." A similar observation was made by R. Alschuler and W. Hattwick [7a] on the basis of drawings by 150 children. They noted that those children who worked mostly with single straight-line strokes seemed definitely grouped together by their relatively assertive, outgoing behavior. Some typical traits for this group were: "realistic interests," "initiative for play," "aggressive," and "negativistic." On the other hand, those children observed to work with curved, continuous strokes seemed grouped together by their more dependent, more compliant, more emotionally toned reactions. Some typical traits for this group were: "affectionate," "lack of confidence," "seek adult attention," "random work habits," and "fanciful imagination."

The characteristic associations accompanying certain graphic patterns can be investigated on the basis of introspective reports. Johannes Walther [441] from the Psychological Laboratory of the University of Munich, had subjects describe their feelings when writing garlands, arcades, and angular lines. His report of a uniformity of feelings experienced with certain graphic movements was partially supported by my own experiments. I asked thirty students to describe their feelings when writing thready, waved lines. Seventy-five per cent of the subjects described their feeling as "nice," "free," "easygoing," "relaxed," while 25 per cent described it as "disagreeable," "awkward," "sloppy." The feelings when making angular lines were in 85 per cent of the cases "harsh," "sharp," abrupt," "aggressive," and in 15 per cent "forceful," "domineering." The feelings when making arcades were in 55 per cent related to "effort," "obstacle," "insecurity," and in 45 per cent to concepts like "systematic," "precise," "co-ordinated." The feelings when making garlands were in 50 per cent of the cases described as "gay," "natural," "simple," "enjoyable," and in the other 50 per cent as "difficult," "sinking," "retreating," "unpleasant." When I asked the subjects to write their names and the words "Bard College" smaller than usual, bigger than usual, with a slant towards the left and with a slant toward the right, and to describe their feelings while performing these movements, the answers again were not scattered but fell into a few groups. Their feelings with the smaller writing were described as follows: "It is more confining, less free," "a feeling of frustration," "restricted," "strained,"— others said: "more precise," "much more significant because it seems to be less superficial," "more real, natural and very personal." Their feelings with the bigger writing were described as "excessive," "grandiose, a little false," "impatient"; others said: "free, lighthearted, lazy," "an enjoyable decrease of control." The left slant was experienced as an expression of "thoughtfulness." One student wrote: "I can write faster with a right slant but feel as if I was running ahead of my thoughts; I like to write this way if not much thought is involved." Others said it felt "strained," "unnatural," "tense," "reactionary," "self-involved." The right slant was experienced by some as "pleasing, artistic"; by others as an expression of "haste," as "sluggish and weak." About 40 per cent of the subjects found it easier to change the graphic movement of their own name, 20 per cent found it easier to change the movement when writing "Bard College" and 40 per cent did not find any difference. When comparing the statements on the different graphic movements with the genuine graphic movement of each subject, 67 per cent of the subjects preferred that movement which they used in their own writing, 33 per cent preferred movements opposite to their own. Of subjects who wrote with their left hand, or admitted doing various things such as driving and eating with their left hand, 80 per cent used arcades; while, of the right-handed subjects, 40 per cent used arcades, 40 per cent garlands, and 20 per cent the angular pattern. A relationship between left-handedness and a preference for arcade writing has also been observed by Roman-Goldzieher [354a]. Although not all of our subjects agreed in their feelings related to certain graphic movements, we observed several characteristic patterns of reactions. We found again that graphic expression cannot be fully interpreted on the basis of single signs but only in relationship to the complex movement pattern.

THE EXPRESSIVE VALUE OF SAMPLES

If graphic expression is an instrument for diagnosis of personality, is it then possible to interpret *each* graphic expression successfully? We must consider this question very carefully, because skeptical persons, suspicious of each analysis of expressive behavior, try to decide the possibility of analyzing expressive behavior by experiments which neglect interrelationships. They submit objects for interpretation, arbitrarily selected, to persons whom they select arbitrarily also; they evaluate the results obtained according to chance expectancy. With this procedure some interpreters have achieved only negative results. Consequently, they dispute any possibility of personality interpretation from expressive behavior.

The successful results of another group of interpreters indicate, however, that the conditions for the experiment are decisive for success or failure. These conditions either refer to the personality of interpreters or to the choice of objects to be analyzed. If interpreters have strong prejudices, they will not succeed in making an analysis. If the objects show the writer's expressiveness to a low degree, the conditions for personality analysis are less favorable than if the objects are very expressive of the writer's personality. Thus a failure with certain subjects cannot decide whether a form of expression is indicative of personality. To decide the preliminary problem concerning the expressive value of graphic samples we should either select or train our subjects. For untrained judges the choice of samples should be determined by their distinctiveness of expression, because the power of perception and distinction of expressions must be trained and sharpened. If we try to guess the leading projection of a subject from his graphic expression, we should take graphic samples from persons who have a certain dominant idea.

The manifold character of human personality shows that certain persons find their expression in certain ways which others do not use. In some persons it is the voice which is especially expressive, in others, the face, and in still others, the handwriting. The expressive value of each medium need not necessarily coincide with the total personality. On the contrary, certain inhibitions of personality may be projected on certain forms of expression, because the inhibition is related to them. Some people may be inhibited in trying to write because of certain childhood experiences, but be free from inhibitions in other forms of expression. In other cases, an ideal of simplicity or an opposition to the written word as a fixed expression, or the dominance of certain compensations, may lower graphic expressiveness. For instance, the signature of Albert Einstein does not express the genius of his personality (Fig. 191). We must also consider that in some instances the signature alone may be revealing, in others only the text, and in yet others signature and text may reflect

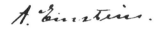

FIG. 191.—The expressive value of samples.

different expressions. In any case, one cannot expect equally successful results from all samples.

Personality is a fusion of many tendencies and attributes, and each characteristic receives its value only from the combination in which it stands. If handwriting expresses personality, each single element of expression must be viewed with respect to the total impression. But also each single interpretation must be made with a view toward a total interpretation. We cannot evaluate isolated traits such as activity, passivity, and intelligence, since each trait can be conceived only in its relationship to the others. Thus we might deduce only that a person is active or passive in certain respects, for instance, in social relationships; or in intellectual matters; or in scientific research.

The conditions of writing, such as the necessity to shape the letters so as to make them readable, limit expressiveness to a certain degree. But we may transform this drawback into an advantage for a personality diagnosis. In life, when judging personality, we frequently proceed under conditions described in the proverb: "One cannot see the forest because of the trees." Graphic expression, giving a reduced picture of personality,

FIG. 192.—Pictograph (a) and oscillograph (b) in the graphic expression of young children.

may make it possible to pick out a dominant tree in the forest of personality. Such a Leitmotif may elucidate an autobiography or biography of a person where the mass of described events obscures a clear pattern.

The first task for an interpretation of graphic expression is to collect the graphic elements; the second is to recognize dominating trends; and the third task is to relate all traces to the center or axis of personality for building up a personality picture. This technique of reconstruction corresponds to that of a criminologist, who collects data, searches for leading traces, and reconstructs the case; and to that of an archaeologist, who restores missing pieces to rebuild an ancient monument.

PICTOGRAPH AND OSCILLOGRAPH

We have an opportunity to investigate the development of projective processes in observing the act of graphic expression in children and primitive people. In children as early as four and five years of age there can be distinguished those who in their first attempts draw primitive pictures like the five year old girl (Fig. 192 a) and those who draw abstract curves and lines like the five year old boy (Fig. 192 b). That means, we can distinguish a preference for static pictures or dynamic graphs. Both expressive ways are significant for two types of personality which manifest themselves early, before any training takes place, both ways of graphic expression being structural.

The concrete and abstract types of graphic expression can be distinguished in drawings; in one kind the contents prevail, emphasizing objects and persons, in the other the expressive way of the artist prevails and manifests itself by certain curves, and by a special fluctuation of lines. We call the recordings of these oscillations "oscillographs." Thus, regarding drawings, we may distinguish between "pictographic" and "oscillographic" characteristics. This difference holds also for another type of graphic expression, namely handwriting.

Handwriting shows collective and individual differences. The collective differences appear in the structure of different writing systems used by various peoples. Egyptian, Chinese, and Aztec graphic symbols show pictures, while our alphabet shows abstract symbols. Writing systems frequently show both characteristics; Chinese letters, for instance, demonstrate these two factors in their development. Take the sign for "heart" in different epochs (Fig. 193). The basic structure of this sign can be recognized in the different epochs, but the projected images are different, and these images were given a special name in each period. The writings of different epochs were called Dragon-writing (a), Flower-writing (b), Bird-writing (c), etc. In the development of writing the original pictures disappeared more and more, and an abstract sign was substituted for the concrete picture (d). As another example, take the development of the Chinese sign for "elephant" (Fig. 194). Similarly, the concrete images of Egyptian hieroglyphics developed into the abstract pattern of the demotic script. A sign, then, usually is a reduced picture and both, pictures and signs, are symbols of associations. Explorers recount of

193   194

FIGS. 193-194.—Development of Chinese signs.

the Melanesian "thread plays" (like our "cat's cradle") that they were not able to recognize the pictures of persons and animals formed by interlaced threads, but that to the natives they appeared clear-cut pictures of the objects represented. These observations suggest that in some cases pictures can be identified and in others not; in the latter case pictures may be so reduced that we do not perceive them as pictures.

We must consider a corresponding phenomenon in personal writing. Images can be projected upon letter formation, but in such an abbreviated way that it is possible to recognize their significance only if we know the corresponding associations; the graphic signs are then mere diagrams of associations. A detailed study of signatures showed that different kinds of pictures may be projected on the letter shape. There are pictorial signs for actual impressions, signs for recollections of the past, for imaginings of the future, and signs for dominating ideas which we shall later demonstrate in handwriting samples.

The relationship between pictures and letters usually starts in the first writing attempts of children. We give as an example the lettering of a five-year-old girl for whom printed letters were either images of a rabbit (e.g., letters A, D) or of sun-rays (e.g., letters F. E.) (Fig. 195).

Summarizing, we call "pictographic" not only pictorial signs which

FIG. 195.—Relationship between pictures and letters in first writing attempts.

FIGS. 196-197.—Pictographic and oscillographic patterns in musical notations.

can be identified as such, but a certain pattern of expression in which the pictorial quality of letters is emphasized. This is the case with an ornamentation of letters and with a distribution of graphic elements, characteristic of a visual type (see page 238).

Contrasted with the pictographic pattern is the oscillographic one. Here, curves and waves may predominate in such a way that the letter shape can hardly be recognized. Signatures made in different stages of an epileptic attack show clearly how graphic expression in an oscillographic manner reflects the energetic processes in personality (see Fig. 55). Here, the writer is not moved by his vision but by his motor principles. He does not observe how he makes his graphic forms but is carried on by his motor impulses, disregarding the appearance of his writing. His emphasis is not upon the impression the writing gives but upon the discharge of his expression.

The pictographic and oscillographic patterns of writing appear at all times, in all peoples, and under all conditions of mind. The old civilizations, primitive peoples, children, mentally diseased persons—they all offer both patterns of expression, sometimes one form exclusively, sometimes both forms combined with each other. These characteristics appear in all forms of graphic movement, in handwriting, musical notations, drawings, ornaments, and doodlings.

Characteristics of the oscillographic pattern are wave-like movements, trembling strokes, isolated forms, an absence of shape or concrete features, a reduction of forms, a swing of curves, a lack of pressure and a quick movement.

Characteristics of the pictographic pattern are pictures, architectonic forms, definite shapes, an ornamental interlacing of strokes, an intentional configuration of elements, an emphasis on the structure of letters, a frequently slow movement. Both types appear distinctively if persons symbolize concepts graphically (see page 238 ff.).

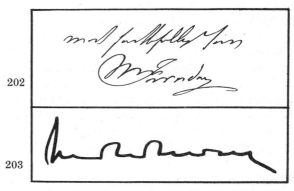

FIGS. 198-203.—Oscillographs in signatures.

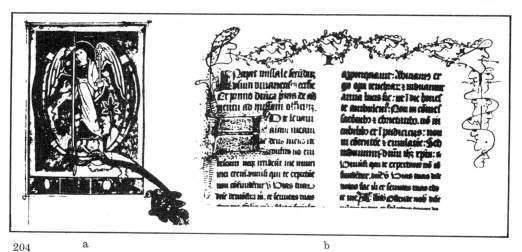

204   a   b

If we compare the musical notations of Paganini (Fig. 196) with those of Bach (Fig. 197), the former reveal a dynamic movement pattern while the latter show a static picture-like elaboration. The oscillographic type seems to be very characteristic of musicians who may pro-

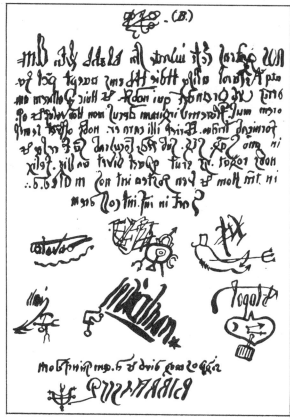

205

FIGS. 204-205.—Pictographs.

ject the concept of musical vibrations upon their graphic expression. The symbol of these oscillations frequently appears at the end of the signature, as in the signatures of Beethoven (Fig. 198), Haydn (Fig. 199), Mozart (Fig. 200), and Suppé (Fig. 201). Further examples of an oscillographic pattern are the signatures of Faraday (Fig. 202) and of Millard Caldwell, Governor of Florida (Fig. 203).

The mediaeval writers and illustrators of manuscripts frequently projected images upon their letters. In an old Anglo-Saxon manuscript the form of the "P" is described in the following way: "The hero bears a long rod with a golden point, always swinging it against a grim enemy." We give an example of such an illustrated letter (Fig. 204 a) and of the projecting activity of a mediaeval illustrator (1493 A.D.), who surrounds his manuscript with doodlings of faces (Fig. 204 b). The handwriting of Urban Grandier (Fig. 205), who made a contract with the devil which was accepted as evidence in court, has the characteristics of picture-like hieroglyphics, and so has the writing of a young graphic artist (Fig. 206). Here we see similar elements in drawing and writing,

FIG. 206.—Similar elements in drawing and writing.

such as the spiral (a), the curve and vertical line (b), the wavy line (c), and the circle (d).

A nice pictographic sample is the menu of a German seafood restaurant the specialty for which was flounders, in German "Flunder" or "Butte." The shape of this fish appears in the letter "B" of the menu (Fig. 207).

The oscillographic and pictographic patterns of graphic expression seem to correspond to two groups of personality characteristics which we might call types. The concept of a "type" has to be taken with great reservations because it leads to a static approach to personality and to a simplification of the given data. But as a mere working hypothesis the concept of a type guides us to recognize characteristic relationships of traits and patterns of behavior. It is in this sense that we attempt to

FIG. 207.—Pictographic sample of a menu.

correlate the pictographic and the oscillographic pattern with certain aspects of personality, which seem to appear with a significant frequency. Our use of the terms "pictographic or oscillographic person" are constructs from which the personality of each single individual deviates in varying degrees.

The pictographic person tends to be dependent on objects. He will like to surround himself with pictures, bibelots, objects of art, etc. He will prefer sculpture and handicraft; he observes and depends on the impression he is making upon others. Abnormal cases of pictographic expression are exemplified by persons who are dominated by symbolic thinking, the structure of which becomes especially manifest in dreams. Such persons are overwhelmed by unconscious images and symbols so that they also realize them in their graphic expression.

Extreme cases of the opposite kind of imagination, the oscillographic one, are persons who are extremely receptive. They can be played upon like a musical instrument. Among them we find mediumistic persons, whose personalities vibrate with each impression. The oscillographic person is in many cases without any relation to objects or their aesthetic value. He is impressionable, sensitive, irritable, nervous, and upon the whole more of an introvert.

A tendency for concretization in intellectual processes expresses itself in pictographs, a tendency for abstraction in oscillographs. A dominance of unconscious processes as, for instance, in mental disease may be expressed by images, realized in pictographs—as in Lombroso's example of a mentally diseased person who drew pictures into his letters (Fig. 208) ; or in oscillographs—as in Crépieux-Jamin's example of a maniac's handwriting which expresses the concept of energetic forces (Fig. 209). Although everybody seems to develop toward one of the two types, the emphasis of one type or the other may change considerably during the individual's life. We give as examples the signatures of two personalities who in their earlier life (a) tended to a pictographic expression and who in their later life (b) developed more oscillographic patterns: the states

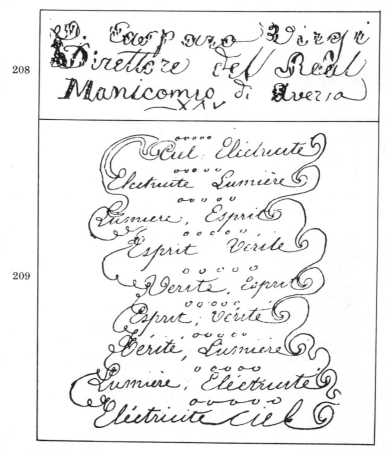

FIGS. 208-209.—Pictographic and oscillographic expression of insanes.

man Bismarck (Fig. 210) and the painter George Cruikshank (Fig. 211). Of course, we seldom find pure types, but in each analysis of graphic forms the degree of their appearance and frequency is decisive. Becoming familiar with the characteristics of both types, experience enables us to distinguish the degree and to select the type of corresponding projections, which get their specific color and shape in connection with all other graphic elements to which they are related. The degree of expressiveness in a

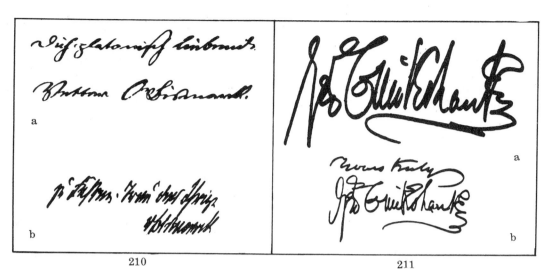

210   211

FIGS. 210-211.—Change of pictographic to oscillographic expression.

pictographic or in an oscillographic way gives us the possibility of predicting certain reactions. We may thus understand that certain deductions from graphic expression, which up to now were attributed to intuition or even telepathy [124, 373], do not always need this explanation, but may be due to a capacity for reconstructing details from a basic structure.

RHYTHM OF GRAPHIC EXPRESSION

Analyzing the determinants of graphic expression we find first that graphic patterns result from movements of the hand. The basic determinants of movement are the factors of time and space. In terms of time we speak of a quick, slow, or moderate movement; in terms of space we speak of a small, large, or medium-sized movement.

Let us first analyze further the factor of space. Any movement is limited from without by the given space and from within by the energy invested in the movement. If we have to write a letter, and only a small piece of paper to write upon is at our disposal, we necessarily contract the movements in order to get our message on the paper. Here the height and width of our movements are limited by the given space. If we write upon a glossy surface which does not absorb the ink very well, we tend to press the pen in order to penetrate the paper. Thus, not only the two dimensions of height and width but also the third dimension of depth is determined by the given condition of writing [90].

But our movement may also be limited from within. If we are exhausted, our movements are likely to show distortions; if we are overexcited our movements tend to expand; and if we are hesitant our movements tend to shrink. In this case inner psychological factors modify the movement which is projected upon paper. Thus inner as well as outer limitations modify the natural movement.

The natural movement is that which is conditioned by training and experience. For instance, the end-stroke in the loop of the written letter "g" is conditioned to go from left to right; however, some people make this movement from right to left. The dot over the "i" is conditioned to be put over the stem of the letter, however, some people put it forward, some back. What are these inner conditions which modify the learned direction of movements?

Centrifugal and Centripetal Movements. We call a movement which leads the hand away from the writer on to the right side of the paper in a horizontal and to the top side in the vertical a centrifugal movement (driving away from the center). The opposite movement comes back to the writer, reaching inside—the inside being on the left side of the paper in the horizontal and on the bottomside in the vertical. We call a movement which leads the hand toward the writer a centripetal movement (driving back toward the center).

These two basic movements, the outgoing and the ingoing, are characteristic of the rhythmic alternation of up- and down-strokes, and of the alternation of progressing and regressing curves. The alternation of ingoing and outgoing movements is characteristic of organic processes such as the inhaling and exhaling of breathing and the systole or contraction and diastole or expansion of the heart muscle. Inhaling is a collecting of air, diastole a collecting of blood; exhaling is giving forth of air, systole a giving forth of blood. If we relate these characteristics of collecting and giving away to mental processes, we may say that we are collecting impressions and we are giving forth expressions. If graphic movements reflect inner psychological processes we may compare the change of strokes which go toward the writer (centripetal strokes) and strokes which go away from the writer (centrifugal strokes) to the basic phenomena, impression and expression. In this sense centripetal movements would reflect the coming in of impressions and centrifugal movements the going out of expressions. Expression can be an immediate reflection of an impression as, for instance, if a terrible impression immediately causes a painful reaction. However, higher forms of expression are not mere reflections, but transformations of impressions. Here expression is an expressive act. A rigid correspondence of centripetal and centrifugal strokes would indicate an absence of transforming and creative acts. A dynamic alternation of centripetal and centrifugal movements is a basic characteristic of rhythm. It does not seem to be chance that musicians like to emphasize such movement in a large loop below their signature, going in a centripetal way from right to left and centrifugally returning to the right. We find this loop, for instance, in the signatures of Johannes Brahms (Fig. 212), Edward Grieg (Fig. 213), Felix Mendelssohn-Bartholdy (Fig. 214), Piotr Ilyich Tchaikovsky (Fig. 215), Richard

Wagner (Fig. 216), Giuseppe Verdi (Fig. 217). We also find this loop in initials as in the signature of Robert Schumann (Fig. 218).

One movement pattern may be especially emphasized, as the centripetal movement of Dorgelès (Fig. 219), and the centrifugal movement of Pascal (Fig. 220). Centrifugal and centripetal movements can be observed in all details of handwriting. They appear in a proclination or reclination of letters, the degree of inclination remaining rather stable in the handwriting of each person. Centrifugal or centripetal movements also de-

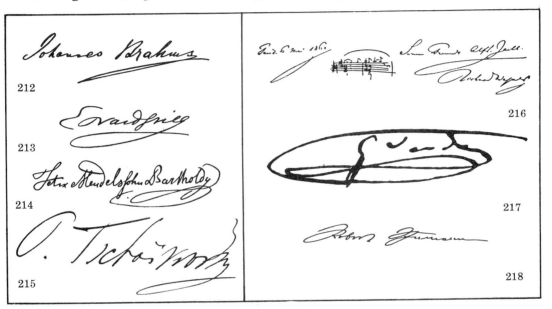

FIGS. 212-221.—Centripetal and centrifugal movements in signatures of musicians.

termine the form of letters. The letter "m" may be written in convex form, having the arcs at the top, or in a concave form, having the arcs at the bottom (see page 246). The movement in the convex form goes from top to bottom, turning toward the writer; it is a centripetal movement. The movement in the concave form goes from bottom to top, turning away from the writer; it is a centrifugal movement. The dot over the "i" may run forward, as in the writing of Emily Dickinson (Fig. 220), or it may be put backward, as in the word "friend" written by Hawkyns (Fig. 221) who emphasizes all regressive movements.

Obviously, we cannot make a diagnosis from the direction of movement alone since, as we have emphasized, each characteristic gets its value only within the context in which it stands. Thus centrifugal and centripetal movements would mean something different in pictographic or in oscillographic writing. However, what we may diagnose is the relationship between centrifugal and centripetal movements, which constitutes what we call rhythm. Rhythm has been considered as the main

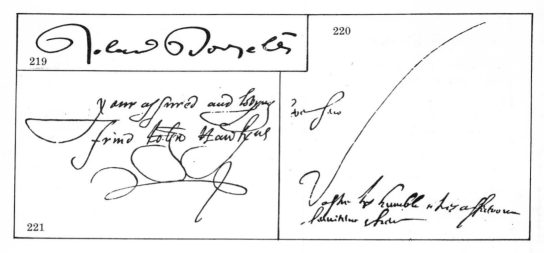

FIGS. 219-221.—Centripetal and centrifugal movements.

problem of graphic expression and Ludwig Klages [205, 211, 247] put it into the center of his graphological system. Several investigators explored organic rhythms in relationship to thought processes [150, 221, 244, 260, 281, 401] and distortions in graphic rhythm have been used for diagnostic purposes [449].

The relationship between impressionability and expressiveness seems to be fundamental in a person's attitude toward his environment and toward himself. An extreme lack of this balance, significant for a disturbance of the individual's relation to his environment, consists in weakness of response, generally due to discouragement; or in an overemphasis of expression, generally due to suppressions and compensations in personality.

Thus, considering the phenomenon of rhythm from the basic movement of centrifugal and centripetal strokes, we can apply it also to the total distribution of graphic elements. We consider the distribution as to the right and to the left, to the upper and to the lower section; the handling of distances between words and rows, and the handling of the margin. Overemphasis as well as neglect of distances points toward psychological disturbances, often being an indication of a neurotic personality. We give a few examples of rhythmical disturbances: arrest of movement and disregard of distances (Fig. 222); lack of distribution (Fig. 223); transposition of pressure (Fig. 224); exaggerated pressure (Fig. 225).

The manifestation of rhythmical movements in relationship to personality trends has been studied on the basis of children's drawings. Schmidl-Waehner [437] found an increasing preference for rigid symmetry among depressive neurotics (60 per cent); and a rigid repetition of uniform rhythm was found among the demented and feebleminded children. Elkisch's [111] studies confirm the relationship between rigidity

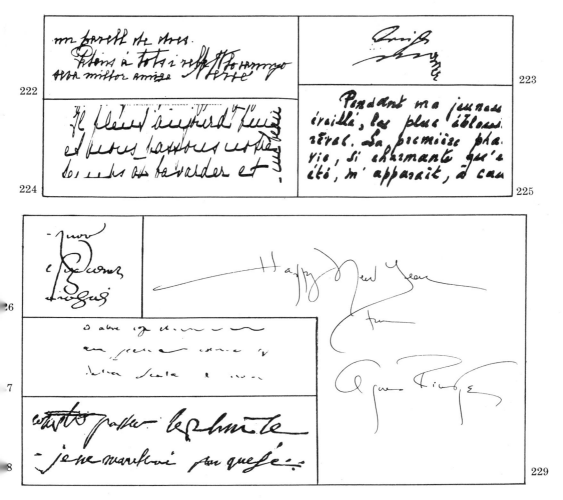

FIGS. 222-225.—The expression of rhythm and its disturbance.
FIGS. 226-229.—Irregularity of movement and conservation of rhythm.

and maladjustment and Brick [53a] notes that stereotypy, in a persistent repetition of a pattern, gave evidence of deeper disturbances. The present author found these tendencies also in drawings of preschool children [464, 467].

However, not every irregular distribution of graphic elements is a rhythmical disturbance. The disregard of distance between rows may be compensated for by a harmonious distribution of graphic forms (Fig. 226) (mediaeval manuscript); the dissolution of letter shape may be compensated for by the vibration of movement (Fig. 227) (Verdi); the lack of balance in pattern, size, and distances of letters may be compensated for by the swing of connecting strokes (Fig. 228) (Napoleon), and the change of directions by the integration of patterns (Fig. 229) (artist).

FIGS. 230-234.—The imaginary line.

The dynamics of expression must be judged dynamically, that is, considering each element with regard to its configuration. The principle of configuration determines also the significance of an emphasis on centripetal and centrifugal movements. Since the natural movement of our writing hand progresses from left to right, any deviation from the natural direction is called regressive. The regression may become manifest in a contraction or arrest of the movement. Such an arrest may be the symptom of a psychobiological disturbance, especially if the natural movement is converted to pressure, as is the case in Figs. 224 and 225.

However, a contraction of movement without transpositions of pressure is an indication of self-discipline, self-control, and concentration on the very meaning of the word; e.g., in Bismarck's writing (Fig. 210 b).

While usually contraction is an expression of self-control up to rigidity, expansion characterizes a lack of self-control with positive and negative implications. An expansion of regressive movements frequently is an expression of uncontrolled day-dreaming (Fig. 221). On the other hand, if expansive movements flow naturally, the dreaming activity is creatively integrated and harmonized with the expression of movement, as is the case with creative personalities (Fig. 229).

THE IMAGINARY LINE

Our graphic movements are limited by spatial norms. The size of graphic movements, originally determined by lined paper, becomes automatic and usually shows a remarkable degree of consistency in one graphic

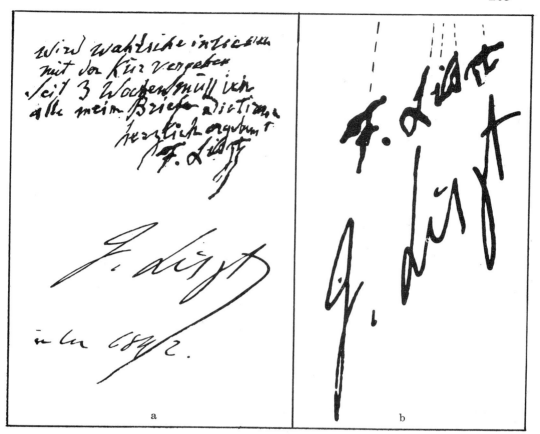

FIG. 235.—The formula of direction.

specimen. If we compare the difference between all big and small letters
in the words of a written sentence we see that they generally have exactly
the same height and same width as if they were produced by measuring.
Partial signs, as the bars of the "t" and dots of the "i," may in different
words of a written sample have exactly the same position so that we can
draw a line through all bars and show them all lying in the same line. The
inclination in strokes of different letters usually shows parallel lines and
the angles of adjoining strokes have the same degree. See, for instance,
the parallels of bars and end-strokes in the French writing of Empress
Eugénie of France (Fig. 230), parallelism of starting-strokes and down-
strokes in Spanish and Italian handwritings (Fig. 231, 232) and in some
examples of the same address written by American writers (Fig. 233).
A lack of parallelism appears in the signature of a German schizophrenic
murderer (Fig. 234, cf. Fig. 96). It seems that the parallel elements are
based upon a formula of direction. The formula of direction seems to
remain stable in graphic movements, and although it is frequently not
visible it can be reconstructed as with Liszt's writing (Fig. 235) when
he was a young man (Fig. a) and an old man (Fig. b).

FIGS. 236-241.—Lines of support and lines of direction.

Besides the formula of direction which creates *parallel* imaginary lines of movement, there is always present in writing a *traditional* imaginary line that is the basic line. While school children have a printed line for balancing their letters, adults do not need this support. The imaginary traditional line effects the balance of the letters. But the writing of certain persons indicates that this traditional imaginary line of support conforms with the parallel imaginary line. Such persons, for instance, underline their names, as did Napoleon (Fig. 236), or they emphasize the upper part of a letter (see Frederick the Great, Fig. 237) so that they get the form of overlines. It often occurs that the signature is put between two of these lines as between rails (cf. André Rivoire, Fig. 238). There are other persons whose loops, broken to a triangle, form such an underline by means of the end-stroke (Fig. 239). Even the middle letters may form a line (Fig. 240).

As the printed line indicates a limitation for the graphic movement and is like a roadbed on which the letters are running, those artificial underlinings and overlinings are projections of limitations. Underlinings seem to reflect the writer's desire to build an artificial ground, a material basis for his living, while overlinings seem to reflect the desire to build a roof as a protection. Since the lower sphere of writing as we shall discuss below, is connected with ideas of physical and material support, and the upper sphere of writing with ideas of mental directives, we call the lower artificial lines "support lines" and the upper artificial lines we call with Klages [211] "directive lines." These directive lines are usually developed at puberty. We frequently observe their growth in successive years of a person's development. We give an example of such a growth in signatures of the same person from his fifteenth to his twentieth year of life (Fig. 241 a-f).

PRESSURE AND PROJECTION

The paper which is covered by lines, reflecting associations of the writer, frequently is treated as a substitute object. We observe this with young children, who sometimes project their aggression on the paper in beating movements and in mutilating the paper or the figures drawn upon it. One of the children we investigated remarked when pressing the letters together tightly: "Oh, how glad I am to press and beat the letters!" (Fig. 322 a, page 351). We can observe children's tendency toward expansion if they cover the paper entirely with lines. There are other children who, through discouragement, are afraid to make graphic forms. The graphically expansive children usually are the same who not only dominate the paper but also their environment, and the graphically timid ones are also timid in other respects. The paper, the material on which the writing process is realized, becomes the screen for the writer's projections. These projections either are a copy of the writer's attitudes to his environment or they are a compensation for a very opposite behavior, a projection of wishes and fears, not expressed in his daily life.

If the writing covers the paper completely, without leaving any space free, this expression may correspond to a real or desired tendency toward domination and greed. Such a writer will not only use up the paper to the last inch but he may also wish to disregard the limits of his environment. A person who overemphasizes width of margin and intervals between words also may show this attitude of reserve or aesthetics toward his environment. If the graphic movement begins with an emphasis of ornamental strokes this graphic expression may correspond to a person who likes to exhibit his treasures. Overstrong pressure manifests a special effort which may have psychological or biological reasons. Roman-Goldzieher [354] measured speed and point pressure by means of her graphodyn which transfers graphic movements to a registering kymograph on which graphic records are obtained. Investigating the average speed and pressure with 2145 Hungarian schoolchildren at various age levels these standard values can be utilized as an index of maturation and mental growth. The deviations from the norm were investigated with 600 individuals, including 100 stutterers, 43 deaf mutes, 46 backward children, and 77 juvenile delinquents. Stutterers showed a prevalence of heavy pressure and of retarded speed, which, after correction, approach the average [353]. A lack of normal pressure was characteristic for delinquent girls. It was noted that poor pressure, denoting lack of will power, was especially characteristic for those girls who were committed for "sexual offenses." Backward children showed notably slow speed. Pascal's [318] investigation of handwriting pressure by means of an apparatus connected with a kymograph indicates a significant correlation between "energy," "impulsiveness," "dominance," "determination" and handwriting pressure. By asking seven psychologists to rate 21 of their students according to these traits, it was found that "no person who is rated five or better on energy has a light pressure. And the reverse is also true; i.e., no person with a heavy pressure is ever rated low in energy by the judges." It was also found that "the men tended to write with greater average pressure and greater pressure range than the women."

Pressure, however, as one manifestation of movement can be a reflection of actual behavior or of compensation. Some persons use pressure as an experience of actual energy or masculinity, others with a lack of energy or feminine structure may express their wish for an energetic personality and their movement is a compensation for a missing trait. Frequently it is only through an interrelationship of characteristics that the pressure can be evaluated. Just as the movement of pressure is an act that is symbolic of certain personality characteristics, so the paper, the object toward which the movement is directed, is a screen for the writer's projections. The object for which the paper stands may represent the environment of family or friends; and the wishful idea of caressing or beating a person may correspond to the act of caressing or beating the paper. The pen beats the paper with heavy strokes, as in the writing of a German Nazi girl student (Fig. 242), or caresses the paper with light strokes and sudden pressures.

If shadings make the graphic patterns indistinct, such a fogginess is frequently the expression of a free-floating anxiety, as it was equally recognized in persons' responses to patterns of inkblots (Rorschach). If the shadings appear together with distinct graphic forms, they suggest a high sensibility for touching sensations which is in general an erotic phenomenon; together with pointed vertical strokes it may be

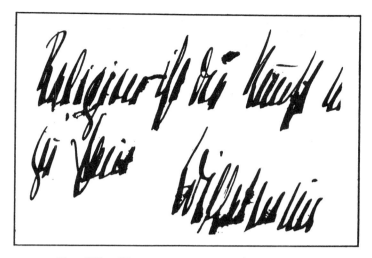

FIG. 242.—The paper as screen for projections.

a symptom of sadism (see the writing of de Sade (Fig. 243); together with curved horizontal strokes it may be a symptom of masochism (see the writing of Sacher Masoch (Fig. 244). The transposition of pressure frequently seems to be a symptom of transposed (perverted) sexual urges. Characteristic of Casanova's "libidinous" handwriting (Fig. 245) is a combination of equal pressure, movement and graceful forms. Some persons confessed that the writing process itself evokes agreeable sensations, and the frequent fetichism connected with writing instruments is an instance of this peculiarity [201].

IMAGINARY DIMENSIONS OF WRITING

In some writing the highest emphasis on expressive forms lies in strokes above the basic writing line, in the upper section of writing; in others beneath it, in the lower section of writing; and in a third group in the middle section. This difference of expression not only appears in an emphasis of strokes in one region of writing, but also in a misalignment of letters; e.g., Michelangelo (Fig. 246) puts the "v," "s," and "c" in the lower region instead of the middle one. This difference can be observed also in old manuscripts, of which we give examples for the different emphasis on these three sectors: the upper sector (Fig. 247), the lower sector (Fig. 248), and the middle sector (Fig. 249). The three sectors of writing, which can be distinguished in most graphic patterns, seem to be a characteristic of man's general triple division of phenomena. The triple division of space (height, width, depth) and of time (past, present, future) has from ancient times on been extended to a triple division of many cosmological, biological, psychological and social phenomena. The ancients divided the world into three basic regions: heaven—above, earth—middle, underworld—below; they divided man's body (considered

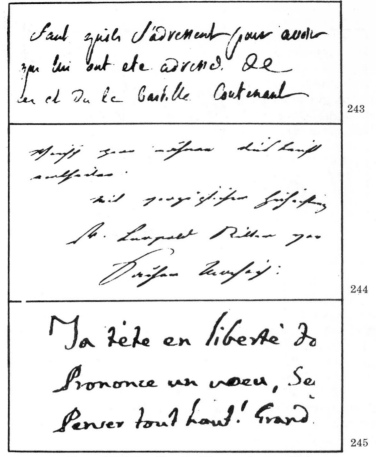

FIGS. 243-245.—Handwriting and sexuality.

to be a microcosm corresponding to the world's macrocosm) into three sectors: head—above, thorax—middle, abdomen—below.

Each of the three regions was given a meaning which was equally significant for the world scheme and for the human organism:

Above (heaven, head) .... Symbol of mental force

Middle (earth, thorax) .... Symbol of social activities

Below (underworld, abdomen) .... Symbol of impulses and unconscious forces

It seems that such a scheme of triple organization still has an effect on our unconscious. Freud, for instance, was led to distinguish three psychological entities which he called the Ego, the Id, and the Superego. It seems that the concept of a triple organization is also projected upon the formation of our letters. Max Pulver [336] was the first who found the diagnostic value of the emphasis on three sectors of writing. An extreme emphasis on strokes in these spheres either by their length or by their width, or by pressure, is supposed to indicate an emphasis

on the corresponding fields of personality. Especially characteristic is
the emphasis on the lower sphere of writing. We have observed that the
total graphic movement of persons who have a mental breakdown correspondingly may emphasize the lower sphere of writing which, however,
is also emphasized by persons with strong impulses related to the
sexual sphere and to other driving powers of the inner personality. Disturbances in the lower strokes frequently go together with disturbances
in impulses, especially sexual ones [190, 279, 335, 336, 449], but they
also may be accompanied by signs indicating sublimation and control of
these impulses. Generally we find either a high emphasis on or inter-

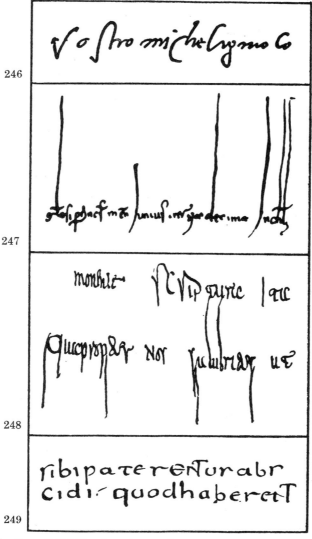

FIGS. 246-249.—Imaginary dimensions of writing.

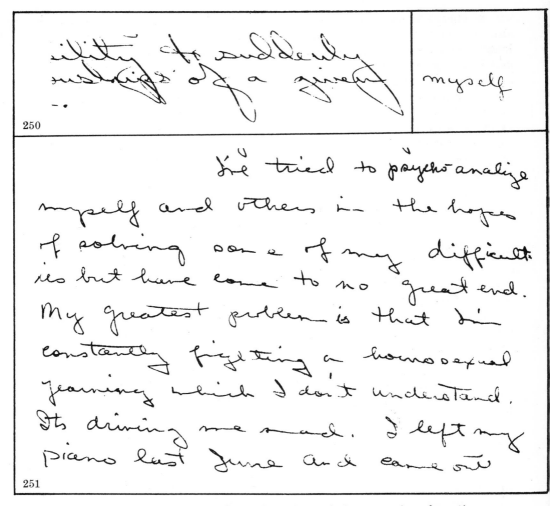

250

251

FIGS. 250-251.—The lower sphere of writing and the expression of emotions.

ference with the lower strokes in the writing of adolescents, when the growing forces of puberty are either emphasized (Fig. 250 a) or restricted (Fig. 250 b). It has been observed that writers with sexual perversions frequently show strange distortions in the lower loops of their letters. Sometimes we may observe that these distortions appear especially when the writer thinks of his sexual perversion. I present a cut from a letter of a young man who asked me for advice about curing his homosexual urges (Fig. 251). The writer states: "I've tried to psychoanalyze myself and others in the hope of solving some of my difficulties but have come to no great end. My greatest problem is that I'm constantly fighting a homosexual yearning which I don't understand. It's driving me mad. . . ." The lower loops in the letters of all words are normal until the writer speaks of his difficulties. Suddenly the lower loops are broken off and turned inward. This pattern is emphasized with the loops of the words "constantly fighting," where the formerly rounded curve of the loop has become angular. Having observed that associations modify letter formations, we deduce that the association of the sexual perversion modified the pattern of the loops.

While the pattern of the lower strokes seems to be related to an expression of emotional processes, the pattern of the upper strokes seems more to reflect mental processes. An exaggeration, perseveration and distortion of movements in this sphere may be found in graphic movements of mentally disturbed persons (see Figs. 208, 209). We often find a change in the emphasis on strokes during the development of the same person. Assuming that movement toward the right indicates a progressive tendency expressing activity and movement toward the left a regressive one expressing reflection, we may interpret progressions and regression in the three spheres of writing. In the lower section of writing, symbolizing impulses, a progressive tendency would indicate activity, dominance, aggression; a regressive tendency in this section of writing would point toward retrospection, need for protection, and infantile tendencies. In the upper section of writing, symbolizing mental activities, a progressive tendency would indicate speculation and a regressive tendency reflection. In the middle section of writing, symbolizing social activities, a progressive tendency would indicate extraversion and a regressive one introversion. These empirical observations lose their oddity if we consider the mechanisms of empathy, projection, and symbolization which can be demonstrated experimentally. The associative connections mentioned before seem to be developed in everybody as the result of collective experiences, and become conditioned reactions.

Assuming that the upper sphere of graphic movement indicates projections of mental tendencies, and the lower section projections of impulses, we may find a relationship between both spheres. It seems significant whether the graphic movement starts from the upper or the lower section, and whether the movement generally ends in strokes directed toward the upper or the lower section. We can investigate whether the relation between both sections is a fluent one or whether there are inhibitions. The flow between both sections may be emphasized in the swing of the graphic movement or in rhythmic intervals between the single letters, a phenomenon which we frequently find in the writings of artists. Inhibitions in the graphic flow in both sections may appear in a break or other disturbances of lower strokes or in their interference with the row underneath.

As already mentioned, the writing plane permits not only two-dimensional movements but also a movement toward the third dimension, a movement into the depth, manifested in pressure [90, 279, 336]. The pen spreads open, because the paper hinders the graphic movement from penetrating into the depth. If we ask a person to write in the air, we can observe the depth-direction of this movement. As we have mentioned before (page 204), the depth of writing can be demonstrated by taking different sheets of tissue paper with inserted sheets of carbon paper, and having a subject write on the top sheet. Certain strokes will not show traces on the carbon copies, while others will show traces on the first and second copies, but not on the third and fourth, and some strokes may show traces on all copies [used by 24, 35]. We thus observe that different persons employ various degrees of pressure to penetrate into the depth of the paper. However, the degree of pressure is not identical with the thickness or thinness of a stroke. Thin strokes may cut deeply into the paper. Both low and high pressure are characteristic of two types of movements which also find their reflection in artistic expression.

Modern art emphasizes two trends of expression which have appeared as long as man has expressed himself graphically: the so-called abstract and the realistic. The chief feature of abstract art is non-objective ornamentation and the chief feature of realistic art is its imitation of nature. One goal of imitation of nature is approached by the technique of perspective, which represents objects to be seen in three dimensions. The graphic object is handled with reference to its depth as if it were represented by a sculptor. The object is, so to speak, modeled out of the paper or canvas.

The aim of ornamentation is an opposite one. The canvas, considered as a plane, is covered by signs; ornamentation, such as tattoo and printed cloth, is like a mantle hung over an object. A graphic artist can treat the paper in two basically different ways: either he treats the paper as a plane and draws upon it in a two-dimensional way as in ornaments, or he sees the paper as a plastic material modeling it in a three-dimensional manner. We can also distinguish these two different expressions of graphic forms in handwriting. The writer may cover the writing plane as if he wanted to envelop it, resulting in two-dimensional strokes. A

FIG. 252.—Enveloping movement.

significant example is the handwriting of Princess Charlotte of Belgium (Fig. 252). But the writer may also imagine a third dimension, as if he wanted to engrave the paper (cf. Maurice Bedel, Fig. 253). In two-dimensional writing a thick stroke originates by being thickly brushed with ink; this corresponds to the trend of covering with ink as much paper as possible. In three-dimensional writing a thick stroke originates through pressure, by being engraved into the paper. This corresponds to the trend of aiming toward the depth of the paper. The two-dimensional stroke which "covers" the paper can be recognized by its uneven margins, which result from a low pressure. The three-dimensional stroke which penetrates the paper can be recognized by the sharp edge, resulting

FIG. 253.—Engraving movement.

from the decided pressure. The writer of two-dimensional strokes adapts his expressive movement to the conditions presented by the paper. Owing to the unity of personality, such persons are usually not only adaptive in their writing but also in all other respects. They may have the ability for intuitive understanding, frequently accompanied by dreaminess. In

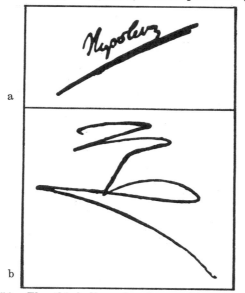

FIG. 254.—The third dimension in graphic expression.

extreme cases their adaptability coincides with a lack of activity. Three-dimensional writing, indicating a person's intention to model the paper, corresponds to a tendency to handle objects actively and to treat the environment in a dominant way.

Another way of expressing a three-dimensional graphic movement is writing in perspective. Leaving the horizontal plane, the movement aims at the background of the paper. The letter "B" in Fig. 253 shows such an attempt at perspective. Another example is the signature of Napoleon with a progressive perspective at the time of his success (Fig. 254 a) and a regressive perspective at the time of his abdication (Fig. 254 b). Such a tendency corresponds to an imagination which is not related to present facts or conditions but expresses an anticipation of future and a dwelling on past possibilities. As the rising line corresponds to an

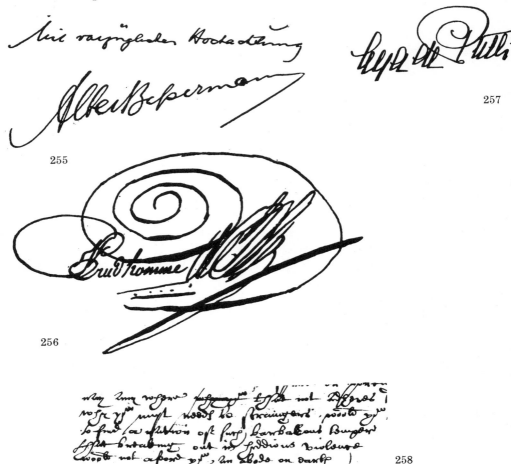

FIGS. 255-258.—The third dimension in graphic expression.

elation, this movement may represent a positive anticipation of the future. If rising lines are accompanied by sinking lines in the same writing specimen, we may suppose that a positive anticipation, a hope, is based on a present negative situation (Fig. 255). The graphic expression of a rising or falling line may, like other graphic elements, change at different times in a person's life.

The entire writing may diminish perspectively, thus resulting in a perspective of rails which seem to meet in the distance (Fig. 255). There is also an expressive movement which seems to start from the depth behind the paper, coming forward to the surface. One expression of such a movement is a spiral turning counter-clockwise (Fig. 256), whereas a spiral movement turning clockwise (Fig. 257) seems to express the intention to screw into the depth of the paper.

DR. THOMAS MANN

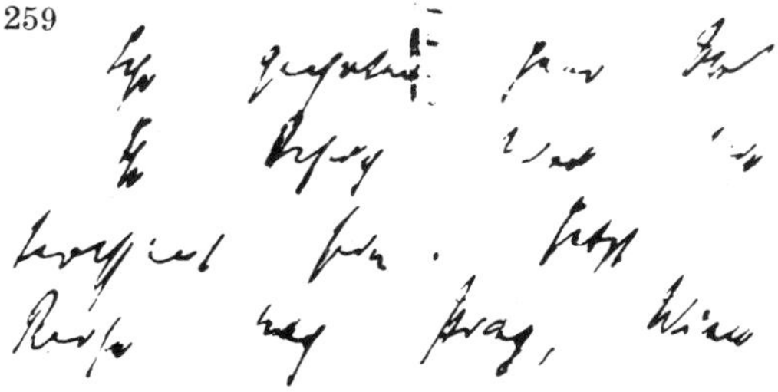

FIGS. 259-263.—The third dimension in graphic expression.

The manner of penetrating an imagined third dimension on the paper sometimes proceeds in steps. The trend toward the depth is here accompanied by a stopping of this movement, expressing a tendency toward analytic and reflective thinking; as examples the writing of Shakespeare (Fig. 258) of Thomas Mann (Fig. 259) and of Nietzsche (Fig. 262 a). Three-dimensional strokes which are engraved into the paper are frequently isolated from each other, each movement of hewing a stroke into the paper being a separate act. A writer who treats the paper three-dimensionally ignores the condition of two-dimensional space given by the paper. This disregard of given conditions may correspond to an emphasis on private imagination, going as far as the actual construction of a private world. We find such construction of a private world in artists in whom imagination prevails (cf. writing of the playwright Gerhardt Hauptmann, Fig. 260), or in scientists (cf. Michelet, Fig. 261) absorbed in their studies; but this may also be the case when the normal personality is affected by a disease which deprives the individual of a normal relationship to the world. The latter becomes especially visible when we compare the writings of the same person in health and in mental disease. Here we often observe an alteration of the graphic movement in a sudden appearance of the direction toward the third dimension which was lacking in healthy days. We demonstrate this by the writing of the healthy (Fig. 262 a) and mentally ill (Fig. 262 b) Nietzsche. The sudden depth-pressure also may appear after an epileptical seizure (Fig. 263 b). In our example of an epileptic's signature, the signature after the seizure (b) shows the sudden depth-pressure, while the signature before the seizure (a) shows a regular pressure without the tendency toward the depth. Psychological isolation is not only expressed by isolating letters

FIGS. 264-270.—Surroundings and dots of the "i."

and words but also by isolating the signature with a surrounding flourish, as it appears in artists (Verdi, Fig. 217), scientists (cf. Gay-Lussac, Fig. 265) and equally with persons who isolate themselves from society (cf. example of a criminal by Lombroso, Fig. 264). The isolation may also be expressed by flourishes which "lock" the signature, as in that of Maximilian I, the Great Elector of Bavaria (Fig. 266).

The difference of expressive movements can be studied in the smallest graphic signs, which are the dot of the "i" or, in German writing, the hook of the "u." The dot of the "i" can be made without pressure, representing a two-dimensional spot; or it can be made with pressure, thus getting the characteristic of a three-dimensional element. If the dot of the "i" has the form of a coin or an arrow, the penetration into the third dimension is made with special emphasis. If this penetration is directed toward the right we seem to have an indication of active mental exploration (cf. John Kepler, Fig. 267). If the penetration is directed toward the left (Fig. 268), we may deduce that the imagination is focused in a retrovert way upon one's own personality. I found that such persons dream very much. If the dot of the "i" has the form of a circle (Fig. 269), such a movement substitutes a perseveration on the spot for the impulse of penetration. This is a characteristic expression of self-involvement which we find often in the narcissistic structure of young persons and artists. The dot of the "i" or the hook of the "u" may also show a wavy form representing a movement that penetrates in steps an imagined third dimension on the paper. We have mentioned that this movement appears to be typical of persons with psychological interests, probably reflecting the tendency of penetrating to psychological roots. Sigmund Freud (Fig. 270) shows this characteristic with his hook of the "u." (See the step-like movement of the hook in the word "Anregung," first word of the last line in our sample, and the hook in "Befriedigung," first word of the first line.) The same movement appears with the end-stroke of his signature, where we not only see the step-like movement but a pressure at the end-point of the stroke, showing the tendency to penetrate the depth of the paper by means of pressure.

Some of these fundamental characteristics of writing can be measured and evaluated statistically. We can measure the size of letters; their respective deviation from the horizontal and vertical norm; the angle formed by up- and down-strokes; the distance between letters, words, and rows; the proportion between curves and straight lines; the diameter of curves; the degree of pressure; the frequency of periodic repetitions in letter shapes; the emphasis laid upon curved or straight lines; curved or angular letter linkings; the enhancement of letters in the upper, middle, or lower section of writing—on the right or on the left side. But all these factors have to be considered in relationship to each other and it is not possible to draw conclusions from one isolated factor; it is on the crossroad of all these expressive values that the axis of personality may be found.

CHAPTER XII

THE SELF

THE IMAGE OF OURSELVES

Images of present, past, and future may prevail for certain periods of time as stable nuclei around which the fluctuating patterns of personality are configurated. While our reactions to stimuli change according to the different environmental conditions, one reaction assumes a more or less stable pattern: this is our reaction to the image we have of ourselves. The image of our own personality has its stereotyped reflection in our signature. If we compare various handwriting specimens of the same person with reference to text and signature, it appears that the pattern of the signature remains more stable than does the pattern of the text. Our measurements indicate that even considerable changes in the signature that are due to either maturation or fundamental experiences, follow a certain stereotyped pattern of proportion. As suggested by psychoanalytical observations the image of ourselves is patterned in early childhood. The importance which a certain graphic expression has for the writer appears in the emphasis he gives to it. One expression of emphasis is the size of graphic movements. A relationship between the size of graphic movements and personality trends has been investigated, especially in drawings of school children. Careful observation of the children's daily behavior made it possible to identify significant correlations between certain characteristics of their graphic movements and their personalities. Maria Brick [53a], who made her observations over a two-year-period on about 200 children from three to fifteen years of age, found that compulsive and neurotic children excelled in diminutive drawings, and that rejected and deprived children used only a small part of the paper, usually at the bottom. T. S. Schmidl-Waehner [437], studying 38 normal and abnormal children, reports that 86 per cent of the pictures drawn by depressive children were small in size, and 80 per cent of the pictures by the feeble-minded were large in size. The small size seems to be a result of an overcontrol of movements, while the large size seems to result from a lack of movement control. The increase of size in the stages of fatigue, exhaustion, and emotional upheaval, and the decrease of size in stages of inhibition and frustration, both support the above interpretation of movement (see page 74). Paula Elkisch [111] who studied 2200 drawings and paintings, concludes from her observations:

"Painting and crayoning done in isolated or restricted areas have in general parallel withdrawing and emotionally dependent behavior tendencies.—Expansion stands for a direction toward the surrounding world, for the potential ability of making contact. . . .

The present author found a unity between graphic movements as expressed in children's drawings and their bodily movements, recorded in photographs and moving pictures.* A study on the preference of size in the drawing of a man by children of various age groups gave the following percentages with 10 children in each group [467] as shown in Table 12.

TABLE 12

Preference of size in drawings of children in percentages

Ages	Large size	Small size
5	80	20
6-10	70	30
11-13	30	70
14-16	30	70

This observation seems to indicate that the size decreases corresponding to maturation, which is accompanied by a development of self-control. The degree of vertical as well as of horizontal extension of graphic patterns reflects the presence, or the lack, of an economy of movements, which also appears in a reduction or enrichment of graphic patterns. In handwritings a reduction appears in a simplification of letters, an enrichment in additional ornamental strokes and flourishes.

The signature, symbol of a self-portrait, may show a special emphasis on flourishes, on size, extension of letters, and large space between first and second name. Emphasis does not always lie in an extension, but sometimes in a contraction of movement. In this case the signature covers less space than the letters in the text written by the same writer. The patterns are narrowed, intervals are reduced, the letter shape is poorer, and the letter size is diminished. The interval between two words denotes the degree of accompanying emotional associations. Association experiments have shown that the interval between stimulus and response is longer if a subject's associations are disagreeable ones. The disagreeable associations are kept at a distance. Graphic expression indicates a similar phenomenon. As the graphic movement is accompanied by projections, the sudden appearance of a large interval between two written words seems to correspond to a sudden appearance of a large interval in a chain of associations. In such a case we have reason to believe that an emphatic interval indicates an emotional content related to the word written after the interval.

We give as an example the signature in a medieval manuscript, represented by the words "Ego Alfanus" (Fig. 271). The word "Ego" (self) has an enormous extension which indicates that the projection of self prevails for a long time and asks for a long space. The expressive movement related to this projection is directed toward the right** and toward the left,*** thus indicating a unification of opposite tendencies.

---

*Illustrations in [464]; also in the author's film: "Unity of Personality," distributed by the Psychological Cinema Register, The Pennsylvania State College.
**letter "e"
***letter "g"

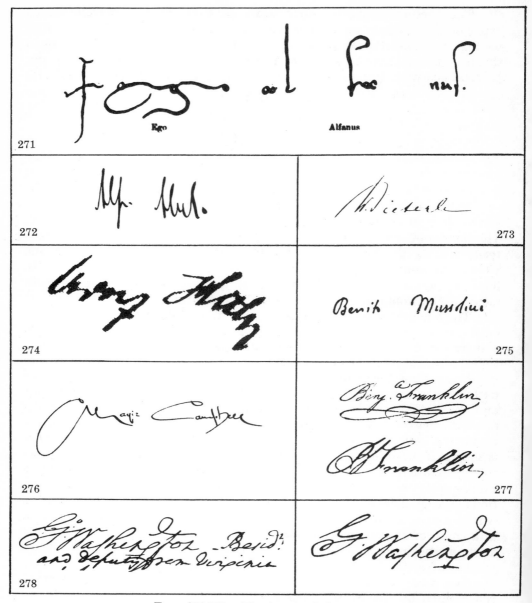

FIGS. 271-278.—The image of the self.

The name "Alfanus," however, is divided into its three syllables by long
intervals. Comparing the movement of the name and its interruptions
with the movement of "Ego" made as a unit, we may suppose that the
unity expressed by the concept of the Ego preceding the split of the name
represents a projection of a wishful tendency to unite a split personality.
The process of projection suggests that the first name, by which the

child is called, is related to man's youth and past, while the family name, with which the adult signs, is related to man's present. If the projection of self is much more emphasized in the second name than in the first, it might follow that the image of self prevails more satisfactorily in the present and that recollections of youth are disagreeable. The distance between first and second name seems to express the gap which the writer feels to be between his present life and his past. Exploratory studies in such cases could check up on this conclusion.

Below we shall discuss several signatures of moving-picture actors; they were written under autobiographical sketches which allow us to compare deductions made from the graphic expression with facts indicated by the autobiographies.*

In the signature of Alfred Abel (Fig. 272), the first name is abbreviated, and the second name is written at quite a distance from the first and is situated on a lower plane. We would deduce a withdrawal from his youth. Abel begins his short autobiography with the words: "It was an accident that on March 12 I was born." (It surely is no accident that Abel omits the year of his birth.) He then immediately begins to report his most terrible experience, which occurred when he was fifteen. It was the murder of his patron, a forester. "I never will forget this moment until my death." It may have been this terrible remembrance which induced Abel to separate himself from his youth.

We find opposite tendencies in the signature of Wilhelm Dieterle (Fig. 273), although he writes only an initial for his first name. Here we see how the stronger initial letter of the second name protects the smaller first letter of his first name like an embracing arm. The writer seems to love the time of his childhood, which is always present in his imagination and breaks through his present associations—the arm of the "W" through the embrace of the "D." In his short biography we see Dieterle emphasize a deep love for the time of his youth. He actually speaks about this time only in his autobiography—of farm life, of the street battles of the boys, of his life as apprentice, etc.

The signatures of Hitler and of the young Mussolini indicate that both tried to separate themselves from their youth; Hitler (Fig. 274) by writing his first name with Gothic letters and the second name with Roman letters, Mussolini (Fig. 275) by emphasizing the interval between first and second name. A split between over-emphasis and under-emphasis of graphic patterns in the first name is expressed in the signature of Dr. Campbell (Fig. 276), one of the presidents of the American Psychiatric Association. Besides such an ambivalent attitude toward oneself there also appear changes in the image of oneself. Benjamin Franklin's signature to the Declaration of Independence shows a separation between first name and last (Fig. 277 a) while the initial of the first name is carried by that of the second name in the signature to the Constitution (Fig.

---

*"Wir vom Film" (We of the Movies), edited by Stefan Lorant.

277 b). George Washington, in his signature to the Constitution (Fig. 278 a), links up the initial of his first name with his last name, but sometimes separates both (Fig. 278 b).

SELF-IMAGE AND HETERO-IMAGE

As we have mentioned previously, our associations modify our total movement pattern in general and our centrifugal-expansive and centri-petal-withdrawing movements in particular. The change of pattern can be observed in the signature of Emperor Wilhelm II, if we compare the signature under a successful treaty with Russia in 1905 (Fig. 279 a)

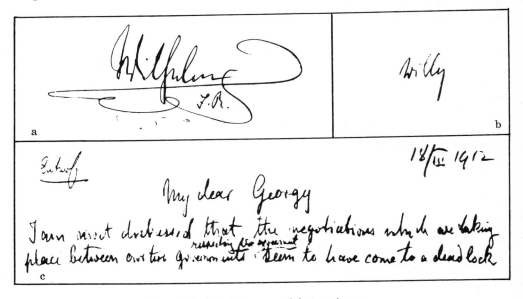

FIG. 279.—Self-image and hetero-image.

with the signature under a letter (b) in which he tries to come to an understanding with George of England (c). The signature in the former case (a) is expansive and arrogant while in the latter it is contracted and insecure (b). Thus, emphasis and reduction, related to progressive and regressive movements, become significant of the writer's attitude toward himself, his "self-image," and of his attitude toward others, his "hetero-image." We do not use here the two more familiar terms of "in-troversion" and "extraversion" because they describe more complicated dynamic processes of personality. A person with a predominant "self-image" is more concerned with himself than with others; he is aware of his activities and self-conscious. A person with a predominant "hetero-image" is more concerned with others than with himself, and usually more spontaneous. The two terms cannot be identified with a person's manifest social behavior, because a person may use social activities merely to enhance his self-image, or he may be an isolated individual but thinking mainly about the improvement of social conditions. The dominance of a self-image leads to a self-awareness of movements, which finds its graphic reflection in the degree of movement accentuation, in the direction of movements, their expanse, and in the degree of interconnections of patterns.

A dominance of centripetal movements, i.e., of movements turning toward the writer, would be one characteristic of a dominant self-image, whereas a dominance of centrifugal movements, i.e., of movements turning away from the writer, are one characteristic of a dominant hetero-image. Narrowness of movements in the spacing of letters as well as a slow-writing speed being symptoms of restriction, self-control or self-consciousness are indicators of a dominating self-image; while width in the spacing of letters as well as a quick writing speed often are signs of an influencing hetero-image. An isolation of letters, an absence of interconnections and cut-off end-strokes of letters, especially at the end of words, are characteristics of restrictions and of self-consciousness, while emphasized interconnections indicate that the writer does not stop in his progressing movement. The signature of the German emperor Wilhelm II (Fig. 279) * shows various characteristics of a dominant self-image, the overaccentuation of movements in the signature to the Russian treaty, centripetal movements in both signatures, a narrow spacing and cut-off end-strokes. Thus, various manifestations of graphic movements can demonstrate one and the same basic expression, and the frequency of traits related to the same principle indicates its degree in the system of personality.

THE LEITMOTIF

Our movement patterns are determined by three main factors: their objective adequateness, the environmental stereotype, and the individual expressiveness. With respect to handwriting the intention of writing a certain letter requires certain movements adequate for this purpose. However, the functional letter pattern is modified by the letter style of the epoch we live in and by our individual characteristics. The handwritings of some persons seem to be especially "functional," emphasizing legibility at the expense of any personal expression; this was required by writings in "courthand" (Fig. 280). There are some writers who identify themselves with the ideals of a past epoch. We give as an example the script of a young modern Spanish poet (Fig. 281) whose poetry and imagination are related to the Moorish-Spanish epoch. The typical Arabic style, with its interlacing ornaments, is projected on the shape of his letters.

Ornaments which characterize the style of a certain epoch indicate that a large number of individuals have common ties of expression in handwriting. Similarities in the shape of letters of different persons are not surprising if the form of letters is similar to the models of letters

---

*From: Ein Jahrhundert deutscher Geschichte; Reichsgedanke and Reich 1815-1819, edited by Hans Goldschmidt, Hans Kaiser and Hans Thimme. Berlin, 1928.

learned in school. But if we find similarities in letter forms and flourishes of unlearned patterns we might deduce a similarity in those intra-individual tendencies to which these expressions correspond. In spite of a very different environment some persons may have in common a cor-responding wish image which they hope to realize at some future time. Compare the signature of the Russian poet, Alexander Pushkin (1799-1837) (Fig. 282) with that of the German actor Ernst Deutsch, living in our time (Fig. 283); the signature of the French novelist Paul de Kock (1794-1871) (Fig. 284) with that of a member of the French government, living in the twentieth century (Fig. 285).

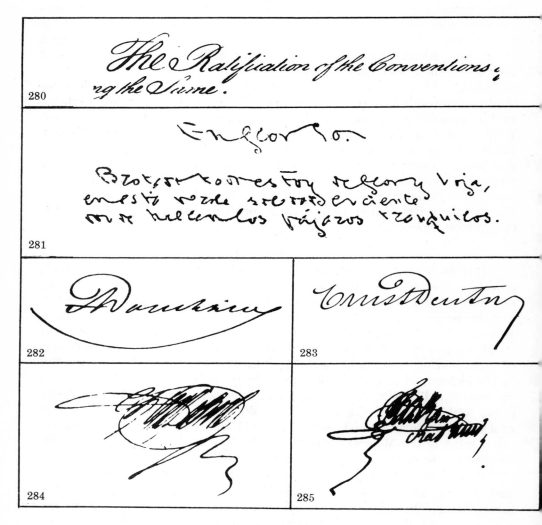

FIGS. 280-285.—Styles of graphic expression.

As our observations suggest, the main leitmotif in graphic movements is neither legibility nor the style of an epoch, but the individual personality. Although individuality involves the principle of uniqueness, members of the same profession, with similar ideas, may have certain expressive characteristics in common. Such professional leitmotifs can be discovered in signatures, if the profession became a determining factor of the writer's associations. Pictographic writings may show the individual leitmotif in the form of images which can easily be identified, whereas oscillographic writings would show the leitmotif in certain ab-

FIGS. 286-291.—Leitmotifs in signatures.

stract symbols which can be discovered only by the associations of the writer himself, as we have described in our experimental approach (see page 235 ff.).

Searching for graphic leitmotifs in pictographic writings of persons who have clear-cut dominating ideas, we chose some signatures of theologians, composers, painters, warriors, and members of various other professions. There seems to be no possibility of treating such material statistically or of verifying exactly whether the symbols discovered are representations of the dominating ideas. But a considerable number of cases where such graphic symbols were found corresponding to the dominating idea of the writer suggest that these patterns were not merely made by chance. We give in the following a list of signatures, classified according to professions, selecting for each group three writers who express their professional leitmotif graphically.

Group I: *Theologians*

Symbol of the cross:
    Pope Alexander VI (Fig. 286)
    Harry Emerson Fosdick (Fig. 287)
    Francis J. Spellman (Fig. 288)

Group II: *Composers*

Musical symbols, as musical keys and notes:
    Johann Sebastian Bach (Fig. 289 a)
    Friedemann Bach (Fig. 289 b)
    Franz Abt (Fig. 290)
    Piotr Ilyich Tchaikovsky (Fig. 291)

Group III: *Painters*

Symbol of painting, as palette:
    Rembrandt van Rijn (Fig. 292)
    Jean Baptiste Greuze (Fig. 293)
    George Cruikshank (Fig. 294)

Group IV: *Warriors*

Symbols of war, as sword, flag, gun, sabre, found in handwritings of warrior-kings and generals:
    Francis II (Fig. 295)
    Emperor Charles (Fig. 296)
    General Linnardt Torstenson (Fig. 297)

Group V: *Creative Personalities*

Carl Linnaeus, classifier of animals and flowers (Fig. 298)
Count Ferdinand von Zeppelin, inventor of the dirigible (Fig. 299)
Sergei Eisenstein, creator of the moving picture, "Potemkin," which made him famous (Fig. 300)

Linnaeus seems to project upon his signature the outlines of an embryo and of a calyx (Fig. 298). Count Zeppelin makes forms resembling the shape of the dirigible (Fig. 299). In Eisenstein's signature appears a pattern resembling that of a cruiser (Fig. 300).

FIGS. 292-297.—Leitmotifs in signatures.

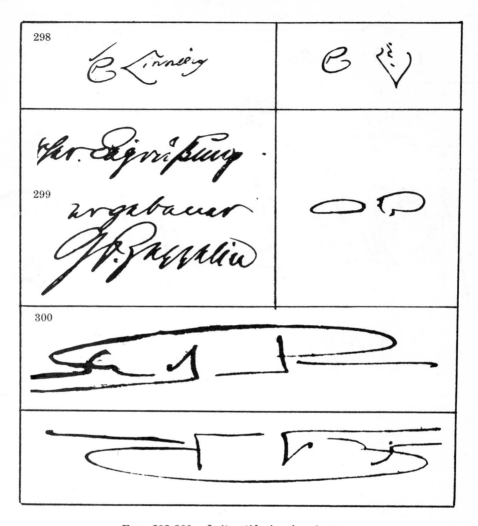

FIGS 298-300.—Leitmotifs in signatures.

Diagnostically, all these patterns of leitmotifs have a different value; whether they are expressions of empathy into the transient object dealt with (Eisenstein); whether they are projections of persistent dominant associations (Zeppelin); or whether they are symbolizations of larger concepts (Linnaeus). An understanding of such symbolizations, however, demands a detailed analysis of the writer's life-history, as we shall attempt to demonstrate in a later chapter.

CHANGES OF PERSONALITY

Since we consider graphic expression as a diagram of the unconscious, indicating the flow and direction of intrapersonal energy, a comparison of several diagrams of one person allows us to follow the centers of his movement. Some persons' movement pattern changes especially in the lower sphere of writing, others in the upper sphere; some show a higher degree of change at the right side, some at the left side. Transformations in the lower sphere of writing appear in unconscious processes, as in the various stages of an epileptic seizure (see Fig. 301) or with

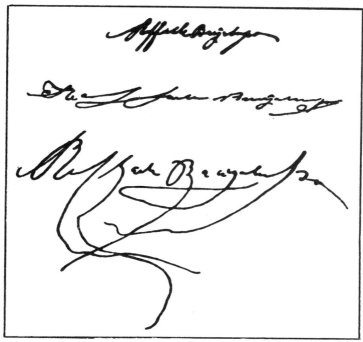

FIG. 301.—Changes of personality and changes in the lower sphere of writing.

emotional persons, such as Napoleon, whose flourishes change according to their moods (Fig. 302). Oscillations in the upper sphere of writing may appear in one and the same graphic expression, as for instance in the handwriting of Goethe, in which the hooks of the "u" go in all directions (Fig. 303). This seems to indicate a flexibility in the mental sphere. Thomas A. Edison's signature (Fig. 304) shows changes in the upper flourish, the progressive direction of which (a) becomes changed to a regressive one in old age (b).

Changes in the sphere of writing appear during disease and at the time of a person's decline. Such changes are not necessarily disturbances of expressiveness. On the contrary, disease may sometimes increase the expressiveness and release inhibitions. If we compare the handwriting of the poet Friedrich Hölderlin (Fig. 305) in his normal days (a) and during his mental disease (b) we see that the specimen from the time of disease shows a higher decomposition in its totality; but if we compare the identical words in both writings (Fig. 305 c), the rhythm of movement is more fluent in the writing of the mentally diseased man (b) than

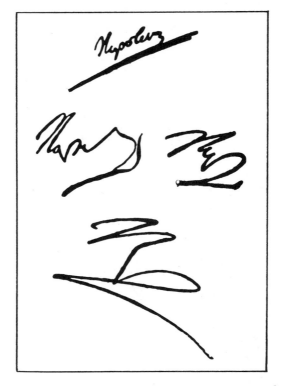

FIG. 302.—Changes of personality and changes in the lower sphere of writing.

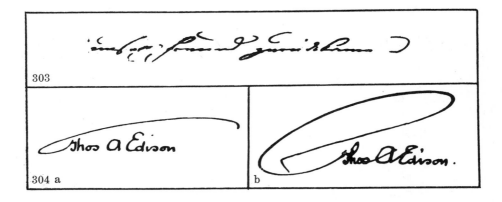

FIGS. 303-304.—Changes of personality and changes in the lower sphere of writing.

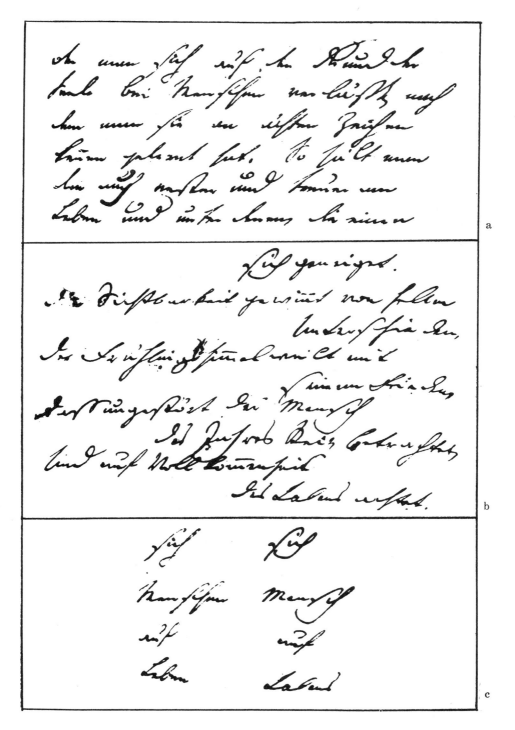

FIG. 305.—Changes of graphic expression during disease.

in the normal (a) ; it seems that the disease had released some inhibitions. We can observe a similar change in the writings of Heinrich Heine (Fig. 306) at the height of his vigor (a) and on his deathbed (b). Identical words in both writings show that the movement is more fluent and more expressive in the writing of the invalid. Thus, a decline of physical force does not necessarily correspond to a decline in the projection of psychological processes. A similar observation has been made

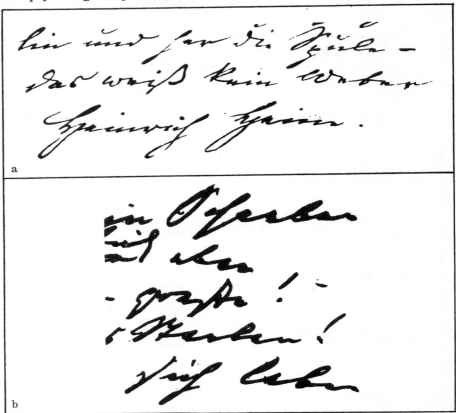

FIG. 306.—Changes of graphic expression during disease.

with some mentally diseased and brain-injured patients [355] who after their disturbance suddenly showed creative forms of expression; also their graphic movements became more original and more expressive. It seems that in these cases the bio-psychological disturbance had removed certain controls and inhibitions of expressiveness.

PSYCHOTHERAPY AND GRAPHIC EXPRESSION

A special object of investigation in studying the transformation of handwriting is to consider the phases of the graphic movement in psycho-therapeutic treatment, for here we can observe more distinctly the relation between graphic movement and psychological changes. We shall now discuss ten graphic specimens written in succeeding steps of psychoanalytic treatment during two and a half years. The patient, a woman, developed a grave neurosis, originating in an erotic conflict which consisted of being attracted and repelled by homosexuality. A second origin of her split was her manic-depressive temper, alternating between

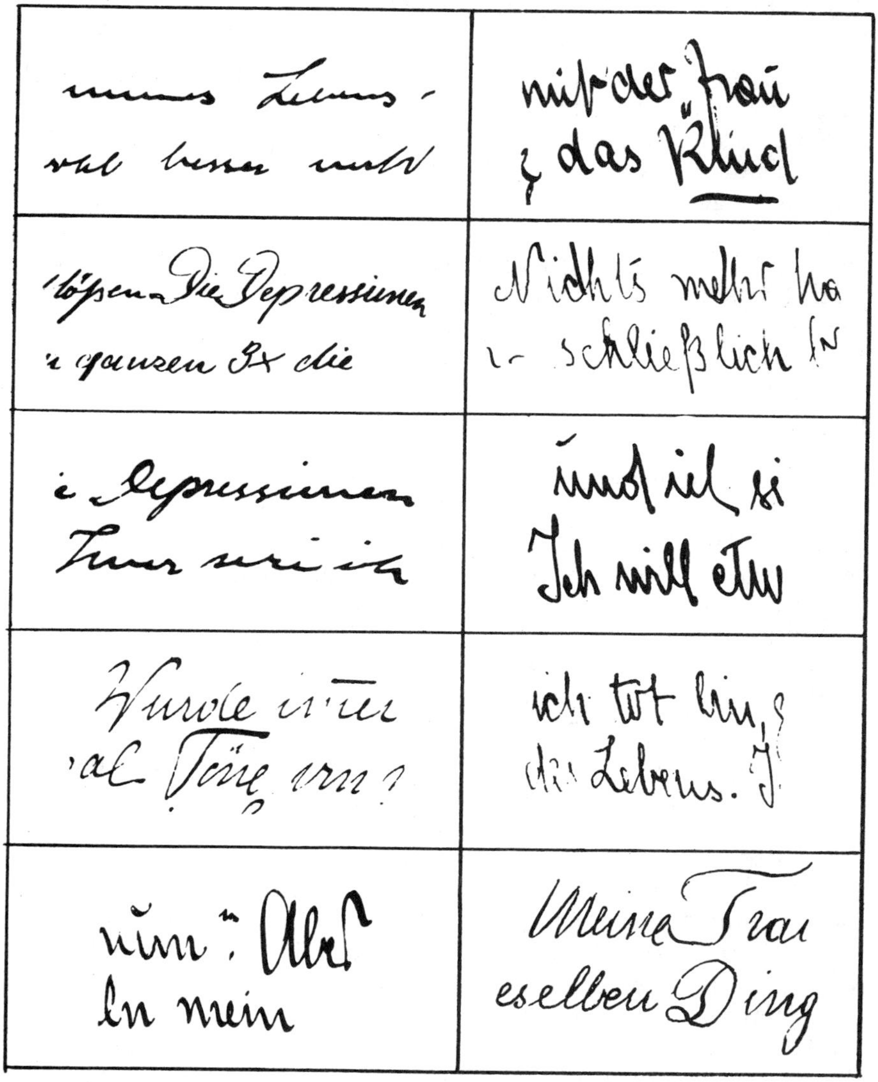

FIGS. 307-312.—Psychotherapy and changes of graphic expression.

active and passive, euphoric and melancholic phases. Our samples are from her diary and we give below the sentences from which the graphic specimens derive* (Fig. 307):

*The words appearing in the graphic samples are italicized.

(a) January 1928: Ich werde mit meinen Empfindungen hin und her gerüttelt, ich bin *meines Lebens* nicht mehr sicher." (I am shuttled by my feelings. I'm no longer sure of my life.)

(b) September 1928: "Meine Leistungen fangen an mir selbst Respekt einzu*flössen. Die Depressionen* sind verschwunden." (My work begins to give me respect for myself. My depressions have disappeared.)

(c) January 3, 1929: "Alles is wieder da, auch die *Depressionen* nachts. Der Kampf in den Träumen." (All has come back, also the depressions at night. The battle in my dreams.)

(d) January 28, 1929: "Als ich das Stichwort für die Musik gab, sah ich nur die Kleine unten. Ich stand da, als ob eine innere Kraft von mir ausginge. Ich *wurde immer* beherrschter und hörte mit einem Male *Töne von* mir, die wie dunkle Glocken klangen. Ich möchte ihr die ganze Welt geben." (When giving the cue for the music I only saw that little girl. I was standing there as if an inner force were emanating from me. I steadily became more controlled and suddenly I heard my voice sounding like deep bells. I should like to give her the whole world.)

(e) November 10, 1929: "Ich laufe dauernd mit einer Angst he*rum. Aber* ich weiss nicht vor was. Am meisten fürchte ich mich im Dunke*ln mein* Schlafzimmer zu betreten. Wenn ich einschlafen will, werde ich plötzlich aus den Daunen gerissen, weil ich mir einbilde, dass der ganze Fussboden voll von Schlangen wimmelt." (I am always running around with fear, but I don't know of what. Mainly I'm afraid to enter my bedroom. When trying to sleep, I am suddenly aroused, imagining that the whole floor is alive with snakes.)

(f) November 23, 1929: "Aber *mit der Frau* suchen ist so ein Kapitel. Ich glaube ich suche *das Kind.*" (To search for the woman is a doubtful matter. I think I'm searching for the child.)

(g) December 1929: "Ich hatte das Verlangen mit ihm zusammen zu sein. Weihnachten war mir viel zu lange zum Heiraten. Als ich mit ihm zusammen war, war ich masslos enttäuscht. Angeödet. *Nichts mehr hatte* ich für ihn übrig, . . . *Schliesslich.*" (I had the desire to be with him. It seemed too long to me to wait till Christmas to get married. When I was together with him I was completely disillusioned. Bored. I had no more feeling for him at all. . . . Finally . . .)

(h) January 19, 1930: "Ich spiele mit Puppen, ein Mann und ein Mädel. Der Mann kommt immer mit ins Bett. Ich bin in den schönsten Kinderjahren, *und ich spiele* mit Bällen zum Schreck meiner Wirtin. *Ich will . . .*" (I'm playing with dolls, a man and a girl. I always take the man to bed with me. I'm in the best years of my childhood, playing with balls, to my landlady's consternation. I wish . . .)

(i) March 1930: "Wär ich ein Skorpion, eine Natter, Schlange, Giftfliege, ich würde mich fanatisch auf das ganze Menschenpack stürzen, sie alle zu zerstören. Seit zwei Tagen bin ich mir klar, dass ich eine Gefangene seit Jahren bin, dass *ich tot bin.* Ich bin eine Gefangene *des Lebens.*" (Oh, were I a scorpion, a viper, a snake, a poisonous fly, I would pounce fanatically upon the whole human rabble in order to destroy them all. For two days I have realized that I have been a prisoner for years, that I am dead. I am a prisoner of life.)

(k) June 1930: "In X. liebe ich nicht ihn bewusst, sondern ihn als Kind und grossen Bruder. *Meine Traurigkeit is verschwunder. Dieselben Dinge . . .*" (As to X., I don't love him consciously, but as a child and an older brother. My sadness has disappeared. The same things . . .)

We can distinguish different phases in these writings, those of a depressed state of mind, expressed by small and flat or thin letters (samples a, c, g, i), and a manic state of mind, expressed by steep and large letters (samples b, d, e, f, h, k). The same characteristics appear in the signature of this patient (Fig. 308) which in the depressed state

FIG. 309.—Depressed and manic periods reflected upon the signature.

of mind is flat and compressed (a) while the manic period enlarges the signature in all dimensions (b). The depressed as well as the manic signatures show characteristics of a psychic tension which disappeared after the healing. Her drawings also reflect the manic and depressed moods. The faces in a manic drawing are big (Fig. 309) and with emphasized features, shown in motion, the drawing being made with a pressure of strokes. The faces in the depressed drawings (Fig. 310) are small, without emphasis on features, shown in calmness, the drawing made without pressure on strokes. We shall analyze such a dream-drawing below (Fig. 310).

There are three objects (Fig. 310): Dominating and taking up the greatest space is the figure of a woman; on the lower part of the paper, pressed into the corner, is an officer of the Frederician period whose helmet and shoulder approach the lower part of the woman; the third object is a tree which separates the figures. The face of the woman has a dreamy expression, and her eyes are closed. The eyes of the officer are open. His face has a similarity to that of the woman; it has a frankly feminine expression. The right epaulet of the officer seems to stand for

309

310

FIG. 310.—Manic and depressed period reflected upon drawings.

a sexual symbol. The flight from reality is expressed by transposing the figures into a past time, that of the Frederician period, and by the woman's representing herself in a state of sleep or dream. The figure of the officer, similar to her own, seems to represent her alter ego in the mask of a man and, moreover, in that of a soldier of the Frederician period which, historically, is related to an emphasis on discipline. Her sexual impulse appears in a hidden representation, and the tree, symbol of the tree of life in her own association, seems to represent a state of vitality which her state of depression and dissatisfaction makes the most desirable thing. Since graphic movements and graphic representations reflect our associations, which are largely determined by our intentions and wishes, we may explain the graphic characteristics of our subject as an expression of her wishes, namely, to escape from her present situation, to be a man and to have self-discipline.

It is interesting to note that the patient's graphic expressiveness decreases after her cure. One handwriting specimen (k) dates from the time when the patient recovered from her neurosis. By then her psychological troubles had disappeared, but her graphic movement became stiff and the forms of letters became conventional. This case again shows that tensions of personality may increase the expressive value of forms of expression, since associations and inner psychological stimuli seek expression in some form.

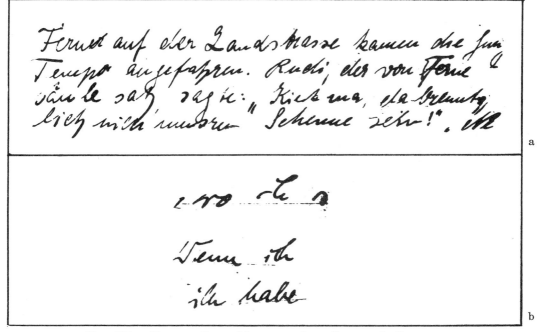

a

b

FIG. 311.—Change of graphic expression after psychotherapy.

The influence of psychotherapeutic treatment in a productive as well as in an inhibiting way may be demonstrated in another example. The writing of a neurotic boy, at that time sixteen years of age, reflects his maladjustment in its completely arhythmical movement (Fig. 311 a), in the change of shape and height of letters, pressure, inclination, and direction of writing. After a psychotherapeutic treatment the boy lost his neurotic anti-environmental manifestations (aggression, kleptomania, vagabonding, etc.). He developed intellectual and artistic interests and a social behavior, but, in addition, strong inferiority feelings. This phenomenon, which was due to a restriction of impulses, becomes visible in his writing one year after the beginning of the psychotherapeutic treatment, when the boy was unable to write the word "ich" ("I"). Either he completely omits the letter "c" in "ich" (a) or he introduces it later on (b), or he enlarges this letter (c), so often omitted before, in a special manner (Fig. 311 b).

Roman-Goldzieher [353] found, on the basis of several hundred handwritings of stutterers, that their graphic movement is rhythmically disturbed, and that omissions of letters, sudden pressures and lack of differentiation are characteristic signs. The graphic picture in the handwriting of stutterers tends to show inhibitions of movement and the lack both of balance and of aesthetic patterns.

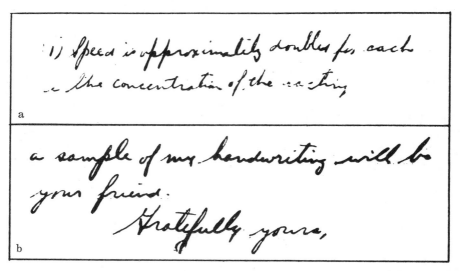

FIG. 312.—Graphic expression of a stutterer before and after speech therapy.

Two writing examples of a stutterer (Fig. 312) demonstrate how psychotherapeutic treatment can influence the graphic expression. The first specimen shows how the writing movement is inhibited (a). The pressure and even the shape of the letters sometimes disappear. The connection between the letters is broken, and the letters lack all balance and direction. After a treatment of three months this person was able to speak fluently and in a corresponding sense the handwriting also became fluent (b), the writing movement became regular, the letters regained normal pressure and shape, the connection between the letters became a continuous one, and the letters attained balance and direction.

As graphic expression is a reflex of intrapersonal dynamics, transformations of personality appear in the oscillations of graphic movement, in changes of directions, and in transformations of patterns.

CHAPTER XIII

INDICATORS OF GRAPHIC EXPRESSION

The Expression of Consistency

If we compare a writer's graphic forms over a long period of time, we frequently find a high degree of consistency in his patterns. Does such consistency express certain personality trends? We observed that different persons have different degrees of consistency. A high degree of consistency, based upon a strong fixation of movements, may reflect, positively, strong stability of personality patterns and negatively, rigidity. On the other hand, a low degree of consistency may reflect, positively, creative flexibility and, negatively, insecurity, and unreliability. Since the consistencies of form appear in a different degree in different graphic elements, the emphasis on certain forms may express certain trends in personality. The projection of associations upon graphic movement indicates that first and second name may be accompanied by different associations. As already mentioned, the first name is usually accompanied by associations with youth and the past life of the individual, the second name, with associations of the self-formed personality of the more mature age. The first name is the call-name of the child, and the second is employed in the signature of the responsible individual. If there are still more consistencies in the first name, we may conclude that the writer emphasizes his past, while a greater number of consistencies in the second name would indicate an emphasis on the present life situation.

Consistencies may furthermore be emphasized in the three dimensions of movement: the horizontal plane, the vertical plane, and movements toward the depth of the paper. On the horizontal plane we may find consistencies in movement toward the right, expressing progression, or toward the left, expressing regression. The vertical movement connects the upper and the lower planes of writing. We found that associations related to the conscious sphere of personality are expressed preferably in the upper plane, and associations related to the unconscious in the lower plane of writing. Consistencies in vertical movement, therefore, seem to express the relationship between the conscious and unconscious organization of personality.

Movement toward the depth appears in dots which are pushed into the depth of the paper. The relation to the other factors indicates whether such stabilization is a genuine trend of asserting one's individuality, or the attempt to find a position within an unstable environment. The relation of consistencies manifested in the three dimensions of movement is an indicator of the dynamics in the structural scheme of personality.

The consistencies may be emphasized at the beginning or at the end of movements. Consistencies at the beginning of movement seem to express the degree of initiative; those at the end of movement, the stability of the goal.

PREDOMINANCE OF DIMENSIONS IN GRAPHIC PATTERNS

Each graphic specimen, be it drawing or handwriting, has a predominant emphasis on one of the three dimensions. We give below an exploratory interpretation for the predominance of each dimension.

Height. The movement toward height seems to correspond to a tendency toward prominence, therefore, to an emphasis on the Ego.

Breadth. The movement toward breadth seems to correspond to a tendency towards expansion, characteristics of which are in the realm of personality trends toward self-assertion.

Depth. The movement toward depth aims to penetrate, to dig into the material. An emphasis on units in this dimension seems to point to the fact that it is a main aim of the writer to find his position within an unstable environment, to secure the ground on which he is standing; on the other hand, the movement aiming toward depth suggests an intention to explore the background and the root of things.

PREDOMINANCE OF REGIONS IN GRAPHIC PATTERNS

Graphic patterns usually show their predominance in one of the regions of the paper. We again give an exploratory interpretation of their expressive values.

The Start (left). If the patterns are emphasized at the start of the graphic movement, the immediate appearance of expression may correspond to impulsiveness.

The End (right). An emphasis of expressive characteristics at the end of the movement seems to hint at a personality which comes to a conclusion after all preceding steps have been taken. Rational consideration seems to be a more important factor than impulse.

The Middle. If the expressiveness is emphasized in the middle of a word, we frequently find a conflict between emotional and rational tendencies of the writer.

The Upper Plane. The emphasis on the upper region of writing seems to correspond to a predominance of ideas related to the concept of height, such as elevation, loftiness, sublimity, and speculation in a positive and negative sense.

The Lower Plane. The emphasis on the lower plane seems to correspond to a predominance of ideas related to the concept of resources, such as materialistic aspects (the ground on which one stands) or emotional aspects (the unconscious and vital resources).

PREDOMINANCE OF CHARACTERISTICS IN GRAPHIC PATTERNS

Total and Partial Emphasis. If the graphic pattern is emphasized as a whole, for instance by surrounding flourishes and other ornamentations, it seems that the personality is led by *one* definite concept with which the individual wishes to show his "indivisibility," his singleness and originality. If only certain graphic elements are emphasized in the overall pattern, this seems to express a tendency for differentiation, or for solving problems.

*Motor and Visual Characteristics.** A predominance of motor characteristics which appear in oscillographic writings and in simple proportions between beginning and ending of graphic movements seems to correspond to an emphasis on motor activities. A predominance of visual characteristics, which appear in pictographic writings and in simple proportions between the limits of graphic movements, seems to indicate a high visual impressionability. The visual type, as opposed to the motor type, seems to be more determined by impressions than by actions; here static appearance is more important than dynamic process. If visual characteristics appear at the beginning and motor characteristics at the end, the interpretation is suggested that impressions lead to expressions or actions. If the opposite is true, that motor characteristics appear at the beginning and visual characteristics at the end, expressions or actions seem to fade into dreams.

The Expression of Balance. We speak of balance if weights are equally distributed. A drawing immediately shows us such a balance in the distribution of graphic elements. In a signature we may speak of a balance if its main parts, that is, right, left, upper, and lower, show an equal amount of emphasis. Such balance appears also if the signature shows a center from which proportions radiate into all directions. Such a center may be more or less distinct; it may appear in the different significant sections of the writing, in the first name or in the second; at the start, middle, or end of the signature; in the upper, middle, or lower plane.

Balance can be expressed by repetition of the same or by interrelationship of different elements. Balance through repetition is a static expression of stability. Balance through interrelationship is a dynamic expression of reciprocity. Most graphic patterns are a mixture of both balancing principles, and, also, in different graphic patterns of the same

---

*See page 125 ff.

person the type of expression may change, indicating that the specific type of balance used does not reflect a fixed "mark of personality" but is influenced by the momentary attitude toward the world.

PERSONALITY TRAITS AND TRAIT-CLUSTERS

Our experiments and empirical observations established a basis for the statement which is the fundamental hypothesis of the present study: that graphic movements depend on inner factors of personality rather than on outer factors of environment. Although the influence of outer factors such as choice of writing material, conditions of writing, national characteristics of graphic pattern, training of form principles, and chance factors cannot be denied, the inner factors of personality are strong enough to modify the material which got its crude form through outer factors.

Besides our main aim of verifying the thesis that graphic movements have expressive values, our next step was to make the reader familiar with their possible meanings. Focusing upon various characteristics of graphic expression, we tried to convey some main principles of the graphic language of expression. As with every other language, the student has to familiarize himself with his object of study, he has to think in terms of his object before he becomes able to work with it productively. The inner factors of personality which determine graphic expression are a characteristic whole in each individual. Just as a picture or a piece of music is a whole which cannot be broken down into its single elements without losing its characteristic expressive quality, so a graphic pattern, whether drawing or handwriting, has to be seen as a whole, namely, considering its constituents in their interrelationships. However, if we are trained to understand the whole, the additional analysis of the elements will increase our understanding. Thus an interpreter of graphic expression, an art expert, or a graphologist, works with particular details as "signs" but in relationship to the total expression. Crépieux-Jamin [81], one of the few scientific graphologists, remarked that the study of graphic elements is to graphology what the study of the alphabet is to the reading of prose. Prose is not treated alphabetically, but the knowledge of the alphabet is essential. It is not the sum of letters, but their interplay, which forms the meaning of the word. Just as the same signs form many words, so the same graphic indicators form many meanings; what Crépieux-Jamin calls the "resultants" are decisive. There are as many "resultants" as there are human beings; it is, therefore, impossible to classify these innumerable groups. It is also impossible to enumerate all personality traits forming the "resultants." A "resultant" depends on two variables: on the intensity and on the interrelationship of its factors. For instance, "activity" is the high *intensity* of a trait of which the low intensity is "passivity." The activity of an artist is structurally so different from the activity of a businessman that these two *relationships* of the same trait change the value of the trait.

The main observation of our study is the discovery of lawful inter-relationships of expressive movements, as reflected upon their "form" and upon their "expression." If the pattern of expressive data corresponds to certain personality traits, it should be possible to reconstruct and to predict personality traits from a few given data. However, the interpretation of data always straggles behind the observation and we have not yet found the means of adequately describing personality traits in terms of their structural interrelationship. Our observation of Gestalt patterns in expression demands a new technique of describing and diagnosing personality in Gestalt patterns. The assumption that personality is not a bundle or sum of isolated traits, related to each other by chance, but rather follows principles of organization, has developed from the observations of psychoanalysis and of Gestalt theory. However, as R. B. Cattell remarks [70]: "Actual studies dealing with the intercorrelation of personality variables, either as clusters or as factors, or on an adequate scale and by methods which permit of mutual confirmation of findings, are, nevertheless, still distinctly rare, perhaps because of the considerable labor or technical skill which they require."

Although there is still much disagreement about basic personality traits and their interrelationship to "syndromes," namely, several traits which repeatedly occur together in individuals, there is some agreement about an intensity scale of traits. We can distinguish trait pairs of opposites such as emotional-unemotional or reflective-unreflective. We furthermore can establish a relationship between two and successively more trait pairs such as the manifestation of emotion and thought, as for instance, impulsive-deliberate. There is another relationship in terms of the traits' effect upon the individual himself, such as cheerful-depressed, or contented-dissatisfied; in terms of his reactivity: excitable-phlegmatic, or tough-sensitive; in terms of his social responsiveness: affectionate-frigid, or sociable-seclusive; in terms of self-assertion: bold-timid, or dependent-independent; in terms of emotional and rational disturbances: balanced-neurotic, or clearthinking-incoherent. Further interrelationships can be built up, such as between emotional and rational disturbances and social responsiveness: responsible-irresponsible, and so forth. A long and detailed analysis would be necessary to establish systematically a system of personality clusters. Cattell [70], investigating studies on personality clusters by 14 independent researchers on the basis of over 4500 cases, found 50 nuclear clusters gathered in 20 distinct spheres of personality. But a correlation of such trait clusters to certain patterns of expressive movement needs a large body of empirical material, and in order to find one's way through the complex scheme of interrelationships and correlations, we have to simplify our approach.

We tried to classify factors in groups of intensity, constituting trait-groups. We described each group by three high and three low values of intensity. In order to bring some scheme into our selection of groups we classified them according to the alphabet, selecting a trait for each letter of the alphabet and thus developing an intensity scale. Certainly, the choice of primary trait-names is arbitrary, but this does not matter since we are interested only in groups of factors. Our list of factors can easily be dealt with since the letter indicating a factor is the same as the initial letter of a trait in a group. The arrangement of letter and initial coincidence made it impossible always to start with a high or a low value; we simply divided each group into characteristics which develop from opposite basic traits. Since our trait-selection is limited we add to each trait-group Cattell's nuclear clusters. The present author's concept of factors and their graphic representation appeared to be fruitful for his attempts at graphic interpretation, and future research will indicate the degree of validity of these observations. They are here presented as suggestions and should serve mainly as a basis for identifying expressive values of graphic patterns. We present an alphabetical list of trait-names with their corresponding factor symbols. (See further, Tables 14 and 15, for grouping of trait names into factors of expression.)

TABLE 13

List of Trait Names

Trait-name	Factor	Trait-name	Factor
active	P	calculating	D
adaptable	R	careless	E
adjusted	F	changeable	Q
adventurous	X	confident	J
aesthetic	A	contracted	X
aggressive	Y	conventional	O
altruistic	B	co-operative	B
anal	A	co-ordinated	C
analytical	K	courageous	H
apathetic	W	cramped	T
artistic	A	creative	V
ascetic	L	critical	K
asensual	L	crude	S
assertive	Y	curious	I
		cynical	N
benevolent	B		
blindly following	K	decisive	H
brilliant	W	defiant	H

TABLE 13. *(Continued)*

List of Trait Names

Trait-name	Factor	Trait-name	Factor
deliberate	D	intuitive	D
determined	D	inventive	I
dictatorial	M	irrational	X
disorganized	A	irregular	C
dreaming	D	isolated	G
dreary	W		
dull	S	jealous	J
easygoing	Z	knowing	K
eccentric	O		
egoistic	B	libidinous	L
elated	P	loyal	J
eloquent	P		
exact	E	malevolent	B
expansive	X	manic	T
extravert	G	masculine	M
		masochistic	Y
faithful	J	mature	C
fearful	H	mechanical	O
feeble	V	mediumistic	S
feminine	M	melancholic	P
flabby	V	meticulous	E
free	F	modest	M
frigid	L	moody	T
frustrated	U		
		naive	K
gregarious	G	narrowminded	I
		natural	N
		neurotic	R
hesitant	H		
hostile	M	optimistic	Z
humorous	W	original	O
hypochondriacal	P	overdoing	Q
		oversexed	L
Idealistic	H		
impulsive	U	paranoid	J
inarticulate	O	passive	P
incoherent	E	pedantic	E
infantile	C	perverted	L
ingenious	A	pessimistic	Z
inhibited	Q	placid	R
insecure	R	playful	O
insensitive	S	productive	V
insincere	N		
integrated	F	quick	Q
intelligent	I		
introvert	G	rational	X

TABLE 13. *(Continued)*

List of Trait Names

Trait-name	Factor	Trait-name	Factor
regular	C	tense	T
reluctant	Z	timid	H
reserved	F	traditional	X
restful	R		
restless	R	unadjusted	F
		unaesthetic	A
sadistic	Y	uncontrolled	U
scatterbrained	U	unco-operative	B
schizoid	T	unco-ordinated	C
self-conscious	U	unintegrated	F
self-controlled	U	unintelligent	I
self-effacing	Y	uninteresting	W
sensitive	S	uninventive	I
sentimental	K	unnatural	N
sexual: *see* libidinous		unproductive	V
sincere	N	unwilling	Z
sloppy	E		
slow	Q	vital	V
social	G	withdrawn	G
spontaneous	D	witty	W
stable	Q		
suggestible	S	yielding	Y
suspicious	J		
tactful	M		
temperamental	T	zealous	Z

The list of trait names which we selected is not purely subjective, as might be objected. The list originated on the basis of a large amount of expressive material which elicited the trait names which we collected. When I had finished this list and arranged the trait clusters, my attention was drawn to Cattell's list of personality clusters which, as mentioned before, resulted from 14 independent workers. It appeared that one nuclear trait of each of his 53 personality clusters was represented in our 26 clusters. Therefore, our choice of nuclear traits coincided with those used by other workers on the basis of over 4500 analyzed cases. There follows a list of 26 basic factors, each with six degrees of intensity, so that the table covers 156 trait names. A subsequent table gives the graphic indicators which, according to the author's empirical observations, seem to be significant for each factor. Needless to repeat, such a correlation is tentative, serving as a working hypothesis for a first approach to an interpretation of graphic expression.

The list of graphic indicators corresponding to each trait group also originated on the basis of a large amount of comparative material which was validated according to empirical criteria. I furthermore compared my formal criteria for graphic analysis with those of other investigators [79, 211, 319, 336, 339, 365, 437]. Although there is considerable agreement about the meaning of graphic expression, the principles of graphic expression cannot be measured as we did with the principles of graphic forms. The following graphic indicators appeared to be characteristic of certain personality clusters; a handwriting specimen may comprise one or several factors, and of each factor one or several indicators.

In the following, we present the two tables which attempt to classify the factors of expression (Table 14) and their corresponding graphic indicators (Table 15). The grouping of traits according to their interrelationship and according to intensity groups may be controversial in some cases, but for practical purposes the present arrangement seemed to be the most adequate one. We have to keep in mind that any classification of factors of expression is rigid and no more than a guide to deal with the complex dynamics of expressive behavior.

TABLE 14. Factors of Expression

Symbol of factor	Intensity Group I	Intensity Group II	Cattell's Personality Clusters
A	Aesthetic artistic ingenious	unaesthetic disorganized anal	General aesthetic interests, thoughtfulness, constructiveness. (1)
B	Benevolent cooperative altruistic	malevolent uncooperative egoistic	Integrity, altruism vs. dishonesty, undependability. (2) Interest in group life, liking to participate vs. self-sufficiency. (3) Friendliness, generosity, cooperativeness vs. hostility, meanness, obstructiveness. (4)
C	Coordinated regular mature	uncoordinated irregular infantile	Emotional maturity, clarity of mind vs. infantilism, dependence. (5)
D	Deliberate determined calculating	spontaneous dreaming intuitive	Practicalness, determination vs. daydreaming, evasiveness. (6) Thrift, tidiness, obstinacy vs. lability, curiosity, intuition. (7) Creativity, curiosity, intuition vs. stability, insensitiveness. (8)
E	Exact meticulous pedantic	incoherent sloppy careless	Conscientious effort vs. quitting, incoherence. (9) Alcoholism, rebelliousness, carelessness vs. piety, reverence, thrift. (10)
F	Free adjusted integrated	reserved unadjusted unintegrated	Intrusiveness, frivolity, neurotic instability vs. deliberateness, seriousness, reserve. (11)
G	Gregarious social extravert	withdrawn isolated introvert	Gentlemanly, disciplined thoughtfulness vs. extraverted, foolish, lack of will. (12)
H	Hesitant timid fearful	decisive defiant courageous	Energy, boldness, spiritedness vs. apathy, timidity, languor. (13) Independence, cleverness, confidence vs. timidity, dependence, languidness. (14) Physical strength, endurance, courage vs. physical inactivity, avoidance, danger. (15)
I	Intelligent inventive curious	unintelligent uninventive narrowminded	Intelligence, penetration, general talent vs. lack of general talent. (16) Verbal skill, interesting ideas, inquisitive vs. narrow interests, absence of flattery. (17) Curiosity, wide interests vs. limited interests. (18)

TABLE 15. List of Graphic Indicators

Factor	Indicators Group I	Indicators Group II
A	good arrangement of patterns, well-proportioned and original forms, simplified, frequently printed letters, rhythm of movement	bad arrangement of patterns, unproportioned letter forms, overloaded shapes, arhythmical movement
B	emphasis on interconnections, progressive movement, long end-strokes, garland connections, broad, more round patterns, spaced units	isolated elements, regressive movement, short-cut end-strokes, arcade connections, narrow, more angular patterns, small-spaced units
C	coordinate movements, direct movement, regularity of patterns, unified inclination	unco-ordinate movements, wavy movement, irregularity of patterns, change of inclinations
D	meticulous forms, exact position of dots over the "i," punctuation, limitation of curves, letters connected, medium pressure	variety of expression for the same form, position of dots right or left from the letter, lack of punctuation, extension of curves, letter connections broken, slight pressure
E	lack of variety, traditional forms, exact details, e.g., punctuation, bars	neglect of correctness, indistinct letters, lack of details
F	details interconnected with letters, simplification of forms, medium intervals, size of letters related to size of paper, medium width of capitals and letter connections	details isolated, elaboration of forms, lack of uniformity of patterns, big or narrow intervals, capitals low, letter connections narrow
G	progressive movement, large, horizontal patterns, garland connections, terminals long, t-bars high, i-dots dashed	regressive movement, large vertical patterns, emphasis on curves and spirals, terminals short, t-bars low, i-dots round
H	evasive strokes, narrow movements, interruptions, weak pressure, small size, abruptly stopped end-movements, t-bars light, descending movements	straight strokes, broad, uninterrupted movements, strong pressure, large size, outgoing end-movement, t-bars heavy, ascending movements
I	clear, graceful forms, simplified patterns, connection of different, even unrelated patterns, emphasis on essentials, medium or small letters, predominance of upper features, speed moderate to fast	unclear, ungraceful forms, awkward elaborations, lack of connections, unnecessary details, large letters, neglect of upper features, slow speed

TABLE 14. *(Continued)*

Symbol of factor	Intensity Group I	Intensity Group II	Cattell's Personality Clusters
J	*J*ealous suspicious paranoid	confident faithful loyal	Cynism, suspicion, dishonesty vs. idealism, trustfulness, respecting self and others. (19) Benign emotional maturity vs. slanderous, jealous, self-pitying infantilism. (20)
K	*K*nowing critical analytical	naive sentimental blindly following	Sociability, sentimentalism, warmth vs. independence, hostility, aloofness. (21)
L	*L*ibidinous oversexed perverted	asensual ascetic frigid	Personal attractiveness, sociability, pleasure seeking, frivolity vs. earnestness, a s c e t i c i s m, mirthlessness. (22)
M	*M*asculine dictatorial hostile	feminine modest tactful	Crude social assertion, exhibitionism vs. modesty, obedience to authority. (23) Shrewd, dictatorialness vs. naive, unassertiveness. (24) Rigidity, d e s p o t i s m, egotism vs. adaptability, friendliness, tactfulness. (25)
N	*N*atural sincere idealistic	unnatural insincere cynical	Obstructionism, cynicism, unstable hostility vs. idealism, affection, sensitive consideration. (26) Grateful, kindness, Christian idealism vs. hostility, cynicism, selfish withdrawal. (27) Cynicism, suspicion, dishonesty vs. idealism, trustfulness, respecting self and others. (28)
O	*O*riginal playful eccentric	conventional inarticulate mechanical	Asceticism, eccentricity vs. comfort-loving conventionality. (29) Amorousness, playfulness vs. propriety. (30) Eloquence, affectedness, amusing conversationalism vs. self-efface-ment, inarticulateness, naturalness. (31)
P	*P*assive hypochondriacal melancholic	active eloquent elated	Agitation, melancholy, obstinacy vs. placidity, social interest. (32) Hypochondriacal, taciturn retroversion vs. eloquence, interest in future. (33)

TABLE 15. *(Continued)*

Factor	Indicators Group I	Indicators Group II
J	regressive movements opposite to progressive ones, curves and spirals combined with angular patterns, transposed pressure, sudden emphasis on details, strokes ending in sharp points, disturbance in the depth movement, slant to the left	progressive movements, regular up-and-down strokes in predominantly angular pattern, medium pressure, equable emphasis on forms, movements ending smoothly, slant to the right
K	emphasis on details as well as on connections, emphasis on upper sphere of writing, closed patterns, oscillating step-like movements	lack of details and connections, certain emphasis on lower sphere of writing, open patterns, pictorial forms
L	emphasis on lower sphere of writing, especially on loops, loops ink-filled (distortions in lower loops in cases of perversion), swelling pressure, shading effect (lack of parallelism between lower loops in cases of endocrine disturbances), graceful forms, downstrokes firm	neglect of lower sphere of writing, thin loops or avoidance of loops, low or transposed pressure, cut end-strokes, broken forms, down-strokes thin or unsteady
M	high pressure up to dirty appearance, block type, straight lines, movements, sharp strokes, strong vertical loops, capitals large, t-bars heavy, speed fast	low pressure up to fading strokes, filigree-like patterns, curved lines, small movements, bending strokes, feeble horizontally directed loops, capitals small and simple, t-bars light, medium speed
N	well-shaped circular movements, regular ratios, precise connections, distinct features, fluent movements, constant writing angle, equal pressure, forms legible, ovals open	circular letters, open at bottom, irregular ratios, thready connections, indistinct features, slow movements, varying writing angle, varying pressure, ambiguous forms, ovals closed or open at base
O	original forms up to odd patterns, unexpected interconnections, variety of rhythmical distribution, good configuration	conventional forms, learned connections, stereotyped, rigid symmetry
P	sinking movements, broad forms, light pressure, blurred, fuzzy strokes, shadings, emphasis on horizontals, light pressure, small capitals	rising movements, angular forms, high pressure, oscillating strokes, emphasis on verticals, firm pressure, large capitals

TABLE 14. *(Continued)*

Symbol of factor	Intensity Group I	Intensity Group II	Cattell's Personality Clusters
Q	Quick changeable overdoing	slow stable inhibited	Austerity, thoughtfulness, stability vs. playfulness, changeability, foolishness. (34)
R	Restful adaptable placid	restless insecure neurotic	Neuroticism, self-deception, emotional intemperateness. (35) Generally emotional, dissatisfied, intense vs. content, placid, temperate. (36) Inflexibility, wandering vs. adaptableness, ease of settling down. (37) Realism, reliability vs. neuroticism, changeability. (38)
S	Sensitive suggestible mediumistic	insensitive dull crude	Poised sociability, inertia, toughness vs. introspectiveness, sensitivity, haste. (39)
T	Tense cramped schizoid	temperamental moody manic	Paranoid schizoid vs. trusting cyclothyme. Profligacy, planlessness, friendliness vs. austerity, hostility, perseverance. (40) Sthenic emotionality, hypomania, instability vs. self-control, patience, phlegm. (41)
U	Uncontrolled impulsive scatterbrained	self-controlled self-conscious frustrated	Infantile, demanding, self-centeredness vs. emotional maturity, frustration, tolerance. (42) High-strungness, impulsiveness, anxiety vs. apathy, relaxation, deliberateness. (43)
V	Vital productive creative	feeble unproductive flabby	Creativity, self-determination, intelligence vs. narrowness of interests, fogginess. (44)
W	Witty humorous brilliant	uninteresting dreary apathetic	Cheerful, enthusiastic, witty vs. coldhearted, sour, mirthless. (45) Creativity, wit, emotional color vs. dullness, banality, stability. (46)
X	eXpansive adventurous irrational	contracted traditional rational	Lack of restraint, adventurousness vs. general inhibition, fearfulness. Sociability, adventurousness, heartiness vs. shyness, timidity, reserve. (47)

TABLE 15. *(Continued)*

Factor	*Indicators* Group I	*Indicators* Group II
Q	increased size of left-hand margin toward bottom of page, dotting the "i" ahead, rising alignment, medium width, t-bars high, dashed, quick movements	decreasing size of left-hand margin, dotting the "i" exactly over its stem, sinking alignment, narrowness, t-bars low, short, even, slow movements
R	graphic elements are balanced, centered, determined, continuity of movement, medium width, good shape, distinct forms, uniform slant in loops, parallelism, even size of letters, round forms, moderate speed	graphic elements are unbalanced, scattered, continuous change of direction, interruptions, narrowness, shapelessness, indistinct forms, differences of slant in loops, lack of parallelism, small letters of uneven heights, hesitant forms, variable speed
S	thin lines, wavy movements, original interconnections, shading, rhythm	thick lines, disproportionate movements, lack of interconnections, lack of shading, lack of rhythmical quality
T	angular, narrow movements, isolation of letters, regressive inclination of letters, frequently distorted loops (disturbance in the height or depth of movement in cases of schizophrenia), small sized letters	round, wide movements, emphasis on connections, frequently combined with pressure, progressive inclination of letters, large loops (disturbance in the breadth of movement in cases of manic-depressive psychosis), large sized letters
U	introductory movements, blots and details, geometrization, rigid or disturbed rhythm, large difference between the size of small and tall letters, extreme variation of narrowness and width, terminal long, speed fast	immediate start with the essential pattern, neat differentiation, interruptions, regressive movements, inhibitions, reduced size, narrow movement, terminals short, speed moderate to slow
V	vivid distribution of features, movement starting from the depth, original forms, movement in upper and lower spheres of writing, open forms, interconnections and isolation of letters, down-strokes firm, straight	poor distribution of features, lack of depth movement, conventional forms, rigidity in upper and lower spheres of writing, closed patterns, perseverations, down-strokes light, bent
W	simplified forms with original and surprising reductions, fluency of movement, round patterns with pressure, "i"-dots curved and high, speed moderate to fast	empty regularity or unnatural additions to the letters, lack of fluency in movement, lack of differentiating patterns, extremes of pressure (either to low or to heavy), "i"-dots round and low, speed slow
X	expansive movement, variety of patterns, movements aiming toward the depth, emphasis on upper sphere of writing, broad curves, upper and lower extensions inflated	constricted movement, uniformity of patterns, lack of depth, emphasis on middle sphere of writing, lack of curves, upper and lower extensions reduced

TABLE 14. *(Continued)*

Symbol of factor	Intensity Group I	Intensity Group II	Cattell's Personality Clusters
Y	Yielding self-effacing masochistic	assertive aggressive sadistic	Stubbornness, pugnacity, clamorousness vs. tolerance, self-effacement. (48) Assertion, rivalry, conceit vs. modesty, unassumingness. (49) Smartness, assertiveness, independence vs. unsophistication, submissiveness, reverence. (50) Eager, self-assertion vs. lack of ambition. (51)
Z	Zealous optimistic easygoing	unwilling pessimistic reluctant	Balance, frankness, sportsmanship vs. pessimism, secretiveness, immoderateness. (52) Gratefulness, easygoingness, geniality vs. hardness, vindictiveness, coldheartedness. (53)

TABLE 15. *(Continued)*

Factor	Indicators Group I	Indicators Group II
Y	weak pressure, diffuse features, sometimes overexactness of patterns, leveled forms, wobbly margin of lines, long thin strokes, t-bars light and low, capitals small	sharp contrast of thin and thick strokes, large features, emphatic lines, sharp outlines, pointed strokes, endings frequently with pressure, t-bars flung down and pointed, capitals large
Z	quick and secure movement, consistency of forms, good connections, emphatic inclination of letters, emphasized pressure, "i"-dots advanced, t-bars high and long	slow and insecure movement, inconsistency of forms, lack of connections, opposition in the inclination of letters, change of the basic line of letters, transposed pressure, emphasis on dots put exactly over the letter, t-bars hooked

As stated before, our list of factors and of indicators cannot be used like a cookbook, since the complex patterns of personality cannot be diagnosed by ready-made recipes. Factors and indicators are presented only as guiding principles for that interpreter who has familiarized himself with graphic expression as a whole and with the general psychological principles underlying the expressive act. Such an interpreter will be able to use the following list of graphic characteristics, which is meaningless as an isolated dictionary of signs, but merely serves as a frame of reference for basic connotations. What we call "characteristic" is under no circumstance a fixed meaning, but a basic expressive value which changes in different configurations.

TABLE 16. Main Characteristics of Graphic Expression

I. *Texture of Strokes*

Appearance	*Characteristics*
1. high pressure	force, vitality, lack of differentiation*
2. three-dimensional pressure	activity, domination
3. two-dimensional pressure	receptivity, adaptability
4. broad spotting	anal stage, uncleanliness, disorderliness
5. low pressure	sensitivity, dreaminess, weakness*
6. faint, wobbly lines	vagueness, passivity
7. changing pressure, shadings	tactile sensitivity, anxiety*
8. straight lines	quickness, decisiveness
9. oversharp lines	decisiveness, definiteness
10. margin of lines unsharp	imagination
11. jittery lines	irritation

II. *Impulses of Movements*

12. continuity of movement	purposefulness, security
13. determination of movement	decisiveness, security
14. interrupted determined movement	stubbornness, carefulness, negativism, pre-meditation*
15. vacillating movement	inhibitions, insecurity
16. interrupted vacillating movement	inhibitions, insecurity
17. sudden movements	impulses
18. change of movements	impulses
19. contrasting movements	contradictory trends
20. confinement of movements with pressure	urges
21. confinement of movements without pressure	dreaminess
22. monotonous movements	passivity, lack of differentiation
23. narrow movements	restriction
24. wide movements	expansion
25. big movements	aspirations
26. small movements	control

*The application of the proper trait name depends on the relationship of the graphic element to pressure

TABLE 16. *(Continued)*

III. *Direction of Movements*

Appearance	*Characteristics*
27. direction from top to bottom	introversion, anxiety, masochism, self-involvement, dreaminess*
28. direction from bottom to top	extraversion, domination, aggression, curiosity*
29. direction from right to left	introversion, self-determination, isolation, discouragement*
30. direction from left to right	extraversion, tendency to leadership, seeking for support*
31. ascending movements	elations
32. descending movements	depressions
33. graduated movements	tendency to penetration

IV. *Forms of Movements*

34. centripetal movements	dominance of impressions
35. centrifugal movements	dominance of expressions
36. horizontal movements	rest, perseverance, weakness, feminine trends*
37. vertical movements	motion, determination, nervous activity, masculine trends*
38. angular movements	tension, reflection, criticism, doubt, restraint*
39. circular movements	balance, changing moods, evading any decision, manic-depressive*
40. wavy or thread-like movements	flexibility, sensitivity, adaptability
41. reduced patterns	simplification
42. elaborated patterns	ambition, speculation
43. pictographic type	dependency on outer objects
44. oscillographic type	dependency on inner processes

V. *Emphasis on Certain Regions of Space*

45. tendency toward right	progression, extraversion
46. tendency toward left	regression, introversion
47. tendency toward depth	activity, domination
48. tendency toward surface covering	receptivity, adaptability
49. upper sphere	speculation, mental activities
50. lower sphere	emotional activities
51. middle sphere	social activities

VI. *Character of Patterns*

52. well-shaped patterns	aesthetic attitude, artistic feeling
53. lack of form principle	lack of observation or imagination
54. good distribution	creative ability
55. bad distribution	rhythmical disturbance
56. differentiation of forms	capacity for adjustment
57. lack of differentiation	lack of orderliness and cleanliness
58. preference for big forms	tendency toward expansion, ambition
59. preference for small forms	discouragement, regression, control*

---

*The application of the proper trait name depends on the relationship of the graphic element to other graphic elements.

TABLE 16. *(Continued)*

Appearance	*Characteristics*
60. great contrast of size	conflicts
61. connection of forms by lines	ability to see relationships
62. embracing of smaller elements by larger ones	ability to integrate
63. free handling of forms	free approach to objects
64. exactness	ability in observing reality
65. fanciful forms	predominance of private world
66. indistinct forms	evasiveness
67. broken forms	psychological or biological disturbances
68. transpositions in forms and arbitrary changes	attempts at suppression, dishonesty
69. consistency of forms	decision
70. surrounding lines	differentiation, protection, isolation
71. imaginary lines (underlinings, overlinings)	projections of limitations or directions of imagination

VII. *Typological Value of Graphic Forms*

1. *The realistic type*

Appearance	*Significance*
(a) realistic or traditional manner of representation	more cycloid temper
(b) exactness	observing
(c) preference for clear-cut outlines	visual type
(d) preference for curves	auditory type
(e) preference for contrasts	emotional type
(f) secure movement	mobility
(g) broad pressure	aggressiveness
(h) pronounced change of movement	manic-depressive moods
(i) dirty appearance	anal phase
(j) overemphasis on details	lack of integration
(k) pictographic expression	visual-mindedness, impressionable

2. *The abstract type*

Appearance	*Significance*
(a) abstract or original manner of representation	schizoid type
(b) lack of exactness	dreamy
(c) preference for small details	self-consciousness
(d) preference for angles	tension, private world
(e) preference for shadings	tactual type, dreaminess, anxiety
(f) insecure movement	instability
(g) sharp pressure	sadistic trends
(h) schematism of movement	rigidity
(i) overexactness	submission
(j) bizarre figures	blocking of natural reactions
(k) dissolution of forms	insecurity, absent-mindedness
(l) oscillographic expression	abstract-mindedness, expressiveness

The characteristics of graphic expression have to be studied in their interrelationships, and they receive their value from their common denominator. The detection of the same principle in the variety of expressions leads us to the "axis of personality," the frame of reference in terms of which characteristics of graphic expression become indicators for factors in personality.

The following is a synopsis of graphic patterns in a simplified form. The graphic characteristics are divided under the categories:

I. The dimensions

   A. Size

   B. Extension

   C. Pressure

II. The movements

   A. Siant

   B. Direction

   C. Distance

III. The patterns

   A. Stroke

   B. Form

   C. Texture

IV. The configurations

   A. Form-level

   B. Accentuation

   C. Transformation

   D. Region

The categories include various elements; we selected eight of the most characteristic ones for each category. The following sample of a recording blank shows how the graphic indicators in a handwriting sample can be checked. The letter abbreviations behind each category and the number behind the elements facilitate the reference when data are grouped together under "General Observations."* (See page 322.)

---

*For practical purposes, a manual is planned which is to include the list of graphic indicators and the factors of expression; recording blanks may be obtained separately.

322   DIAGRAMS OF THE UNCONSCIOUS

RECORDING BLANK for checking GRAPHIC INDICATORS

Name: *Sex*:   *Age*:   *Profession*:

Dimensions

Size (S)	Check	*Extension* (E)	Check	*Pressure* (P)	Check
average	1	average	1	average	1
big	2	extended	2	firm	2
emphasized	3	outreaching	3	heavy	3
inflated	4	increasing	4	turgid	4
small	5	contracted	5	light	5
reduced	6	ends cut	6	low	6
microscopic	7	ends hooked	7	faint	7
threadlike	8	decreasing	8	broken	8

Movements

Slant (Sl)	Check	*Direction* (D)	Check	*Distance* (Di)	Check
vertical	1	bottom-top	1	average	1
right	2	ascending	2	separated	2
forward	3	progressing	3	large	3
oblique	4	stepping	4	gaps	4
left	5	top-bottom	5	connected	5
backward	6	descending	6	together	6
reclined	7	regressing	7	cramped	7
horizontal	8	vacillating	8	entangled	8

Patterns   *Types* (Ty)

Strokes (St)	Check	*Forms* (F)	Check	*Textures* (Te)	Check
angular	1	conventional	1	pictographic	1
piercing	2	accentuated	2	oscillographic	2
hard edged	3	elaborated	3	rhythmical	3
n-shaped	4	confused	4	a-rhythmical	4
round	5	perverted	5	shaded	5
thready	6	simplified	6	transposed pressure	6
soft edged	7	indistinct	7	distortions	7
u-shaped	8	restricted	8	breaks	8

Configurations

Form-level (F)	Check	*Accentuation* (A)	Check	*Transformation* (T)	Check
good distribution	1	determined	1	consistency	1
differentiation	2	sudden	2	surroundings	2
good shape	3	changing	3	enclosures	3
exactness	4	contrasting	4	directives	4
bad distribution	5	persevering	5	transpositions	5
no differentiation	6	interrupted	6	fixations	6
bad shape	7	fading	7	dislocations	7
confused	8	decomposed	8	projections	8

Regions (R)	Check		Check	*General Observations**
above	1	left	5	
middle	2	depth	6	
beneath	3	surface	7	*affix sheet if
right	4	scatter	8	necessary

CHAPTER XIV

HANDWRITING AND BIOGRAPHY

SIGNATURE AND ASSOCIATION

As we have seen, the act of writing is accompanied by associations. These associations may be conscious or unconscious. Muscular and organic activities also are closely linked up with associations, as was demonstrated by experiments with the "conditioned reflex": if a dog gets his food he produces saliva. If a bell is rung at the same time, the dog's association between bell and food becomes so strongly established that if the experimenter rings the bell without giving any food, the dog starts to produce saliva. This demonstrates that a certain association may instantly evoke a certain organic activity. The so-called psychosomatic studies show that psychological changes or disturbances produce bodily changes or disturbances; and conversely, that bodily changes or disturbances have an immediate effect upon psychological processes. The activities of the body and of the mind can therefore not be separated. Our movements are accompanied by mental activities, i.e., conscious or unconscious associations, and it seems probable that our mental activity also is accompanied by certain movements which, however, are perceptible only if they appear in a high degree; they can be noticed in rhythmic movements when hearing music and imitating gestures when seeing moving objects. Since handwriting is an expressive movement reflected upon paper, we understand that here also associations influence the movement pattern, and we have tried to demonstrate experimentally how different associations can be recognized in graphic patterns.

From a writer's various associations influencing his graphic movement some are more dominant than other ones. While many associations only appear as transient reflections upon the writing process, some leave their constant mark upon certain letter formations and they appear especially distinctive in the more stereotyped pattern of a person's signature. By means of measurements we discovered consistencies of graphic formation; and by means of association experiments we found consistencies of expression. Such an expressive consistency reveals a writer's image of himself and in many cases his conception of the world in the form of a stereotyped symbol. Since these symbols are individual ones, we usually recognize them only if we have data of identification, as given by the writer's associations, and his autobiographical data. It might be objected that knowing a man's interests and conceptions it would be possible to find in his signature whatever we search for, so that our findings actually would be conclusions determined by preconceived notions. This danger, however, is greatly limited if the graphic symbol is distinct, if the associations are specific, and if the correlations of both are significant. Such a significance appears if we deal with a pointed, simplified and striking identity between concept and symbol. Our freedom of interpretation is furthermore limited by the observation that leitmotifs usually appear in the signature and with the start of graphic movements; we therefore look for the symbol in the initial of the signature. In some cases, however, the leitmotif patterns the entire graphic movement. Thus, the leitmotif, taken from known data, and rediscovered in the graphic pattern, helps us to interrelate the biographical material and the indications of graphic expression.

We shall try to apply our observations to an analysis of a few handwriting specimens. In order to verify our statements, examples are taken from historical personalities about whom we possess biographical data. In order to unify our examples we take a corresponding graphic pattern in all cases, namely, the signature. Although a graphic analysis should always be based on several graphic specimens of the same person, possibly written at different times of his life, including written texts and signatures, our limitation of space obliges us to refer only to one or two signatures of the same person. From our great mass of material we selected a few cases of individuals whose lives not only show definite consistent patterns, but who are obsessed by one idea the reflection of which we try

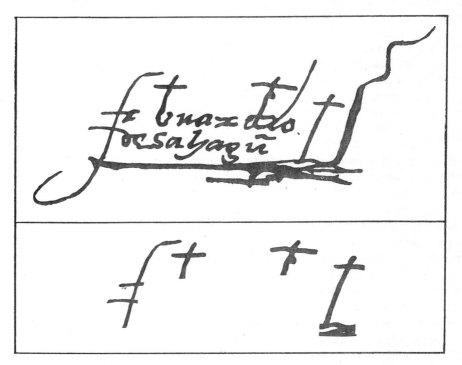

FIG. 313.—Grapho-analysis: Fra Bernardino de Sahagún.

to discover in their graphic expression. Our selection was further determined by using representatives of different professions, of different nationalities, and of different epochs. We present the following cases:

Fra Bernardino de Sahagún, Spanish missionary (1499?-1590)
Baruch de Spinoza, Dutch philosopher (1632-1677)
Blaise Pascal, French philosopher (1623-1672)
Immanuel Kant, Prussian philosopher (1734-1804)
Abraham Lincoln, American President (1809-1865)
Ludwig II, Bavarian King (1864-1886)
Case Gert, Russian child (1915-   )

FRA BERNARDINO DE SAHAGUN

Much of the civilization of the Mexican and Mayan peoples which was destroyed by the covetousness of the Spanish conqueror Cortez in 1520 would have been unknown to us had there not lived one man who devoted sixty years of his life to observing and describing the customs and concepts of these peoples. We use a signature of this man, Sahagún, who was a missionary of the Catholic Church; the signature is published in the French edition of his main work (Fig. 313).

In the following there are listed the graphic characteristics of the signature with their significance as we have presented them in our preceding tables. The numbering of items corresponds to the numbers used in the table and facilitates reference to them.

I. *Texture of strokes*

Appearance	*Characteristic*
1. high pressure	force, vitality, lack of differentiation
2. three-dimensional pressure	activity, domination
10. edge of lines unsharp	imagination
11. jittery lines	irritation

II. *Impulses of movement*

14. interrupted determined movement	stubbornness, negativism
19. contrasting movement	impulses, insecurity, contradictory trends

III. *Directions of movements*

28. direction from bottom to top	extraversion, domination, aggression, curiosity
29. direction from right to left	introversion, self-determination, isolation, discouragement
31. ascending movements	elations
33. graduated movements	tendency toward penetration

IV. *Emphasis on certain forms of movement*

Appearance	*Characteristic*
37. vertical movements	motion, determination, nervous activity, masculine trends
38. angular movements	tension, reflection, criticism, doubt, restraint
43. pictographic type	dependency on outer objects

V. *Emphasis on certain regions of space*

46. tendency toward left	regression, introversion
47. tendency toward depth	activity, domination
49. upper sphere	mental activities

VI. *Character of patterns*

54. good distribution	creative ability
56. differentiation of forms	capacity for adjustment
60. great contrast of size	conflicts
61. connection of forms by lines	ability to see relationships
65. fanciful forms	predominance of private world
69. consistency of forms	decision
71. imaginary lines	projections of limitations or directions of imagination

Graphic indicators	*Factor of expression*
T-factor, Group I	
angular movements, isolation of letters, disturbance in the depth of movement	tense, cramped, schizoid

The most significant traits are those which appear with several graphic characteristics; they form the center for our interpretation. They are the following:

Traits	*List-numbers of characteristics*
domination	2, 28, 47
irritation tension conflict	11, 38, 60, T-factor
determination stubbornness	14, 29, 37
introversion private world	29, 46, 65

The characteristics of "domination" and "determination" seem to contradict the characteristic of "introversion." We suppose that this contradiction is one source for the predominating "tension" and "conflict," which seem to determine the entire graphic pattern (Factor T).

Besides these dynamic indicators we also observe a static image, the picture of the cross. We suppose that this image is the leitmotif of the writer, the center for the contradictory trends of domination and introversion, the origin of his conflict. These basic characteristics, together with the other indications, will guide us now in an analysis of the total expression.

If we look upon the signature of this man—Fra Bernardino de Sahagún of the Franciscan Order—we remark the expression of a tremendous force and an unusual expression of personality in the emphasis on the picture of the cross. The crosses grow from the letters and from the flourish, highly erected like menacing magic symbols. The projection of the cross is known to us from other Church men, as we have seen it in several signatures (Figs. 286-288); but there the cross was an element of the letter and not a separate unit as in Sahagún's writing. So we ask what this particular emphasis may mean. The extreme clearness of the cross, as demonstrated in the signature, leads us to the supposition that the significance of this symbol was similar to that of the Inquisition, namely, to show the invincibility and menacing force of the power of the Church. But considering that the signature shows limiting movements at the beginning and at the end and an especial emphasis at the basis, it seems that the projection of this idea was not so much determined by environmental as by inner-personal forces.

The signature indicates tension and conflicting tendencies born from a psychic conflict. The tension of personality is characterized by the tremendous pressure on strokes, visible in all graphic elements. There is the basic underlining which with force and determination is as straight as though drawn with a ruler but which ends in the outburst of a stroke, like a blazing flame. In all letters there appear knots and patches, typical expressions of restrained energy, and the movement in two opposite directions—toward the left side (as in the regressive bow of the "d," "h," and "g") or to the upper right side (as in the curve of the penultimate letter)—suggests the diagnosis of a conflict between introvert and extravert tendencies. The two parallels in the first letter, the distribution and distance of letters, the placing of the crosses and the limiting lines at the right, left, and lower sides of the writing seem to reflect an attempt to bring order and system into chaos.

But these tendencies seem to be an artificial mask. The harmonious flow of the first letter contrasts too much with the outburst of the end-stroke; the consistency of the underlining line in the beginning, contrasted with the split strokes at the end, reflect vibrations of the inner-personal struggle. The tension is even reflected upon the movements with which the cross is made, indicating inner conflicts related to this symbol. Tension is always an expression of opposite tendencies in personality, and if the symbol of the cross has a key position within this tension of opposites it might follow that the cross of Sahagún is not only a symbol of faith, but also of its opposite. This key to Sahagún's signature may lead our attempt to relate it to the few autobiographical notes extant to form a picture reflecting the dark time of the conquest of the New World.

Sahagún was one of the missionaries sent by the Apostolic Church to convert the natives of the newly conquered New Spain. All these missionaries might have undertaken the task of conversion with the same prospect which Alexander gave Manuel the Fortunate of Portugal: that by converting the children of the Devil he "might win eternal life and the blessing of the Holy See." Thus a young missionary like Bernardino might have gone to the New World not only to win the natives to the faith but also to win for himself "Eternal Life," and the symbol of the cross would have accompanied Bernardino in his task.

When Sahagún came to Mexico in 1529, eight years after the conquest he found in the country the traces of acts which—according to the Mexican reporter Ixtlilxochitl—were "horrible cruelties." The natives were so frightened that they apparently did all that was commanded of them, being excellent subjects for conversion. But in secret they continued to exercise their rites and ceremonials. When Sahagún asked his colleagues for the meaning of these customs, they either had not observed these rites and were satisfied with the external deceptive behavior of the natives, or they had found them too unimportant to take them seriously. But how convert the natives, if one could not discuss with them the error of their idolatry, and how, if one could not understand their language and their behavior, could one know whether they were continuing the old worship of their gods? Thus, before undertaking any militant action, Sahagún decided to become acquainted with the arms of his enemies and with their battle plans.

For his act of conversion Sahagún used for the first time a psychological and even a therapeutic method. He wrote in his book:*

> A physician cannot give any medicine to a sick person without knowing first in which mood or by what cause an illness originates; that means that a good physician should have knowledge of medicines and diseases to be able in an adequate manner to apply for each disease the opposite medicine; and the preachers and psychotherapists, for healing psychic diseases, should have experience of medicines and of psychic diseases, and the preacher should know devices for directing his doctrine against them.

Sahagún was the first missionary who took the faith of the natives seriously; he wrote:

> "I, Fray Bernardo de Sahagún, friar of the Franciscan Order . . . wrote twelve books *of the divine or better said idolatrous things*** and human and natural ones of this New Spain . . . Concerning the religion and cult of their gods, I do not believe that there exists any-place else in this world where idolatries are practiced with such reverence and with such lavishness as in New Spain."

---

*Historia universal de las cosas de la neua españa repartida en doze libras en lengua mexicana y española, fecha por el muy reurendo padre, fra bernardino de Sahagún, frayle de sant francisco de obseruancia." (Tomo I, Mexico 1938)

**"escribi doce libros de las cosas divinas, o por mejor decir idolatricas, y humanas y naturales."

This sentence, "I wrote twelve books of the divine or better said idolatrous things" and the emphasis on the "reverence" and "lavishness" of the natives' worship seems strange in a man who went out to destroy these very things. But during the time Sahagún spent with the natives, his emphatic occupation with the devilish poison seems to have intoxicated Sahagún himself. He surrounded himself with natives whom he taught to write with Latin letters, asking them to write down their recollections of their customs. But such an impulsive and emphatic man as Sahagún appears, from his words and his signature, to be, was not only influenced by the anthropological significance of the native customs, but became also emotionally affected by their spiritual meaning. He might have begun to understand too well the soul of these people and to love the natives, thus finally sacrificing his life more for the sake of the natives than for the Holy Church. When a terrible pestilence broke out in 1545, Sahagún devoted all his care to the natives and he himself buried more than 10,000 men.

Sahagún probably fell into a tragic conflict. His task was a militant battle for Christ; on the other hand there was his deep understanding of the Antichrist. And now the battle began in his own soul: "What does it mean, O Lord, that you have permitted the enemy of the human race so long to dominate at his pleasure this sad . . . nation. . . ."*

It seems that on this occasion Sahagún began to doubt. If God admitted this worship, either the power of the devil was stronger than God's power or this worship was also a religious manifestation of man. In these conflicts the identification with his mission was crumbling, the devilish enemy got access to his soul. As Sahagún said:** "It is an old custom of our enemy the Devil to look for a hiding place where he can attend to his occupations, following the word of the Gospel that the evildoer is afraid of the light." There remains nothing to do but surround himself with walls of crosses, symbols of the faith.

For the Church, Sahagún was not militant enough. The Church was displeased at Sahagún's showing so much interest in the Indians. According to a special edict of the Spanish king on April 22, 1577, all original papers of Sahagún and their translations were taken away from him and publication of any of his material which was related to the old rites and customs was forbidden.

Knowing that he wrote "divine or better said idolatrous things," that "it is an old custom of our enemy the Devil to look for a hiding place," Sahagún seems to have feared that the Devil's hiding place was in him, and he tried to expel him with the conjuration of the cross.

It is through this leitmotif that his graphic characteristics become interrelated (see page 325). The characteristics of "irritation," "tension"

---

*The whole text was suppressed in the edition of Bustamente and is not represented in the editions of Kingsborough, or in the French edition of Jourdanet, but only in the Spanish edition, Mexico, 1938.

**cit. E. Seler: Gesammelte Abhandlungen, Vol. II.

and "conflict" seem to result from the split between his "private world," stimulated by his identification with the mystical world of the natives and his "determination" to carry out the fight for the practical world of the Church.

Baruch de Spinoza
Blaise Pascal
Immanuel Kant

Spinoza, Pascal, and Kant (Figs. 314 a-c) have no more in common than their devotion to philosophy, to an interpretation of the meaning of existence. Each of them led a life in which the values of everyday reality did not mean much but the values of mental and spiritual existence meant everything. Each of these men represents a pattern of thought which became characteristic of our civilization: Spinoza, the great advocate of mental-emotional balance; Pascal, the prophet of an emotional philosophy; and Kant, the herald of the mind's supremacy.

Before analyzing the three disparate approaches, which converge in one common goal, namely, the view of life from a philosophical perspective, we compare the graphic indicators of their handwriting according to our classifications (Spinoza, Fig. 314; Pascal, Fig. 315; Kant, Fig. 316).

In order to see more clearly their similarities and dissimilarities of expression, we classify their characteristics side by side.

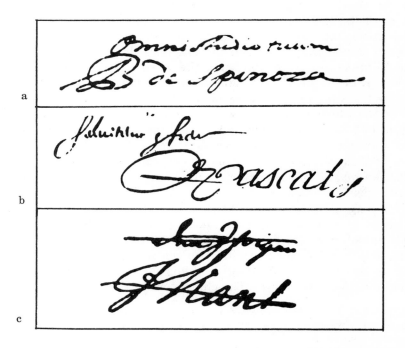

FIG. 314.—Signatures of Baruch de Spinoza, Blaise Pascal, Immanuel Kant.

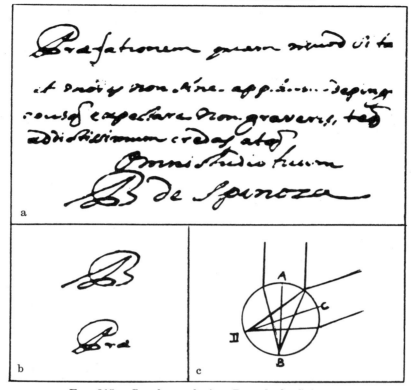

Fig. 315.—Grapho-analysis: Baruch de Spinoza.

I. *Texture of Strokes*

Spinoza (Fig. 314)	*Pascal* (Fig. 315)	*Kant* (Fig. 316)
3 two-dimensional pressure, receptivity, adaptability	3 two-dimensional pressure, receptivity, adaptability	2 three-dimensional pressure, activity, domination
7 changing pressure, shadings, sensitivity	7 changing pressure, sensitivity, anxiety	1 high pressure, force, vitality, lack of differentiation
10 edge of lines unsharp, imagination	9 oversharp lines, decisiveness, definiteness	10 edge of lines unsharp, imagination

II. *Impulses of Movements*

14 interrupted determined movements, stubbornness, negativism	15 interrupted vacillating movement, inhibitions, insecurity	12 continuity of movement, purposefulness, security
18 change of movements, impulses	17 sudden movements, impulses	23 narrow movements, restriction

III. *Directions of Movements*

27 from top to bottom, introversion, anxiety, masochism, self-involvement, dreaminess	28 from bottom to top, extraversion, domination, aggression, curiosity	28 from bottom to top, extraversion, domination, aggression, curiosity

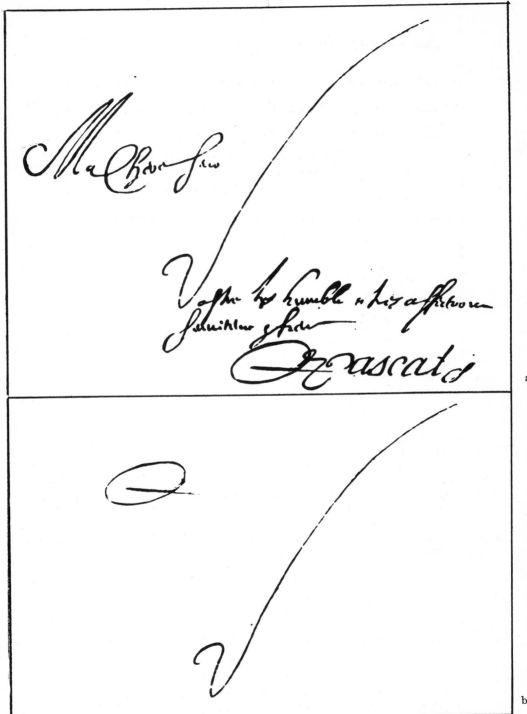

a

b

FIG. 316.—Grapho-analysis: Blaise Pascal.

29 from right to left, introversion, self-determination, isolation, discouragement

30 from left to right, extraversion, tendency to leadership, seeking for support

29 from right to left, introversion, self-determination, isolation, discouragement

31 and 32 ascending and descending movement, elations and depressions

32 descending movement, depressions

IV. *Emphasis on Certain Forms of Movements*

34 centripetal movement, dominance of impressions

35 centrifugal movement, dominance of expression

34 centripetal movement, dominance of impressions

39 circular movement, balance, changing moods, evading any decision, manic-depressive

37 vertical movements, motion, determination, nervous activity, masculine trends

38 angular movements, tension, reflection, criticism, doubt, restraint

40 wavy or thread-like movement, flexibility, sensitivity, adaptability

42 elaborated patterns, ambition, speculation

41 reduced patterns, simplification

V. *Emphasis on Certain Regions of Space*

46 tendency toward left, regression, introversion

49 upper sphere, speculation, mental activity

49 upper sphere, speculation, mental activity

VI. *Character of Patterns*

54 good distribution, creative ability

52 well-shaped patterns aesthetic attitude, artistic feeling

55 bad distribution, rhythmical disturbance

56 differentiation of forms, capacity for adjustment

60 great contrast of size, conflicts

61 connection of forms by lines, ability to see relationships

Graphic Indicators

R-factor, Group I
graphic elements are balanced, centered, determined, continuity of movement, good shape, distinct forms

X-factor, Group I
expansive movement, variety of patterns, depth-movements, emphasis on upper sphere, broad curves, extensions inflated

K-factor, Group I
emphasis on connections, on upper sphere of writing, closed patterns, oscillating step-like movements

N-factor, Group I
well-shaped circular, movements, well-sized ratios, precise connections, distinct features, fluent movements, constant writing angle

A-factor, Group I
good arrangement of patterns, original forms, rhythm of movement

U-factor, Group II
start with the essential pattern, regressive movements, reduced size, narrow movement

Factors of Expression

R-factor, Group I	*X-factor, Group I*	*K-factor, Group I*
restful, adaptable, placid	expansive, adventurous, ir-rational	knowing, critical, analyti-cal
N-factor, Group I	*A-factor, Group I*	*U-factor, Group II*
natural, sincere, idealistic	aesthetic, artistic, ingeni-ous	self - controlled, self - con-scious, frustrated

Dominating Trends

Spinoza	*Pascal*	*Kant*
receptivity 3, 40, 56	speculation 42, 49	determination 2, 28
introversion 27, 29, 46	emotional conflicts 7, 15, 31, 32, 60	criticism, simplification, seeing relationships 38, 41, 61
restfulness R-factor	irrationality X-factor	criticism K-factor
idealism N-factor	aestheticism A-factor	frustration U-factor

Taking the trends as guiding factors, the single indicators can be related to them and with reference to all the integrated data personality sketches may be constructed. But, as we have demonstrated in our preceding example, the depth of personality may be approached if we take into consideration the leitmotif. As we have stressed, the leitmotif can be found only with the help of available data; it is a key which may fit one of

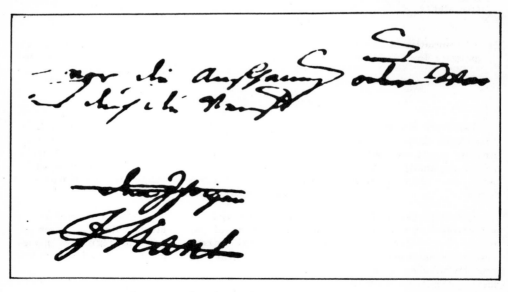

FIG. 317.—Grapho-analysis: Immanuel Kant.

the many given locks and serves to draw our attention to a dominant association of the writer. Of outstanding graphic patterns Baruch de Spinoza's initial "B" shows a combination between an angle and a circular pattern, both connected by a loop like an infinity sign ∞ (Fig. 315 b). Blaise Pascal's initial "B" (Fig. 316) shows a perfect ellipse crossed by a horizontal bar, a form which hardly reminds us of the traditional pattern of this letter. Characteristic, furthermore, is the overemphasized vertical up-stroke of Pascal's letter "V" in the word "voster" (your) (b). The most characteristic patterns in the writing of Kant (Fig. 317) are the long horizontals which superimpose his signature. We shall now try to discover the writers' associations which may be related to their graphic symbols.

BARUCH DE SPINOZA

Biographical Data. With reference to Spinoza's graphic pattern of an angle and a circle a letter may be cited which he wrote to Jarig Jelles on March 3, 1667; he writes of the circle, in connection with a discussion on Déscarte's "Dioptrics":

> It is certain that in this matter the circle surpasses all other figures which can be discovered. For *the circle has everywhere the same property.** For instance, the circle A B C D has this property, that all rays parallel to the axis C D, and coming from the direction C, will be refracted at the surface in such a way that they will all come together at the point D. This can be said of no other figure.

Spinoza illustrates this statement by a figure with those elements which are dominant in the initial of his signature (Fig. 315 c). Discussing in the same letter the properties of the angle, Spinoza remarks:

> . . . the angle is formed by the rays coming from different points, at the surface of the eye, when they cross each other there. And this *angle also becomes greater or less according as the foci* of the glasses put in a telescope are more or less distant.

For Spinoza the circle represents the idea of a structure which remains everywhere the same, which has "everywhere the same property," while the angle changes with regard to the focus.

In another letter of October 1674 to Hugo Boxel, Spinoza describes angular and circular forms as symbols of projection:

> I believe that a triangle, if only it had the power of speech, would say in like manner that God *is eminently triangular* and a circle would say that the *Divine Nature is eminently circular,* and in this way each thing would ascribe its own attributes to God, and make itself like unto God, while all else would appear to it deformed.

---

*Italicized by the present author, also in the following quotations.

The examples imply that the circle is for Spinoza a symbol of nature and of constancy and the angle a symbol of God and of change. The emphasis on geometrical images is characteristic of Spinoza's philosophy, expressed in his ethics: "Ethica more Geometrica Demonstrata" (Ethics demonstrated geometrically): "I shall consider human actions and appetites just as if I were considering lines, planes, and bodies." For Spinoza the highest form of reason is represented in geometrical order for limiting and directing the passions; the conflicts of forces in the human soul have to be ruled as in the physical world. These conflicts derive from opposite tendencies; but reason can perceive a common origin in them.

While the world is like the circle and God like the rays which, as angles emanate from the circle's center, man has to construct in himself both the harmony of the circle and the dynamics of the angle. Just as the circle embraces the angles, so the principle of harmony should embrace the dynamics of passions, ruling and limiting them. The rays of the circle symbolize Spinoza's concept of a duality in a unity, like God and nature, change and stability, passion and reason. It is in his signature that Spinoza binds both together, the symbol of the circle and the symbol of the angle, by the third symbol, ∞, the sign of infinity. But also the dynamism of man's individuation postulated by Spinoza in the act of retroversion seems to have its graphic reflex. The whole writing is covered with retrovert curves, especially emphasized in the "d" of the "de" between the given name and the surname. According to Spinoza man establishes his center of balance by means of retroversion, thus discovering in himself the forces of God from whom he originates. The leitmotif of uniting the principles of harmony and dynamics, of stability and change, of reason and of passion, seems to unify the various characteristics of Spinoza's graphic expression (see page 334) of which we listed the characteristics of "idealism" and "restfulness," of "receptivity" and "introversion." These characteristics, almost contradictory at the first glance, are reconciled with each other in Spinoza's geometrical system of soul and universe.

BLAISE PASCAL

With reference to Pascal's distinctive graphic patterns (Fig. 316), the ellipse in his initial "B" and the long curve of the letter "V," we quote a statement from his "Pensées":

> Let man contemplate the whole of nature in her full and grand majesty and turn his vision from the low objects which surround him. . . .
> Let the earth appear to him a point in comparison with the vast circle described by the sun; and let him wonder at the fact that this vast circle is itself but a very fine point in comparison with that described by the stars in their revolution round the firmament. . . .
> We only produce atoms in comparison with the reality of things. *It is an infinite sphere* the center of which is everywhere, the circumference nowhere.

For Pascal the vast world-circle is the expression of the boundlessness in which man is lost. Thus he writes, again in the *Pensées:*

> Returning to himself, let man consider what he is in comparison with all existence; let him regard himself as *lost* in this remote corner of nature; and from the little cell in which he finds himself, I mean the universe, let him estimate at their true value the earth, kingdoms, cities, and himself. What is a man in the *Infinite?* . . . A Nothing in comparison with the Infinite, an All in comparison with the Nothing, a mean between nothing and everything. Since he is infinitely removed from comprehending the extremes, the end of things and their beginning are hopelessly hidden from him in an impenetrable secret; he is equally incapable of seeing the Nothing from which he was made, and the Infinite in which he is swallowed up.

The world-circle gives Spinoza a feeling of protection, like the embracing arm of a mother in which the child feels secure; but, according to Pascal, man facing the Infinite lives in a vacuum and suffers from this hopeless condition.

Spinoza found an actual correspondence between his spiritual concept and his profession of polishing lenses. Pascal's concept, however, led him to occupy himself with the vacuum. He was the first who experimented with a vacuum within a vacuum, proving that air pressure produces "that redoubtable void that frightens all Nature."

For Spinoza the concept of mathematics is a model of calculation and construction, a model of man's self-containedness. For Pascal the concept of mathematics is the infinite curve, and man can do no more than escape with his thought into infinity. Pascal writes: "In comparison with the Infinites all finites are equal, and I see *no reason for fixing our imagination* on one more than on another. The only comparison which we make of ourselves to the infinite is painful to us." These associations of world sphere, vacuum and infinite may underlie Pascal's graphic symbolism of the ellipse crossed by a curve and the "unending" curve, the curve of infinite with which he signs the letter. This leitmotif seems to interrelate Pascal's graphic factors of expression (see page 334), of which we listed as the most characteristic ones: "aestheticism," "receptivity" and "speculation" on the one hand, and "irrationality," "inhibition," "conflict" and "anxiety" on the other.

IMMANUEL KANT

The most characteristic element in Kant's signature is the horizontal line superimposed on his name and on the words of the close, "der Ihrige" (Yours) (Fig. 317). Kant refers to the concept of a "line" at the beginning of his career, at the age of twenty-two:* "I have already *fixed upon the line* which I am resolved to keep. I will enter on my course, and nothing shall prevent me from pursuing it." Kant kept this concept until the end of his life when he was 80 years old. Wasianski, who nursed Kant in his advanced days, reports one of Kant's later self-characteriza-

---

*Introduction to Kant's Critique of Practical Reason, London, 1901; p. 13.

tions:* "Kant spoke of himself under the figure of a gymnastic artist who had continued for nearly fourscore years to support his balance upon the tightrope of life, without once swerving to the right or to the left."

The line was for Kant a symbol of the "line of living" and the "line of balance." This was Kant's main aim: to fix a line of living for himself and for others. He draws a line between fact and speculation, between reality and metaphysics, between man and God. The *Critique of Pure Reason* prescribes the line reason must follow. We cannot extend our reason to grasp things as they are, because all things depend on the way in which we see them, on the function of our sense organs, and we never can have knowledge of anything nonperceivable, such as metaphysical ideas. However, our world of experience is made possible by certain general mechanisms of our thinking. Nature, as we perceive it, depends on the forms of our intelligence and not vice versa, as was believed before. Our understanding prescribes its laws to nature. With this revolutionary thought Kant draws a line for nature. But the line of reason has a correlate in the line of morality. The moral law in us prescribes the ethics; the line of living and thinking, as drawn by Kant, limits man's aspirations. From this aspect the line becomes a symbol of limitation, and in the highest degree of limitation it gets the function of crossing out the freedom of life.

Kant actually lived this example, leading the most impersonal life that any philosopher lived. He never left his home town, Königsberg, and saw nothing of the world. He never had a love affair and said that his only mistress was metaphysics. Twice he thought of getting married, but in one case he reflected so long that the girl married a more decisive man, and in the other case the lady moved from Königsberg before Kant declared himself. He never had spontaneous joys in life; even eating, drinking, sleeping and resting were exactly scheduled. Thus his personal life was completely repressed, and life was considered merely as a training ground. We give below some observations made by Wasianski which illustrate the artificial clockwork of Kant's personal life.

> Precisely at five minutes before five o'clock, winter and summer, Lampe, Kant's footman, who had formerly served in the army, marched into his master's room with the air of a sentinel on duty, and cried aloud, in a military tone, "Mr. Professor, the time is come." This summons Kant invariably obeyed without one moment's delay, as a soldier does the word of command—never, under any circumstances, allowing himself a respite, not even on the rare occasion of having passed a sleepless night. As the clock struck five Kant was seated at the breakfast-table, where he drank what he called *one* cup of tea; and no doubt he thought it such; but the fact was, in part from his habit of reverie, and in part also for the purpose of the refreshing warmth, he filled up his cup so often that in general he is supposed to have drunk two, three, or some unknown number.

---

*"The Last Days of Immanuel Kant," publ. 1804, Engl. transl. by Thomas de Quincey.

Heinrich Heine wrote of Kant:

> Rising, coffee-drinking, writing, reading, dining, walking, each had its fixed time. . . . When Immanuel Kant in his gray coat, a cane in his hand, appeared at his house-door . . . the neighbors knew it was exactly half past three by the clock.

The consequence of Kant's time complex was that all delays were extremely disagreeable to him, and his constant exclamation if he wanted anything was to bring it "on the spot." Kant's time complex seems to have originated in his basic insecurity in matters of his personal life, and this insecurity, as Wasianski remarked, was related to Kant's habit of reverie. His life was a life in imagination and not in reality. It is very significant that he had an excellent memory for all intellectual problems and a very poor one for all things of everyday life. This split between reality and imagination seems to be reflected upon the graphic discrepancy between the expressive features of his signatures and the text above it. The writing of the text shows movement, swings, and a very original pattern of letters. There is, especially, a great movement in the upper sphere of the writing which is completely missing in the signature. The compression of letters in the signature, as the line which crosses out his name, is a symbol of inhibitions and suppressions, whereas the free movement in the upper sphere of the text writing is a symbol of freedom of thought and expression.

Thus the leitmotif of Kant's signature accentuates his split between reality and imagination, between the personal life and the search for eternal truth. The leitmotif interrelates the main characteristics of his graphic expression (see page 334), which we listed as "determination," "criticism" and "frustration."

ABRAHAM LINCOLN

Abraham Lincoln united in himself great contradictions which are not visible in his signature (Fig. 318 a). This signature became stereotyped, as is frequently the case with men who sacrifice their private lives to the public. Lincoln's inner personality appears in the graphic movements of his private notations. We selected a poem which Lincoln wrote in 1844 (Fig. 318 b), in which the general characteristics of his graphic movements become more apparent than in his signature.

I. *Texture of Strokes*

2	three-dimensional pressure	activity, domination
6	faint, wobbly lines	vagueness, passivity
7	changing pressure, shadings	tactile sensitivity, anxiety
10	margin of lines unsharp	imagination

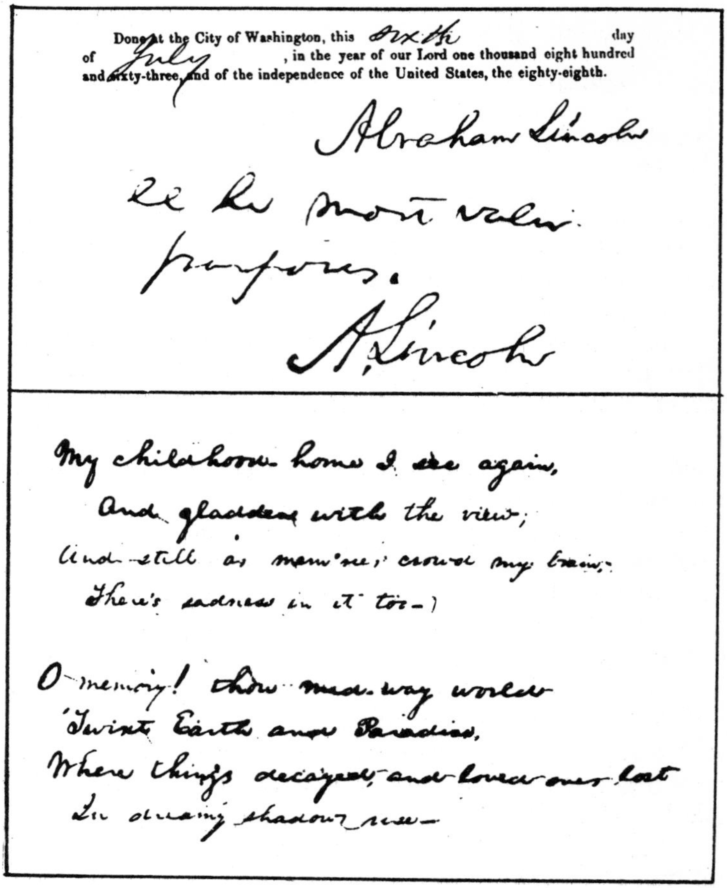
Done at the City of Washington, this sixth day of July, in the year of our Lord one thousand eight hundred and sixty-three, and of the independence of the United States, the eighty-eighth.

Abraham Lincoln

A. Lincoln

My childhood home I see again,
And gladden with the view;
And still as mem'ries crowd my brain,
There's sadness in it too—

O memory! thou mid-way world
'Twixt Earth and Paradise,
Where things decayed and loved ones lost
In dreamy shadows rise—

a

b

FIG. 318.—Grapho-analysis: Abraham Lincoln.

II. *Impulses of Movements*

14	interrupted, determined movements	stubbornness, negativism
23	narrow movements	restriction
26	small movements	control

III. *Directions of Movements*

20	confinement of movements with pressure	urges
21	confinement of movements without pressure	dreaminess
27	direction from top to bottom	introversion, anxiety, masochism, self-involvement, dreaminess
30	direction from left to right	extraversion, tendency to leadership, seeking for support
31	ascending movements	elations
32	descending movements	depressions
34	centripetal movements	dominance of impressions

IV. *Emphasis on Certain Forms of Movement*

37	vertical movements	motion, determination, nervous activity, masculine trends
38	angular movements	tension, reflection, criticism, doubt, restraint
40	wavy movements	flexibility, sensitivity
41	reduced patterns	simplification
44	oscillographic type	dependency on inner processes

V. *Emphasis on Certain Regions of Space*

47	tendency toward depth	activity, domination
51	middle sphere	social activities

VI. *Character of Patterns*

55	bad distribution	rhythmical disturbance
57	lack of differentiation	lack of orderliness and cleanliness
59	preference for small forms	discouragement, regression
67	broken forms	psychological or biological disturbances

Graphic Indicators

S-Factor, Group I

Thin lines, wavy movements, original interconnections, shading rhythm

T-Factor, Group I

Angular, narrow movements, isolation of letters, small sized letters, disturbance in the depth of movement.

Factors of Expression

S-Factor, Group I	sensitive, suggestible, mediumistic
T-Factor, Group II	tense, cramped, schizoid

The following characteristics are dominant:

passivity, restriction, negativism	6, 14, 23, 38, 59
psychobiological disturbance	55, 67, Factor T
dreaminess, introversion	21, 27, 44
sensitivity	7, 40, Factor S
activity, determination	14, 37

Although Lincoln's graphic expression exhibits indications of activity, the trends of introversion and passivity seem to dominate. The indications of psychobiological disturbances seem to be related to the dual aspect of activity and passivity, which, as we shall discuss in the following, alternated periodically.

Lincoln's most characteristic graphic pattern (Fig. 318) is the duality of expression in different words appearing in a change of shape, height, pressure, and connection of letters as well as in a change of speed. This repeated change of expression indicates rapid changes of moods. We notice that in the first and second line the words,

> "My childhood home I see again
> and gladden with . . .,"

are written with pressure, while the pressure disappears completely in the following words:

> ". . . the view
> and still as mem'ries crowd my brain
> There's sadness in it too."

The pressure recurs in the next exclamation:

> "O . . . .,"

and disappears in the following word:

> ". . . memory";

it reappears in the exclamation mark and the following three lines and vanishes in the last line. The height of letters is in general greater in the writing with pressure. Considering the linking of letters, we notice a continuity of strokes and connections in those periods which are written with pressure, while the continuity often is interrupted in disconnected strokes of the words written without pressure.* In the writing without pressure we frequently find broken strokes in the same letter,** and an isolation of letters.***

This contradictory manner of graphic expression seems to correspond to two different personalities; but both forms, so different in expression, have one principle in common: the lack of patterning of the letters. In the part written with pressure, the shape of the letters is effaced, and the loops are filled up. In the part written without pressure, the shape of the letters is broken. The first part, the obscuring of letters, is typical of an obscuring of ideas, a case we find in the state of depression where the world seems to be veiled in melancholy. The second part, with decomposition of letters, is typical of a state of weakness: the force for projecting images and directions diminishes; absentmindedness is noted. The thin and disconnected strokes of the second part are like a sieve which lets through an influx of impressions; such type of graphic expression is characteristic of a high impressionability and sensitiveness to influences. But the high pressure of strokes and the filling up of loops

---

*Compare the "o" of "childhood" and "home" (1st line) with the "o" of "crowd" (2nd line) and "too" (3rd line). Compare the "a" of "again" (1st line) and "gladden" (2nd line) with "brain" (3rd line) and "sadness" (4th line).

**See the "l" of "still" (3rd line), the "w" of "crowd," the "y" of "my," the "b" of "brain" (3rd line), the "h" of "there's," the "n" of "sadness," the "t" of "it" (4th line).

***See the "a" of "and," the "s" of "still" (3rd line), the "n" of "in" (4th line).

in the first part show just the contrary, an opposition to influences, a lack of impressionability. Such opposite characteristics must result in a high tension of personality. The retroversion of strokes and the rooting of the starting lines* is characteristic of the first part, and if such a movement is accompanied by pressure, it shows that the movement of progression is interrupted. Such a movement together with the emphasis on the starting point is characteristic of a perseverance on images of the past. For the second part just the opposite is characteristic; here the progressive way is emphasized, expressing the stimulus of ideas turned toward the future. Lincoln found in his associate, William H. Herndon,** an observer who possessed unique psychological qualities. Herndon was a friend and associate in the law office of Lincoln and he observed his associate during twenty-five years. Herndon remarked in a letter of July 17, 1887:***

> *He was a man of opposites, of terrible contrasts.* One man today would see Lincoln in one state, and the man would say this was Lincoln. Tomorrow this same man would see Lincoln in a totally different state and say that was not Lincoln, and yet it was, for Lincoln was under his law, and that ruled him with the iron of logic. This caused these contrasts in Lincoln, caused the differences of opinions among men in relation to Lincoln.

In a letter of February 21, 1891, Herndon wrote:****

> Mr. Lincoln was a peculiar, mysterious man. I wrote to you once that Mr. L. had a *double consciousness, a double life.* The two states, never in a normal man, coexist in equal and vigorous activities though they succeed each other quickly. One state predominates and, while it so rules, the other state is somewhat quiescent, shadowy, yet living, a real thing. This is the whole reason why L. *so quickly passed from one state of consciousness to another and a different state.* In one moment he was in a state of abstraction and then quickly in another state when he was a social, talkative, and a communicative fellow.

Lincoln himself had this feeling of a dual personality which became manifest for him in strange sensations of split personality. Emil Ludwig in his book on Lincoln quotes a happening recorded by a friend in Lincoln's own words:

> Once, after a tumultuous and tiring day, I threw myself down on an old sofa at home. Opposite where I lay was a bureau with a swinging glass upon it, and looking in that glass, I saw myself reflected nearly at full length; *but my face, I noticed, had two separate and distinct images,* the tip of the nose of one being about three inches from the tip of the other. I was a little bothered, perhaps startled, and got up and looked in the glass, but the illusion vanished. On lying down again, I saw it a second time, plainer, if possible, than before; and then I noticed that one of the faces was a little paler— say, five shades—than the other. I got up, and the thing melted away, and

---

*e.g., the "m" of "my" (1st line).
**The Hidden Lincoln. New York, 1938.
***Ibid., p. 190.
****Ibid., p. 263.

> I went off, and in the excitement of the hour forgot all about it—nearly, but
> not quite, for the thing would once in a while come up, and give me a little
> pang, as if something uncomfortable had happened.*

The duality of personality projected upon his graphic expression here
seems to be visible to Lincoln in his facial expression. The adolescent
Lincoln had already told a friend:**

> I may seem to enjoy life rapturously, when I am in company. But when I
> am alone, I am so often overcome by mental depression that I never dare
> carry a pocketknife.

Lincoln's main feature is his melancholy. Herndon said:***

> Mr. Lincoln was a sad, gloomy and melancholy man and wore the signs of
> these in every line of his face, on every organ and every feature of it.

and:

> His melancholy oozed from him as he walked.

Friends found him "sitting alone in a corner of the bar remote
from anyone, wrapped in abstraction and gloom." He was not only
dominated by sadness, but sadness attracted him. Victor Hugo said,
"Melancholy is the pleasure of being sad." When Lincoln heard sad songs
he asked the singer to write down the words for him. Thus we find among
his papers poems with phrases like: "Do ye know some spot where mor-
tals weep no more?" He himself expressed this feeling in poems like the
one from which we took our writing specimen:****

> My childhood home I see again,
> And gladden with the view;
> And still as mem'ries crowd my brain,
> There's sadness in it too—
> The friend I left that parting day—
> How changed, as time has sped.
> Young childhood grown, strong manhood gray,
> And half of all are dead—
> I range the fields with pensive tread,
> I pace the hollow rooms;
> And feel (companion of the dead)
> I'm living in the tombs—

This melancholy came from within, out of the depth of his personality,
and from without, when he identified himself with the suffering of men.
The image of slavery persecuted Lincoln. "It exercises," as he said, "the
power of making me miserable." The feeling of his own melancholy and
the identification of it with the melancholy of the world seemed to evoke
the tension in his personality, obliging him to overcome his passivity by

---

*See other similar observations in the author's book: The Expression of Per-
sonality.

**Emil Ludwig, Lincoln (transl. by E. & C. Paul) Boston, 1930, p. 43.

***Herndon, p. 121.

****Herndon, pp. 447-8.

forced action. These opposite tendencies evoked dynamics which on the one hand made him absent-minded and on the other hand gave him tremendous energy.

In Lincoln's graphic expression inhibitory elements seem to dominate (see page 341). "Passivity, restriction, negativism, psychobiological disturbances, dreaminess, introversion, sensitivity." But there are also opposite elements of "activity and determination." The graphic expression indicates this potentiality although it does not show that Lincoln made his own passivity an element of activity and turned his melancholy into power.

LUDWIG II OF BAVARIA

The figure of Ludwig II of Bavaria is of especial interest, because he is representative of those typically German characteristics which culminated in Kaiser Wilhelm II and in Hitler. The mixture of self-love, ambition, and introversion drove his country into bankruptcy and himself to suicide. It was not chance that Ludwig's best friend was Richard Wagner, composer of that epoch which was the prelude to Germany's "Götterdämmerung."

a   b

FIG. 319.—Grapho-analysis: Ludwig II of Bavaria.

The Elemental Approach. Using the signatures of the young prince (Fig. 319 a) and of the king (Fig. 319 b), we collected the following indicators of his graphic expression.

I. *Texture of Strokes*

3	two-dimensional pressure	receptivity, adaptability
10	edge of lines unsharp	imagination
4	broad spotting	anal stage, unclean

II. *Impulses of Movement*

12	continuity of movement	purposefulness, security
13	determination of movement	decisiveness, security
20	confinement of movements with pressure	urges
24	wide movements in initials	expansion

III. *Directions of Movements*

27	from top to bottom	introversion, anxiety, masochism, self-involvement, dreaminess
29	from right to left	introversion, self-determination, isolation, discouragement

IV. *Emphasis on Certain Movements*

34	centripetal movements	dominance of impressions
36	horizontal movements	rest, perseverance, weakness, feminine trends
39	circular movements	balance, changing moods, evading any decision, manic-depressive
42	elaborated patterns	ambition, speculation
43	pictographic type	dependency on outer objects

V. *Emphasis on Certain Regions of Space*

46	tendency toward left	regression, introversion
48	tendency toward surface-covering	receptivity, adaptability
49	upper sphere	speculation, mental activities
50	lower sphere	emotional activities

VI. *Character of Patterns*

52	well-shaped patterns	aesthetic attitude, artistic feeling
62	embracing of smaller elements by larger ones	ability to integrate
65	fanciful forms	predominance of private world
68	transpositions in forms and arbitrary changes	attempts at suppression, dishonesty

Graphic Indicators

Factor A, Group I

Good arrangement of patterns, original forms, rhythm of movement.

Factor L, Group I

Emphasis on lower sphere of writing, especially on loops; swelling pressure, lack of parallelism between lower loops.

Factors of Expression

A-Factor, Group I	aesthetic, artistic, ingenious
L-Factor, Group I	libidinous, oversexed, perverted

The following criteria appear repeatedly:

introversion	27, 29, 46, 65
receptivity	3, 34, 48
aesthetic attitude	52, Factor A
urges	4, 20, 50, Factor L

The characteristics of introversion and receptivity combined with an aesthetic attitude and emotional urges are typical of the so-called narcissistic personality. Besides these dynamic indicators we also observe a static image—oddly enough, the image of a swan. Actually artists frequently used this animal as a symbol of narcissistic erotism, as for instance in pictures of Leda with the swan. But for Ludwig, the swan seems to have been a decisive, individual experience.

When comparing two signatures of Ludwig II of Bavaria, one written by the prince, the other by the king, we notice a contrast in both expressions. While the prince writes in Gothic letters, the king writes in Roman letters. The signature of the prince is directed forward, that of the king is directed backward. Both movements become especially visible in the letter "d." The signature of the prince is written very conventionally, while in the signature of the king the initial starts with a very unconventional pattern: it is turned 90 degrees to the right. This very subjective patterning of the initial suggests that Ludwig's writing was accompanied by very specific associations.

Each visitor at Ludwig's bizarre castle Neu-Schwanstein (New Swan's Rock) is surprised to find himself surrounded by symbols of the swan (Fig. 320). We see here the swan in pictures accompanied by mythical figures; in the ornaments of carpets; in the chandeliers; in the writing-desk sets, etc. Relating this main idea to the signature of the king, we actually discover the image of the swan in the starting movement of the king's signature (Fig. 319 c), an image which is not present in the signature of the prince. Searching for the roots of this extraordinary image, I studied the writing of Ludwig's parents. Actually, there appears an outer resemblance in Ludwig's later writings with that of his father, Ludwig I (1786-1868), but there the picture of the swan is missing (Fig. 321).

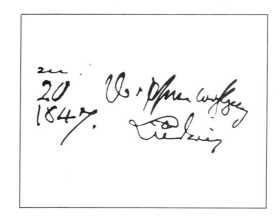

320   321

FIG. 320.—The emblem of Ludwig II.
FIG. 321.—Signature of Ludwig I.

As documents reveal, the king had a swan which he fed every day at a certain hour in an artificial and isolated lake. It seems that for Ludwig the swan was a symbol of isolation. Let us follow this motive of isolation to its first manifestations. Documents record* that in his childhood the French governess of the prince taught him sentences like: "L'état c'est moi" and "Tel est notre bon plaisir," emphasizing that all was made for him and that he was an absolute monarch. The child was mostly alone and he often retired to a darkened room, lying down on a couch. The king remarked: "It was not annoying for me; I thought of different things and entertained myself quite well." The idea of isolation also dominated Ludwig when he was king. He ordered performances given in the theater with himself as the only spectator. In identification with Louis XIV of France, who had built a dining table which could be dropped through the floor, so as to be set for his orgies without the intrusion of the servants, Ludwig II of Bavaria imitated this invention, though he ate alone at his table. One of his castles was called by him "Meicost Ettal," an anagram of "L'état c'est moi." In this castle the king had his own artificial firmament shining over his bed, artificial orange trees surrounded his bed, and the sound of an artificial waterfall put him to sleep.

It was not only the swan, which, aloof and proud, makes its way over the water, that was the symbol of loneliness, but also the water itself. As a little boy, Ludwig liked to fish in an isolated lake, and as a king he ordered the construction of artificial lakes and a subterranean water grotto in which he had himself driven around in a boat which had the form of a swan. It was with Friedrich I, the Emperor Barbarossa, who drowned in a river, and whom the German saga transposed to a cave in a mountain, that Ludwig liked to identify himself. Pictures of this king decorated a main room of his castle.

There was a third element related to the swan: the blue color of the waters of Bavarian lakes, the swan's element. This color was determined for Ludwig by his mother, who chose the color blue for his garments, jewelry, and book-bindings, while she chose the color red for his brother Otto. A complicated installation of artificial lights gave a blue color to the water of Ludwig's subterranean grotto. In this blue grotto, dressed as the swan-prince Lohengrin, driving around in a golden boat, the king fed the swans.

The well-known German painter Wilhelm Kaulbach obtained the king's order to paint Lohengrin with the swan. But Ludwig was not pleased with the portrayal of the swan, and the royal painter, Ille, got a separate order to paint the swan of this picture. Leinfelder, the adjutant of the king, wrote the following letter to Ille:

> I would suggest that you consider whether the head of the swan is not too big, and whether his breast which lies on the water is not too small; I must tell you that the king since his earliest childhood has observed and studied this favorite animal of his.

---

*L. V. Kobell: König Ludwig von Bayern und die Kunst.

The king said that the swan was present even in his earliest imaginations. It was a symbol of his family, which also called their castle "Hohenschwangau" (High Country of the Swan). The libretto of the opera *Lohengrin* made the greatest impression upon the prince. It became his only wish to hear the performance of this opera, when it was no longer on the list of productions. His desire was so strong that he went on his knees to his stern father, pleading with him to order a performance. The king fulfilled this desire on the prince's sixteenth birthday. The impression of this opera became determining for the prince, and the music had, as his adjutant legation secretary, von Leinfelder, reports, "an almost demoniacal effect" on him. Leinfelder describes this influence on the occasion of the second opera he heard, *Tannhäuser*—especially when the hero enters the Venusberg with its swans:

> . . . it made a tremendous impression upon his nervous system. His reactions during the opera performance were almost pathological ones. At the passage when Tannhäuser goes back into the Venusberg, Ludwig's body was shaken by such convulsions that I was afraid it might be an epileptic attack.

From then on the prince identified himself with the characters of Wagner's mystical operas which were centered for him in the figure of Lohengrin and the swan. When Ludwig became king, his first action was to bring Wagner to his court. Herr von Pfistenmeister, who had to search for Wagner, at this time poor and rather unknown, was instructed to direct the following words to Wagner:

> His Majesty asked me to deliver this ring. As this stone burns so he is burning ardently to see the creator of the verses and music of Lohengrin.

Many years after the ardent friendship between the king and Wagner had been formed, Ludwig determined to marry his cousin Sophie. He called her his "Elsa" and himself her "Lohengrin," remarking that they had found each other in the spirit of Wagner. He wrote her: "You're the dearest of all women alive—but as you know the God of my life is Richard Wagner." The wedding day was fixed, and tapestries with the Lohengrin figures were chosen for Sophie's room. But the world of his imaginary Wagner figures was too strong for him to bear the reality. He postponed the wedding day from one date to another. When Sophie's family let Ludwig know that "another postponement is no longer compatible with Sophie's honor," Ludwig made his decision. He wrote: "Beloved Elsa: It is the wish of your parents to dissolve our engagement, and I am willing to accept their offer."

He wrote in his diary: "The vision which depressed me has disappeared. I wanted to be free, I thirst for liberty, to be delivered from the depressing nightmare."

Lohengrin, the swan-prince, the lonesome pilgrim whose name should never be asked, becomes the ideal of Ludwig. Lohengrin, dreaming, is the motive which had to be used for an album of the king.

When Wagner died, Ludwig fell into an apathy which lasted many hours. He cried: "Wagner's body is mine, it belongs to me." From that time on the world of reality, in which Ludwig in spite of his dominating dreams had been rather active, disappeared. His only wish was to build castles and more castles as a realization of his dreams. Millions and millions were devoured, and the parliament refused to procure more money. Ludwig wanted to dissolve the parliament; he was taken by attacks of rage. He wrote to Hesselschwerdt:

> Tell them that the only joy of my life is building, that now, when all has come to a standstill, I feel terribly unhappy. I am considering abdication, even suicide. Tell them that this state of mind must be stopped, that the progress of the building no longer should be hindered.

The mania of dream realization ruined the country, and thus the parliament decided to dethrone the king. Declaring that Ludwig II was suffering from a mental disease, he was secluded in his castle "Berg." On June 13, 1886, Ludwig asked to go for a swim in the lake with his physician, Dr. Gudden. They did not come back. The dead body of Dr. Gudden was found sitting upright in the water, and that of the king floating face downward on the surface of the lake. Injuries in the face of Gudden revealed that there had been a battle in the water.

The swan, symbol of royalty, loneliness, and death, had shadowed the life of the dreamy king. As the swan in folklore is related to death, singing his most beautiful hymns before dying, thus also for Ludwig the swan represented the bird of death, which symbolically pulled the king down into the water of death, into the Lake of Starnberg.

The signature shows that the swan, related to Ludwig's leading concepts, becomes a key picture, incorporated into his graphic movement.

CASE GERT T.

Although the handwriting of children already shows individual differences, their writing is in general more adapted to the school model. If we notice an extreme deviation from the customary letter shape we have to assume the presence of strongly determining individual associations. The handwriting of a child, observed by the author, shows such very individual characteristics when writing a German text in Roman as well as in Gothic letters. (Fig. 322a) These individual characteristics disappear completely when writing in his native language, Russian. (Fig. 322b) Many of the Russian letters have the same shape as the Roman letters, but we notice that their shape is normal in the Russian text, and distorted in the German text. We therefore may assume that the distortion is due to associations related to the new environment. It is characteristic of the distortions that the letters are pressed together, that they are forced into unnatural positions and that the heads of letters are strangled. The general aspect is, on the one hand, that of an extreme aggressiveness; on the other hand, pressure and slowness

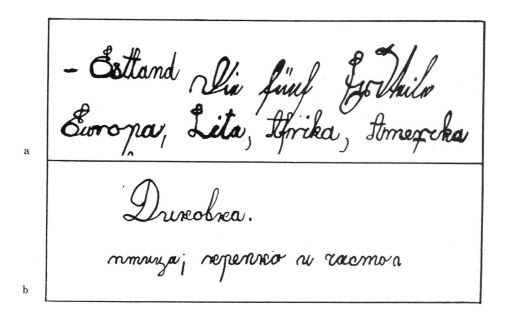

FIG. 322.—Handwriting, language and neurosis.

suggest an attempt to anchor the movement, probably due to a drive for security.

The case was observed in Berlin during the years 1928-29. Gert T., an only child, was born in Russia which the family left at the time of the Russian Revolution. After traveling through different countries the family, which was wealthy, settled in Berlin where they lived in very comfortable surroundings. A short time after moving to Berlin the parents of the boy were divorced, Gert remaining with his mother and his grandparents. When I began my educational supervision, Gert was 13 years of age. He gave the impression of infantile and schizophrenic behavior. The main symptoms were a complete lack of understanding of reality, and expressions of fear and aggression. The question to be considered at the outset was whether the disturbance originated in a fundamental pathological disposition or in a neurotic technique of escape from outward reality.

His early domestic life had been troubled for a long time by the vicissitudes of the Russian Revolutionary War which subjected him to horrible sights and forced his family to migrate from one place to another. His nurses and private teachers were often changed. Apparently he took all changes with nonchalance, but more and more he felt alienated from outside events in such a way that his teachers believed him to be dull and without any interests. His spontaneous memory was exceedingly poor. His abnormal behavior was marked by an increasing anxiety and by an increasingly habitual attitude of doubt and negation. A typical symptom of his anxiety was his continuous fear of being alone and abandoned by all his family. He refused to leave his home to go to school. At night he arose and walked through the apartment in order to make sure that his family was still with him. When I was sitting opposite him in the trolley car and the conductor passed by between us, he burst out in a fearful cry, supposing that, not seeing me for a moment, I might have disappeared. He asked me if it would be possible that I might be annihilated like a rubbed out pencil-stroke. These symptoms showed his continuous indiscriminate fear of possible sudden evaporation of anything around him. "Don't be afraid," I told him, "you are not alone," but he answered: "Is it possible that one is not alone?"

On the intellectual plane his feeling of insecurity of existence and his lack of relationship to the objective world became apparent in his complete scepticism and doubt of even the most obvious and evident phenomena. Asked how many legs a dog has, he answered: "I've only seen four legs but perhaps some have less?" He doubted the evidence of his memory just as much as his immediate apperception. Thus he was not certain which was his own overcoat when, after a visit, he found it hanging among others on the wall. When we took a walk he asked me: "Would it be possible for us to walk here and at the same time be at home playing? Can other people divide themselves and may they become different from what they are? Are there green objects which may turn red? Can you, being dark-haired, turn blond?" When his mother made up her lips and face, she became a different person in his eyes. The changing appearances of all objects in nature, as from day to night, from summer to winter, struck him so deeply that he could not identify the same objects as still remaining the same under these different circumstances. The continuous metamorphoses which he could not understand provoked in him an intense desire to safeguard himself against these changes.

His vision of a possible and complete change from one thing to another, even its opposite, was based on real experiences he had had. The radical sudden changes in the milieu of his early childhood during the revolutionary war, and the sudden inexplicable hostility of previous friendly acquaintances were some of these. He tightened his emotional attitude into a wary and mischievous aggressiveness in order to escape the incalculable elusive influences of the object-world, to experiment with it, and eventually to dominate it.

When I crossed the street with him he tried to stop me midway across, shouting, "I hope you will be knocked over by the car." Under the pretext of telling me a secret he came near my ear and roared into it in order to make me deaf. He repeatedly assaulted me slyly and tried to scratch out my eyes. In the crowded trolley car he pushed along and trampled on other people's feet.

When writing, he distorted and compressed the letters, crying, "I'll push the letters and torment them!" In a similar manner he distorted his spoken words.

Neurotic tendencies are usually projected upon the formation of letters. These neurotic tendencies are manifested in the writing of the boy when he was 13 years old. In the writing of 13 and 14 years of age, in the neurotic state, the slow movement is related to an extremely high pressure which apparently is the expression of an actual psychic pressure. At the same time, when the boy wrote this neurotic specimen in German words (Fig. 322 a), he wrote the other specimen in Russian words without this neurotic stamp (Fig. 322 b). This difference of graphic expression of specimens written at the same time indicates that the neurosis might be related to the German environment in which the child seemed to feel unfamiliar. In the writing of his native language no neurotic trends are manifest. The graphic expression of this boy reveals that his flight from reality may be due to a non-acceptance of the new environment in a foreign country. This flight from reality is accompanied by an aggression against all objects of his reality, the aggression also being projected upon the letters of his writing. The aggression appears in the pressure of letters; in their pressing against each other; in the curving back of letters like "d" in "Erdteile" (continents); and in the strangling of the heads of the letters "E" and "L" (Fig. 322 a).

Considering a drawing of the same period when the boy in school was asked to draw a rainy day at the fair, we observe that he does not draw the movement and life at the fair, but a house with cells in which he puts single men and women (Fig. 323). He asked the teacher how

FIG. 323.—Drawing of a neurotic child.

to draw women and copied the teacher's drawing but he omitted to give the women feet and a face. Instead of the face he made a cross, like that found among the rock carvings (petroglyphs) of primitive peoples in Africa. We find a marked difference in the drawing of male and female figures, the hands of men being emphasized and the face, arms, hands, and feet being omitted on the women. We may explain the emphasis on men's hands as an expression of the boy's dominating idea of grasping the objects of the world in order to become familiar with the reality. The boy who had grown up under the influence of his mother and grand-mother and who had female teachers was in effect more familiar with women than with men. But since these persons represented reality for him, and since this reality was completely incomprehensible to him, he was not able to project images of familiarity on these persons. Thus they were without shape, and he could draw only the men according to the image of himself.

The Pattern of Personality

As our personality sketches indicate, it is the interrelationship itself between graphic and biographical data that enables us to approach the depth of personality. Man's direct and indirect expressions complement each other, and a comparison between life history or "case material" and graphic expression may in many cases lead to a new understanding of the persons concerned, because the leitmotifs thus crystallized serve to bring into focus a person's dominating trends. The ability to apprehend the leitmotifs of personality is an intuitive process, but like all intuitive processes it can be trained. Such training seems to be possible only upon the basis of the material itself. By studying descriptions of life his-tory the student of personality will get a sense of understanding and of discovering the leitmotifs. Focusing upon certain distinctive trends and upon the leitmotifs, the complexity of material becomes limited, disclosing the profile of expressiveness, so that the signature may serve as a guide in the search for the leading factor in the labyrinth of happenings that compose the story of a man's life.

The supposition that many of our manifestations are arbitrary and ac-cidental is in contradiction to the findings of biology and physiology and results in a gap between psychology and physiology concerning the or-ganization of man's structure. Our finding of an unconscious organiza-tion of graphic form and of graphic expressiveness enables us to apply the physiological aspect of organization to the psychological field.

In describing expressive movement from a behavioristic point of view we would say: This man puts a dot over the "i," or he puts it on the left or on the right side. This descriptive statement would not reveal the essential phenomenon that, for instance, the dot is the central point of his graphic pattern. In the mere enumeration of graphic elements, the same value would be given to the dot as to some other graphic elements, without considering the role that a part plays within the whole and without establishing a hierarchic order of features. Personality and each of its expressions follow a pattern, and it is the pattern which we have to discover in graphic movement. Our present study indicates that graphic expression is patterned according to unifying principles. Not only the principles of form, but also the principle of expression, follows the law of integration and unification. Chance and accident seem to have no place in this concept of personality; the diagrams of the unconscious actually show patterns, integrated like those of a design. Understanding these diagrams of the unconscious helps us to understand the unity of personality.

BIBLIOGRAPHY

1. Adler, G. S.: Graphologische Untersuchungen an Schriften psychiatrisch begutachteter Rechtsverbrecher. (Graphologic investigations of the handwritings of psychiatrically appraised criminals.) Stetten-Basel: Dissertation, 1939.

2. Albertini, L.:Lehrbuch der Graphologie. (Textbook of graphology.) ed. 16. Stuttgart, 1932.

3. Allen, C. N.: Individual differences in delayed reaction of infants. Arch. Psychol. *19*:5-40, 1931.

4. Allport, G. W.: Change and decay in the visual memory image. Brit. J. Psychol. *21*:133-148, 1930.

5. ———: Personality, a Psychological Interpretation. New York, 1937.

6. ———, and Odbert, H. S.: Trait names: a psycho-lexical study. Psychol. Monog. *47*: no. 211, 171, 1936.

7. ———, and Vernon, P. E.: Studies in Expressive Movement, New York, 1933.

7a. Alschuler, R. H., and Hattwick, B. W.: Painting and Personality. Chicago, 1947.

8. Alten, E. H.: The psychology of handwriting and its importance to the physician. Med. Rec. *150*:71-74, 1939.

9. Anders, P.: Über den individuellen Eigenrhythmus beim menschlichen Gange und seine Beziehungen zum Rhythmus der Herz–und Atemtätigkeit. (The individual rhythm of the human gait and its relationship to the rhythm of the heart and of breathing). Pflüg. Arch. *220*:287-299, 1928.

10. Anderson, M.: A study of the data on the results gathered from repeated mental examinations of 200 defective children attending special schools over a period of 8 years. J. Appl. Psychol. *7*:54-64, 1923.

11. Andagua y Garimberty, J. de: Arte de escribir por reglas y sin muestras. (The art of writing after rules and without models.) Madrid, 1781.

12. Arkin, E.: The problem of the stability of the human organism. J. Genet. Psychol. *42*:228-236, 1933.

13. Arnheim, R.: Experimentell psychologische Untersuchungen zum Ausdrucksproblem. Psychol. Forsch. *11*:1-32, 1928.

14. Arrington, R. E.: Interrelations in the behavior of young children. Child Development Monog. *8:* 1932.

15. Astillero, R.: Grafologia scientifica. (Scientific graphology) ed. 2. Milano, 1928.

16. Audebrand: Graphologie et psychophysique. (Graphology and psychophysics.) Soc. Dauphinoise d'ethnol. et d'anthropol. *15*:59-181, 1908.

17. Bachmann, J.: Graphologie und Berufsberatung. (Graphology and vocational guidance.) Ztschr. pädag. Psychol. *37*:381-385, 1936.

18. ———: Das graphologische Gutachten und seine Bewährung. Ein Bericht. (The graphological testimony and its verification. A report.) Ztschr. f. Menschenkunde *13*:131-144, 1937.

19. Bagger, E. S.: Psycho-graphology, a Study of Rafael Schermann. London, 1924.

20. Baldi, C.: Trattado come da una lettera missiva si conoscano la natura e qualita dello scriviente. (Judging the nature and quality of a writer from his letters.) Bologna, 1644.

21. Baley, S.: A handwriting scale for children of primary schools. Collaborative study by students of the Pedagogical Institute of the Association of Polish Instructors. Psychol. wychow. *11*:97-109, 1938-39.

22. Barratinskaya, M. S.: Character as Revealed by Handwriting. London, 1924.

23. Baughan, R.: Character Indicated by Handwriting. London, 1890.

24. Baxter, M. F.: An experimental study of the differentiation of temperament on the basis of rate and strength. Am. J. Psychol. *38*:59-96, 1927.

25. Bayer, K.: Experimentelle Untersuchung über die Schreibzeit und den Schreibdruck. (Experimental investigation of duration and pressure in writing.) Würzburg, 1939.

26. Baylay, N.: A study of the crying of infants during mental and physical tests. J. Genet. Psychol. *40*:306-329, 1932.

27. Bechterev, V. M.: General Principles of Human Reflexology. (Transl. by E. and W. Murphy.) New York, 1932.

28. Becker, M.: Graphologie der Kinderschrift. (Graphology of children's handwriting.) Freiburg i. B., 1926.

29. Berna, H.: Die Graphologie und andere Testversuche. (Graphology and other methods of testing.) Schweiz. Z. Psychol. Anwend. *1*:270-273, 1943.

30. Bernstein, E. G.: El caracter y su interpretación grafológica. (Character and its graphological interpretation.) In Mouchet, E.: Temas actuales de psicología normal y patológica. Buenos Aires, 1945.

31. Béroud, G.: L'expertise des faux en écriture par altération. (The investigation of forgery in handwriting.) Lyon, 1923.

32. Berri, M. de: The Secrets of the Alphabet; A Study in Graphology. New York, 1942.

33. Berthelot, P.: La graphologie. In La Grande Encyclopédie, Paris (without date), pp. 220-235.

34. Biäsch, H.: Graphologische Bemerkungen über die Bindungsform. (Graphologic remarks about forms of connection.) Psychol. Rundschau *1*:230-234, 1929.

35. Bills, A. G.: The influence of muscular tension on the efficiency of mental work. Am. J. Psychol. *38*:227-251, 1927.

36. Binet, A. L.: L'âge et l'écriture. (Age and handwriting.) La Rev. des Rev., ser. 4, *48*:182-195; 326-341, 1904.

37. ———: La graphologie et ses revelations sur le sexe, l'âge et l'intelligence. (Graphology and its revelations of sex, age and intelligence.) L'année psychol. *10*:179-210, 1904.

38. ———: Les révélations de l'écriture d'après un controle scientifique. (Revelations of handwriting by scientific control.) Paris, 1906.

39. ———: Une expérience crucial en graphologie. (A crucial experience in graphology.) Rev. philos. *64*:22-40, 1907.

40. Birkhoff, G. D.: Aesthetic Measure. Cambridge, 1933.

41. Bobertag, C.: Ist die Graphologie zuverlässig? (Is graphology reliable?) Heidelberg, 1929.

42. Bois, J. S. A.: La pression verticale dans l'écriture. (Vertical pressure in handwriting.) Ann. Ass. canad.-franç. Av. Sci. *5*:119, 1939.

43. Bolton, T. L.: Rhythm. Am. J. Psychol. *6*:145-238, 1893.

44. Booth, G. C.: The use of graphology in medicine. J. Nerv. Ment. Dis. *86*:674-679, 1937.

44a. ———: Objective techniques in personality testing. Arch. Neurol. Psychiat. *42*:514-530, 1939.

45. Booth, M. H.: How to Read Character in Handwriting. Philadelphia, 1910.

46. Boraas, H. O.: An experimental study of the relative merits of certain written letter forms with respect to legibility, with speed and stability as related factors. J. Exper. Educ.. *5*:65-70, 1936.

47. Born, W.: Unconscious processes in artistic creation. J. Clin. Psychopath. & Psychother. *7*:253-272, 1945.

48. Bracken, H. v.: Das Schreibtempo von Zwillingen und die sozialpsychologischen Fehlerquellen der Zwillingsforschung. (The writing tempo of twins and the socio-psychologic sources of error in twin research.) Ztschr. mensch. Vererb.-u. Konst.-Lehre *23*:278-298, 1939.

49. ———: Erbbiologische Untersuchungen über die Handschrifteigenart. (Heredobiologic investigations on handwriting characteristics.) Dtsch. Z. ges. Gerichtl. Med. *33*:64-72, 1940.

50. ———: Untersuchungen an Zwillingen über die quantitativen und qualitativen Merkmale des Schreibdrucks. (Investigations with twins concerning quantitative and qualitative characteristics of handwriting pressure.) Ztschr. f. ang. Psychol. *58*:367-384, 1940.

51. Braun, F.: Untersuchungen über das persönliche Tempo. (Investigations concerning personal tempo.) Arch. f. d. ges. Psychol. *60*:317-360, 1927.

52. Bray, C. W.: Transfer of learning. J. Exper. Psychol. *11*:443-467, 1928.

53. Breitkopf, A.: Grossbewegungen und Kleinbewegungen. Ein Beitrag zu einer vergleichenden Ausdruckslehre. (Macromovements and micro-movements—a contribution to comparative analysis.) Ztschr. f. ang. Psychol. *58*:1-92, 1939.

53a. Brick, W.: The mental hygiene value of children's art work. Am. J. Orthopsych. 14:136-146, 1944.

54. Britt, S. H., & Mensh, I. N.: The identification of one's own handwriting. J. Crim. Law & Criminol. 34:50-60, 1943.

55. Brooks, C. H.: Your Character from Your Handwriting. London, 1930.

56. Broom, M. E., Thompson, B., and Bouton, M. T.: Sex differences in handwriting. J. Appl. Psychol. 13:159-166, 1929.

57. Bruel, O.: Graphologische Diagnostik. (Graphologic diagnosis.) Beiheft. Schweiz. Ztschr. psychol. Anwend. 6:56-65, 1945.

58. Buehler, C.: The Social Behavior of the Child. In Handbook of Child Psychology, Worcester, 1931; pp. 392-431.

59. Bunker, M. N.: Case Book Number One. American Institute of Graphoanalysis, Kansas City, 1936.

59a. ——: Grapho-analysis Dictionary. American Institute of Grapho-analysis, Kansas City, 1938.

60. Burt, C. L.: The Measurement of Mental Capacities. Edinburgh, 1927.

61. Byerly, T.: Characteristic Signatures. London, 1823.

62. Byram, J. H.: Character. New Jersey, 1935.

63. Caftale, R.: Psicoanalisi e grafologia. (Psychoanalysis and graphology.) Rev. italiana di psichoanalisi, 1932.

64. Callewaert, H.: Physiologie de l'écriture cursive. (Physiology of cursive writing.) Bruxelles, 1937.

64a. ——: La rééducation de l'écriture chez les multilés et amputés de la main droite. (Re-education of writers with multilation or amputation of the right hand.) Arch. Serv. san. Armée belge 99:71-77, 1946.

65. Cantril, H., Rand, H. A., and Allport, G. W.: The determination of personal interests by psychological and graphological methods. Char. & Pers. 2:134-143, 1933.

66. ——, and ——: An additional study of the determination of personal interests by psychological and graphological methods. Char. & Pers. 3:72-78, 1934.

67. Carmena, M.: Schreibdruck bei Zwillingen. (Degree of handwriting pressure in twins.) Ztschr. f. d. ges. Neurol. u. Psychiat. 103:744-752, 1935.

68. Carvalho, C.: Crime in Ink. New York, 1929.

69. Caspar, P., and Kügelgen, G. v.: Dichter in der Handschrift. (Poets in their handwriting.) Hannover, 1937.

70. Cattell, R. B.: The principal trait clusters for describing personality. Psychol. Bull. 42:129-161, 1945.

71. Chao, W. H.: Handwriting of Chinese mental patients. In Lyman, R. S., Maeker, V., and Liang, P.: Social and Psychological Studies in Neuropsychiatry in China. New York, 1939.

72. Chipman, C. C.: The constancy of the intelligence quotient of mental defectives. Psychol. Clin. 18:103-111, 1929.

73. Cole, A.: A successful experiment in the teaching of handwriting by analytic methods. J. Psychol. 1:209-222, 1936.

74. Cooper, J. B.: A comment on graphology. J. Psychol. 17:263-267, 1944.

75. Coyhill, G. E.: Anatomy and the Problem of Behavior. New York, 1929.

76. Crépieux-Jamin, J.: Traité pratique de graphologie, étude du caractère de l'homme d'après son écriture. (Practical treatise of graphology, a study of the human character through handwriting.) (without date.)

78. ——: L'écriture et le caractère. (Handwriting and Character.) Paris, 1888.

79. Crepieux-Jamin, J.: Handwriting and Expression (transl. by J. Holt Schooling). London, 1892.

79a. ——: Les éléments de l'écriture des canailles. (Graphological characteristics of delinquency.) Paris, 1924.

80. ——: L'âge et le sexe dans l'écriture. (Age and sex in handwriting.) Paris, 1925.

81. ——: The Psychology of the Movements of Handwriting (transl. by L. K. Given-Wilson.) London, 1926.

82. ——: A. B. C. de la graphologie. (A. B. C. of graphology.) Paris, 1930.

83. Crider, B.: The reliability and validity of two graphologists. J. Appl. Psychol. 25:323-325, 1941.

84. Cuff, N. B.: Is the I.Q. constant? Peabody J. Educ. 8:32-34, 1930.

85. Czapigo, W.: Pismo typów Kretschmera. (The writing of Kretschmer's types.) Psychoteknika 11:120-126, 1937.

86. Dantzig, B. v.: Writing, typing and speaking. J. Speech Disorders 4:297-301, 1939.

87. Daumerlang, E.: Gibt es eine Vererbung der Handschrift? (Is handwriting inherited?) Krim. Mh. 10:175-176, 1936.

88. Davenport, B. F.: Logical Analysis of Subscribed Signatures. Boston, 1914.

89. Dearborn, G. V. N.: The emotion of joy. Psychol. Rev. Monog. 2: no. 5, 70 ff., 1899.

90. Delhougne, A.: Dreidimensionale Graphologie. (Three-dimensional graphology.) Ztschr. f. Menschenkenntnis 7: 1931.

91. Demmler, H.: Eignungsfeststellung aus den Merkmalen der Handschrift. (The determination of aptitude from the characteristics of handwriting.) Industr. Psychotech. 14:182-191, 1937.

92. Desbarolles, A.: Système de graphologie. (System of graphology.) Paris, 1875.

92a. ——: Méthode pratique de graphologie. (Practical method of graphology.) Paris, 1878.

93. Deschamps, L.: La philosophie de l'écriture, exposé de l'état actuel de la graphologie. (The philosophy of handwriting after the present state of graphology.) 1892.

94. DeWitt, B. L.: Handwriting and Character. Philadelphia, 1925.

95. Dietrich, W.: Statistische Untersuchungen über den Zusammenhang von Schriftmerkmalen. (Statistical investigation of the interrelationship of criteria in handwriting.) Neue psychol. Stud. 11:73-143, 1937.

96. Dobrzynska-Rybicka, L.: Un cas d'automatisme graphique. (A case of automatic handwriting.) Kwart. Psychol. 11:41-51, 1939.

97. Donnini, R.: Il carattere rivelato della scrittura. (Character revealed through handwriting.) Perugia, 1925.

98. Douglas, A. W.: What's in a Signature. Saint Louis, 1931.

99. Downey, J. E.: Preliminary study of family resemblances in handwriting. U. of Wyoming Dept. of Psychol., Bull. no. 1. Laramie, 1910.

100. ——: Judgments on the sex of handwriting. Psychol. Rev. 17:205-216, 1910.

101. ——: Graphology and the Psychology of Handwriting. Baltimore, 1919.

102. ——: The Will-Temperament and Its Testing. Yonkers on Hudson, 1923.

102a. ——: Creative Imagination. New York, 1929.

103. Drever, I.: Notes on the study of handwriting. Exper. Ped. 2:25, 1913.

104. Drope, D.: Kritische Gedanken über Rorschach-Versuch und Handschriftenkunde. (Critical reflections on the Rorschach procedure and graphology.) Arch. f. d. ges. Psychol. 104:353-379, 1939.

105. Duparchy-Jeannez, M.: Les maladies d'après l'écriture. (Diseases revealed in handwriting.) Paris, 1919.

106. Duraud, M.: De l'écriture en miroir, étude sur l'écriture de la main gauche dans ses rapports avec l'aphasie. (Mirror writing, a study on left-handed writing and its relationship to aphasia.) 1882.

107. Eagelson, O. W.: The success of sixty subjects in attempting to recognize their handwriting. J. Appl. Psychol. 21:546-549, 1937.

108. Eaton, S.: How to Read Character from Handwriting. Boston, 1893.

109. Eisenberg, P.: Judging expressive movement: I. Judgments of sex and dominance-feeling from handwriting samples of dominant and non-dominant men and women. J. Appl. Psychol. 22:480-486, 1938.

110. Eliasberg, W.: Political graphology. J. Psychol. 16:177-201, 1943.

110a. ——: Graphology and medicine. J. Nerv. & Ment. Dis. 100:381-401, 1944.

110b. ——: Methods in graphology. J. Psychol. 18:125-130, 1944.

110c. ——: Prognosis and prevention of untoward events on the basis of the driver's case history. J. Clin. Psychopath. & Psychother. 6:132-143, 1944.

111. Elkisch, P.: Children's drawings in a projective technique. Psychol. Monog. 266:1-31, 1945.

112. Eng, H.: The Psychology of Children's Drawings. New York, 1931.

113. Enke, W.: Die Psychomotorik der Konstitutions-Typen. (Psychomotor processes of the constitutional types.) Ztschr. f. ang. Psychol. 36:237-534, 1930.

114. ——: Handschrift und Charakter im exakten Versuch. (Exact experiments on the relationship of handwriting and character.) Klin. Wchnschr. *17*:1624-1627, 1938.

115. Erickson, M. H.: The experimental demonstration of unconscious mentation by automatic writing. Psychoanalyt. Quart. *6*:513,1937.

115a. ——, and Kubie, L. S.: The use of automatic drawing in the interpretation and relief of a state of acute obsessional depression. Psychoanalyt. Quart. *8*:443-466, 1938.

116. Erlenmeyer, D.: Die Schrift. Grundzüge ihrer Physiologie und Pathologie. (Handwriting: Fundamentals of its physiology and pathology.) Stuttgart, 1879.

117. Erskine, L. G.: Your Signature, What it Reveals. Larchmont, 1931.

118. Eysenck, H. J.: Graphological analysis and psychiatry: and experimental study. Brit. J. Psychol. *35*:70-81, 1945.

119. Fairbairn, W. R. D.: Prologemona to a psychology of art. Brit. J. Psychol. *28*:288-303, 1938.

120. ——: The ultimate basis of aesthetic experience. Brit. J. Psychol. *29*:167-181, 1938.

121. Fechner, G. T.: Vorschule der Aesthetik. (Introduction to aesthetics.) Leipzig, 1897-98.

122. Fenz, E.: Körperbau und Handschrift. (Physical type and handwriting.) Ztschr. f. Menschenkenntnis *12*:187-204, 1936-37.

123. Ferrari, H., Héricourt, J., and Richet, C.: La personnalité et l'écriture, essai de graphologie expérimentale. (Personality and handwriting, an essay on experimental graphology.) Rev. Philos., 1886.

124. Fischer, O.: Experimente mit Raphael Schermann. (Experiments with Raphael Schermann.) Wien, 1924.

125. Fontes, V.: Drawing and writing in psychiatric diagnosis. Clin. Hig. Hidrol., May, 1938.

126. Frazer, P.: A Manual of the Study of Documents to Establish the Individual Character of Handwriting and to Detect Fraud and Forgery. Philadelphia, 1894.

127. ——: Handwriting. In Encyclopedia Americana, *13*:673-677, ed. 1941.

128. Freeman, F. N.: An experimental analysis of the writing movement. Psychol. Monog. *17*: no. 4, 1914.

129. ——: An evaluation of manuscript writing. Elem. Sch. J. *36*:446-455, 1936.

130. French, W. L.: The Psychology of Handwriting. London, 1922.

131. Freud, S.: The Psychopathology of Everyday Life. New York, 1914.

132. ——: The Basic Writings. New York, 1938.

133. ——: New Introductory Lectures on Psycho-Analysis. New York, 1933.

134. Furman, M., and Priv, Z. N.: Handwriting and Character. London, 1930.

135. Fursac, J. R. de: Les écrits et les dessins dans les maladies nerveuses et mentales. (Handwriting and drawing in nervous and mental diseases.) Paris, 1905.

136. Galamini, A.: Azione della stimolazione del senso cinestesico speciale sui movimenti volontari. Nota II. (Stimulating action of the special kinesthetic sense on voluntary movements. II.) Valsalva *8*:330-398, 1936.

137. Galton, F.: Inquiries into Human Faculty and Its Development (1883). New York, 1937.

138. Garrett, H. E.: Personality as habit organization. J. Abnorm. & Soc. Psychol. *21*:250-255, 1926.

139. Garrison, S. C.: Retests of adults at an interval of 10 years. Sch. & Soc. *32*:326-328, 1930.

140. Garth, T. R., Mitchell, M. J., and Anthony, C. N.: The handwriting of negroes. J. Educ. Psychol. *30*:69-73, 1939.

141. Geering, R.: Handbook of Facsimiles of Famous Personages. Basle, 1925.

141a. Geigy Hagenbach, K.: Handbook of Facsimiles of Famous Personages, comp. by Ch. Geigy. Basle, 1925.

142. Gerstner, H.: Lehrbuch der Graphologie. (Textbook of graphology.) Celle, 1925.

143. Gesell, A.: Accuracy in handwriting as related to school intelligence and sex. J. Psychol. *17*:394-405, 1906.

144. ——: The Developmental Psychology of Twins. In Handbook of Child Psychology, Worcester, 1931, 158-203.

145. ——: Some observations of developmental stability. Psychol. Monog. *47*:35-46, 1936.

146. ——, and Ames, L. B.: The development of directionality. J. Genet. Psychol.
68:45-61, 1946.

147. Gibson, J.: The reproduction of visu-
ally perceived forms. Exper. Psychol.
12:1-39, 1929.

148. Gillingham, A., and Stillman, B. W.:
Remedial training for children with specific disability in reading, spelling and
penmanship. (Rev. ed.) New York, 1940.

149. Giraud, A.: Petit dictionnaire de
graphologie. (A brief dictionary of
graphology.) Paris, 1896.

150. Golla, F. L., and Antonovitch, S.: The
respiratory rhythm in its relation to the
mechanisms of thought. Brain *52*:491-
509, 1929.

151. ——: The relation of muscle tonus
and the patellar reflex to mental work.
J. Ment. Sc. *75*:234-241, 1929.

152. Goodenough, F. L.: Measurement of
Intelligence by Drawings. Chicago, 1926.

153. ——: Sex differences in judging the
sex of handwriting. J. Soc. Psychol.
22:61-68, 1945.

154. ——, and Brian, C. R.: Certain factors underlying the acquisition of motor
skill by preschool children. J. Exper.
Psychol. *12*:127-155, 1929.

155. Graewe, H.: Zwillinge und ihre
Schriften. (The handwriting of twins.)
Umschau *42*: no. 15, 1938.

156. Granit, A. R.: A study in the perception of form. Brit. J. Psychol. *12*:223-
247, 1921.

157. Grant, A., and Marble, M.M.: Results
of Cincinnati handwriting survey. Sch.
Rev. *48*:693-696, 1940.

158. Gray, P. D., and Marsden, R. E.: Constancy of the intelligence quotient. Brit.
J. Psychol. *17*:20-26, 1926.

159. Green, C.: La graphologie est-elle une
branche de la médecine? (Is graphology
a branch of medicine?) Avenir méd., 7-17,
1944-45.

160. Grohmann, J. C. A.: Ideen zu einer
physiognomischen Anthropologie. (Ideas
for a physiognomic anthropology.) Leipzig, 1791.

161. Gross, K., and Bauer-Chlumberg, M.:
Handschrift und Geisteskrankheit. (Hand-
writing and mental illness.) J. Psychiat.
Neurol. *54*:312-329, 1937.

162. Grünberg, H.: Els pintors i la grafologia. (Painters and graphology.) Rev.
Psicol. Pedag. *4*:261-265, 1936.

163. Hagen, H. von: Reading Character
from Handwriting. New York, 1902.

164. Hambidge, J.: Dynamic Symmetry.
Boston, 1919.

165. Hansen, R.: The three R's of handwriting. Train. Sch. Bull. *39*:2-8, 1942.

166. Hartge, M.: Eine graphologische Untersuchung von Handschriften eineiiger
und zweieiiger Zwillinge. (Graphologic
study on monozygotic and dizygotic
twins.) Ztschr. f. ang. Psychol. *50*:129-
148, 1936.

167. ——: Graphologie in der Pädagogik
und Berufsberatung. (Graphology in
pedagogy and vocational counseling.)
Ztschr. f. ang. Psychol. *54*:92-127, 1938.

168. Hartshorne, H., May, M. A., and Shut-
tleworth, F. K.: Studies in the Organization of Character. New York, 1930.

169. Harvey, O. L.: The measurement of
handwriting considered as a form of expressive movement. Char. & Pers. *2*:310-
321, 1934.

170. Hauff, L. v.: Absichtslos entstandene
Kritzeleien als Ausdruck der seelischen
Lage jugendlicher Mädchen. (Uninten-
tional scribblings as expressions of the
psychologic state of adolescent girls.)
Jena: Dissertation, 1940.

171. Hearns, R. S.: The use of graphology
in criminology. J. Crim. Psychopath.
3:462-464, 1942.

172. Hegar, W.: Graphologie par le trait.
(Graphology according to the character
of the stroke.) (2 vols.) Paris, 1938.

173. Hehlmann, W.: Handschrift und Erbcharakter. (Handwriting and hereditary
character.) Ztschr. f. ang. Psychol.
54:128-137, 1938.

174. Heiss, R.: Die Deutung der Handschrift. (The interpretation of handwriting.) Hamburg, 1943.

175. Hempstead, L.: The perception of
visual form. Am. J. Psychol. *12*:185-192,
1901.

176. Henze, A.: Lehre der Handschriftendeutung. (Manual of graphology.) Journal published from 1863.

177. Héricourt, J.: La graphologie. Rev.
philos., Novembre 1885.

178. Hermann, E.: Messungen an Handschriftproben von Zwillingspaaren unter 14 Jahren. (Measurements of handwriting samples of pairs of twins less than 14 years old.) Ztschr. f. Psychol. *147*:238-255, 1939.

179. Hildreth, G.: Developmental sequences in name writing. Child Developm. *7*:291-303, 1936.

180. ———: Comparative speed of joined and unjoined writing strokes. J. Educ. Psychol. *36*:91-102, 1945.

181. Hill, G. E.: The handwriting of college seniors. J. Educ. Res. *37*:118-126, 1943.

182. Hirt, E.: Untersuchungen über das Schreiben und die Schrift. (Investigations concerning the act of writing and of handwriting.) Psychol. Arb. *6*:531-664, 1914.

183. Hocquart, E.: L'art de juger de l'esprit et du caractère des hommes sur leur écriture. (The art of judging human intentions and character from handwriting.) Paris, 1812.

184. Holt, E. B.: Animal Drive and the Learning Process. New York, 1931.

185. Homma, T.: On the direction or order of the strokes in writing Chinese characters. Jap. J. Psychol. *12*:608-613, 1937.

186. ———: On the natural formation in the writing orders of Japanese letters. Jap. J. Psychol. *13*:429-440, 1938.

187. Hull, C. L., and Montgomery, R. P.: Experimental investigation of certain alleged relations between character and handwriting. Psychol. Rev. *26*:63-74, 1919.

188. Inni, T.: A critical experiment of graphology. Jap. J. Psychol. *11*:60-80, 1936.

189. Jacobson, E.: Progressive Relaxation. Chicago, 1929.

190. Jacoby, H. J.: Handschrift und Sexualität. (Handwriting and sexuality.) Berlin, 1932.

191. ———: Über die Veränderungen in Schriften todnaher Menschen. (Changes in the writing of persons near death.) Schrift *1*:56, 1935.

192. ———: Analysis of Handwriting; an Introduction Into Scientific Graphology. New York, 1940.

193. ———: Self-knowledge Through Handwriting. New York, 1941.

194. Jäger, F. M.: Lectures on the Principle of Symmetry. Amsterdam, 1920.

195. Jersild, M. T.: The constancy of certain behavior patterns in young children. Am. J. Psychol. *45*:125-129, 1933.

196. Johnson, B.: Changes in muscular tension in coordinated hand movements. J. Exper. Psychol. *11*:329-341, 1928.

197. Johnson, W. H.: The improvement of handwriting. Elem. Sch. J. *43*:90-96, 1942.

198. Judd, C. H.: The difficulty of acquiring a social mode of behavior. Bull. Sch. Educ. Ind. Univ. *12*: no. 4, 46-47, 1936.

199. Jung, C. G.: The Integration of Personality. New York, 1939.

200. Kaempffert, W.: Handwriting revelations. Science in the News. The New York Times, November 26, 1939.

201. Kapp, F.: Schreibübungen eines greisen Homosexuellen als Lustgewinn und infantile Regression. (Writing exercises of a senile homosexual as a source of pleasure and infantile regression.) Monatschr. f. Krim.-Biol. *28*:516, 1937.

202. Karfeld, K. P.: Das Wunder der Handschrift. (The marvel of handwriting.) Berlin, 1935.

203. Kiken, I.: Badanie osobowsci zapomoca omy lek w pisaniu. (Investigation of personality by the aid of mistakes in writing.) Polsk. Arch. Psychol. *8*:126-135, 1935-36.

204. Kinder, J. S.: A new investigation of judgments on the sex of handwriting. J. Educ. Psychol. *17*:341-344, 1926.

205. Klages, L. R.: Die Probleme der Graphologie. (Problems of graphology.) Leipzig, 1910.

206. ———: Ausdrucksbewegung und Gestaltungskraft. (Expressive movement and creativity.) Leipzig, 1913.

207. ———: Einführung in die Psychologie der Handschrift. (Introduction to the psychology of handwriting.) Heilbronn, 1924.

208. ———: Die Grundlagen der Charakterkunde. (The foundations of Characterology.) ed. 6. Leipzig, 1928.

209. ———: The Science of Character (Transl. from ed. 5 of Grundlagen der Charakterkunde.) London, 1929.

210. ———: The so-called "religious curve." Z. ges. Psychiat. *16*:575-584, 1938.

211. ——: Handschrift und Charakter; gemeinverständlicher Abriss der graphologischen Technik. (Handwriting and character; popular treatise on graphological technic.) Leipzig, 1940.

212. Kloos, G. The so-called "religious curve" of Klages: a critical contribution on psychological expression by handwriting. Ztschr. f. d. ges. Neurol. u. Psychiat. *162*:716-727, 1938.

213. Koch, U.: Trattato scientifico de grafologia. (Scientific treatise on graphology.) ed. 2. Bologna, 1920.

214. Koffka, K.: Principles of Gestalt Psychology. New York, 1935.

215. Köhler, W.: Gestalt Psychology. New York, 1929.

216. Korff, E.: Handschriftkunde und Charakterererkenntnis. (Graphology and character recognition.) Bad Homburg, 1936.

217. Koster, R.: Die Schrift bei Geisteskrankheiten. (Handwriting of the mentally diseased.) Leipzig, 1903.

218. Kramer, E., and Lauterbach, C. E.: Resemblance in the handwriting of twins and siblings. J. Educ. Res. *18*:149-152.

219. Krauss, R.: Über graphischen Ausdruck. (Graphic expression.) Ztschr. f. ang. Psychol. (Suppl.), no. 48, 1930.

220. Kretschmer, E.: Physique and Character. (Transl. by W. J. H. Sprott.) New York, 1926.

221. Krieger, L.: Rasse, Rhythmus und Schreib-innervation bei Jugendlichen und Erwachsenen. (Race, rhythm and the innervation of writing in children and adults. Ztschr. pädag. Psychol. *38*:15-31, 1937.

222. Kroeber-Keneth, L.: Unfallneigung und Handschrift. (Handwriting and liability to accident.) Ztschr. Menschenkenntnis *14*:17-32, 1938.

223. ——: Bericht über eine "Qualifikationskartei." (A report on a "qualification chart." Industr. Psychotech. *15*:238-243, 1938.

224. Kröner, A. R.: Schreiben und Zittern als Ausdrucksbewegung der Hand. (Writing and trembling as expressive movements of the hand.) Arch. ges. Psychol. *100*:68-132, 1938.

225. Kubie, L. S.: Experiments with the use of hypnagogic states and automatic writing for the recovery of unorganized forgotten sensory impressions. Tran. Am. Neurol. Ass. *77*:178, 1944.

226. Kügelgen, H. von: Graphologie und Berufseignung. (Graphology and vocational aptitude.) Industr. Psychotech. *55*:311, 1928.

227. Kuhlmann, F.: The results of repeated mental reexaminations of 639 feeble-minded over a period of 10 years. J. Appl. Psychol. *5*:195-224, 1921.

228. Kuroda, M.: Über die Messungseinrichtung für die Geschwindigkeit und den Druck der Pinselschrift. (On the measuring apparatus of the speed and the pressure of brush writing.) Tohoku psychol. Folia *8*:47-62, 1940.

228a. ——: Eine Untersuchung über die Beurteilung des Schreibdrucks und der Schreibgeschwindigkeit an der Pinselschrift. (A study on the judgment of writing pressure and writing speed in brush writing.) Tohoku psychol. Folia *8*:151-204, 1940.

229. Lacy, G. J.: Handwriting and forgery under hypnosis. J. Crim. Law & Criminol. *34*:338-343, 1944.

230. Landis, C., Gulette, R., and Jacobsen, C.: Criteria of emotionality. Ped. Sem. *32*:209-234, 1925.

231. Langenbruch, M.: Praktische Menschenkenntnis auf Grund der Handschrift. (Practical knowledge of human behavior through handwriting.) Berlin, 1929.

232. Lashley, K. S.: Brain Mechanism and Intelligence. Chicago, 1929.

233. Lavater, J. K.: Physiognomische Fragmente. (Physiognomic fragments.) Leipzig, 1774-78.

234. Lavay, J. B.: Disputed Handwriting. Chicago, 1909.

235. Leggitt, D.: Perceptual learning in penmanship. Elem. Sch. J. *40*:764-770, 1940.

236. ——: A comparison of abilities in cursive and manuscript writing and in creative art. Sch. Rev. *49*:48-56, 1941.

237. Legrün, A.: Über die Handschrift von Geschwistern. (The handwriting of siblings.) Ztschr. pädag. Psychol. *37*:151-157, 1936.

237a. ——: Vier eineiige Zwillingspaare im Lichte ihrer Handschrift. (The handwriting of four identical twins.) Z. Volks- und Rassenlehre, 20, 1936.

238. ——: Über die Handschrift der Trinkerkinder. (The handwriting of children of alcoholics.) Ztschr. Kinderforsch. *45*:234-259, 1936.

239. ——: Zur Deutung von Kinderkritzeleien. (The interpretation of children's scribblings.) Ztschr. Kinderforsch. *47*:236-249, 1938.

240. ——: Schriften Geisteskranker aus ihrer Jugendzeit. (The adolescent handwritings of psychotics.) Ztschr. pädag. Psychol. *40*:85-91, 1939.

241. ——: Die absteigende Linie in Geschwisterschriften. (The descending line in the handwriting of siblings.) Ztschr. pädag. Psychol *41*:104-111, 1940.

242. Leibl, M.: Grafologia psicologica. (Psychologic graphology.) Milan, 1935.

243. ——: Il tipo estrovertito e il tipo introvertito studiati grafologicamente. (The extraverted type and the introverted type studied graphologically.) Riv. Psicol. norm. pat. *33*:184-187, 1937.

244. Leumann, E.: Die Seelentätigkeit in ihrem Verhältnis zum Blutumlauf und Athmung. (Psychologic processes in their relationship to blood circulation and breathing.) Philos. Stud. *5*:618-631, 1889.

245. Lewin, K.: Environmental Forces in Child Development and Behavior. In Handbook of Child Psychology, 94-127. Worcester, 1931.

246. Lewinson, T. S.: Graphologie in Amerika. (Graphology in America.) Schrift *1*: 77 ff, 1935.

247. ——: An introduction to the graphology of Ludwig Klages. Char. & Pers. *6*:163-170, 1938.

248. ——: Dynamic disturbances in the handwriting of psychotics; with reference to schizophrenic, paranoid and maniac-depressive psychoses. Am. J. Psychiat. *97*:102-135, 1940.

249. ——, and Zubin, J.: Handwriting Analysis; a Series of Scales for Evaluating the Dynamic Aspects of Handwriting. New York, 1942.

250. Lewis, N. D. C.: The practical value of graphic art in personality studies. Psychoan. Rev. *12*:316-322, 1925.

250a. ——: Graphic art productions in schizophrenia. Nerv. & Ment. Dis. Proc. *5*:344-368, 1928.

251. Lewitan, C.: Untersuchungen über das allgemeine psychomotorische Tempo. (Investigations concerning the general psycho-motor tempo.) Ztschr. Psychol. *101*:321-376, 1927.

252. Lindemann, E.: Experimentelle Untersuchungen über das Entstehen und Vergehen von Gestalten. (Experimental investigations on the origin and the disappearance of configurations.) Psychol. Forsch. *2*:5-60, 1922.

253. Lipps, T.: Aesthetik. (2 vols.) Leipzig, 1903-06.

254. Lippuner, O.: Die Schrift des Mörders Irniger. (The handwriting of the murderer Irniger.) Beih. Schweiz. Ztschr. Psychol. Anwend., no. 6, 66-72, 1945.

255. Little, M.: Current opinion, experimentation, and study on handwriting problems. Elem. Sch. J. *43*:607-611, 1943.

256. Lombroso, C.: Grafologia. Milano, 1895.

257. Long, W. F. and Tiffin, J.: A note on the use of graphology by industry. J. Appl. Psychol. *25*:469-471, 1941.

258. Lumley, E.: The Art of Judging the Character of Individuals From Their Handwriting and Style. London, 1875.

259. Lundholm, H.: The affective tone of lines. Psychol. Rev. *28*:43-60, 1921.

260. MacDougall, R.: The relation of auditory rhythm to nervous discharge. Psychol. Rev. *9*:460-480, 1902.

261. Mach, E.: Untersuchungen über den Zeitsinn des Ohres. (Investigations concerning the sense of time in the ear.) Wien, Sitzungsbericht *2*:1865.

261a. ——: Untersuchungen über das Endorgan des nervus octavus. (Investigations concerning the end organ of the nervus octavus.) Wien, Sitzungsbericht *2*: 1865.

262. ——: Popular Scientific Lectures. Chicago, 1894.

263. ——: The Analysis of Sensations and the Relation of the Physical to the Psychical. (Transl. by C. M. Williams.) Chicago, 1914.

264. Mach, L.: Lese- und Schreibschwäche bei normalbegabten Kindern. (Reading and writing deficiencies in normal children.) Ztschr. Kinderforsch. *46*:113-197, 1937.

265. Mandowsky, A.: Vergleichend-psychologische Untersuchung über die Handschrift. Ein Beitrag zur Ausdrucksbewegung Geisteskranker unter besonderer Berücksichtigung der Schizophrenen und des manisch-depressiven Irreseins. (Comparative psychologic investigation of the handwriting of schizophrenics and manic-depressive patients.) (Dissertation.) Hamburg, 1933.

266. Mansfield, W. W.: Disguise in handwriting. Med.-leg. Crim. *March:* 23-29, 1943.

267. Marcendes, D.: Un caso de agraphia de evoluçao, forma pura. (A case of developmental agraphia, pure form.) Rev. Neurol. & Psychiat., S. Paulo, *2*:40-45, 1936.

268. Marcus, H.: Contribution à la localisation de l'agraphie. (Contribution to the localization of agraphia.) Acta psychiat., Kbh. *12*:431-446, 1937.

269. Marcuse, I.: Applied Graphology. New York, 1945.

270. Margadant, S. V.: Eine tiefenpsychologische Grundlage zur Klages'schen Graphologie. (A depth-psychologic foundation for Klages' graphology.) Amsterdam, 1938.

270a. Marguerite, R., and Mannheim, M. J.: Vincent van Gogh im Spiegel seiner Handschrift. (Vincent van Gogh's personality reflected in his handwriting.) Basel, 1938.

271. Marum, O.: Character assessment from handwriting. J. Ment. Sci. *91*:22-42, 1945.

272. Matumoto, K.: On the writing of Chinese characters by children. Jap. J. Psychol. *13*:441-450, 1938.

272a. ———: Supplementary report on the writing of Chinese characters by children. Jap. J. Psychol. *13*:561-563, 1938.

273. Mayer, G., and Schneickert, H.: Die wissenschaftlichen Grundlagen der Graphologie. (The scientific foundations of graphology.) ed. 3. Jena, 1940.

274. McAllister, C. N.: Researches on movements used in handwriting. Yale Psychol. Lab. Stud. *8*:21-63, 1900.

275. Melcher, W. A.: Dual personality in handwriting. J. Crim. Law & Criminol. *11*:209-216, 1920.

276. Meloun, J.: Experimentelle Graphologie. Ztschr. f. ang. Psychol. *32*:518-525, 1929.

277. Meloun, H. A., et al.: Handwriting measurement and personality traits. Char. & Pers. *2*:322-330, 1934.

277a. Meloun, J.: Does drawing skill show in handwriting? Char. & Pers. *3*:194-213, 1935.

278. Mendel, A. O.: Personality in Handwriting. New York, 1947.

279. Mendelsohn, A., and Mendelsohn, G.: Der Mensch in der Handschrift. (Man in his handwriting.) 1928.

280. Mentz, P. von: Die Wirkung akustischer Sinnesreize auf Puls und Athmung. (The effect of auditory stimuli upon pulse and respiration.) Philos. Stud. *2*:61-124, 371-393, 563-602, 1895.

281. Meumann, E.: Untersuchungen zur Psychologie und Aesthetik des Rhythmus. (Investigations into the psychology and aesthetics of rhythm.) Philos. Stud. *10*:249-322, 393-430, 1894.

282. Meyer, G.: Die wissenschaftlichen Grundlagen der Graphologie. Vorschule der gerichtlichen Schriftvergleichung. (The scientific foundations of graphology. An introduction to the forensic comparison of handwritings.) ed. 3. Jena, 1940.

283. Meyer, J. S. Mind Your P's and Q's. New York, 1927.

284. Michon, J. H.: Système de graphologie. (System of graphology.) Paris, 1875.

284a. ———: La méthode pratique de graphologie. (The practical method of graphology.) Paris, 1878.

285. Middleton, W. C.: The ability to judge sex from handwriting. Sci. Mon., N. Y., *46*:170-172, 1938.

286. ———: The ability of untrained subjects to judge dominance from handwriting samples. Psychol. Rec. *3*:227-238, 1939.

287. ———: The ability of untrained subjects to judge neuroticism, self-confidence, and sociability from handwriting samples. Char. & Pers. *9*:227-234, 1941.

288. ———: The ability of untrained subjects to judge intelligence and age from handwriting samples. J. Appl. Psychol. *25*:331-340, 1941.

289. Miles, W. R.: Correlation of reaction and coordination speed with age in adults. Am. J. Psychol. *43*:377-391, 1931.

290. Minogue, B. M.: The constancy of the I.Q. of mental defectives. Ment. Hyg. *10*:751-758, 1926.

291. Mira, E.: Myokinetic psychodiagnosis: a new technique for exploring the conative trends of personality. Proc. Roy. Soc. Med. *33*:9-30, 1940.

292. ——: Psychiatry in War. New York, 1943.

293. Molnár, I.: Kéziráshibák elemzése. (Analysis of errors in handwriting.) Psychol. Stud. Univ. Budapest *3*:18-25, 1939.

294. ——: Szándékrealizálások torzulásai az irásban. (Distortions in the realization of intentions in handwriting.) Pázmány Péter Univ., Phil. Dept., 1939.

295. ——: Szándektorlódások az iráshibákban. (Intentional accumulations in handwriting mistakes.) Mag. psychol. Szle *12*:82-108, 1939.

296. Moreau de la Sarthe: L'art de connaître les hommes par la physiognomie. (The art of recognizing persons by means of physiognomy.) Paris, 1805-09.

297. Morlass, J.: Écriture en mirroir et bilatéralisme humain. (Mirror writing and human bilateralism.) Encéphale *34*:493-516, 1939-41.

298. Mühl, A. M.: Automatic writing as an indication of the fundamental factors underlying the personality. J. Abn. & Soc. Psychol. *17*:162-183, 1922-23.

299. Münsterberg, H.: Die psychophysische Grundlage der Gefühle. (The psychosomatic foundation of sentiments.) Proc. II. Int. Cong. of Exper. Psychol. 132-135, London, 1892.

300. Murphy, G., Murphy, L. B., and Newcomb, T. M.: Experimental Social Psychology. (rev. ed.) New York, 1937.

301. Murray, H. A., et al.: Explorations in Personality. New York, 1938.

302. Nagel, V.: Graphologische Ahnenforschung. (Graphologic genealogy.) Ztschr. f. Menschenkenntnis *13*:77-86, 1937.

303. Naumburg, M.: The drawings of an adolescent girl suffering from conversion hysteria with amnesia. Psychiat. Quart. *18*:197-224, 1944.

304. Newell, H. A.: Your Signature. A Guide to Character from Handwriting. London, 1926.

305. Newhall, S. M.: Sex differences in handwriting. J. Appl. Psychol. *10*:151-161, 1926.

306. Newmann, H. H., Freeman, F. N., and Holzinger, K. J.: Twins: A Study of Heredity and Environment. Chicago, 1927.

307. Nicolay, E.: Messungen an Handschriftproben von Zwillingspaaren über 14 Jahren. (Measuring handwriting samples of twins over 14.) Arch. ges. Psychol. *105*:275-295, 1939.

308. Nielsen, J. M.: Cerebral thrombosis causing deletion of artificial writing center in left cerebral hemisphere of left-handed man. Bull. Los Angeles Neurol. Soc. *2*:176, 1937.

309. Noel Mo: American Foundation of Grapho-analysis. The Trail You Leave in Ink. Kansas City, 1941-46.

310. Norcross, W. H.: Experiments on the transfer of training. J. Comp. Psychol. *1*:317-363, 1921.

311. Obst, J.: Über graphischen Ausdruck und graphische Sprache. Versuche mit Kindern. (Graphic expression and graphic speech. Experiments with children.) Seestadt-Rostock, 1938.

312. Olyanowa, N.: Handwriting Tells. New York, 1936.

313. Omwake, K. T.: The value of photographs and handwriting in estimating intelligence. Publ. Person. Stud. *3*:2-15, 1925.

314. Osborn, A. S.: Questioned Documents. London, 1929.

315. Oseretsky, N.: Psychomotorik. Ztschr. f. Psychol. (Suppl.) no. 57, 1931.

316. Ostermeyer, G., and Sterzinger, O.: Graphologische Untersuchungen. (Graphologic investigations.) Ztschr. f. ang. Psychol. *52*:1-23, 1937.

317. Paisley, M. A.: Problems in cursive, manuscript and mirror handwriting. Winston-Salem, 1937.

318. Pascal, G. R.: Handwriting pressure: its measurements and significance. Char. & Pers. *11*:234-254, 1943.

319. ——: The analysis of handwriting; a test of significance. Char. & Pers. *12*:123-144, 1943.

320. Paskind, H. A., and Brown, M.: Constitutional differences between deteriorated and non-deteriorated patients with epilepsy: IV. The handwriting. Arch. Neurol. & Psychiat. *43*:507-516, 1940.

321. Perkins, F. T.: Symmetry in visual recall. Am. J. Psychol. *44*:473-490, 1932.

322. Peter, H.: Handschrift und Schwachsinn. (Handwriting and feeblemindedness.) Ztschr. f. Kinderforsch. *45*:134-142, 1936.

323. Pfister, H. O.: Farbe und Bewegung in der Zeichnung Geisteskranker. (Color and movement in drawings of insanes.) Schweiz. Arch. Neurol. & Psychiat. *34*:325-367, 1934.

324. Piéron, H.: Le problème scientifique de la graphologie. (The scientific problem of graphology.) Rev. scientif., ser. 5, *6*:616-622, 1906.

325. Piscart, R.: Echelle objective d'écriture. (Objective handwriting scale.) Louvain, 1939.

326. Pohl, U.: Experimentelle Untersuchung zur Typologie graphologischer Beurteilung. (Experimental study of typology in graphologic judgments.) Untersuch. Psychol. Phil. *11*:1-46, 1936.

327. Pophal, R.: Grundlegung der bewegungsphysiologischen Graphologie. (The foundation of motor-physiologic graphology.) Leipzig, 1939.

328. ——: Zur Psychophysiologie der Spannungserscheinungen in der Handschrift. (Psychophysiology of tension phenomena in handwriting.) Ztschr. f. ang. Psychol. *60*:129-315, 1940.

329. Powers, E.: Graphic factors in relation to personality. Dartmouth Coll. Library, 1930, unpubl.

330. ——: The Present Status of Experimental Graphology. In Allport and Vernon: Studies in Expressive Movements. New York, 1932, 185-211.

331. ——: Matching Sketches of Personality with Script. In Allport and Vernon: Studies in Expressive Movement. New York, 1932, 212-223.

332. Pratt, K. C., Nelson, A. K., and Sun, V. H.: The Behavior of the Newborn Infant. Columbus, Ohio, 1930.

333. Preyer, W. T.: Zur Psychologie des Schreibens. (Psychology of handwriting.) Hamburg, 1895.

334. Proskauer, G.: Graphometrische Untersuchungen bei Gesunden, Schizophrenen und Manisch-Depressiven. (Graphometric studies of normals, schizophrenics and manic-depressives.) Berlin, 1936.

335. Pulver, M.: Trieb und Verbrechen in der Handschrift. (Urge and crime in handwriting.) Zürich, 1934.

336. ——: Symbolik der Handschrift. (Symbolism of handwriting.) ed. 3. Zürich and Leipzig, 1940.

337. ——: Grundsätzliche Bemerkungen zur Ausdruckspsychologie. (Fundamental considerations on the psychology of expression.) Schweiz. Ztschr. psychol. Anwend. (Suppl.) no. 6, 5-28, 1945.

338. Quinan, C.: Kinetic aspects of growth: a graphic study. J. Genet. Psychol. *57*:199-205, 1940.

339. Rand, H. A.: Graphology. Cambridge, Mass., 1947.

340. Randall, F. B.: A study of the constancy of the I.Q. Sch. & Soc. *26*:311-312, 1927.

341. Ranitzsch, S.: Ein ungewöhnlicher Fall von Handschriftennachahmung und Anonymschreiberei. (An unusual case of imitation of handwriting and anonymous writing.) Ztschr. f. Menschenkenntnis. *13*:193-200, 1938.

342. Raymond, G. L.: Proportion and Harmony. New York, 1909.

343. Ream, M. J.: The tapping test: a measure of motility. Psychol. Monog. *31*: no. 1, 293-319, 1922.

344. Reinhardt, J. M.: Heredity and environment: a reexamination of some evidence from studies of twins with emphasis upon the graphological method. Char. & Pers. *5*:305-320, 1937.

345. Reis, H.: Die Handschrift — dein Charakter. (Handwriting and your character.) Bad Homburg, 1940.

346. Remmers, H. H., and Thompson, Jr., L. A.: A note on motor activity as conditioned by emotional states. J. Appl. Psychol. *9*:417-423, 1925.

347. Reuthe-Fink, L. v.: Gedanken über die Rolle der Graphologie in der Wehrmachtpsychologie. (Thoughts concerning the role of graphology in army psychology.) Soldatentum *4*:77-78, 1937.

348. Rexford, G.: What Handwriting Indicates. New York, 1904.

349. Reymert, M. L.: The personal equation in motor capacities. Scann. Sci. Rev. 2:177-222, 1923.

350. Ricci, A.: Dinamismo della parola scritta, parlata e pensata. (Dynamism in written, spoken, and thought language.) Cervello 15:181-196, 1936.

350a. ——: Dinamismo della scrittura dettata, copiata e pensata. (Dynamism in dictated, copied, and self-initiated handwriting.) R. C. Accad. Sci. med. chir. 90:225-236, 1936-37.

351. Rice, L.: Character Reading from Handwriting. New York, 1927.

352. Roback, A. A.: Meaning in Personality Manifestations. Proc. IX Int. Cong. Psychol., pp. 362. Princeton, 1930.

352a. Roback, A. A.: Writing slips and personality. Char. & Pers. 1:138-146, 1932.

353. Román-Goldzieher, K.: Untersuchungen über die Schrift der Stotterer, Stammler und Polterer. (Investigations on the handwriting of stutterers, stammerers and blusterers.) Ztschr. f. Kinderforsch. 35:116-139, 1929.

354. ——: Studies in the variability of handwriting. The development of writing speed and point pressure in school children. J. Genet. Psychol. 49:139-160, 1936.

354a. ——: Untersuchungen der Schrift und des Schreibens von 283 Zwillingspaaren. (Investigations on the handwriting of 283 twins.) Schweiz. Psychol. Anwend. (Suppl.) no. 6, 29-55, 1945.

355. Román-Goldzieher, K., and Feuchtwanger, E.: Handschriftuntersuchungen an Hirnverletzten. (Studies on the handwriting of brain-injured persons.) Schweiz. Arch. f. Neurol. u. Psychiat. 1, 1934.

356. Rougemont, E. de: Une nouvelle science sociale, la graphologie, cours gradué professé au Collège Libre des Sciences Sociales. (Graphology, a new social science, graduate course of the College Libre des Sciences Sociales.) Paris, 1932.

357. Roxon-Ropschitz, I.: The act of deleting and other findings in writings of neurotics. Psychiatry 9:117-121, 1946.

358. Ruesch, J., Finesinger, J. E., and Schwab, R. S.: The electromyogram of handwriting. Psychosom. Med. 2:411-437, 1940.

359. ——: Muscular tension on psychiatric patients. Pressure measurements on handwriting as an indicator. Arch. Neurol. & Psychiat. 50:439-449, 1943.

360. Rugg, L. S.: Retests and the constancy of the I.Q. J. Educ. Psychol. 16:341-343, 1925.

361. Ruml., W.: Links- und Rechtshandschrift ein und derselben Person. (Left-handed and right-handed writing of the same person.) Krim. Mh. 10:25-30, 1936.

362. ——: Ein Schreibphänomen. (A writing phenomenon.) Krim. Mh. 11:49-52, 1937.

363. Rüth, G.: Die Schreibfehler und ihre Bedeutung für die Schülerbeurteilung. (The meaning of mistakes in writing for the judgment of pupils.) Ztschr. pädag. Psychol. 40:91-96, 1939.

364. Ruthenberg, M.: Rechtschreibfehlleistung und psychischer Konstitutionstypus. (Faulty acts in handwriting and type of psychological constitution.) Ztschr. f. Kinderforsch. 48:73-115, 1939.

365. Saudek, R.: The Psychology of Handwriting. London, 1925.

366. ——: The methods of graphology. Brit. J. Psychol. 7:221-259, 1927.

367. ——: Experiments with Handwriting. New York, 1928.

368. ——: Das zentrale Nervensystem und der Schreibakt. (The central nervous system and the act of writing.) Jahrb. Charakterologie 6:277-303, 1929.

369. ——: Zur Psychologie der amerikanischen Handschrift. (Psychology of American handwriting.) Ztschr. f. Menschenkenntnis 6: 1931.

370. ——: Writing movements as indications of the writer's social behavior. J. Soc. Psychol. 2:337-373, 1931.

371. ——: Pubertätsjahre im englischen Internat. (Years of adolescence in British boarding schools.) Char. & Pers. 1:12-26, 1932.

372. Schade, W.: Handschrift und Erbcharakter. (Handwriting and hereditary character.) Ztschr. f. ang. Psychol. 57:303-381, 1939.

373. Schermann, R.: Schicksale des Lebens. (Destinies of life.) Berlin, 1932.

374. Schneidemühl, G.: Handschrift und Charakter, ein Lehrbuch der Handschriftenbeurteilung. (Handwriting and character, a textbook of graphology.) Leipzig, 1911.

375. Schneikert, H.: Leitfaden der gerichtlichen Schriftvergleichung. (Textbook of forensic comparisons of handwriting.) Leipzig, 1918.

376. ——: Zur Lehre von den primären und sekundären Schriftmerkmalen. (The theory of primary and secondary characteristics of handwriting.) Arch. Krim. 98:140-144, 1936.

377. Schorn, M.: Untersuchungen zur Kritik der graphologischen Gutachten. (Studies in criticism of graphologic diagnoses.) Industr. Psychotechn. 4:359-368, 1927.

378. Schorsch, G.: Die Ausdruckskunde in der psychiatrischen Diagnostik. (The study of expression in psychiatric diagnosis.) Ztschr. f. d. ges. Neurol. u. Psychiat. 87:705, 1938.

379. ——: Die prämorbide Persönlichkeit bei Schizophrenen. (The prepsychotic personality of schizophrenics.) Ztschr. f. d. ges Neurol. u. Psychiat. 167:154-157, 1939.

380. Schröder, H. E.: Lebendige Charakterbildung. (Formation of character by experience.) Ztschr. f. Menschenkenntnis 13:182-193, 1938.

381. Schryver, S.: Psychomotility in behavior disorders as seen in the handwriting of children. J. Nerv. & Ment. Dis. 100:64-69, 1944.

382. Schuler, R. A.: Mussolini à travers son écriture. (Mussolini in his handwritings.) Paris, 1925.

383. Schultze-Naumburg, B.: Handschrift und Ehe. (Handwriting and marriage.) München, 1932.

384. Seeling, O.: Zwillingsindividualität und Zwillingsgemeinschaft. (Individuality and common traces in twins.) Hamburg, 1932.

385. Seeman, E., and Saudek, R.: The self-expression of identical twins in handwriting and drawing. Char. & Pers. 1:91-128, 1932.

386. ——: The handwriting of identical twins reared apart. Char. & Pers. 1:268-285; 1:22-40, 1933.

387. Seesemann, K.: Bewährungskontrolle graphologischer Gutachten. (Control of validity in graphologic testimonies.) Industr. Psychotech. 6:104-108, 1929.

388. Sellers, C.: The handwriting evidence against Hauptmann. J. Crim. Law & Criminol. 27:857-873, 1937.

389. Severino, M. A. (1580-1656): Vaticinator, sive tractatus de divinatione litterali. (Prophetic book, treatise on divination from letters.)

390. Sheldon, W. H., and Tucker, W. B.: The Varieties of Human Physique. New York, 1940.

391. Sherman, I. C.: The Franz dot tapping test as a measure of attention. J. Appl. Psychol. 7:353-359, 1923.

392. Shirley, M.: The First Two Years, vol. II, p. 56. Minneapolis, 1931-33. (3 vols.)

393. Sidor, E.: Graphology in forensic medicine. The handwriting of criminals. Rev. Med. leg., Rumania 3:510-524, 1940.

394. Silver, A. H.: Graphograms for Instant Analysis of Character Through Handwriting. London, 1928.

395. Smith, A. J.: Applied Graphology. Chicago, 1920.

396. Smukler, M. E.: Mirror writing in school children. Penn. M. J. 43:21, 1939.

397. Solange-Pellat, E.: Les lois de l'écriture. (The laws of handwriting.) Paris, 1927.

398. Spadino, E. J.: Writing and laterality; characteristics of stuttering children. Teach. Coll. Contr. Educ., no. 837, 1941.

399. Spearman, C. E.: The Abilities of Man. London, 1927.

400. Spencer, S.: What Handwriting Reveals. New York, 1927.

401. Squire, C. R.: A genetic study of rhythm. Am. J. Psychol. 12:492-589, 1901.

402. Stainbrook, E., and Löwenbach, H.: Writing and drawing of psychotic individuals after electrically induced convulsions. J. Nerv. & Ment. Dis. 99:382-388, 1944.

403. Steif, A.: Ikrek megegyezö firkálámódja. (Similarity of scribbling in twins.) Psychol. Stud. Univ. Budapest 3:51-66, 1939.

404. Stern, W.: Person und Sache. (Person and thing.) Leipzig, 1923.

405. ——: General Psychology from the Personalistic Standpoint. New York, 1938.

406. Stocker, R. D.: The Language of Handwriting. New York, 1901.

407. Storch, D.: The similarity of brothers and sisters in mental traits. Psychol. Rev. 24:235-238, 1917.

408. Storey, A.: A Manual of Graphology. London, 1922.

409. Streletski, C.: Graphologie du practicien. (Graphology of the practitioner.) Paris, 1927.

409. Super, D. E.: A comparison of the diagnoses of a graphologist with the results of psychological tests. J. Consult. Psychol. 5:127-133, 1941.

410. Sylvus, N.: Neue Wege in der Handschriftendeutung. (New ways of interpreting handwritings.) Zeichen der Zeit, no. 4, 1-40, 1931.

411. Takemasa, T.: Sho oyobi shoji dôsa no shinri—Sho no shinrigakuteki kôsatsu ni kansuru nisan no mondai. (Psychology of calligraphy and writing action. Some problems concerning the psychology of writing.) Kyôiku Shinri Kenkyû 15:339-354, 1940.

412. Tchang, T. M.: L'écriture chinoise et le geste humain; essai sur la formation de l'écriture chinoise. (Chinese script and human gesture; essay on the formation of Chinese script.) Shanghai, 1937.

413. Teltscher, H. O.: Handwriting: The Key to Successful Living. New York, 1942.

414. Theiss, H.: Zur experimentellen Graphologie. (Experimental graphology.) Ztschr. f. Menschenkenntnis 5:237-245, 1929.

415. ——: Experimentelle Untersuchungen über die Erfassung des handschriftlichen Ausdrucks durch Laien. (Experimental investigations concerning the apprehension of graphic expression by the layman.) Psychol. Forsch. 15:276-358, 1931.

416. Thelen, E.: Zuordnungsversuche an Schriftproben von Zwillingen. (Matching experiments with samples of the handwritings of twins.) Ztschr. f. Psychol. 147:215-237, 1939.

417. Thorndike, E. L.: The Principles of Teaching. New York, 1906.

418. ——: Handwriting. Teach. Coll. Rec. 9:83-175, 1910.

418a. Thorndike, E. L.: Resemblance of young twins in handwriting. Amer. Nat., 49, 1915.

419. Thumm-Kintzel, M.: Psychology and Pathology of Handwriting. (Transl. from the German by M. Kintzel-Thumm). New York, 1905.

420. Trey, M. de: Der Wille in der Handschrift. (The will in handwriting.) Bern, 1946.

421. Unger, H.: Schriftveränderungen bei Verbrechern. (Changes in the handwriting of criminals.) Ztschr. f. gerichtl. Med. 27: no. 4, 1936.

422. ——: Die Bedeutung der Arkadenbindung. (The meaning of loop connections.) Ztschr. f. Menschenkenntnis 13:21-29, 1937.

423. ——: Graphologische Berufsberatung. (Graphologic vocational guidance.) Industr. Psychotech. 15:78-84, 1938.

424. ——: Weibliche oder männliche Schrift. (Feminine or masculine script.) Ztschr. f. ang. Psychol. 58:213-235, 1940.

425. Ungern-Sternberg, I. C.: Portrait intime d'un écrivain d'après six lignes de son écriture. (Intimate portrait of a writer by six lines of his handwriting.) Paris, 1898.

425a. Usnadze, D.: Ein experimenteller Beitrag zum Problem der psychologischen Grundlagen der Namengebung. Psychol. Forsch. 5:24-43, 1924.

426. Uzdanska, R.: Przypadek wybitnych trudnosci w czytaniu i pisaniu. (A case of particular reading and writing disability.) Psychol. wychow. 11:10-27, 1938-39.

427. Valentine, W. L.: Experimental Foundations of General Psychology. (rev. ed.) New York, 1941.

428. Vanzanges, L. M.: L'écriture des musiciens célèbres. (The handwriting of famous musicians.) Paris, 1913.

429. ——: L'écriture des créateurs intellectuels. (The handwriting of creative intellectuals.) Paris, 1926.

430. Varty, J. W.: Manuscript writing and spelling achievement. Teach. Coll. Contr. Educ. no. 749, 1938.

431. Vernan, P. E.: A new instrument for recording handwriting pressure. Brit. J. Educ. Psychol. 4:310-316, 1934.

432. ——: The evaluation of the matching method. J. Educ. Psychol. *27*:1-17, 1936.

433. ——: A note on the standard error in the contingency matching technic. J. Educ. Psychol. *27*:704-709, 1936.

434. ——: The matching method applied to investigations of personality. Psychol. Bull. *33*:149-177, 1936.

435. Vértesi, E.: Handschrift und Eigenart der Krebsgefährdeten. (Handwriting and peculiarity of persons threatened by cancer.) Budapest, 1939.

436. Vetter, A.: Ausdruckswissenschaft. (Science of expression.) Ztschr. f. Psychol. *53*:233-250, 1937.

437. Waehner, T. S.: Formal criteria for the analysis of children's drawing. Am. J. Orthopsychiat. *12*:95-104, 1942.

437a. ——: Interpretation of spontaneous drawings and paintings. Genet. Psychol. Monog. *33*:3-70, 1946.

438. Wagner, L.: Goethe's Handschrift. (The handwriting of Goethe.) Ztschr. f. Menschenkenntnis *8*:180-186, 1932.

439. ——: Der Unterschied männlichen und weiblichen Selbstgefühles in der Handschrift. (The difference between male and female self-confidence in handwriting.) Ztschr. f. Menschenkenntnis. *10*:129-143, 1934.

440. Wagoner, L. C., and Downey, J. E.: Speech and will-temperament. J. Appl. Psychol. *6*:291-297, 1922.

441. Walther, J.: Die psychologische und charakterologische Bedeutung der handschriftlichen Bindungsarten. (The psychologic and characterologic significance of forms of connection in handwriting movements.) Neue psychol. Stud. *11:* no. 3, 63-158, 1938.

442. Washburn, R. W.: A study of the smiling and laughing of infants in the first year of life. Genet. Psychol. Monog. *6:* nos. 5-6, 1929.

443. Wells, F. L.: Personal history, handwriting and specific behavior. Char. & Pers. *14*:295-314, 1945-46.

444. Wenzl, A.: Graphologie als Wissenschaft. (Graphology as science.) Leipzig, 1937; Arb. Psychol. Inst. Univ. München *8:* 1937.

445. Werner, R.: Über den Anteil des Bewusstseins bei Schreibvorgängen. (The role of consciousness in the writing process.) Neue Psychol. Stud. *11*:1-72, 1937.

446. Wertheimer, M.: Über Gestalttheorie; Symposion I, 1925.

447. Westerman, D.: Die Glidyi-Ewe in Togo. Berlin, 1935.

448. Wheeler, A. W.: A study to determine the errors that appear in written work of rural and urban pupils in certain school systems of Kentucky. J. Exper. Educ. *8*:385-398, 1940.

449. Wieser, R.: Der Rhythmus in der Verbrecherhandschrift; systematisch dargestellt an 694 Schriften Krimineller und 200 Schriften Nicht-krimineller. (Rhythm in the handwriting of criminals; systematically demonstrated by means of 694 scripts from criminals and 200 scripts from noncriminals. Leipzig, 1938.

450. Wiles, M. E.: Effect on different sized tools on the handwriting of beginners. Elem. Sch. J. *43*:412-414, 1943; see Child Developm. Abstr. *17:* 576.

451. Wills, A. R.: An investigation of the relationship between rate and quality of handwriting in a primary school. Brit. J. Educ. Psychol. *8*:229-236, 1938.

452. Wilson, F. T., and Fleming, C. W.: Reversals in reading and writing made by pupils in the kindergarten and primary grades. J. Genet. Psychol. *53*:3-31, 1938.

453. Wirtz, J.: Druck- und Geschwindigkeitsverlauf von ganzheitlichen Schreibbewegungsweisen. (Sequence of pressure and speed in writing–movements considered as a whole.) Neue psychol. Stud. *11:* no. 3, 5-55, 1938.

454. Wittlich, B.: Ein Beitrag zur Frage der Geschlechtsbestimmung nach der Handschrift. (Contribution to the question of the determination of sex according to handwriting.) Ztschr. f. Menschenkenntnis *3*:42-45, 1927.

455. ——: Handschrift und Erziehung. (Handwriting and education.) Berlin, Leipzig, 1940.

456. Wixted, W. G., and Curoe, P. R. V.: How well do college seniors write? Sch. & Soc. *54*:505-508, 1941.

457. Wohlfart, E. W.: Der Auffassungsvorgang an kleinen Gestalten. (The perceptual process with small configurations.) Neue psychol. Stud., 347-414, 1928.

458. Wolberg, L. R.: Hypnoanalysis. New York, 1945.

459. Wolfe, H. K.: Some judgments on the size of familiar subjects. Am. J. Psychol. 9:137-166, 1898.

460. Wolff, W.: Gestaltidentität in der Charakterologie. (Configurational identity in characterology.) Psychol. u. Medizin. 4:32-44, 1929.

461. ——: Über Faktoren charakterologischer Urteilsbildung. (Factors in the formation of characterologic judgments.) Ztschr. f. ang. Psychol. 35:385-446, 1930.

462. ——: Experimentelle Tiefenpsychologie. Ein Report. (Experimental depth psychology; a report.) Imago 20:104-122, 1934.

463. ——: Das Unbewusste der Handschrift im Experiment. (The expression of the unconscious in handwriting by experimental methods.) Die Umschau 40: no. 28, 1936.

464. ——: Projective methods for personality analysis of expressive behavior in preschool children. Char. & Pers. 10:309-330, 1942.

465. ——: "Graphometry": a new diagnostic method. Psychol. Bull. 39:456, 1942.

466. ——. The Expression of Personality, Experimental Depth Psychology. New York, 1943.

467. ——: The Personality of the Preschool Child. New York, 1946.

468. Wulf, F.: Über die Veränderung von Vorstellungen. (On the change of concepts.) Psychol. Forsch. 1:333-373, 1922. Reported in W. D. Ellis: A Sourcebook of Gestalt Psychology. New York, 1939.

469. Wundt, W.: Vorlesungen über die Menschen- und Tierseele. (Lectures on human and animal psychology.) Transl. by J. E. Creighton & E. B. Titchener. New York, 1894.

470. Yates, D. H.: Psychological Racketeers. Boston, 1932.

471. Ziegler, A.: Ist die Graphologie von diagnostischer Bedeutung für den praktischen Arzt? (Is graphology of diagnostic significance for the practical physician?) Ztschr. Menschenkenntnis 13: no. 9, 1937.

472. Zillig, G.: Über ein Phänomen beim Schreiben mit der linken Hand. (A phenomenon found in writing with the left hand.) Nervenarzt 12:512-515, 1939.

473. Zinke, H.: Der Druck in der Handschrift. (Pressure in handwriting.) Ztschr. f. ang. Psychol. 56:217-227, 1939.

474. ——: Der Verbundenheitsgrad in der Handschrift. (Degree of connectedness in handwriting.) Ztschr. f. Psychol 58:246-260, 1940.

474a. ——: Die Bindungsformen in der Handschrift. (Connecting forms in handwriting.) Ztschr. f. Psychol. 60:96-115, 1940.

INDEX

For easier use of the Index, it has been subdivided into the following four sections: Subject Index, Index of Main Graphic Indicators, Author Index and Index of Handwriting Specimens.

SUBJECT INDEX

Abasement, graphic expression of, 243
Abbreviation of images in handwriting, 252
Ability
  for empathy, and reconstruction of doodlings, 231
  to express emotions by letters, 180
Abnormal
  cases of pictographic expression, 257
  and normal conditions, consistencies of movement made under, 27
  and normal people, experiments with doodlings of, 227
Abstract
  art, non-objective ornamentation in, 274
  and concrete types of drawings, 251
  and concrete way of symbolization of concepts, by graphic patterns, 238
  expression, tendency for, in oscillographs, 257
  and realistic expression, 274
Associations, accompanying act of writing, 191ff, 323
Achievement, graphic expression of, 243
Acoustic-minded and visual-minded subjects, interpretation of graphic forms by, 193
Actions
  motor type, determined by, 303
  symbolization of, by graphic pattern, 235
Activities, co-ordination of, 150
Activity
  attitude of, graphic expression of, 312
  progression in lower sector of writing, indicating, 273
Adaptability, graphic expression of, 314
Adaptation
  correlation of round movements with, 247
  diagnosis of, 136ff
  graphic, of husband and wife, 137
  of graphic movements, 137
  graphic, of political leaders to each other, 137
Addicts, morphine and opium, 217
Addressee, writer and, empathy in relationship between, 196
Aggressiveness
  angular strokes as indicators of, 247
  graphic expression of, 316
Adjustability
  curved strokes as indicators of, 247
  graphic expression of, 310
Adolescents, handwriting of, 10, 272
Adventurous attitude, graphic expression of, 314
Aesthetic
  analysis, 5

attitude, graphic expression of, 310
expression in graphic movement, 267
expression, symmetry in, 43
patterns, lack of, in handwritings of stutterers, 300
relationships, 93
Aesthetics
  Greek concept of, 58
  principle of proportions in, 58
Age
  factors of, 15
  old, graphic expression of, 197, 198
  old, proportional contraction of move- in, 78-80, 156
Agreement in the Crimea, signatures to, 138, 139
Aggression
  expression of, 216
  graphic characteristics of, 180, 181, 197, 201
  hidden, 136
  indicated by pressure of letters, 353
  inferiority feeling as motive for, 216
  and oppression, fantasies of, 216
  progression in lower sector of writing, indicating, 273
  projection of, by young children, 267
Agraphia and handwriting, 10
Agreement and disagreement among judges of the same specimen, 15
Alphabet
  and national projections, 212
  and individual associations, 216
  national and size of letters, 245
Alternation
  dynamic, of centripetal and centrifugal movements, rhythm as, 260
  of ingoing and outgoing movements, 260
  of progressing and regressing curves, 260
  rhythmic, of up- and down-strokes. 260
Altruism, graphic expression of, 310
America, frequency of publications on handwriting in, 6
Analogous
  expressiveness, 177
  graphic expression and wish images, 286
  projection of concepts upon letters, 180, 181
Anal tendencies, graphic expression of, 310
Analysis
  aesthetic, 5
  contradictory statements in, 15
  of determinants of graphic expression, 259
  of a dream-drawing, 297, 298
  essential statements in, 15

375

Chi-square test, 52, 53
Cinematographic studies of handwriting, 9
Circular
  and angular forms, as symbols of projection, 335, 336
  dot over the "i," indicating self-involvement and narcissism, 279
Classification
  of data, 14
  of factors of expression, 309ff
  of graphic movements, 123, 124
  of signatures, 29
  visual, 30
Clockwise and counter-clockwise movements, 277
Closed and open eyes, comparison of writing with, 21ff, 202, 203
Clusters
  nuclear, of traits, 306
  personality, studies on, 305, 306ff
Coined dot over the "i," indicating dreaminess, 279
Cold and rigid character, degree of inclination as related to, 246
Collective and individual differences of handwriting, 251, 252
Colors
  graphic expression of associations to, 199
  matching of graphic forms to, 192, 193
  primary, experiment with matching of concepts to, 235
Columbia University Teachers College, experiment at, 169-171
Common denominator of expression, 184ff
Comparison
  of an author's original manuscript with his final copy, 212
  of dream images with spontaneous drawings, 225, 226
  of geometrical forms of children and their parents, 136
  of left- and right-handed writing, 20ff, 212
  and relationship of different associations, 216
  between Rhythmical Quotient and Intelligence Quotient, 167
  of a writer's different headings or addresses to the same person, 205
  of writing with eyes closed and open, 21ff, 202, 203
  of writing in health and sickness, 294
  of writings of the same person in health and mental disease, 278, 291
Compensation
  for change of directions by integration of patterns, 263
  for dissolution of letter shape by vibration of movement, 263
  for irregularity by harmonious distribution of graphic forms, 263
  for opposite behavior, projections as, 267
  pressure as reflection of actual behavior or of, 268
Complex
  movement pattern, 248
  and neutral words, difference of length of, in normal state and hypnosis, 222, 223

words, 136, 207, 221
Composers, professional leitmotifs in signatures of, 287, 288
Compression and distortion of letters, 267, 350, 352
Compulsion to complete the law of configuration, 101
Concentration indicated by contraction of movements, 264
Concepts
  matching of graphic forms to, experiments with, 192, 193
  and symbols, identity between, 324
Concrete
  and abstract way of symbolization of concepts, by graphic patterns, 238
  and abstract types of drawings, 251
  features, absence of, as characteristic of oscillographic pattern, 254
  images, symbolization of abstract elements into, 226
Concretization, tendency for, in pictographs, 257
Conditioned reflex, 323
Conditions
  artificial experimental, 180
  consistencies of movement made under normal and abnormal, 27
  environmental
    change of, 27
    influence of, 15, 17, 18, 20, 121, 158, 177
  different, of writing, percentage of consistencies in the same movement pattern done under, 26
  disregard of given, 277
  experimental, importance of, 249
  outer, of writing, 3, 131, 259, 304
  unfamiliar, of writing, 20ff
  unusual, of writing, 20ff
  varying, of writing, 20ff
  of writing, limiting expressiveness, 250
Confidence, graphic expression of, 312
Configuration
  ability of, 150
  and balance, 129, 130, 173, 174
  basic, 96
  and brain processes, 172, 173, 174
  centripetal and centrifugal movements, determined by, 264
  change of expressive value in change of, 318
  characteristics of, 150ff
  as characteristic of proportion, 120
  in a child's signature, 153, 154
  concept of, and a theory of brain mechanism, 172, 173
  conservation of formula of, during interrupted movements, 126-128
  consistency of
    and identification of handwriting, 124
    over a person's life period, 161ff
  degree of, 151, 165
  and development of personality, relationship between, 168, 169
  diagrams of, in graphic movement, 100ff
  different symbols of the same, 98
  disturbance and conservation of, 126
  in drawings of preschool children, 167, 168

Self-recognition
  and non-recognition, 184
  of one's own writing, experiment on, 182
  self-characterization of handwriting, in
    absence of, 171
Sensations
  connected with writing process, 269
  kinesthetic, 71
Sense for symmetry of the blind, 43
Sensibility, degree of inclination as related
    to, 246
Sensitivity, graphic expression of, 314
Sentience
  graphic expression of, 243
  lack of connections related to, 243
Sentimental attitude, graphic expression of,
    312
Sex
  characteristics
    and handwriting, 7, 13
    physiological and psychological, 13
  differences, and handwriting, 10, 12, 68
  symbolization of concept of, by graphic
    pattern, 235
Sexual
  characteristics
    expressed in lower sector of writing,
      271
    expressed by shadings, 269
  perversions, and distortions in lower
    loops of letters, 272
  problems, diagnosed by handwriting, 11
  symbolism in analytical drawings, 298
  urges, perverted, and transposition of
    pressure, 269
Shading
  as expression of anxiety, 268
  as expression of sadism or masochism,
    269
  sensibility for touching sensations, sug-
    gested by, 268
  sexual characteristics, expressed by, 269
Shape
  absence of, characteristic of oscillographic
    pattern, 254
  change of, 341
  of curves, determined by measure-unit,
    125
  definiteness of, characteristic of picto-
    graphic pattern, 254
  and diameter, of curves, 108
  of letters
    compensation for dissolution of, by vi-
      bration of movement, 263
    frequency of periodic repetitions in, 279
  projection of likes and dislikes, wishes
    and fears, by, in children's drawings,
    201
Shock, emotional, proportional increase of
    movement during, 92
Siblings
  handwriting of, 123
  movement patterns of, 123
  symbolization of concept of, by graphic
    pattern, 235
Sickness, comparison of handwriting in
    health and, 294
Signatures (see also Name)

to the Agreement in the Crimea, 139
and associations, 323ff
to the Atlantic Charter, 140
authenticity of, and formula of propor-
    tions, 144
centers of, 124
center of movement in, 55, 58, 124, 303
made on checks, 28, 29
classification of, 29
of composers, 287, 288
configuration in a child's, 153, 154
configurational relationships between first
    and second names of, 54
consistencies in length of total, and their
    parts, 36
consistency of
  if disguised, 21ff
  movement in, 25
  if written bigger than usual, 21ff
  if written smaller than usual, 21ff
to the Constitution, 29, 46, 49, 51
constitutive elements of, 124-126
contraction of, during depressed state of
    mind, 297
of creative personalities, 288, 290
to the Declaration of Independence, 29,
    46, 48, 49, 51
to the Declaration by the United Nations,
    138
decrease of extension in, 76ff
detection of symbols in, 235ff
difference of movement concerning first
    and second names in, 76
made in different stages of an epileptic
    attack, 253, 278, 291
distortions in, 132
dot over the "i" as center of, 101, 102
elements of, 32, 124
end-stroke as main element of, 124
an example of mosaic, 126
experiments on symbols in, 235ff
extension of, 32, 45, 46, 54, 125
  during manic state of mind, 297
flourished, samples of, 60
flourishes surrounding, 279
form of, 125
frequency distribution of, concerning pro-
    portional length of first and second
    name, 48, 49, 78
graphic disturbances in, 131
increase of movement in, 80ff
lack of center of movement in, 55
leitmotif in, accentuating split between
    reality and imagination, 339
leitmotifs in, 286, 324
measurement of, from left to right limit,
    32, 46, 54
measurement of, from start to end, 32, 45,
    54
middle-stroke as main element of, 124
of musicians, rhythm in, 260, 261
overlining of, 335, 337
of painters, 288, 289
part-movements in, 124
of presidents of the American Psychia-
    atric Association, 246
proportions between measure-unit and ex-
    tension of, 125

width of, 243

Strong pressure, indicating lack of impressionability, 342, 343

Structure
of graphic expression, 239
of graphic patterns, 193
of letters, emphasis on, characteristic of pictographic pattern, 254
of personality, 19, 244
theories on, 93, 94
of symbols, 191
type of social, 156

Structurization, gestalt and, 96

Stutterer, writing of a, before and after psychotherapeutic treatment, 300

Stutterers
handwritings of, 10, 299, 300
lack of aesthetic patterns in handwritings of, 300
lack of balance in handwritings of, 300
pressure and speed of, 268
rhythmic disturbance in handwritings of, 299, 300
sudden pressure in handwritings of, 300

Style
of a certain epoch, characterized by ornaments, 285
of expression, 3
of graphic expression, 285, 286
of retelling, matched with handwriting, 13

Subjective
and objective degree of proportions, 167
and objective symbols, 221

Subjective Objective Quotient and Objective Rhythmical Quotient, 167

Sublimity, indicated by emphasis on upper sector of writing, 302

Submission, graphic characteristics of, 180, 181

Substitute object, writing-paper treated as a, 267

Success
of graphological experiments, 12
of matching experiments, 12

Suggestibility, graphic expression of, 314

Suicide, writing before, 217

Summary of studies on handwriting, 8

Superego, Id, Ego, and, 270

Supernormal personality, 18

Support, lines of, 266, 267

Suppression
indicated by crossing out of name, 339
of unconscious trends, 20

Survey
on experimental graphology, 13
historical, 5

Suspicion, graphic expression of, 312

Swing of curves, characteristic of oscillographic pattern, 254

Symbolic
expression of ideas, 221
gestures, 98
meaning of drawings, 226
relationship of concepts, 235
representations, 68
thinking, and dreams, 257
value of gestures, 220, 221

Symbolization
in ceremonies, 221

of concepts, 299
concrete and abstract way of, by graphic patterns, 238
by graphic patterns, experiments on, 235
oscillographic and pictographic type of, 238
in customs, 221
and diagnosis, 233
in doodlings, 224, 227ff
in drawings of preschool children, 221, 238
in dreams, 221
of family relationships, by graphic patterns, 237
in graphic expression and in dreams, 225
graphic, of insanes, 233, 234
in handwriting, process of, 227
in hypnosis, 221
imagination and, in graphic expression, 238
of inner psychological processes, 220
mechanism of, 226
process of, 219ff
projection and, difference between, 220
as transfer of expressiveness, 191
as transformation of abstract elements into concrete images, 226

Symbols
alphabetic, connected with the same group of associations, 216
of associations, graphic signs as, 252
Aztec graphic, 251
of balance, 68
Chinese graphic, 251, 252
and concepts, identity between, 324
of the cross, 288, 327
different, of the same configuration, 98
Egyptian graphic, 251, 252
of expression, 244
graphic
and art, 221
distinction of, 324
hidden, 227, 231
of impulses and unconscious forces, 270
indirect reflection of expressiveness in, 191
of mental force, 270
and movement, 220
musical, 288
of musical expression, 256
objective and subjective, 221
of painting, 288
of projection, angular and circular forms as, 335, 336
of security, 68
sexual, in analytical drawing, 298
in signatures
detection of, 235ff
experiments on, 235ff
of social activities, 270
stereotyped, 323
structure, of, 191
of war, 288

Symmetry
in aesthetics, 43
in artistic expression of mentally diseased, 42

INDEX OF MAIN GRAPHIC INDICATORS

See Tables 14-16. Compare with corresponding terms in Subject Index.

Narrow
forms, 311(B), 315(R)
movements, 311(H), 315(Q,T), 318(23)

Open or closed forms, 313(N), 315(V)
Original forms, 313(O), 315(V)
Oscillating movements, 313(K,P)
Oscillographic patterns, 319(44), 320(1)
Outline of strokes, 315(Y)
Overloading of shapes, 311(A)

Parallelism of strokes, 313(L), 315(R)
Perseveration of movement, 315(V)
Pictographic patterns, 313(K), 319(43),
320(K)
Pressure
emphasis on, 317(Z), 318
high or low, 311(D,H), 313(M,P), 315-
(W), 317(Y)
three-dimensional, 318(2)
two-dimensional, 318(3
variations of, 313(N)
swelling of, 313(L)
transposition of, 313(J), 317(Z)
Printed letters, 311(A)
Progressive movements, 311(B,G), 313(J)
Punctuation, careful or careless, 311(D,E)

Ratios, regular or irregular, 313(N), 315-
(S)
Reduction
of patterns, 319(41)
of movements, 315(W,X)
Regressive
inclination, 315(T)
movements, 311(B,G), 313(J), 315(U)
Regularity of movements, 311(C), 313(J),
315(W)
Rhythm
of movement, 311(A), 315(S)
of distribution, 313(O)
rigidity of, 315(U)
Rigidity and schematism of movements,
315(V), 320(h)
Rising movements, 313(P)
Round
movements, 315(T)
patterns, 311(B), 315(R,W)

Secure or insecure movements, 317(Z), 320-
(f)
Shadings of letters, 313(P), 315(S), 320(e)

Sharpness
of pressure, 320(g)
of strokes, 313(M)
Simplification of patterns, 311(A,F,I), 315-
(W) (see also Reduction)
Sinking movements, 313(P)
Size
differences of, 315(U)
even or uneven, 315(R)
increasing or decreasing, 315(Q)
of letters, related to paper size, 311(F)
reduction of, 315(U)
small or large, 311(H,I), 315(T)
Slant of letters, 313(J), 315(R) (see also
Inclination)
Small movements, 318(26), 319(59)
Spacing of patterns, 311(B)
Speed, 311(I), 313(M,N), 315(Q,U,W)
variability of, 315(R)
Spheres of writing, emphasis on, 315(X)
(see also upper, lower, middle)
Stereotyped forms, 313(O)
Straight lines, 311(H), 313(M), 318(8)
Sudden movements, 318(17)
Surrounding lines, 320(70)
Symmetry, emphasis on, 313(O)

T-bars
form of, 317(Z)
position of, 311(G), 315(Q), 317(Y)
pressure of, 311(H), 313(M)
Terminals
emphasis on, 311(G)
long or short, 315(U)
Texture of strokes, 318
Thickness of lines, 315(S)
Traditional forms, 311(E)
Transposition of forms, 320(68)
Typological value of graphic forms, 320

Upper sphere, emphasis on, 311(I), 313(K),
319(49)

Vacillation of movement, 318(15)
Vertical
movements, 319(37)
patterns, 311(G), 313(P)

Wavy movements, 311(C), 319(40)
Width
degree of, 315(Q,R)
of movements, 318(24)
variation of, 315(U)

AUTHOR INDEX

INDEX OF HANDWRITING SPECIMENS